SILENTS TO DIGITALS

THE MEMOIR OF HOLLYWOOD PRODUCER & DIRECTOR ROBERT CAWLEY

RENA WINTERS

Copyright (C) 2022 Rena Winters

Layout design and Copyright (C) 2022 by Next Chapter

Published 2022 by Next Chapter

Edited by Elizabeth N. Love

Cover art by Lordan June Pinote

Mass Market Paperback Edition

All rights reserved. No part of this book may be reproduced or transmitted in any form or by any means, electronic or mechanical, including photocopying, recording, or by any information storage and retrieval system, without the author's permission.

PROLOGUE

"QUIET ON THE SET! QUIET ON THE SET!

IT MUST BE QUIET SO THE ACTORS CAN HEAR THE DIRECTOR."

The voice of the assistant director boomed through the huge megaphone. The crowd of over three thousand watched the filming of the comedy.

"IF SILENCE IS NOT MAINTAINED DURING THE FILMING OF EACH SCENE, THE POLICE WILL HAVE TO REMOVE THE AUDIENCE. I KNOW YOU WANT TO SEE THIS MOVIE MADE. PLEASE COOPERATE!"

Frank Kirby, the director, was the man in charge. A Hollywood veteran who had won acclaim as assistant director for his work on two of the greatest silent film classics. The original *Ben Hur* that starred Francis X. Bushman and *The Big Parade* starring Rene Adore and matinee idol John Gilbert. Producer/writer Hal Roach had selected Kirby to helm this "Our Gang Comedy" titled *The Pie Eating Champeen*.

Mr. Kirby, who had a quiet way of handling children, walked slowly toward the three-and-a-half-year-old actor playing the role of "Wheezer" who was standing on the sidewalk at the beginning of the Bank Block where the scene was to be played.

Kirby always spoke to his young actors by the names of the characters they played in the film rather than their real names. "Wheezer," he said in a soft voice, "we are going to film this scene just the way we rehearsed it except this time there will be real watermelon in front of the store. You will walk down the street to the grocery store which has a stand with slices of watermelon on ice in front. You will take a slice, take a bite, and then you will hear the grocer yell at you and start rushing to the door of the store. You will drop the melon and run as fast as you can to the far end of the block where the scene ends. Do you understand?"

"Yes, Mr. Kirby."

Frank turned and started to walk back to a spot between the cameras as he yelled, "Slate for Take One," The cameramen started grinding their cameras and recorded the slate information. "*The Pie Eating Champeen*. Hal Roach Productions, Take One," the director called "Action" and Wheezer started his walk. Reaching the grocery, he grabbed a slice of melon, took a bite and stood eating the melon as the grocery owner rushed out the door. Kirby yelled, "Cut," as the crowd roared with laughter.

Kirby's sweating face was flushed as he raced to his actor still eating melon. "Wheezer, where's your mind? We're making a movie and you are to take my direction. I told you to drop the melon and run."

This tiny actor answered with watermelon juice running down his chin, "I never tasted watermelon before and it's so good."

"Okay, I'll grant you it's good and you can have all the slices you want after we complete this scene. This time, take a bit, drop the melon and run."

"I'll do it, Mr. Kirby."

"Swell, let's go. You get on your mark. Slate boys, let the cameras know this will be Take Two."

Kirby called "Action". Wheezer started his walk. Once in front of the grocery, he grabbed a slice of melon, took a bite, then dropped the melon and ran as the grocery owner came running out the door.

Kirby yelled, "Cut! We'll print that," as he ran to Wheezer, picked him up hugged him while whistles, applause and laughter filled the air.

The date was August 13, 1928, when the first scene of *The Pie Eating Champeen* was filmed. There are only a few who remember. I remember. You see, I was "Wheezer" and this was the real start of a wonderful life full of interesting people, places and events.

CHAPTER ONE

I was born at 3:55 AM on Saturday, January 24, 1925, at Grant Hospital in Columbus, Ohio. There was an eclipse on the sun. On January 28th I was named Robert Mason Cawley, Jr.

This was near the end of an era known as "The Roaring Twenties" and "The Jazz Age." Women now had the right to vote. Many servicemen had returned disillusioned after the horrors of the Great War. Cars were cheap and money was loose. The Government was still fighting Prohibition and many types of crime. "Scarface" Al Capone was taking over the crime syndicates in Chicago. Boy's suits cost $9.75 with a vest and two pairs of pants, one of them being knickers, and girl's coats were $5.00.

At the grocery, butter was 35 cents a pound while Maxwell House Coffee sold for 49 cents a pound.

This was a time of wealth and wild excess. This was the era of 'Flappers' dancing the 'Charleston' in shimmy dresses with bobbed hair. Endless parties, bathtub gin, gangsters, and lots of jazz music and bootleggers.

Americans had left the farms and small towns and

immigrated to the cities in huge numbers in hopes of finding a more prosperous life, lured by the expanding industry the cities offered.

My mother, Kathryn Fry, and my father, Robert Cawley, had been told not to attempt to have another child after their baby girl died a short two years before. My mother had been adamant that she wanted a child of her own so, with a great deal of worry regarding the results, my mother became pregnant, and now, if we both survived, she would have her son. She was on the critical list and I was not far behind. Both of us had to have private nurses. Mine was a lovely lady named Rena Gillmore. Rena was to play a major role in my life in the far distant future.

My mother kept a clipping from the Columbus Dispatch the day I was born that read: "Persons born on this day have great possibilities. Although you will encounter many difficulties, you will have no trouble in forging ahead if you are sure you are right before starting. A strong religious tendency controls your actions to a great degree. Your love affairs will bring you many worries, but in the end will bring you your greatest happiness."

I have no idea who wrote that but I can tell you it was right on target.

After six weeks in the hospital, I was sent to live at my Aunt Minnie Agee's until Mother was allowed to come home and could take care of me. Aunt Minnie soon found out that when I was fussy after dinner, she could make me instantly happy by putting the radio headphones over my little ears and I would listen to the endless dance music, without commercials, that played from the big bands in remote locations. I waved my little hands with pleasure until I went to sleep. I have always thought that gave me the love for music that has been with me all of my life.

In time, Mother and I went home with my father and my twelve-year-old cousin, George Cawley, and started family life. In our long family history, recorded in the family Bible brought from Ireland when the family first immigrated to the USA, was listed farmers, bankers, coal miners, railroad workers, and various other jobs as the family grew and prospered. There was never a single person listed in the world of entertainment.

My father, born to a coal mining family in West Virginia, had been an outstanding scholar until he was forced to quit school at the age of eight and work a mile deep in the earth trapping a door in the Raymond City coal mine to help support their family. Looking at his old report cards revealed an 'A' student who had a great thirst for knowledge. His greatest regret was that he was never able to go to college to improve his lot in life. After his oldest brother, Shelby, was killed in the mines, leaving a wife and five children, my father left West Virginia and came north to Ohio where he found work on the Hocking Valley Railroad (later to become the C & O) as a brakeman. My dad had an upbeat personality. He laughed a lot and his deep baritone voice with the Southern accent was often heard in song with a variety of mountain and railroad tunes. He and my mother were always very much in love and there was lots of hugging and kissing in our family. I thought this happened in every family. When I grew older and visited other kids' homes, I was surprised to find parents who acted as if they hardly knew each other.

My mother, Kathryn, a very good-looking blond,

was a high school graduate. As a girl she had taken music lessons and played the piano. After high school, she was employed by the Bell Telephone Company as an operator and was soon promoted to supervisor.

For three years, before they met, she had talked to my father on her home telephone when he would call for her brothers, Tink and Charley, who also worked for the railroad. She loved my father's soft Southern voice and asked her brothers to introduce her to him. They refused. Two years later, they relented and told my father that their sister wanted to meet him. A date was set and my mother awaited his arrival. The doorbell rang; she opened the door and heard the soft Southern voice say "Miss Kitty, I'm pleased to meet you."

Over the years this was always a story my mother told. "I heard the voice but there was no one there. My brothers were both six feet four and I was looking straight forward expecting to see someone the same size. Then I looked down and saw Bob who was five foot eight. I opened the screen door and let this little man in."

This always brought a lot of laughs. My father had muscular shoulders and his entire body was like a piece of steel, a result of hard work. He was five foot eight inches tall. My mother, five foot seven.

They fell in love, were married, and now we were a family of four. My father's oldest brother Shelby left his wife Mary and five children when he died. A year to the day after his death his widow, Mary, had a fatal heart attack while being fitted with a pair of glasses, leaving five children. The three oldest sons, Archie, Emmett and Clifford, were already working, but the two youngest, daughter Lena Mae and son George, were in school without a mother and father. Lena Mae went to live with Aunt Lena, Mary's mother, and in 1922 George came to live with my mother and father. He was the image of my dad, always easy going and fun to be around. My mother left her job to be a full-time mom. They rented the bottom floor of a brick duplex at 95 Thurman Avenue, on the South side of Columbus. On one side was the parking lot for employees of the Godman Shoe Factory whose four floors were in an "L" shape around the parking lot. We were separated from the lot by a long stand of lilac bushes. On the other side of our big yard lived Mr. and Mrs. Milausen. An elderly couple who had come to America from Germany before the War.

The Kline family, father, mother and daughter, Mary Jo, two years older than I, had the upstairs of our duplex. Mr. Kline was a butcher. For the most part our area of the south side had blue-collar workers who worked at the Wagner Brewery, the Seagrave Company (builders of fire engines), Buckeye Steel Casting, and the railroad. We did have a police officer, an accountant and a baker who lived down the tree-lined street.

I was just another toddler in the neighborhood. There were very few kids my age, so I played with my toys and spent time with mother and George. My dad was on eight-hour call. The railroads were very busy and he had little free time at home.

It seemed he always came home from trips around 12:45AM. After he showered he would sit by our old Atwater-Kent radio and listen to the WLS Barn Dance from Chicago. He was a fan of the Barn Dance star Louise Massey, a first-rate vocalist/composer and her musical group that often featured her young brother, Curt Massey, a fine singer who also played thirty-two instruments. My father never dreamed that one day his little son would be producing and directing *The Curt Massey Show* on NBC-TV.

Destiny was starting to gently move me toward the world of show business.

Although Hollywood was still producing silents, the end of that era was in sight.

Before "Our Gang" came upon the scene, I had made my show biz debut singing "The Wreck of Old 97" on WCAH Radio – Columbus on March 2, 1928.

Soon after this, my mother read in the *Columbus Dispatch* that the newspaper was going into partnership with producer/writer Hal Roach to produce an "Our Gang Comedy" movie with central Ohio children making up the entire cast. If interested, they should fill out the application form that appeared in the paper and mail it to the Our Gang Editor of the *Dispatch*. This idea was a stroke of genius on Mr. Roach's part. He had pitched twenty-six different newspapers in twenty-six different cities around the USA to enter this project where current "Our Gang" films had started to lose viewer interest, and a salesman like Mr. Roach wasn't about to let that happen. He was aware that in 1926 Warner Brothers had released an experimental short sound film titled "April Showers" featuring the voice of the world's greatest entertainer, Al Jolson. The experiment was a huge success, and in 1927 Jolson was the star of the *Jazz Singer*, the world's first feature-length talkie in which he said the immortal phrase, "You ain't heard nothing yet."

Out of the twenty-six films to be made, one of the children in a film cast would be taken to Hollywood for a cameo role in a regular "Our Gang" film. The young actor would be paid all expenses, to and from Hollywood, plus expenses while in Hollywood for the parents would be paid by Hal Roach Productions.

Mother showed me pictures of the "gang" and asked me if I would like to be in a movie. I had never seen a movie, but I made "Wheezer" my choice. In the picture in the paper, "Wheezer" was wearing a vest and that's who I wanted to be because my dad wore a vest. Mother cut out the application and sent it in along with a current photo that was required and we waited.

Mr. Roach had written twenty-six different screenplays for the twenty-six cities competing and the *Dispatch*-sponsored film would be called *The Pie Eating Champeen*.

The principal cast would number six, plus the dog "Pete," who would also audition. Each cast hopeful, including the dog, would appear on stage at Loews Broad Theater before a live audience and judges on separate evenings with a winner selected each night until the cast was complete.

Grandview, a suburb of Columbus, had been selected as the location for the shoot.

One day in early July of 1928, a letter arrived saying I had been selected to compete and was to report to the Lowes Broad Theater in the heart of downtown Columbus at 7 PM on August 1, 1928, dressed as "Wheezer" when the boy to play that role would be selected.

CHAPTER TWO

My mother, father and I rode on the streetcar to Broad and High Street, the center of Columbus. I had never been to town at night and the many lights and displays of the department store windows proved to be a fairy land. We crossed High Street and walked the block west to Lowes Theater where the huge marquee spelled out "Wheezer Contest Tonight."

The street outside the theater was bedlam. All I could see were potential "Wheezers" and their mothers pushing and shoving their way into the theater as they kept saying things like, "You're going to be a movie star" (whatever that was) or " You will soon be in Hollywood" (wherever that was), plus constant reminders to smile, not muss their hair, and not to blow their nose. Some little guys cried and others told their mothers they didn't want to go into the theater and got slapped for that remark.

My father showed our letter from the *Dispatch* to an usher and we were seated in the center of the theater. I was in awe of the beautiful interior and could hardly wait to see my first movie which was Jackie Coogan in *The Bugle Call*. I was thrilled by what I saw on the screen and it was a good thing it was a silent film because the mothers were making so much noise telling their sons how to act that you could have never heard the soundtrack had it been a talkie.

When the film was over, the lights came on in the theater and all the contestants were told to line up in the aisles and theater people would take them back stage. I moved into the line where mothers were holding onto their sons demanding they go back stage with them. Someone came onto the stage and announced ONLY the contestants would be allowed back stage and mothers must go back to their seats.

At last, we slowly moved backstage and I was amazed and thrilled by all the sets, the lights and everything I could see. This was a wonderland. It was love at first sight.

Some of the boys were blubbering and crying for their mothers and were calmed by theater workers as we were placed in long rows across the stage. Two or three who screamed and cried were returned to their mothers and were out of the contest.

Those remaining stood in their line behind the closed curtain, and then, wonder of all wonders, the pit orchestra began to play. A voice from somewhere announced, "The selection for the Wheezer contest is about to begin. Here is the evening's host for this event, vaudeville star, Mister Al Herman."

The band played a fanfare as there was a roar of applause. The curtain slowly opened and we saw the huge audience out front. From the wings came Al Herman singing "Toot, Toot, Tootsie", a huge Al Jolsen hit.

The crowd was going wild with applause and whistles, but on stage many of the boys were screaming, crying and calling for their mothers, while others tried to climb the curtain at the back of the stage.

Al Herman, as the great Jolson often did, was working in blackface, but none of the children on stage had ever seen a black person and they were reacting in terror.

Al had the conductor stop the music then turned to the contestants and asked, "Isn't anyone going to say hello to old Al?"

Who will ever know what made me do it? While the others huddled at the rear of the stage, I walked out to the footlights and up to Al and stuck out my hand.

"Hi, Al."

"Hi, young man, what's your name."

"I'm Robert Mason Cawley, Jr."

Al knelt down and said something to the musical director.

"Come here, Robert."

I went to him and he sat me on his knee and sang "Sonny Boy" to me, greeted by big applause. When the other boys saw that nothing bad had happened to me, they all got back in their lines and the crisis was over. Al sang "April Shows", then started to explain to the audience how the contest would work with a combination of audience applause and the decision of the judges. Al was explaining the rules, but the audience was laughing at something going on behind him. When he turned around, he saw that I was moving kids from one line to another. Telling them where to stand. He laughed and turned to the crowd.

"My God, Robert Mason is already directing."

The audience loved it. For all intents and purposes, the contest was over and the audience and judges awarded me the role of "Wheezer" in the Hal Roach Our Gang Comedy *The Pie Eating Champeen*.

After the evening was over, Al Herman, with his makeup removed, met with my mother and father and urged them to give me a few tap dance lessons then bring me to Hollywood where he thought I had a great future. He told them (and he was right) that a great era was going to be opening soon for kids who could sing and dance, and with my personality, I would get all the work I wanted. He even gave my dad the names of several Hollywood agents that he felt would be right for me.

Hollywood is three thousand miles from Columbus and my father had a steady paycheck from a solid company. He did not realize the future, that in just over a year, the stock market would crash and that he would be walking the streets trying to find work. If his decision would have been different, I would have arrived in Hollywood before Mickey Rooney and who knows what could have happened?

CHAPTER THREE

Each night at Lowes Broad Theater, a new cast member including the dog that was to play "Pete" were selected.

The picture of the cast was front page material, but it was the WRONG cast.

I was the only one in the photo who was really in the cast. The next day the paper made the correction with photos of the real cast.

On August 7, 1928, the cast met each other for the first time at the Grandview Community Center. Pretty blond Betty Jane Fulmer would play the role of "Jean Darling," the vamp of the comedy. Cute Betty Jane Wright, with her dark bangs, was cast as "Mary Ann." The freckled Walter Lee Dunlap had won the part of "Harry Spear," and Joe Comella, of Bellefontaine, Ohio, who at thirteen years of age tipped the scales at 190 pounds, would be "Joe Cobb." Little Beatrice Carter was "Farina", and Rex, a Boston terrier, had won the role of "Pete" and would be with me for the bulk of the film.

I shook Rex's paw and met Betty Fulmer, Betty

Jane Wright, Walter Dunlap and Joe Comella, plus a kid named Hugh Winkle, who had been selected for a minor role as a bully. All this time all of our mothers were meeting each other. Then little Beatrice C. Carter, who would play "Farina" and her mother arrived. Kirby introduced them to everyone. You must remember, I had never seen a black person and I thought she was wearing 'blackface' makeup. I walked up to her and ran my finger down her cheek then showed my mother that the black didn't come off. Needless to say, my mother was really upset by my actions and apologized over and over for her son. Mrs. Carter smiled and told her not to think about it; she understood. As it turned out, Beatrice and I became good friends and always played together when we were not in a scene.

After introductions were over, we sat down with Frank Kirby, the director, and his assistants and crew to go over the story.

"This is a comedy with fun elements that will appeal to audiences. Our story starts small and will build toward the rip-roaring climax of a gigantic pie-throwing scene that will involve over one thousand kids; every child who made an application to play roles in the film has been invited to take part. Up to that point, you will be involved in a big field day that will include races. There will be races for fat boys, three-legged races, tugs of war, and many events of this kind that will include kids who did not win major roles as you did.

"We are scheduled to film starting Monday morning, August 13th, and will continue through the 16th when we should wrap the production. If we are forced to go into an extra day, we will, but with your help and attention to my direction, we should be able to get every scene with just one take. This will be the first full-length movie ever to be filmed in Columbus, so let's make it a good one. You will be here at the Grandview Community Center each day no later than 9:30AM for wardrobe and makeup. Filming will start at 10 AM and we will film rain or shine so be ready for a full day's work. Always listen close to my directions and the directions of my assistants. We're going to have lots of fun and make a really good movie."

For the most part, we did as were told and it was fun. The only hitch came on the afternoon of the 14th when Kirby was directing Jean Darling and another actor in a scene. I suggested we play soldier, so we went to the people who catered lunch to borrow pots and pans for helmets. The catering people had run out of pots but I was not going to play soldier without Farina. Somewhere I found a clean porcelain 'chamber pot' and put it on her head. The handle was up too high to go under her chin. I pulled the pot down until it covered her eyebrows; now, the handle fit tight. We had played for maybe ten minutes when an assistant called on everyone to come to the area off the cameras for the next scene that included the entire cast. Everyone took pots off their heads, gave them back to the catering crew and ran to the set. That is everyone except Farina who called me to help her. The heavy pot was stuck and I was unable to pull it off. Soon assistants were there, and then Director Kirby, my mother, Bernice's mother, and all the mothers of the principal actors. Kirby wanted to know how this happened and I told him. Bernice was crying but the pot remained jammed. Kirby told an assistant to call the Grandview Fire Department, "Tell them to get over here fast. We have an emergency."

I realized that the film, which had been ahead of schedule, was now at a standstill. Soon daylight would fade and Kirby would have to call it a day. Beatrice continued to cry and her mother tried to calm her as my mother was reading the riot act to me while apologizing to Mrs. Carter and Kirby while his staff grew grimmer by the second.

The fire department arrived with bottles of spray that the firemen shot up under the pot, and then presto, Beatrice's head was free. She wiped her tears and hugged me then we both ran hand in hand ahead of Kirby and his crew to the set.

As it turned out, we were able to make up time and finished that day on schedule.

The next day was the big climax, and close to four thousand spectators and more police were on hand. There were at least a thousand kids on the set plus the principal actors. We got right into the pie-eating contest and then into the mob scene where hundreds, if not thousands, of pies were thrown or pushed into faces. Pies enough to feed all the kids in a dozen villages were used during that film's wild scene, which had for its background the Grandview Avenue shopping area.

Where was Wheezer?

I was on my mark under a picnic table where I shared my cherry pie with my pal Pete. Mr. Kirby had made me a gift of my first pair of sandals, and I worried all through the scene that he would be upset because I had caught a piece of lemon pie on the toe of one of new shoes.

Over the yelling and the mêlée, I heard Kirby and his assistants yelling, "CUT, CUT." Pete and I crawled out from under the table to see kids smeared with pie from head to toe. Little Farina's smiling face wore what remained of a marshmallow pie. The audience was roaring with laughter. From out of the mob Kirby found me and carried me around the set, stopping to praise his crew. "Well, Wheezer, we did it. *The Pie Eating Champeen* is a wrap." He took me to my mother and thanked her for letting her son be in the movie. He left and told the other principals and their mothers goodbye.

The cast, along with my mother and I, went back to the Community Center, picked up our personal belongings, then got a streetcar and headed home. I didn't want it to end. I knew I was going to miss Mr. Kirby and his crew. I would miss Grandview and the cast but that was my first lesson about show business. People are put together to make a film, either in front of or behind the camera. You become family and very close, then in a few weeks or months it's over and, for the most part, you never see any of those people again.

It hit really hard the evening our family went to Lowes Broad to see *The Pie Eating Champeen*. The title of the film was up in lights. On stage was a Mexican review that starred the Perezcaro sisters, great dancers, who put on a super act different from any other in vaudeville.

Once again, we sat through the screening of Jackie Coogan in *The Bugle Call*, now enjoyable without all the noise the mothers made previously.

Then it came up on the screen and there I was, larger than life. The movie got great applause and we sat through the entire program once more and left for home near midnight. I fell asleep on the streetcar. My father carried me home.

CHAPTER FOUR

After the weeks of build-up, the contest, and the filming, it seemed there was a huge void in my life. I played with other little kids but I missed the thrill that show business had provided. At last I talked with Mother and Dad about following Al Herman's advice and to take dancing lessons.

The folks put it like they always did.

I could try dancing lessons and they would pay for them; however, if a time came I did not want to practice or continue, I only had to tell them I wanted to quit and the lessons would stop.

After checking out teachers, I was enrolled in a class at Oscar School of Dance. Mr. Conrad was considered the best teacher in central Ohio. Being in a class filled with girls and boys proved to be lots of fun, but Oscar soon moved me to two private lessons a week. He was a real taskmaster. He reminded me that this was a part of show business, and it WAS a business.

By October, I was appearing in reviews and was involved in shows he produced. My father had bought a masonite board that he put in the basement along with a wind-up Victrola and a stack of records to dance to. I loved the sound of my taps and was very proud of my black patent leather shoes which I always softened with Vaseline after every practice session.

In December a tragic event took place. Little Ernie Tumeric lived up the street on the other side of the alley that ran behind our backyards. We were the same age and loved to play together. Both our mothers had told us never to play in the alley, but young boys don't listen. Just before Christmas, we had a heavy snow and we were in the alley playing hide and seek and it was my time to hide. I got behind a pile of wood in a neighbor's yard and waited for Ernie. The sky was turning dark and no Ernie. In the gloom of the afternoon, I dimly saw the tail lights on the big garbage truck turning out at the far end of the alley. A few seconds later, I found what remained of my little playmate. He was in a bloody ball, head crushed by the truck he never heard driven by a driver who never saw the tiny tot in the blinding snow. I screamed all the way home for my mother to save Ernie. When I broke into our kitchen and told her what happened she called an ambulance and the police, then put on her overcoat and went to the Tumeric house to break the news to Ernie's mother and to support her until his father came home from work at the factory.

I remember the funeral. A great deal of crying and screams. In an open casket was my friend with his head, from his eyebrows up, wrapped in soft white cloth. Father Gilfillen said that Ernie was playing hide and seek in heaven where there were no trucks, only soft clouds. It was my first contact with death.

The next time I played in the alley, I was a teenager playing basketball.

Oscar featured me in a review on New Year's Eve where I wore my first tux and sang and danced to "When You're Smiling" and "Back in Your Own Backyard," plus a pretty ballad titled, "Jeannine, I Dream of Lilac Time." The adult crowd sang Auld Lang Syne, tooted horns and swung noisemakers as 1928 faded into history.

For this soon-to-be four-year-old, it had been, with the exception of Ernie's death, a very good year.

Life was on a high note for our family and a great deal of the United States. I was happy in our home and George was happy in school. We had no warning that for us, like millions of other Americans, our lives would be violently changed in the days ahead.

CHAPTER FIVE

Starting the first of 1929, I was in high gear. Dancing up and down steps, coming off the steps doing splits, double wings and new fancy footwork. I was in demand for paid engagements on radio singing and dancing as a guest artist to great new musical numbers including "Ain't Misbehaving" and "Honey Suckle Rose." I did a takeoff on popular radio star, Rudy Vallee, complete with a very large megaphone. "Singing' in the Rain" and "Star Dust" were new and I did both often. In that era, how could you be a top male performer and not do some Jolson hits in blackface? The super tear-jerking "Little Pal," the uptempo "California, Here I Come" and the heartbreaking "I Wonder What's Become of Sally" were winners. I worked hotels, lodges, variety shows as well as radio.

Prior to becoming Wheezer, I had spent many late spring, summer and early autumn evenings sitting on our front porch listening to the music from Milhausen's side yard. Someone in their family played accordion, and most evenings they sang songs in German. Songs from their homeland. I had no idea what the words meant but I learned to sing them phonetically. One day I was at Mrs. Milausen's to pick up a pan of sweet rolls she had baked for our family and she was singing a song in German and I sang with her. She couldn't believe her ears and the next evening I was invited over to their yard, and with the accordion playing I sang a list of their songs in perfect German. The next thing I knew my mother, father, and I were invited to the German-American Club located on the south side where many times I would sing a program of German songs backed by a four-piece group. It was lots of fun and the sandwiches and desserts were fabulous and the President of the club always gave me a new twenty-dollar bill at the end of the evening.

In a scrapbook I have a variety of clippings written in German from their newspaper praising my work. We were unable to read them but Mrs. Milhausen read them to us and they were wonderful. I always tried to be available when they called.

CHAPTER SIX

As we went into summer, my mother felt I had all the instruction I could get from Oscar. She had read that Eddie Coleson, a sensational black dancer known as "The Cincinnati Whirlwind" was taking two and half months away from club work to visit his mother who lived in the Mount Vernon District of Columbus. Mother got a hold of Eddie's mother to see if it might be possible for me to take lessons from him while he was in town. Financial arrangements were made and I was slated for three dance lessons a week while he was available.

You must remember that during these years, black entertainers could not work white nightclubs, hotels or theaters. With the exception of Bill Robinson, we never got to see many fantastic black artists. If you desired to see artists like Duke Ellington, Cab Calloway, or any black entertainers, you had to go to New York where you could go up to Harlem and enjoy the shows at the Cotton Club or Apollo Theater.

Eddie had danced at the major black clubs in the United States and had built a national reputation.

Mom and I took the streetcar to the Mount Vernon District and walked four blocks, with never a white face in sight, until we reached a tenement with the correct address. We went up three flights of stairs to the Colesons' apartment where we met Eddie and his mother. Eddie was in his late twenties with a build like Fred Astaire. Our rehearsal hall was the Colesons' kitchen with the table against one wall with the chairs stacked on top. The floor was covered by linoleum.

From the first routine with Eddie, I realized I knew nothing about dancing, but I learned. Eddie was unable to tell me the name of various steps but would dance a step, then tell me to do "one of those things." For two-and-a-half months I was at the Colesons' three days a week for two-hour sessions. I learned and could execute those "things" he taught me. We would dance as a team with the sweat pouring off both of us in that hot kitchen.

Mother asked what song I should workout to. He told her "The Rose Room." We had never heard the song, but following his directions, we found a record shop that had it. That record got played until it wore out. That song would later play an important part in a key decision I would make later in my life.

The summer went by too fast and Eddie was back on the club circuit, but he left behind a "Columbus Whirlwind" that brought a form of dance that white Columbus had never seen. I had reached the peak of my career as a dancer.

On the national scene, Herbert Hoover, the President of the United States, promised that in all the United States there would be "a chicken in every pot and car in every garage." We had chicken often and we had a garage, but no car, so we had high hopes.

That all went out the window on October 24, 1929, when the Stock Market crashed on a day that became infamous as "Black Thursday." The crash did not occur in just one day but was spread out to the end of October, and then came the start of the descent into the Great Depression that would last for ten years.

The newspapers were filled with photos of people jumping to their death from high-rise buildings knowing they were in financial ruin, and the radio kept America abreast of the gloom and doom news.

I only knew my parents were very worried over the future. In November it became evident that my father's job with the railroad would be gone in 1930 and that millions of men, young and old, would be looking for work. Homes would be foreclosed and banks would repossess farms. My dad thought if he were laid off, he could find a job fast, but mother was not so sure. We had rent to pay, bills to pay, and no source of income if dad's job was gone. Mother made a snap but wise decision. "I'm going to see if I can get Robert on a vaudeville circuit. The railroad has said that even if you are laid off, our family passes to travel on any railroad will still be good and we get to the locations on the train." My father protested, but she laid out the cold, hard facts. He and George would keep things going at home while she managed my career on the road. Then, if after Dad was laid off he could get a steady job, we would quit vaudeville. The die was cast. I would have great competition in the theaters, but we had to get bookings and send the bulk of the money home. Mom made the needed calls and I was booked in Cleveland and Detroit theaters over the holidays.

Being four years old I didn't understand the situation we were in. I only knew I was going to sing and dance and, best of all, ride the train.

CHAPTER SEVEN

Mother and I each had a small suitcase. Mine carried my tux and my precious tap shoes in a cloth sack that included my jar of Vaseline. Casual wear, socks, underwear and PJs. Mother had several dresses, undies, makeup and a stack of arrangements for the various orchestras who would back my act.

The family opened what few Christmas presents we had early Christmas morning, then mother and I caught the streetcar to the Union Station to get our train to Cleveland. A few miles out of town, I realized that the next day was Christmas and Dad and George were back home. Mother bought me a little glass railroad engine filled with candy and that little keepsake, minus the candy, sits on a shelf in my office. Cleveland had an excellent pit band, as did Detroit. Both of my jobs at the theaters were contracted. These would be the last contracted jobs in vaudeville. In the future, only the winner would be paid. Normal winnings were twenty-five dollars cash.

What a wild year 1930 was. At times it seemed all I did was sing and dance and then sleep in the coach on a train with Mother next to me. We would get into a town early in the day; my tux would be cleaned and processed while we ate low-cost food. Before the show, Mom would get some things from a grocery or deli which we would eat on the train en route to our next stop. In time, all the towns and theaters looked the same. People on the street begging for food or money. At night whole families slept in doorways, and in the theater the competition was really tough. Many old-timers who had once been headliners on Broadway trying to make enough money to live another week were being booed and mistreated by the customers. At many theaters the admission had been cut to a quarter or, in some, fifteen cents. The crowds were hungry, angry and prone to violence. They brought bags of rotten fruit, worn-out shoes, and pieces of auto tires to throw at the entertainers whose acts they didn't like. Oh yes, there really was a hook. A long wood pole with a shepherd's crook on the end that went around the neck of an entertainer whose act was failing, dragging the poor souls off the stage.

The saddest thing was the old-timers, many husband-and-wife acts who had been at the top of vaudeville, and now their careers were over. They had no food, no money, and no way to get to the next town or go home, if there was a home to go to. Several of these situations led to suicide.

A month into our journey my dad called Mom to tell her he had been laid off and was looking for a job. As of that moment, I was the family's only source of income.

I was on a roll. Town after town, night after night, I won and took the cash. Later we would stand on empty railroad platforms waiting for a train that might not arrive for hours. Not so bad in the spring, but really rough during those cold winters.

The theaters had very good pit bands. Musicians were starving and would work for any wage. As always, the tune smiths kept great songs coming. "Am I Blue," "I May Be Wrong" and Louise" were public favorites.

Shows ran a little over an hour, and you worked only once unless there was a tie for first place. Then you came back with a second chance to win the cash. Most of the time I worked Fridays and Saturdays and we were home the bulk of the week. Dad walked the streets from dawn to dark trying to find any work possible. For three days he got a job moving heavy freight and his ankles swelled over the tops of his work shoes and Mother spent hours bathing his feet.

With spring and summer on the way, Mom spent hours on the phone booking me into county fairs and festivals around the country to generate extra cash between weekend vaudeville dates.

We played them all, large or small. A great deal of the time the backup musicians were less than perfect and several times Mom had to run down the producers for our money, but she always got it.

Although I kept winning, the audiences were more out of control. Several entertainers had been badly injured by thrown objects and a young woman had lost an eye. Dad was still pounding the pavement with few results, so we decided to go into the fall/winter season.

I had success in many major cities and one was Pittsburgh where I had won five times. Two weeks before we returned for a sixth appearance, my mother made the only mistake she ever made as my manager.

She felt that the audience in Pittsburgh had liked my work and now we would give them something different. No snappy songs, no flashy dances, but a musical "reading" with me in drag doing something called "Betty at the Baseball Game."

When I was announced, there was a roar of applause as they expected me to come out singing and dancing. Instead, they saw me in a dress wearing a picture hat over my blond wig.

The audience went ballistic! I was hit by rotten fruit, pieces of tire, and anything they could throw as they booed. My mother cried, begging the manager to give me the hook. He was crying. I was his favorite performer and he refused to pull me off the stage. I was crying after someone in the balcony hit me in the head with a rotten head of cabbage that spun me around. I stayed on my feet and completed my three minutes, although my face and clothes were covered with rotten eggs. As soon as I got cleaned up, we headed for the train station. Mother threw the dress and hat and wig into a dumpster. As we traveled to Cincinnati she cried almost all the way and kept telling me she would never change the act. Again, I went to sleep to the click-clack of the train's wheels.

In Cincinnati I won, singing and dancing. We returned to Pittsburgh in the fall. I came out singing and dancing to a standing ovation and left with the cash.

Home for a brief break I was entered in The Gateway Jubilee contest. No singing and dancing. Just showing up in the best Native American Indian costume. Something set off a battle royal between the contestants. Swinging rubber tomahawks and shooting arrows. When the dust settled, there I was in my war bonnet, made up red skin and a complete Indian outfit the first prize winner, and what a prize it was. A silver monoplane with pedals, plus a leather flight jacket, helmet and goggles. I wanted to stay home and ride around the neighborhood in my plane, but duty called back on the road.

In December my father landed a steady job with the Transient Service Bureau.

The country's transients were almost daily becoming more stabilized through the agency. Service bureaus were set up for their care throughout the nation. Men without funds were fed, given clean beds, baths, haircuts and hospitalization. They were required to work at least sixteen hours a week in payment for the service. My dad was a Senior Registration Clerk who took all the background on the incoming men. My dad had been one of these men and knew how to talk to them. G.E. Hoover, who ran the local operation, told Dad with his know-how and natural ability he could be a superintendent if he had a college education.

I finished my engagements and we came home in time for the holidays. It was wonderful being home. The only sad note was that George had returned to West Virginia to complete high school and live with Aunt Leana who was having physical problems and needed help around the house.

Vaudeville, except in New York and Chicago, had been killed by the talkies. I was finished with vaudeville but felt a new door would open that would send my life in new directions.

CHAPTER EIGHT

A few days before Christmas a gentleman called requesting a meeting with my family to discuss a possible radio series. He said that they would like to sign a contract for me to be Master of Ceremonies, sing and dance for a new radio series for the Theronoid Company; Theronoid was a rubberized belt that resembled a filled tire inner tube that you put around your waist. Plugged into an electrical outlet, it would vibrate and you would shed unwanted fat. The show was to be called *Theronoid's All-Star Juvenile Show*. Did we want a steady radio showcase? You bet. They wanted a regular musical cast of kids consisting of Arlene "Honey" Holestein, Eddie Thompson, and Howard Engels, plus a small studio orchestra. When we became adults, Eddie Thompson would be with the Metropolitan Opera; Howard Engels was an Ohio State Highway Patrol trooper; and "Honey" would get married and retire from show business.

Monday, Wednesday and Friday evenings 8:45 to 9:15 PM on WCAH you could hear us.

Once this show became news, the floodgates of

opportunity opened and the entire decade became a carnival spin.

During this year, I won a variety of local contests with my three fox terriers and my pet duck, Jerry, who would walk in pet parades beside me with just a red ribbon around his neck as a leash. The winnings included three scooters, which enabled me to provide scooters to neighborhood kids who didn't have one, and roller skates that let me play street hockey with an empty tuna can filled with rocks resealed as a puck. That puck really smarted when it hit me in the mouth, taking the bottom of my two front teeth out. I tried to explain to Dad that we had won but the only thing that concerned him was the cost of rebuilding the bottom of my choppers.

Being a kid you did stupid kid things that your family would always remember. Christmas time found Mom baking tins of cookies as gifts. She had a Santa Claus, reindeer and Christmas wreath cutters, but somewhere the Christmas tree cutter was missing. I was sent to the local variety store to buy a new cutter. When I returned I gave my mother the new cutter in the sack. On opening it, she saw the cutter was a fish. Demanding to know why I brought this home, I explained that the old gent at the store was out of Christmas tree cutters but if she stood the fish on its tail and covered the cookie with red and green icing it would look just like a Christmas tree. I never saw Mom put on her coat so fast. Grabbing me by the arm the two of us marched back to the store where she read the old man the riot act for selling a fish as a Christmas tree to a stupid kid. Getting her money back, we got the correct cutter at the hardware store. Hey, Merry Christmas.

I did shows with little Jack Little and his orchestra. Several productions with his talented sister, Gladys, and several shots with Art Kassel and his "Castles in the Air" orchestra. Then I was signed for a featured role with *Uncle Peter Quigley and His Clever Kiddies*, a one-hour show, broadcast before a live audience every Sunday afternoon from the ballroom of the Jefferson Hotel. I did MC work, sang, danced (with the studio guys holding the mic down by my feet), and did "readings" which proved to be a top audience winner. The "readings" were written by my father but the audience thought they just came out of my head. The New Method Laundry was the sponsor and it was a hit that ran for six years.

I played the groom in a musical production *The Mock Wedding*. Old photos prove I was an unhappy camper as my "bride" was five inches taller than me and I had to stand on a ladder to kiss her.

Next, I was MC of the *Kiddies Living Model Style Show* doing a radio broadcast in the High Street display windows of the Boston Store over WSEN. The show, with living kiddy models, ran every hour starting at 10:30 AM on Saturdays and ran for several months.

1930 Easter Sunday morning, we awoke to what seemed the screaming of a million sirens. Rushing to the front porch, we could see huge clouds of smoke from downtown Columbus. The radio told us that the Ohio Penitentiary, a primitive hell hole located just a couple blocks from Lowes Broad Theater, was on fire. This became the blackest mark in Ohio's history as Warden Thomas let over 250 prisoners burn to death because he refused to let them out in the prison yard, surrounded by high walls that had prison guards, US

Army and National Guard troops deployed on the walls and there was no chance of escape.

There were many lodges and social clubs at that time that liked to hire; Maccabeus, Elks, M.E. Brotherhood and others were paying for shows with kiddy talent. Mom booked them all and a new wrinkle was added. Mary Ellen Garrad, a petite blond, and I teamed for long runs as a duet. We did novelty hits of the era including "Darling, I'll See You in Church," "When You Were the Girl on the Scooter," and "Sittin' on the Backyard Fence," which we did in cat costumes.

Away from the entertainment scene, an important incident was shaping up. We would visit friends and I would peck at their piano keys while the adults tried to talk. I told my dad I wanted a piano and he agreed. One day, an old black upright that he had bought for five dollars at a fire sale was delivered. When it was placed in the living room he told me, "If you ever do anything with it, I'll buy you a new one."

Mom got busy looking for the best piano teacher that a little money could hire. It was the Great Depression. I wound up a student of Dr. Frank A. Meier, the Dean of Capitol College and a concert pianist.

He could have been one of the greatest concert pianists of all time, but he had a fear of appearing in public. Now he had a pupil who loved appearing in public and he would use his teaching skills to mold him. Did he ever. He gave me a career that would last a lifetime. A wonderful man and the greatest of teachers. I took my first lesson on Friday, September 19, 1930. In three years, I would win a national championship.

I auditioned and was accepted as a member of the famous Trinity Boys Choir under the direction of Revered Karl H. "POP" Honeig, a native of Germany who was a master organist/pianist and vocal instructor. This was a great honor, as many auditioned but few were chosen. I was assigned the vestment that had been worn by choir boy vocal legend Austin Young. His name was sown into garments before a church worker sewed my name over his. I also had his wooden locker in which he had carved his name. Now known as Austin "Skin" Young, he was the featured male vocalist with the great Paul Whiteman Orchestra. Looking at a Whiteman payroll sheet of that era, you note "Skin" was making $200 per week while a fellow band member named Bing Crosby, who sang as part of a trio called "The Rhythm Boys" with Al Rinker and Harry Barris, was paid $150. Pop was a real taskmaster and teacher. He had one firm rule. If he ever had to speak to you twice about disturbing choir practice, you were out of the choir. There was no shortage of replacements, no matter how good you were. I managed to get a single warning during my third year. Talking with a fellow member as Pop worked with the altos. He smashed his hands down on the keys and the room was silent. "Cawley, when you die you will sit up in the casket and tell the funeral director how to do it. Shut up, this is warning number one." Needless to say, there was never a second warning.

During my final two years with the choir, I won the Agnes H. Johnson Memorial Cross, a solid silver Celtic cross that hung on a red ribbon over my vestment. My friend, Martin Rohe, won the runner-up cross, and he and I would lead the choir as we came up the aisle on Sunday. Should either of us have won our crosses three times, we could have kept them, but our voices changed and that chapter closed. The last half of my final year as a boy soprano, I sang falsetto but there was no way I could fool Pop. My cross went to my friend Ernie Nuzzo, then the outstanding boy singer. If the boy who wears the cross now will look close, he will find my teeth marks in the soft silver. One morning when the front row of the choir knelt down the leg of the board was on my foot. It was bite the cross or scream until I could get the word to all twelve members on the board to rise a little so I could free my foot.

There were many memories created during the choir years. Huge society weddings where I stood by the priest and sang "Oh, Perfect Love" to the newly-weds kneeling below. That always resulted in a five-dollar bill from the groom's best man.

There were all the performances we gave with the favorite being at the famous Mira Mar Restaurant on Christmas Eve where we were served a fabulous dinner, then presented a box of their famous chocolates and a five-dollar bill.

I will always remember one day when Pop took me with him into the church tower where we went into a dust-layered cell-like room where cabled controls led up to massive chimes. What appeared to be wheelbarrow handles acted as keys for Pop's trained hands and feet. When three chime notes are struck simultaneously, Pop would crush two handles and kick number three for a chord. The chimes would start to ring as the pigeons flew out of their nesting place until the evening serenade was finished. Seven days a week he would play the beautiful chimes that would ring out over downtown Columbus. The church faced the state house and was just a block from the fabled Broad and High street intersection.

We all learned a great deal from Pop. He was a wonderful teacher and a fine man.

My last three years at Trinity I was also an altar boy at very early and special services. I served many times with Bishop Hobson as he always requested me.

Otherwise, the radio shows and live performance dates kept rolling.

CHAPTER NINE

Where did 1930 go? Dr. Meier had me practice scales until I thought my fingers would drop off before we started on the classics. My mother saw that I was a member of the Columbus branch of the National Saturday Music Clubs, which enabled us to attend concerts by famous classical artists like the famous operatic contralto, Schumann-Hank and to compete in state contests.

Franklin D. Roosevelt was inaugurated as the 32nd President of the United States which really pleased my folks.

Hit songs included "Brother, Can You Spare a Dime," "I'm Getting Sentimental Over You," "April in Paris," "Let's Have Another Cup of Coffee," and Cole Porter's "Night and Day." Also, a couple of great movies, *All Quiet on the Western Front,* starring Lew Ayers that won the Academy Award, and *Hell's Angels,* were filled with sensational air footage.

Primo Carnera of Italy, whom I would later meet, knocked out Jack Starkey to win the heavyweight boxing crown.

It wasn't all practice or shows. Kids are kids, and

we were playing "Cops and Gangsters" on the Godman fire escapes and basement with toy guns and lots of make-believe. No one wanted to be cops. The newspapers and the radio were filled with stories of outlaws.

Baby Face Nelson, Pretty Boy Floyd and others were starting to grab headlines, and the guy who thrilled kids and their parents the most was John Dillinger, as he robbed banks, and the bankers were those people who foreclosed on farms and homes and destroyed millions of lives. These outlaws became folk heroes. I had a vest, just like John, and a gun moll in tiny red-haired, Louise Vashaw, a daughter of a CPA, so I was Dillinger. Louise's father wasn't too excited over his daughter being a playtime gun moll, but she stayed the course and no one fell from the fire escapes.

CHAPTER TEN

I had a little fox terrier named Ginger, and soon two puppies arrived named Nip and Tuck. With the little money we had, we could not afford more mouths to feed, so Dad put the pups in a burlap sack and headed for the Green Lawn dam to drown them. Mom and I sat in the kitchen, the only room in the house that was heated, crying until a half hour later dad walked in with the pups. He said he just couldn't do it. We would all have to cut back on rations. Mom and I were smiling and dancing while the pups played around Dad's shoes. They were all part of the family until they died of old age.

At Thanksgiving, we faced another crisis. No turkey, no chicken, but we did have a pet chicken we called "Biddy Doyle" who laid eggs. I had won Biddy as a little chick at some contest and she would answer when you called her and was just a sweetheart. Thanksgiving morning we had veggies from our garden. Mom was going to bake biscuits and make a pie. Dad said, "Kitty, put a kettle of hot water on. I'm going to take Biddy behind the garage and then you can prepare her for dinner."

He called to her and she came, was gathered up in one hand, and he picked up his sharpened hatchet with the other, and down the yard he went and they vanished behind the garage. My mother had tears in her eyes and I was choking back emotions when I looked out the back window and saw Dad with Biddy under his arm cackling away.

"Kitty, forget the hot water. Biddy looked me in the eye and I can't do it. I don't care if we never have meat. Biddy has a home here as long as she lives." No wonder my dad was always a hero in my eyes.

This was an era when each day saw at least three men coming to the backdoor asking if they could work for food. We didn't have work for them but not a single one left hungry. After they had eaten, Mother would give them an extra sandwich and a piece of cake in a little sack to take as they moved on.

Marathons and Walkabouts were sweeping the country as couples, mostly, but not always young were willing to dance or walk for twenty-four hours each day with only 10-minute breaks each hour before they collapsed.

Most of these events provided basic food, coffee and soft drinks to the contestants but it was a brutal and cruel competition. If you lost your partner, be it male or female, you could dance/walk solo for eight hours and during that time if someone lost a partner you could continue with them. At the end, the last couple standing won the cash prize. There were medical people there in case someone had to be rushed to a hospital, which was often. This craze hit Columbus along with the rest of the nation and WSEN wanted me on the air from 4 to 10 PM singing and dancing with the orchestra as well as being out on the floor interviewing the contestants. They really wanted me out there until 2 AM seven days a week but I could not work past 10 PM because of the Child Labor Law. I had to be teamed with an adult announcer who could go until 2 AM.

There was one problem that they solved at once. We would go in early Monday, Wednesday and Friday and transcribe *The Theronoid Show* as long as the Walkabout ran. Finding a co-host proved to be a stroke of luck. A guy riding the rails to New York had dropped in. He had been a small-time comic in vaudeville. His deceased father had been a circus clown. He only wanted a few weeks work, as he would be moving on. The station manager liked the young man and thought we would make a good team. I was called in to meet my announcing partner. He was from Vincennes, Indiana, and his name was Red Skelton. We worked the Walkabout at the Columbus Auditorium until it ended. Working with Red was great fun. I sang, danced, and the two us interviewed contestants with Red throwing in some funny lines. Once in a while he joined me in dance and would get me laughing so hard I struggled to complete the routine. I hated to leave at 10 PM and wished I were an adult so we could work the full shift together. I never saw Red again, except in films, after our final night.

CHAPTER ELEVEN

Mom got word that Ted Lewis was looking for a kid performer for a big three-night auto show. Ted was a native of Circleville, Ohio, just down the road from Columbus, and when she told Ted of my credits and that I was from Ohio, I was booked. It proved to be one of the most wonderful experiences of my show business life. In my book, Ted Lewis was the greatest showman of all time. He fronted a show band, his battered old top hat and his not-to-well-played clarinet were familiar trademarks to several generations, but when he sang/talked his super hits "Me and My Shadow," "When My Baby Smiles at Me," "The Cop on the Beat," "The Man in the Moon," and "Me," standing ovations followed. He could make you laugh or cry always asking "Is Everybody Happy?" When he did "I'm Stepping Out With a Memory Tonight" under the soft light of a packed theater, he would have the audience in tears. Even today when I play his recording of that song my eyes grow misty.

Three nights working with Ted was fabulous. His introduction of my act made me feel like the King of Siam. The spotlight would hit me, dressed in a white jacket with orange stripes, white pants sparkling, black patent leather tap shoes and a white beret swinging my juniper-sized polished wood cane with its amber handle that had a small silver snake curled around it as I came dancing down a flight of white stairs singing "Shine On Harvest Moon." After a little interplay with Ted, I closed with a song and dance to "The Sunny Side of the Street."

CHAPTER TWELVE

I worked hard on piano and won first prize at the Saturday Music Club state contest in Cleveland in l931. Although working every week on radio or in live shows I really dogged my efforts on the piano in l932. Now my attention along with other young boys in the neighborhood had discovered baseball and during my practice of scales, I would play my right scales with my left hand using my right hand to open the front door and be out on the porch and into the Godman lot before mom realized I was gone. Dr. Meier, my mother and my dad, everyone, predicted dire results at the state contest in Cincinnati and they were right. I wasn't in the top ten and the new champion of my division was a girl. Not just any girl but a pupil of my teacher Dr. Meier. She was a lovely young lady named Jo Audia Saxbe who lived with her widowed father, an executive of the Pennsylvania Railroad in Arlington. Later, Jo Audia and I would play outstanding twin piano concerts. But at this moment, I never wanted to hear her name. I told Dr. Meier I would never lose a state title again and I never did.

The stakes were high in Cincinnati in 1933. Only

the state winners would be invited to the National Championships that would be held at the Chicago World's Fair (a Century of Progress International Exposition.)

Dr. Meier suggested I step into the top division where I would compete against pianists up to twenty-one years of age. The required song for that division in both state and national contests would be all three movements of the Mozart Sonata in C. The second song the contestant would be judged on was a classic of the contestant's choice. I elected to play the Chopin Nocturne in E flat. This was my mother's favorite song and later became the theme of Eddy Duchin and his famous society orchestra under the title, "My Twilight Dream." After Eddy's death, it was the theme of his son Peter who took over the Duchin orchestra. Today the son can be heard on recordings of the Duchin's orchestra and in the motion picture "The Eddy Duchin Story."

The radio and stage shows went on and there were wonderful new pop tunes like "Blue Prelude," "Easter Parade," "Have You Ever Been Lonely," and "Smoke Gets in Your Eyes." I sang and danced to them but my mind and hard work were on the classics.

The effort paid off as I won first prize at the state with the next stop, the National in Chicago.

CHAPTER THIRTEEN

Columbus, Ohio, was sending three state winners to Chicago. Lodabelle Schmidt, vocalist in her division and Billy Schneider, violinist in his division, while I cast my lot with the senior division.

All of us traveled by train to Chicago five days before the convention and checked into the Astor, a small hotel that had facilities for cooking. The Congress Hotel in Chicago would be the site of musical and vocal competitions and rooms were available where you could rehearse for half an hour at a time. I had assumed that the piano competition would be on a Steinway piano. No, the Baldwin piano had been selected to be the piano for the world's fair. I had trained on a Steinway, which was called "the instrument of the immortals" at the college. The Steinway has fabulous action where you can ripple off runs and give a variety of shades of your work with the pedal selection. Now I was faced with a piano which had a very stiff action and a subpar pedal selection. Mother called the hotel and booked my practice times for the next three days.

Nothing is ever easy and my mother and I didn't

know if we would ever visit Chicago again so we wanted to see all the sights at the fair that we could see missing only Sally Rand and her troop of strippers who captured large crowds and a great deal of publicity. The most thrilling sight for me was being one of the great throng of spectators massed on Chicago's lakefront to welcome General Italo Balboa and his air armada of twenty-four huge Savaio Marchetti seaplanes as they came safely to rest on Lake Michigan. They had lost one plane soon after leaving Europe but the twenty-four white monsters flew in a formation that spelled out "USA" then "Italy" before landing. A United States Navy boat brought General Balboa to the pier, resplendent in his dress white uniform with a sash full of medals, and the gold braid on his cap. A very good-looking man with an athletic build he was an instant crowd favorite as he smiled. This was the first mass flight of aircraft from Europe to the United States.

During the run of the fair certain days honored one of the various states and imagine our surprise when we found out that my competition would be on Ohio Day. That seemed like a good omen.

We ate on the midway and later went into the city to visit the Merchandise Mart, the Wrigley Building and other well known sights. We really made each day special. Knowing we would leave Chicago the day after the big event we tried to see all the sights. We laughed and enjoyed ourselves so much time just slipped away. A little after midnight we were with a group of people on a bridge who were tossing coins to several young black men dancing below. Checking her watch, Mother thought we should be heading back to our hotel since competition started at eight

AM the next morning. The problem was, we didn't know where the hotel was. Mother saw a big Irish cop and told him we were staying at the Astor Hotel and needed to get there.

"Mam, I have been on the beat here in Chicago for twenty years and never heard of such a hotel. The Astor Hotel is in New York."

"I'm telling you there is a Hotel Astor here in Chicago," Mom replied.

"Let me call the station," was the cop's answer as he went to a nearby call box. He talked for several minutes then hung up.

"Mam, you are one hundred percent right. There is a Hotel Astor about five miles away. Let me get you and your son a cab."

It was near 1:00 AM when we arrived at the hotel. The other mothers were about ready to call the police to help locate us. They reminded Mother that we would have to leave the hotel by 7:15 AM to be at the World's Fair and how was Robert going to compete with such little sleep?

"He will either play up to his potential or he won't. Goodnight, ladies."

We had a quick breakfast in our room then joined the others the next morning. Lodabelle was in the wheelchair she had been in since our arrival (to conserve her strength,) Billy was twisting and turning the violin case in his hands.

We were directed to where the various age divisions were competing. Lodabelle, age ten, found her area. Billy age ten found his.

When I found mine, I really had an eye-opener. I was the only kid eight years old and my opponents ranged up to age twenty-one. It was to be a long, long day. First time called you played the entire required Mozart and all the Chopin, my selected number. There were many eliminated after round one and as you were called and re-called you were told to play various arias from all three movements of the Sonata and parts of the Chopin Nocturne. By late afternoon, there were six contestants left. Then four and at last three. The last time around we played the entire Mozart, then the Chopin. At 6:30 PM we were excused and told that the winners would be announced at 8 PM. Mom and I had a snack on the midway and made our way to the big pavilion. The low division winners were announced first and both Billy and Lodabelle, (without the wheelchair,) came on stage to receive their gold medals and since it was Ohio Day, Governor, George White of the Buckeye state was presenting to all the national winners in their division.

At last they reached the senior division and the MC said, "The winner in the senior division is Aaron..." I saw a young man of twenty or twenty-one leave his seat and start toward the stage the MC was interrupted by a man in a tuxedo running in from the wings as the MC said. "One moment please."

Taking a piece of paper from the man in the tux he read, The winner of the senior division is Robert Mason Cawley, Jr. from Columbus, Ohio." I think I danced to the stage with my heart pounding to receive my gold medal as champion. Governor White smiled as he presented the gold to me. "It was quite a day for our state; I'll see you and your mother at the reception."

There was a huge party that followed as we mingled with winners from other states. The Governor told Mother that he was a fan of my radio show and asked her to call his secretary and set a date for a lunch at the Governor's mansion in Columbus.

My mother, like all the mothers whose children had won, were thrilled as were we kids to have won on the big stage. My mother had promised me that if I won I could take her on a speedboat ride on Lake Michigan and she kept her promise although scared half to death.

I was told we could stay a couple of days extra if I desired or go home with Billy and Lodabelle on the afternoon train. I would have loved to stay but I just had to get home to see how my dad and Dr. Meier were reacting.

I sent dad a telegram: "I'm bringing home the bacon."

CHAPTER FOURTEEN

The next evening when the train bearing the three national winners pulled into the Union Station in Columbus the scene was complete bedlam. Hundreds of fans, the media and from somewhere a band was playing. There were photos, autographs, questions from the press and people you had never seen before or would ever see again slapped your back, shook your hand or gave congratulations.

My dad and Dr. Meier were there smiling and hugging as we made our way out to a streetcar. At last we got home where a snack was waiting while mom and I told of all the wonderful sights as well as the hours of competition at the World's Fair.

The following week mom and I had lunch at the mansion with the Governor and the charming first lady, his daughter. Governor White was a widower and his twenty-something daughter had the First Lady title and duties. Governor White wanted me to be his Junior spokesman. A job to which I agreed. My first duty would be to dedicate the flagpoles at the new state office building on Front Street. This led to many speaking and entertainment engagements around the state that the Governor could not attend. Over the next two years, I entertained many times at the Governor's mansion and ate the infamous "rubber chicken" and presented the Governor's good wishes at political dinners.

A week later, Dr. Meier received a letter from Berlin, Germany. I was offered a one-year fully paid scholarship to study piano with the famous Professor Liebling. This man had taught the greatest concert pianists and this could cement my future as a concert performer. My folks were overwhelmed. My father had been recalled by the railroad and he made good on his promise of a new piano. It was a Wurlitzer spinet.

I had until January, 1934, to make a decision. Back to the radio and live performances plus meeting and entertaining guests at the Governor's functions.

My father had been recalled to work on the railroad, and that made all of us happy, but soon after he returned a near-fatal event occurred.

On his way home from work, he was coming under a viaduct and two men accosted him, demanding that he give them his gold railroad watch. That watch was his prized possession and he refused. Both men started swinging and with a quick left, Dad broke one's nose, and he was finished and he started to run away. The other man pulled out a straight razor and started slashing. One slash went across my father's throat and the blood gushed out. Thinking he had killed Dad, he ran after his partner in crime. Dad, holding the slashed throat together, ran to the nearest house. The ambulance was called and he got to the hospital where the doctor sewed up the slash and he was given a quart of blood. The rest of his life he had a wide, white scar across his neck that just missed his jugular vein and he still had his watch.

One day in the fall, I sat down at the kitchen table and told my mother I was not going to Germany to study with Professor Liebling. In fact, although I was still going to study classics, at least for a while, my real interest was swing.

"What are you talking about?"

"Mom, last night Cousin Ken Agee had a great radio show on with Benny Goodman and his orchestra and they play music called 'Swing.' Anyway, Benny announced they were going to play our old favorite 'Rose Room,' and his pianist, a fellow named Jess Stacy was going to be featured. Mom, you should have heard it. What Mr. Stacy did with that tune; well, it was fabulous. Forget playing that concert stuff that you have to play as written. I want to swing."

I know it broke Mom's and Dr. Meier's hearts. I kept up my piano lessons, played twin piano concerts with Jo Audia Saxbe, and had my own classical recitals, but my heart was elsewhere.

CHAPTER FIFTEEN

1934 had a bonanza of great songs that included "Blue Moon," Cocktails For Two," "Deep Purple," and "The Very Thought of You."

A new Warden at Ohio Penitentiary wanted an hour-long radio show on Sundays at noon, and you know who got the call. In memory, I can still hear the announcer: "From within the high grey walls of Ohio Penitentiary, it's the *Sunday Show* featuring Robert Mason Cawley, Jr."

Fanfare from the eighteen-piece prison orchestra, including some former big band sideman, and we were into the theme song, "Dream Train," in front of a packed house of prisoners with armed guards around the walls.

The convicts were a great audience, and so many of them had sons my age who they would never see again. They never took their eyes off of me. The show featured guest artists and the band. And one of their own, "The Lifer" Charley Wilson. Charley, then just twenty had got drunk and killed his date at their high school prom when she paid too much attention to a classmate. Excellent baritone, Charley could have been a star with the big bands.

After the show, the cast was served lunch, and I noticed that each week a prisoner wearing the black and white stripes of the most dangerous would always see I got an extra big piece of pie with a large helping of ice cream. He told me his name was Russell, and in time I discovered he was Russell Clark, the only living member of the Dillinger Gang. He had a life sentence but was released prior to his death.

CHAPTER SIXTEEN

A big event was entering grade school at Stewart Avenue in south Columbus. The press was there to get a photo history for the *Columbus Dispatch*. I liked my school chums, and although not as exciting as show biz, it was mostly fun. In first grade, I was amazed that the teacher, Miss Hayes, an old maid, was so taken by a student named Jeff Papas, who scratched his head and sides while making sounds like a monkey.

It was during this era I started taking notice of girls. Although I had shared dressing rooms and dressed and undressed with girls, I had never paid attention to the fair sex. Mary Jo Kline, the butcher's daughter who lived upstairs in our duplex, got me to realize that girls are "different" when she volunteered to teach me the game of "doctor" deep in the confines of a thick stand of lilac bushes in our back yard. Mary Jo was a year older and a great instructor, so by the time I had reached grade school I knew I would like girls. The year before we graduated from Stewart Avenue to Barrett Junior High, the love bug bit me when I met a very cute girl named Virginia Boyer. She was always dressed pretty and wore light cologne. I thought Virginia was cute and I know she liked me because she would select me for recess games and seemed to like being close to me. Virginia's last name started with a B and mine with a C, so in most classes we set in the front row. But this day we were in the back row of Miss Whitehurst's geography class and the back blackboard was behind us. Virginia whispered to me, "I bet you can't hit her with an eraser." Hey, I'm Virginia's white knight. I reached back, grabbed a felt eraser, and fired a perfect hit on the back of the teacher's head. Miss Whitehurst spun around and demanded to know who threw the eraser. In a split second Virginia jumped to her feet. "Bob Cawley did it." So much for being her white knight.

The principal paddled me in front of the class then marched me to his office and called my mother. Geography was the final class of the day, and before it was over, my mother had arrived with several lilac switches and proceeded to whip me the five blocks to our house with classmates following. Reaching our house she told me to go in the house and announced to the kids, "What you have seen is nothing like what will happen when his father comes home." At 3 AM, Dad pulled me out of bed and you can believe I never assaulted another teacher, until Junior College, but that's another story. Today's bleeding heart parents would be filing lawsuits for child abuse. I had it coming, and although the marks from the lilac switches quickly faded, I knew to act correctly in school and in public, and I, or later my kids, did not yell and run around in eating places or misbehave in any way. The switches get to the brain. All the talking falls on deaf ears.

I remember what my father told me about women. "There are two kinds of women. There is the kind you take home to meet your mother. The kind of woman you would want for a wife and a mother of your children. Then there are the other kind." I never took a girl home that didn't meet the standard he had set. I read that many women betray men and like the wonderful "Noir" films of the 30s and 40s, they are saying "I love you" but they all have other agendas.

CHAPTER SEVENTEEN

In 1935 Cole Porter's "Begin the Beguine" topped the song list that included "Cheek To Cheek," "East of the Sun," "I Can't Get Started," "I'm in the Mood for Love," "Lullaby of Broadway" and George Gershwin's "Summertime," among many other tunes that became standards.

I was being hailed as radio's youngest paid radio announcer in the business and "Baby Orator," thanks to the wonderful scripts my father wrote for me that I memorized and delivered. The sponsored radio shows and recitals had outstanding young talent like violinist Mame Elliot. I was active with the Charity Newsies and sold newspapers on a downtown street corner to help raise money for the poor and homeless. I worked many conventions and dinners at the famed Deshler-Wallick hotel at the crossroads of Columbus, beautiful Broad and High streets. West of the hotel was the beautiful RKO Palace Theater, followed by the AIU Building, later renamed the LeVeque Tower, at the time the tallest building in town. At the time it was connected to the Deshler-Wallick hotel with 400 of the hotel's 1000 rooms being in the Tower. Across the street from the hotel was the Adams Hat store that showcased 8 x 10 photos of famous boxers, like Lou Ambers, who wore Adam Hats. Going west was the Planters Peanut store, once managed by my choir boy pal Ernie Nuzzo, then Doirshams restaurant where all the big band musicians that played the Palace hung out. Heading west next was Lowes Broad Theater where I won the "Wheezer Contest." Going south on High street the State Capital Building and its spacious grounds covered the entire block. Outside was a group of statues of the Ohio generals called "Our Jewels." The Ohio generals who won the Civil War for the Union. These include Grant and Sherman. In the center on the right side was the famous Neil House hotel where the State politicians and visiting football teams stayed. Moving south was Mill Restaurant whose large windows displayed figures of the Ohio State football team and their opponents. You can't talk about Columbus unless you talk about Ohio State football. Several national publications say that Columbus is the most football-crazy town in America. When the Buckeyes win, the town parties like it's the end of the world. When they lose you could shoot a cannon downtown without hitting anyone. No matter what the Bucks do, no season is a success unless they beat a major game rival, the University of Michigan in the final game of each season.

1935 was a glory season and headlines read "Ohio State Annihilates Wolverines 39 to 0 at Ann Arbor. Tippy Dye Streaks Seventy-three Yards in Six Touchdown Avalanche." Dye was 5'8," 142 lbs. and a great field general. Tippy was a basketball All-American and was my first basketball coach in the Columbus Church Youth League. I loved that man. I had added trumpet playing to my skills and although Bunny Berigan and Harry James never had to worry I played with several local bands and with Howard Freytag played "To The Colors" each and every morning when the flag was raised at Barrett Junior High.

Times were changing. Although the radio work stayed at the same level the demand for tap dancers was on the decline. Most bookings were for piano/song and MC jobs.

My mother and father saw a long sought after dream come true when, after years of renting, they built their own home on the corner of North Hague Avenue in Valley View, a suburb on the west side of Columbus. In addition, they bought a second lot by our home where we could have a vegetable garden where we raised a variety of produce that enabled us to have a stand outside our white picket fence where we sold our goods.

It was with mixed emotions, I left the south side. All my school pals would be going to South High School while I was headed for a much more modern area where West Junior High was contained in one huge plant.

I loved our new home and my room with a front window view and another window with a clear view of our second lot and Hague Avenue. West Junior High was to be an exciting experience.

While our house was being built, there were two events I will always remember. I worked a big show at the Auditorium, where I MC'd, sang, danced and played piano. I never guessed this would be the last time I would work with a talented young man I had worked with many times before. Herman Silverman was a very talented dancer but he had extreme asthma and would need thirty minutes rest between numbers. He had traveled the show circuit with his mother, a very nice lady, but because of his illness never got the attention he should have. The strain of dancing was taking its toll and here was a kid who loved show biz. After this show, Herman dropped out of sight. A few years later he came back calling himself Herkey Styles. He became a top comedian working the top clubs across America.

This was also my last time on the road with Mom as my manager. We were off to New York for the *Major Bowes Show* on network radio. It was a great ending to our professional relationship. We stayed at a small hotel in New York City that had a rooftop rehearsal set up. They had tap boards, victrolas for music to rehearse by, plus they had rooms with pianos.

It was at this hotel that I visited the former Heavyweight Boxing Champion, Primo Carnera. Primo had been knocked out the night before in a fight in Brooklyn. It was early afternoon but Primo was recovered yet still in bed. He spoke little English but smiled a lot. We shook hands and his hand covered mine and part of my forearm. He then signed my autograph book. I marveled at the size of his teeth and at his body size. I had never seen anyone that big. I felt very sorry for Primo. The dirty way the boxing game had used this poor soul from Italy. The whole sordid story was captured in the motion picture *The Harder They Fall*.

Mom and I visited the store of Billy Taub, the famous tailor. A heavyweight title fight was coming up and the Heavyweight Belt was on display in his window. I admired the belt and Mr. Taub took it out of the window and placed it around my waist. Needless to say, the belt swallowed me, but Mr. Taub held it around me as my mother snapped a photo. It was a real thrill for a kid and a great memory.

While working stage shows around the city, I met a lovely young lady who was a fabulous dancer and later a major movie star. Her name was Vera Ellen Rohe. Later, as Vera Ellen, she danced with such stars as Fred Astaire and Gene Kelly during the golden era of Hollywood musicals. She had toured with Ted Lewis and later broke into Broadway musicals. Samuel Goldwyn teamed her with Danny Kaye in *Wonder Man* and *The Kid from Brooklyn* and she danced with Gene Kelly. She danced a famous sequence to "Slaughter On 1oth Avenue" in the film *Words and Music* and danced with Astaire in the *Three Little Words* and *The Belle of New York*. She will be remembered for starring roles in *White Christmas* with Bing Crosby and *On the Town* with Frank Sinatra and Gene Kelly. When we met we were working for $50.00 a week working in stage shows. After I went back to Columbus and she stayed and worked Broadway, we kept in touch. She liked strawberry jam and my mother sent her several boxes of homemade jam from our garden. In 1948 I wrote Vera Ellen asking her for a salute to the cadet corps for the Greenbrier Year Book called *The Briar Patch*. She responded and it was a big hit with the corps. We had a secret we laughed about. People always remarked how they liked her singing voice. That was a joke. Vera Ellen couldn't sing. Someone else did the vocals and Vera Ellen just moved her lips.

September 12, 1981, Vera Ellen died of cancer in Hollywood.

CHAPTER EIGHTEEN

1930s – Columbus West Junior High and West High were under one roof. One of the newest public schools in Columbus, it offered large, modern classrooms, a big auditorium for stage shows and concerts, plus an all-around feeling of comfort and a great collection of students. It also meant I would be attending school with my cousins, the Fry sisters, JoAnn, Margie and Elaine, plus we could visit them and their parents, Uncle Charlie and Aunt Fanny. Even closer was Aunt Minnie and Uncle Will Agee, who lived on the far side of Valley View. I could take my two fox terriers, Nip and Tuck, and hike the mile to their home where Aunt Minnie would always have fresh baked goodies and a big glass of milk waiting.

Yes, there were memories from Barett Junior High I kept with me. I missed teaming with Howard Freytag and playing "To the Colors" on our trumpets as the flag was raised each morning. I had loved the fire drills. When the fire alarm sounded, we raced to the cylinder built on the side of the school and jumped on the slide that took us speeding to the yard below. My classmates were headed for South High and I missed them. I had hardly checked in when I was invited to a birthday party that would make life get a new glow for it was there I met the young lady who was to be my first steady girlfriend. I was introduced to all the fellows and girls and the games began. My eyes fell on a beautiful strawberry blond with lovely blue eyes who was wearing a blue velvet dress with a white lace collar. She was about 5'6" and just sparkling. I learned her name was Wanda Jean Deaton, but how would I get to talk to her? This problem was solved when the next game was "Spin the milk bottle."

After a few spins, the bottle lined us up and we went into the closet to kiss and closed the door.

"We don't have to do this," she said.

"Oh yes, we do," I replied and took her in my arms and really enjoyed the meeting of our lips. Flushed and flustered, the new boy in town and Miss Deaton rejoined the party. The bottle lined us up three or four more times and each kiss was better than the one before. We sat together eating cake and ice cream and after the party, I walked her home. She lived on Binns Boulevard which was a half mile south of West High. My home was on the north side of school and was a mile and a half more. I remember my dad asked me if there were no desirable girls on our side of town. I just laughed. Wanda was to be my steady, but it was not to be an easy thing to accomplish. The party was on Saturday.

On Monday, I waited for Wanda when school was over. It had rained that morning, and along with her books, she had brought an umbrella. When she came out, I started to take her books when a guy named Don grabbed her books out of my hand.

"I carry the books, so butt out!" he yelled as he shoved me. I knocked the books out of his hands and the fight was on. A few seconds later he was on the concrete with a bloody nose. The thought that I had become Wanda's white knight vanished as she broke her umbrella over my head, called me a brute, and was down with Don stopping his bleeding with her hankie. She helped him up, gave him her collected books, and with her broken umbrella hanging from her arm, he walked her home. That was the first time I realized that some women can explode. My mother never did, even when she had switched me all the way home from grade school. When I hit the teacher with an eraser she was calm and under control. Like all boys, there would be fist fights along the way but never again over a girl. I took my time walking home. I was unable to figure things out but I knew that sooner or later Wanda would be in my future. West High had dances and other social functions and there were other pretty girls to date.

In 1938, my dad bought his first and only car. A gray and silver Dodge four-door sedan. We all loved that car and it opened the door to a host of one and two-day adventures. Places like Old Man's Cave in the beautiful Hocking Hills and Serpent Mound and the tiny town of Lithopolis, the home of the beautiful Wagnall's Memorial Library which was built by the Wagnall's family to honor their daughter Alice who was the author of *The Rosebush of a Thousand Years*. Gorgeous stained glass windows and a library you could visit a million times and you would never tire of visiting. It was there I saw a message carved in stone that I have carried in my heart. "Dreams long dwelt on amount to prayers and prayers wrought in faith come true."

The car also brought many trips to Poca, West Virginia, to visit Aunt Lena Mae and Uncle Calvin "Bud" Oakes and my cousins, Calvin, who was always called "Junior"; John, always called "Sonny"; and JoAnn Oakes. Vacations to the Great Smokey Mountains, Virginia, and Washington, DC, were highlights.

I was still doing some radio work but the era of kid performers was dying, but I stayed active with the Saturday Music Club.

1937 brought some great new music that would become standards including "Thanks for the Memory," "Rosalie," "Harbor Lights," and "Blue Hawaii." Then 1938 gave us "Bei Mir Bist Du Schoen," "I Married An Angel," "Two Sleepy People" and the unforgettable "September Song" among others. The cinema got our attention with Disney's "Snow White and The Seven Dwarfs," the gritty "Dead End" and Greta Garbo in "Camille."

Meantime there were dark clouds in Europe as Germany mobilized.

West High had some top music makers and we soon put together a swinging group called "The Jive Five." Bob Sinclair, a first-class drummer; Johnny Patterson who played clarinet like Benny Goodman; Bob Gulcher, a super talented alto sax player; Dick Houk with the Tex Beneke-style of tenor sax; and yours truly on piano. The student body loved us and we were present at the majority of school events. The truly top event happened when as a group we played for Benny Goodman. Bob Sinclair's dad was employed by the Palace Theater, which had just started a policy of featuring a name band on stage every Monday, Tuesday and Wednesday. Thursday, Friday and Saturday they would play the Albee Theater in Cincinnati. Mr. Sinclair asked Mr. Goodman if he would listen to five songs, each one featuring a different member of the "Jive Five" and Benny agreed. This was a schoolboy's dream come true. We set up backstage and did our thing backstage. After the band's first show and while the movie was on, we did our thing, and several of the band members looked on. I was thrilled to meet my heroes Jess Stacy and Gene Krupa. Benny advised us to stay in school and go to college. He told Johnny Patterson he was one of the best young clarinet players he had ever heard but to quit playing Benny's style and to develop his own. Gulcher and Houk got high praise for their sax work and Krupa liked Sinclair's drums and passed along some helpful tips to get better. Benny felt I had my own style and had a bright future. We thanked Mr. Goodman for his time and left the theater on cloud nine.

CHAPTER NINETEEN

On a cold October morning in 1939, I had a hot chocolate at the local sweet shop. Outside there were light snow flurries when I announced I was going to California where the warm sun shined daily.

"You're not going anywhere," came from classmates' voices.

"Yes, I am and I'm going now. Anyone want to come with me?"

"I'll go," said Walt Kietzman.

"Me to," said Jim Green.

To the amazement of everyone we crossed west Broad Street at Hague Avenue, put up our thumbs, and in a few seconds, we were picked up by a jolly truck driver who took us all the way to Indianapolis. There we realized that between us we had twenty-three cents. We bought oatmeal cookies with our money and headed for St. Louis. We had to get jobs that paid by cash every night to be able to find sleeping quarters. Walt and Jim got jobs as dishwashers in fast food restaurants, and I ended as a pin setter in a bowling alley. The pay was small but the tips from the various teams bowling were very good. I dreamed of staying around for three weeks, but that vanished the third night as I was under the machine trying to loosen a stuck pin when a weight fell out of the machine, struck my head and caused a lot of bleeding. Jim and Walt found me in the manager's office. He had given me a week's pay plus twenty-five dollars to leave town and forget the accident. We got a warm room for the night and early in the morning were on the road. In time, the ability to thumb rides dropped off and we started riding stock cars or gondolas on the railroad. We were three excited guys who gazed at the palm trees and basked in the warm weather as we pulled into Los Angeles.

After pancakes and sausage, we asked several locals where fourteen-year-olds could find work. The majority said San Pedro. We were directed to Main Street in LA to the electric trolley station and took the famous "Red Reaper" to San Pedro. We wanted jobs that were not too far apart so we could get together on Sundays. Jim got work at a dairy that provided sleeping quarters and food. Walt followed an ad for a ticket taker and nightly clean-up man at a small theater. The man who owned the theater was a toothless old gentleman who was called "Cap." Walt had a sleeping room at Cap's house close to the theater and Cap's wife delivered three good meals a day. While Walt and Cap worked on their deal a very pretty blond my age stopped in front of me with her bike. She was Cap's granddaughter and her name was Jeep. She asked if I was looking for work. I told her I was and she wanted to know if I had ever worked as an actor. When I said yes, she asked me to go with her to meet her mother who just might be able to give me a job. She walked her bike three blocks to a neat white home on a slight hill that had a sign on the lawn that read "Madam Vera Psychic – By Appointment Only" and a phone number. Jeep took me in a side door and I met her mother who had a very pretty face but must have weighed 300 pounds. She was in the market for an Arab who would assist with her clients, mostly older ladies seeking to reach long-dead husbands. Could I act the part of a young Arab boy whose tongue had been cut out by a rival tribe? You bet I could. After being shown what would be my room with a private bath, Madam Vera had me strip to the waist and she used oil that tinted my face, upper body, and hands and forearms dark.

Then I took off my shoes and socks as my feet, which would be clad in sandals only, and she colored my lower legs which were now the Arab color she desired. She took my foot size and wrote it on a slip of paper for Cap to buy me sandals. There was a boy's bike in their garage and Jeep and I rode back to the theater where Cap was teaching Walt his duties.

Next morning, Madam Vera taught me my duties. I was to be at the front door with what passed as a bow and an Arab salute for each client. Then provide them with coffee or tea, milk or sugar. Then later pass by with a tray of cookies. Since I could not talk, there was a lot of pointing and many of the ladies told me how sorry they were that the evil tribe had cut out my tongue. I wore a turban that covered my blond hair and managed to pass as the Arab boy. While Madam did her opening, I vanished into the kitchen and got in position under the table in the "spirit" room. The clients sat around the table as Madam Vera called to their husbands in heaven to let their wives know how much they loved them.

When Vera said a husband was near, I raised my back to a pad fixed under the table and raised it for a few inches, then let it back as the dead husband spoke to his wife from the beyond. When he was returning, I lifted the table, then slowly returned to normal. After the spirit room was vacated, I returned through the kitchen and held the door for the clients as they departed and I gave them my Arab salute. I only worked the front door for the Madam's clients wanting card readings or messages from the crystal ball. Madam liked my work, but by the first week in December, talks of home filled our conversation.

The big adventure ended the second week in December, which found us back in the LA Union Station. I had turned in my costume and sandals, and thanked Madam Vera for the job while Jeep cried, kissed my cheek and told me how much she would miss me. Around 2 PM Los Angeles time, Walt and Jim called their homes. Their parents were wild with joy. The police had been looking for us and their parents were afraid they had been murdered. They were wiring money for first-class tickets on the Super Chief which would depart 6 PM California time plus spending money. We had lunch at Fred Harvey's in the terminal and the guys begged me to call my folks so we could all go home together. I realized this would put a financial strain on my mom and dad that they didn't need. I gave in at 4:45 PM and made the call. My dad answered the phone.

"Hi, Dad, it's Robert."

"Good to hear from you. Where are you?"

"Los Angeles, California."

"That's a place I've always wanted to see. Are

there lots of palm trees, how about orange trees and grapefruit?"

"Yes, dad plenty of those."

"Are Jim and Walt coming home?"

"Yea, Dad, they just called home."

"I bet their folks were glad to hear they're okay."

"They are happy; in fact, they are wiring them money to come home on the Super Chief that leaves at 6 PM California time."

"That's great, they'll be home in plenty of time for Christmas."

"Dad, I miss you and Mom and I want to come home."

There was silence on the line giving me one of the greatest lessons of my life. One that I would have told my children had we ever been in a similar situation. "Son, your mother and I love you more than anything in the world. Look at the reality. You got out there, now you get back." He hung up and at that moment I would have given anything in the world to have their arms around me. I hung around until Walt and Jim left on the Super Chief, then dressed in khaki slacks and a white shirt and started hell-bent for Columbus.

I was ill-equipped for cold and rainy weather. I caught a gondola over the Rockies and had to run all night to keep from freezing. Went back to the highway and had a torrential rain storm in Kansas and got a few hours sleep in a cabin with broken windows in an abandoned tourist camp. By a miracle, I arrived home four days later at dinner time. Looking in the kitchen window, I saw my dad reading the newspaper and my mother cooking dinner.

I opened the door and my mother greeted her Arab-stained son with her great, warm smile. "You're just in time for dinner. Just wash up and we'll be ready to eat."

My father continued to read. I had to say something. "Papa, I came home to die."

Slowly the paper dropped and he looked at me. "Die hell. You came home to eat." I washed up and ate one of the greatest meals of my life.

It was a couple of days before Christmas when, after doing something in the garage, we sat down and I told him about my adventures and he laughed loud and long regarding my being an Arab. Later Mom told me how the two of them had prayed for my safe return. My skin was slowly going back to normal. I was in school and ready for 1940.

CHAPTER TWENTY

At 8 PM, January 11, 1940, West Junior High School presented a musical fiesta that included the boys and girls glee club, school orchestra, and solo and group performers of both music and dance. Prior to the close of the evening by the entire cast, I was featured singing "South of the Border," a popular song of the era. First to congratulate me at the show was Wanda Deaton, and I was told I was her choice to walk her home. We would soon be graduating to West Senior High, but before that happened we both auditioned for a play that would be our swan song to Junior High. The play was a romantic/comedy titled *Digging Up The Dirt*, and Wanda and I were selected by the director to play the romantic leads. A very talented cast would guarantee three acts filled with laughter, mystery and romance. The setting was Mexico where "Professor" was searching for buried treasure assisted by two college boys. "Bill" as played by Lee Schlegel and "Ken" which I played. Along the way the Professor is kidnapped; Bill and I have a "run-in" with a skunk and a group of college girls, including Wanda, as the character "Betty" arrive adding comedy and romance. As you might guess it all works out. The Professor is saved, the treasure is found, and at the close Betty and Ken are alone on the set. Declaring their love for each other and sealing it with a kiss as the curtain closes. Wanda and I had to rehearse this scene many times and we had been instructed to hold the kiss until the curtain was fully closed. We did and the night of the play we were still kissing when the curtain re-opened. The curtain closed then re-opened with the entire cast on stage and we were still kissing. It was the longest kiss in West High history and the peak of our romance.

1940, like every year of that fabulous era, had great songs and this year brought, "Bewitched," "September Song," "Taking a Chance on Love," "How High the Moon," and two novelty songs that took the nation by storm, "Flat Foot Floogie With a Floy Floy" and Ella Fitzgerald's recording of "A Tisket A Tasket" with the Chick Webb orchestra. This was also the year I first heard Bob Eberly sing "The Breeze and I" (later to be his theme song), and "I Hear a Rhapsody" with the Jimmy Dorsey Band and realized I was hearing the greatest singing voice of the big band era which Frank Sinatra later confirmed on the back of one of his albums. I kept my hand in music appearing in several classical concerts with violinist William Polankla, and clarinetist Bill Rundles for the Saturday Music Club. Bill was a track star at Columbus East High and later we would form a potent jazz trio.

In the meantime, my parents were quite concerned over my academic standing. I fell from an A/B standard to C/D report cards, and this would not fly with a mother and father so high on education. The case for this was most weeks I did not go to school except Thursday and Friday. The other three school days were spent at the RKO Palace Theater watching the great name bands performing live. I would arrive at 10 AM when they opened, see the movie, usually a Charlie Chan epic, then see the band at 11 AM to 12N, then the movie. Then at 1 PM see the second show, then the movie, catch the 4 PM show and get home for dinner. I worked Thursday, Friday and Saturday evenings bagging groceries at our local Kroger store so I had spending money.

Many Saturdays I joined my cousins, the Fry sisters, at Redbird Stadium. Then the finest minor league ballpark in America. We were all members of the Knothole Gang. The Redbirds were a St. Louis Cardinal AAA ball club. It was great fun to meet the players like Paul Dean, Enos "Country" Slaughter and radio announcer Jack Buck who later became the voice of the Cards in St. Louis. On Sundays, I would take Miss Deaton to the cinema. It was a terrible time for me. I wanted to work nightclubs but was too young and also too young for radio. Toward the end of the year, I noticed we were getting a lot of catalogs from private schools, and my folks announced that by the start of the 1941/1942 school year I would be in a major school that stressed academics, not name bands so I could build credits to enter college.

Drifting into January 1941, I celebrated my sixteenth birthday and I talked to a club owner to let me have an evening to showcase my vocal and piano talents in his club for one night. I was delighted with the audience response as I told my mother the next morning when she asked "How did it go last night?" "Mom, they loved me." "Would they have loved you if they would have been sober?" Mom always cut to the heart of any subject.

Catalogs from private schools kept coming from all over the United States. They were looking for a school for me. Letters were exchanged and notes pro and con made. Whatever was selected would cost a pile of money but they had saved for this. Dad had been promoted last year to a passenger conductor and retirement was coming up in four years. Then he and mom could travel like they planned. I wondered why they never contacted Greenbrier Military School which was a school designed to take you from the lower two years of Junior College and was a prep school for all the academies including West Point and Annapolis. My uncle, Calvin "Bud" Oakes, was a Greenbrier grad who had played center on the Junior College football team. He always raved about the great faculty and what a fabulous education he had received. However, his Alma Mater was not in the mix. Germany had invaded Poland under Adolph Hitler in 1939 and now took Norway and Denmark, and had invaded Holland, Belgium and Luxembourg. The economy in the USA was booming as we made war materials for Europe. President Franklin D. Roosevelt was re-elected for a third term. Ernest Hemingway wrote *For Whom the Bell Tolls* while Lillian Hellman penned *Watch On the Rhine* and Raymond Chandler published *Farewell My Lovely*. Beloved author F. Scott Fitzgerald died.

The great music kept rolling with Kate Smith's version of Irving Berlin's "God Bless America," Judy Garland thrilled the nation with "Over The Rainbow," Herb Jeffries sang "Flamingo," "Blues In The Night" was another hit from Johnny Mercer, Bob

Eberly owned "I Understand," and a skinny guy named Frank Sinatra made the young girls swoon when he sang "I'll Never Smile Again" with the Pied Pipers and Tommy Dorsey's orchestra. Benny Goodman swung "The Jersey Bounce" while millions of Americans sang their versions of the two novelty hits "Three Little Fishes" and the "Beer Barrel Polka" as they showered.

The catalogs were down to one at our house. The folks had narrowed the field to St. Joseph's Military School in Minnesota. The contract had arrived when another call came.

Major Ivey of Greenbrier was in town and wanted to meet my folks. After meeting Major Ivey and being wined and dined, they signed the contract for me to attend Greenbrier Military School in Lewisburg, West Virginia. My mother delivered me at the beginning of the following school year. After kissing her goodbye on the steps of the school, Major Ivey put her into a taxi and turned to me saying, "You little son-of-a-bitch, you are the property of Greenbrier now."

CHAPTER TWENTY-ONE

Greenbrier Military School

The five hundred students living at the school were formed into companies A through C in the quadrangle while companies D and E were located on the far side of the main building. The quadrangle was a square building built around a grassy yard that held a small "guard house" for the Officer of the Day at morning roll call. The quad had three floors, or stoops, and a ground floor. There were four sides to the stoops with rooms running down each side that housed two cadets and consisted of metal bunk beds, two matching desks and chairs, and two metal lockers for uniforms and shoes. The cadets' trunks were foot lockers. There were large toilets on each stoop. At all four corners of the quad were "suites" where four cadets lived and these had a private bathroom. The one exception to a non-cadet suite was a C stoop that housed Major C. E. "Tite" Turley, the Commandant of Cadets and Head Football Coach and his wife, Verlie. The Major also taught Bible. The band and a portion of a company were on the third stoop. Company B on the second with Company C on the first. On the ground floor was the PX; barber shop; laundry and cleaners; the room used by the Officer of the Day and his staff as well as the Reveille Band; the Varsity Football dressing room, showers for the battalion; the Press Room for the school newspaper and yearbook; and the Office of Major J. W. Benjamin, Public Relations Officer Alumni Secretary, Publication Advisor, English instructor, and my Faculty Advisor.

The main building contained the Executive Offices and the Mail Room. There was a very large Auditorium with a big stage with a Steinway grand piano that served as the Chapel, night Study Hall, rehearsal area for the dance band and glee club also the site of Final Exams in Public Speaking. It was a popular venue for Alumni meetings. Next door was a very large Library filled with books and huge silver trophies won by GMS Rifle and Pistol teams in National Competitions. The area that grabbed my attention was a plaque on one wall that listed, in gold, the names and ranks of former cadets who were honored forever in the GMS Hall of Fame. It also listed what each cadet had been selected for. Each year the faculty met to select three cadets for the Hall. I knew from the moment I saw it this was my goal.

Major Ivey deposited me in C Company, commanded by Captain Bob Peters from Columbus, Ohio. Then I was placed in the second platoon under first Lt. Glenn Osborn from Old Greenwich, Connecticut. His older brother, Maver, was a member of the l931 Hall of Fame and a national champion pistol shot who had received a telegram from mob boss Al Capone, offering him a job. The telegram hung by the

Hall of Fame. Maver didn't take the job but the story was big news in its time.

Although I was very slow getting with the military part of the program other things were going well. I was pianist for both the dance orchestra and the Glee Club, plus I was a member of the Forensic Club and was on the staff of the school paper but the real high was being a halfback on the Colonel's football team which played a high school schedule. This is something I had wanted to do at Columbus West High but coaches are not interested in guys who miss three school days a week listening to big bands. I would like to tell you I was knocking them dead in academics but that wasn't true. The faculty had their work cut out for them but they were more than ready to teach me how to study and in a long haul to make me an Honor Role student.

Each and every cadet is given a book the size of a standard paperback. It has a green cover and it is called the "Green Book" and lists all the rules and regulations of the school and as such is known as "the Greenbrier Bible." The judicial system of the Greenbrier government is the Honor Court. The duty of the Honor Court is to carry out to the best of its ability judgment on those who go against the system. These boys of the Court also try to stop all breaching of the rules. The Cadet Major always sits as President of the Court. The boys on the Court must be honest, conscientious, and judge every claim brought up before them. The Court is made up of all Commissioned Officers and First Sergeants. Major Turley supervised the Honor Court but had no voting power.

CHAPTER TWENTY-TWO

Shortly thereafter my little world came unglued. I was doing okay as a halfback on the Colonel's football team with a big guy named Ben Putnam opening big holes for me and running mate, Howard Johnson. (Years later, Ben's daughter was Lt. Governor of Ohio while Ben was very active with the Alumni Association. Howard became Prosecuting Attorney of Franklin County, Ohio, and sent many criminals to the electric chair.) On this day Ben threw a key block and there was forty yards of running room ahead. My main forte was speed and I was moving in high gear when out of nowhere an opponent hit me with a shoe-string tackle and my right ankle popped like a rifle shot.

Two teammates got me to the sidelines where Doctor Lemon, the school physician stood. "What's wrong Cawley?"

"I think my ankle is broke."

Doc turned to an attendant, "Give him an aspirin and, Cawley, sit down you're blocking my view."

I sat on the bench through the last half, then Ben and Howard got me to infirmary where Doc and the nurse put a cast on my ankle while Doc told stories about when he played "guts football" and never stopped for a broken bone. I was hoping for a nice rest in the infirmary when Doc handed me a pair of crutches telling me to join my platoon and march into evening mess. Doc had me on active duty and I had exercises for my ankle and leg, which healed in record time although a painful process. I would not play again but went to all the practice sessions.

The next week an accident happened that I will never forget. The team was working on blocking punts. Joe Manning, a sixteen-year-old redhead who was always smiling broke through the offensive line, missed the ball but took the full force of the kicker's foot in his mid-section and dropped like a sack of bricks. He was placed in the doctor's car and rushed to the C & O Hospital in Ronceverte where he was diagnosed to have a ruptured appendix. The hospital owned by the C & O Railroad was considered one of the finest in the South. Head Surgeon Dr. Prillerman, whose son was in the GMS Hall of Fame, has a national reputation for surgical work. Manning's parents in St. Albans, West Virginia, were contacted and told the Doctor was ready to operate but needed their permission. Their son's condition was critical. Joe's mother needed time to think and consult with medical sources in Charleston, West Virginia close to their home. The accident happened at a Thursday practice and by Monday no decision had been reached and Joe was getting worse by the hour. On Wednesday, the Mannings notified the hospital that an ambulance was coming that would deliver Joe to a Charleston hospital for surgery. In those days there was no freeway to Charleston only a two-lane highway. That afternoon the area was hit by blizzard conditions and the ambulance did not arrive until late Thursday evening. Joe was loaded in and the exhausted drivers started the long, snow-blanketed trip to Charleston. In spots the ambulance had to wait for road crews to open the snow-packed roads and arrived in the afternoon. Joe was rushed to surgery but it was too late. Our young team mate with the big smile was gone.

When your grades dropped below 85, you had to spend every night in Study Hall in the Auditorium where there were members of the faculty to help you. Good students studied in their rooms I was a charter member of the Study Hall group. After Study Hall, there was fifteen minutes before taps when all lights were out and you were in bed. Every night I would spend ten of those minutes standing in the Library looking at the Hall of Fame.

Someday I would be there. Lt. Osborn had taken notice of my interest in the Hall of Fame and one night he stopped. "Tappo (he always called me that knowing I could tap dance), what's so interesting that you stop here every night?"

"That's where I want to be. One of the best of the best."

"You will get there before any of us because of your music."

"Why, any day Major Richardson will be out sick and you will be called upon to play the piano in Chapel."

"You really think so?"

"Yes, I do. You know I select the three hymns for Chapel. What hymn could you give a special touch to?"

I paused for a moment then said, "'Church In The Wildwood.'"

"Good, I'll make that hymn the closer when you play."

I thought the lieutenant wanted something special. As I later learned, he thought I would play the hymn with vigor, and as the song leader, he would get the corps to put full voice to the last stanza so the walls would reverberate. It proved to be a tragic case of miscommunication. Three days later, the Major was sick and I was called upon to play the hymns, and true to his word "Church in the Wildwood" was the closer. The entire faculty was on the stage as Colonel Joseph Moore did his inspirational Chapel talk. When finished Lt. Osborn called for cadets to stand and sing that beautiful old hymn when we reached the final stanza the lieutenant was ready to urge the corps to the peak of volume, but froze as I broke into a boogie-woogie version of the hymn. I could hear the choked laughter and coughing of the cadets, and I really laid on the "Church in the Wildwood" boogie beat until the final note. Some were laughing so hard tears were running down their cheeks. I had done it! My name would be on that plaque. I would be a member of the Hall. I turned on the piano bench to face school President Colonel Joe Moore. His eyes blazed like the pits of hell. He said, "Come with me," and I followed him into his office. He sat behind his desk and I stood at attention quaking in my shoes. "Cawley, this school is over 100 years old and nothing has ever been as bad as what happened today. I am giving you 200 demerits for your actions. If you reach 201 demerits you will be expelled and your parents will have to pay your full tuition. With your record of getting demerits, I assume you will be gone in a couple of weeks, but if you are able to stay, every single demerit must be off your record by Christmas vacation or you will not be allowed to return for the spring term and no matter what happens, you are forever banished from playing in Chapel. Dismissed!"

Forget the Hall, forget playing in Chapel, how in the hell do you get 200 demerits off in a month and two weeks before vacation? There would be no town leave, no more darts or movies every second not scheduled would be spent walking the "Beat" come rain, shine or snow. How do you keep from getting more demerits? Each demerit means one hour of walking around the football stadium except for Cadet Officers who mostly had more merits than demerits, and should they get excessive demerits, it meant they would be deprived town leave for their demerits.

Two brothers from Mt. Clemens, Michigan, who were first-year cadets, helped me keep my sanity. Down C stoop from my room was a suite where big brother Bob Vermeulen roomed. A high school football star he was a freshman in the Junior College department and at GMS on a football scholarship. Blond, blue-eyed with movie star looks and the build of an Adonis. He was soon the most popular guy in school and all the girls at the Greenbrier College for Women wanted to date him.

Even if it took all night, each and every cadet would be allowed a five-minute conversation with their parents. I guess my call was typical. I talked to Mother, then to my father.

Bob's brother, Don, was three years younger than I was in Company A up on the third stoop. Don later developed into a good-looking guy and played top-notch Varsity football and graduated as a Cadet Captain. Don had brought his record player with him plus a full collection of Glenn Miller recordings. I had his permission to go to his room and play his records. The music was vital for my survival. I took swats with the flat sides of officers sabers and brooms to get double deductions of demerits, plus running the Beat instead of walking to bring the total down. Then came December 7, 1941, when the Japs attacked Pearl Harbor and destroyed most of our Pacific Fleet. It was a warm day in December in Lewisburg, and being Sunday there was no "Beat." We had been to church, had a great lunch that featured fried chicken, and Bob Vermeulin and I were out on the football field tossing a pigskin back and forth. Someone leaned out of the top floor of the quad saying the Japs had attacked the United States. Although we were aware of Hitler and the situation in Europe we told the talking head we did not believe that Japan would attack us. We went back to tossing the football.

Our world exploded when Colonel Joe spoke to us at evening Mess and that after we returned from church the companies were allowed to call their parents. I called my father and asked him to call the school so I could come home and join the Marine Corps before the war was all over. Dad told me, "Stay in school, work on getting your grades up. There would be enough war for all of us."

Of course, he was right, and that was the basic answer every cadet got with one exception. Fred Andrews, a freshman in Junior College from California. His parents were divorced and his father arranged with Colonel Joe to send him home so he could join the Navy. The next morning as we were lined up for morning Mess we watched as Fred Andrews entered a taxi and left for the war. Everyone was filled with envy. Six months later, Fred was the first of our class to die in combat with the Navy in the South Pacific. The following morning of the Japanese attack at Pearl Harbor, it was announced that all our cadet officers age eighteen or over would report to Ft. Campbell, Kentucky to be commissioned Second Lieutenants in the U.S. Army. The war had come home. This was the time I wished I were a homeboy. Cadets, who lived in the area, wore the uniform, did the classes, drills and sports like the rest of us but at 6 PM went home. If I could do that I might be able to get my folks' permission to join the Marines. The Beat brought me back to reality. It was almost vacation time. I really wanted to leave Greenbrier and go home to West High, but I owed it to my mother and father to hang in and stay the year. I was triple timing on the Beat and it looked as though I would lose the battle, but a cadet officer would save my life.

He released me and called a cab saying, "Have a good Christmas." I will never forget it and I was back in full force for the next year, having learned a valuable lesson.

CHAPTER TWENTY-THREE

Prior to leaving GMS, I had several talks with First Lt. Jim Rownd who commanded the First Platoon of Company B. Jim was from Columbus and felt I should get a new start with his Platoon when I returned for the spring term. I could still live on the C stoop. The military office approved my move to B Company. Since my error in Chapel had not been reported to my parents, all I had to deal with was the dismal grade information when I got home.

I was headed home on the old C & O Sportsman for Columbus. Dad picked me up at the depot, and it was the greatest feeling in the world when his arms went around me and he welcomed. There was Mother, my old room, my dogs, Nip and Tuck, civilian clothes, and no Revelry Band to ruin my sleep. Just the wonderful aromas from Mother's kitchen drifting up the stairs. I called Wanda who had written to me at school and we made a date to see the Glenn Miller band live at the Palace. She insisted that I wear my uniform. It's official, the United States is at war with Germany and Italy as well as Japan.

As a family we caught up on films including Academy Award winner *How Green Was My Valley*. Jim Rownd called and I invited him to dinner to meet Mom and Dad. They were impressed by his academic record. Through the vacation that went too fast, Jim and I got together several times to catch a movie or just a bite to eat. My date with Wanda arrived and I got into my uniform and arrived at her home to be checked out by half the neighbors including a pretty little girl named Rosemary Reed who said I looked like a little toy soldier. Nothing told me that someday this little girl would be my wife. Wanda and I were excited to see the Miller Band. The house was packed and we sat in the front row of the balcony, stage center. During the movie we ate popcorn, drank Coke and held hands. Then the house lights dimmed as the strains of Glenn's theme came from the hydraulic stage as it rose out of the orchestra pit and the crowd went wild. The band was fabulous. Our heroes, Tex Beneke, Marion Hutton, Paula Kelly and The Modernaires performed. Glenn stepped to the mic saying "Here's the young man in the romance department, Ray Eberle, with a brand new song "High on a Windy Hill." The band started the song intro and Ray walked out of the wings. He was nineteen years old and handsome. Wanda who had been holding my hand dropped it and said "Oh, my God, he's handsome" and leaned on the balcony rail so far I thought she might fall over. When he started to sing I heard, "So handsome and what a beautiful voice over and over again." When he finished all the girls screamed and Amy Arnell, a real sweetheart and one of my favorite girl vocalists sang.

Later I had lunch with Tommy who had been a school teacher before becoming a bandleader. The whole group was nice.

CHAPTER TWENTY-FOUR

My Father looked out the back window of Cousin Ken Agee's car looking at our home for as long as he could see it as Ken drove him and Mother to Mount Carmel Hospital for tests to find out what was wrong. Prior to this time, I had talked with both parents about taking the Greyhound to Lewisburg to attend the Christmas dance. They both said okay, so I went south to see old friends. During the dance Major Benjamin found me and told me that the hotel had called and that they had a very urgent telegram for me. I got my overcoat and ran in the falling snow to the hill and found my mother had wired my father was critical and come at once. I got the first bus out. The snow got heavier and the two-lane road was iced. It took forever to arrive in Columbus and I grabbed a cab for Valley View.

I raced into our house to find Aunt Fanny in the living room. She told me mom was in her bedroom. I raced up the stairs and into her room. "Your father died calling your name."

Yesterday, Doctor Wells Teachner, one of Ohio's best-known surgeons, had come to the decision that my father had cancer and they had to operate the next morning. At noon he came out and told his nurse to call the country club that he'd be late for lunch. Then turning to my mother, he said "Can't save them all. Your husband is filled with cancer. I just closed him up." With that he vanished through a door. My father died on December 13, 1941. He was fifty-one years of age. He was a fine man, a great husband and the best father in the world. I will always love him. He's my idol. My hero. He was laid to rest in Pleasant Hill Cemetery, West Jefferson, Ohio, on a freezing cold and windy day.

CHAPTER TWENTY-FIVE

Army 1942

In January Army doctors found I was 1-A and I was inducted at Fort Hayes, Columbus, Ohio, and was shipped to Ft. Bragg, North Carolina. This suited me fine as that was the home of the 101st Airborne and that's where I wanted to go. Ft. Bragg is a huge permanent Army base with green lawns and really nice red brick homes for officers. The entrance to Bragg is at Fayetteville, North Carolina. The barracks were large, clean, and the food was equal to any first-class eating establishment. We were under the command of a ninety-day wonder Lt. Shime who would never have been an officer at Greenbrier. The man was worthless. The real trainers were Sergeant Pace, a Cherokee Indian, and Sergeant Clothier, both Army lifers. The First Sergeant was Taslowski, a thirty-year veteran who liked to call us "civilian sons of bitches." Having been to GMS made basic training a snap. I loved the obstacle course, the walk a hundred, run a hundred hikes, the twenty-five-mile hikes, and even the time we slept on the cold, wet sand. I had loved

GMS, so maybe I would make the Army a career, but I wanted to be in the 101st Airborne. Almost as soon as I started basic training, I started going to the Captain and requesting a transfer to Airborne. He explained that at that time all the enlisted men were American Indians and only officers were Caucasian. Well, why not send me to Officer's Candidate School? He told me to go back to my unit. The Captain had found out I had been a professional entertainer and commanding officers got prizes and other considerations if men under their command were top draws in the Ft. Bragg talent shows. That's where I would end up singing songs of the day like "Soldier, Let Me Read Your Letter," "Dear Mom," "You'd Be So Nice to Come Home to," "I've Heard That Song Before" and "Der Fuehrers Face." I was active at the piano with all the standards and the new songs. Ft Bragg had a super dance band that featured Eddie Julian who had been with Vaughn Monroe in civilian life.

I kept up efforts to go the 101st and the Captain kept raining on my parade.

After a series of highlights on the talent side, I told Sergeant Pace that I refused to do the show. The Captain showed up at my barrack and made it very plain. I could either go on the show or could spend the entire weekend crawling inside the ovens and cleaning them. I did the shows.

You always have guys who don't like the rules. I heard a guy who had been a sparring partner of British Heavyweight Champion Tommy Farr, that he would change Sergeant Pace's face if he didn't have three stripes. The Sergeant told him he would be behind the barrack after evening Mess and he would not be wearing stripes. The professional fighter weighed about 250 pounds, Sergeant Pace around 180. The fight lasted all of twenty seconds. Sergeant Pace, a master of "kill or be killed," had the pro whimpering on the ground. No one ever questioned authority again.

We had a guy from Chicago named Fogg who should never been inducted. He fainted when we ran a hundred, walked a hundred. Had real problems on the rifle range, then ended his Army career when he broke both ankles during a field problem. Then there was BoBo Quinn who never showered. After the second week, the Sergeants gave him a shower and he was Mr. Clean after that.

The only time I felt fear was in the grenade pit. We had hiked about ten miles with Lieutenant Schime counting the cadence as he rode in his Jeep. We were stopped at a designed pit where the Lieutenant was going to show us how to throw grenades. We were down in this big deep pit, the Lieutenant pulled the pin then he tossed the grenade. The problem was he couldn't throw it high enough and it fell back into the pit. Like a streak of light Sergeant Pace picked up the grenade and threw it out of the pit as he yelled, "Hit the dirt!" We did and a split second later the grenade exploded. The Lieutenant was never seen near a grenade pit again. Sergeants Pace and Clothier taught us the art of using them.

I had Saturday and Sunday passes and got on the bus and out of Fayetteville as fast as possible. Bartenders had to serve liquor to the Indians in the 101st, something that does not do well with our red brothers. Every weekend there were killings and lots of problems for the MPs.

I went to beautiful Roanoke where I met the Yevelton sisters, Rita and Reiva, a couple of blonde, blue-eyed beauties. We had great times dancing, dining and visiting their home and meeting their folks.

I was selected to be on the Honor Guard for the Easter Sunday Field Mass. You stood with your rifle for two hours. It was a hot, muggy day and several guards passed out from the heat. Early that morning Jonny Wydock and I raced each other over the obstacle course. I won, but it was a crazy way to start the day.

A few days later a guy from Special Services came to see me and offered me a job as musical director for a series of War Bond Tours. I would play piano and sing, lead the sextet, and back a female vocal trio of WACS. I would be promoted to Sergeant. What a deal! However, stupid here told the officer I wanted to be in a combat unit and wasn't interested. He thought I was a mental case.

Next day I went to the Captain about a transfer to a combat unit. He told me to get out of his office. A few days later, I was with a hundred or more GIs being shipped to various parts of the United States. Where was I headed? I could not believe it, San Pedro, California.

In San Pedro, I was quartered in a school damaged by earthquakes and unsafe for students but okay for the Army. We worked the barrage balloons in San Pedro Harbor as a support for all the Anti-Aircraft located all around. We would be at the balloon so many days, and then back to the school; a two-day pass to Los Angeles then the whole routine over again. Why didn't I do the War Bond Tour?

In the harbor, we worked where the Russian freighters docked. Half their crews were women. Big women who worked stripped to the waist. Most were blonds and they didn't shave under their arms. They loved to wink, laugh and shake their hips while calling to us in Russian. We didn't understand them and they didn't know what we said but hand gestures told the story.

Close to our post was a ramshackle bar named "Ollie's." Ollie had to be seventy years old, skinny as a rail and always wore a black dress. Ollie told dirty stories and it was rumored that she had got it on with some of the crew. Some of the guys would eat sandwiches at her place but I settled for a bottle of Coke.

I thought of looking up Madam Vera and Jeep but I passed. I did date a sweet Mexican-American girl named Jenny Trujillo, and once or twice we went to Cap's old theater but Cap had sold it and his house and no one knew where he had gone. Jenny's folks were very nice and her mother made wonderful tacos.

During pass time, I would take Red Reaper into the station in downtown Los Angeles right across from the Main Street Gym where famous fighters trained. The entire trip was dangerous. You had to have the blinds down over the windows because bottles, rocks and rotten fruit would be thrown as you came through Compton. Main Street was very touchy because that was the time of the battles between the Zoot-suited Mexicans and servicemen. Some got killed and many injured. It ended when an entire Marine Division swinging the big buckles on their leather belts filled the street with Zoot suitor's blood, teeth, broken bones and ripped and torn Zoot suits over every square inch of the area.

There was no place to sleep at any price. The hotels would let you sleep in the lobby if you were a serviceman who could find a chair. Otherwise, you bought a ticket and slept in an all-night theater. This was risky because of the muggings.

Although I could have taken a trolley to Hollywood or Beverly Hills, I never thought of it but I did to Santa Monica. It was a beautiful California day and I enjoyed the Midway, the food and the soft ocean breeze. Toward evening, I thought I would ride the famous roller coaster. Why I wanted to do this I will never know since I don't like them. I bought a ticket and the only seat vacant next to a young lady. I asked if it was open and she said it was. I jumped in just as the ride began to move. I was trying to put my field jacket on and my left arm was trapped and we were ready for that first big drop. We started dropping and I started to fall to my death. In a split second, she pulled me back in the seat, keeping her arms around me until the ride was over.

She smiled at me and said, "We're done," and for the first time I realized what a beautiful angel had saved my life. Soft brown hair, an award-winning smile and a great figure encased in a pretty dress. We got out of the ride and I could hardly get my breath.

She started to walk away and I stopped her. "You're not wearing a wedding ring or an engagement ring so I guess you are single."

"Are you married or engaged?"

"No. Since we're both single can I treat you to dinner?"

"I think we could do that, soldier."

"I'm Bob Cawley from Columbus, Ohio."

"I'm Mickey Renar from Los Angeles. I live with

grandparents who came from Ireland and work in a defense plant."

We found a little restaurant, slowly ate, and got to know each other while the blue Pacific lapped at the pilings. It was Saturday night and she didn't work the next day. We went to the Swing Shift dance at the Ballroom. Harry James and his orchestra featuring smooth vocals by Helen Forrest worked from 9 PM until midnight, then Tommy Dorsey and his orchestra played until 3 AM. I think we danced every dance with both bands. By 3 AM we were bushed but happy. Mickey insisted on taking me to her grandparents, as they had an extra room and would be delighted to have a soldier as a guest. Grandma came out in her robe and listened to the tale of our meeting and dancing as we had a piece of fresh baked apple pie. Grandpa came out and welcomed me, and Mickey showed me the big comfortable bedroom that was mine. As we said goodnight Mickey kissed my cheek and, laughing, told me she was glad she had saved me. We both got up late the next morning and Grandma fixed breakfast. Mickey and I took a long walk. She lived about three blocks from the vacant lot where the murdered body of the infamous Black Dahlia would be found. That evening Mickey drove me back to the station where I caught the Red Reaper. When we parted we shared our first kiss. No one paid attention, just a soldier and his girl saying goodbye.

That was the routine into the summer. I would call Mickey's folks and tell them I would be coming and she would pick me up and we would spend hours at the Swing Shift dance where in mid-summer Harry James was replaced by a band that played danceable music but we had never heard of. The leader's name was Lawrence Welk.

There was only one little blip. I would have a few days of coughing every time we refueled the balloons with a different gas.

My thoughts of combat had been replaced with hopes that I would spend the rest of the war and even beyond dancing and having fun with Mickey. We were growing very close.

Then the Army told me I was leaving for a new destination the end of August.

The last trip to Los Angeles was very painful. That night Mickey and I danced very close to all the ballads, and after the dance we took a walk along the beach. Somewhere along the way we kissed and told each other we were in love and I asked her to wait for me and she said she would. When I left Sunday evening, Grandma gave me a sack of her cookies and Grandpa had tears in his eyes. Then I was gone.

On the troop train I was seated by my close GI friend, George Thorpe, a California native and a real upbeat guy. Strong rumor was that we were going to a holding area before being shipped out to Italy. The area proved to be Ft. Custer, Michigan a permanent post in a beautiful setting yet close to Battle Creek and Kalamazoo. George and I got a weekend pass to Kalamazoo and set off to see the sights. In the 21st century it is impossible to believe that two eighteen-year-old men could be virgins. But not for long. We had taken a few steps out of the station when a couple of attractive women, about twenty-five, asked us if we'd like to party. Hell yes, we would like to party. Let the games begin. A bar was the first stop with the ladies, then dinner at an upscale restaurant followed by a stupid comedy movie. Then at last they took us home and we paired off. They never said a word about George and my lack of ability but I bet they were surprised. I didn't think sex was anywhere near what I had heard it could be and wondered what all the fuss was about. The lady was about to go to sleep when I asked her if the photo of the Marine in dress blues was her brother.

The answer made my blood run cold. "Brother? Hell, that's my stupid son-of-a-bitch husband who is somewhere in the South Pacific. I hope a Jap takes him out soon so I can get my ten thousand dollars." She turned out the light, rolled over and went to sleep. I lay in the dark thinking of that man may be dying at this very moment while his wife was in bed with me. After a while, I got out of bed, got my shoes and clothes. I found George, made a signal to be quiet and not wake his woman. We dressed on the front porch in the dark then made our way to the bus station, had breakfast and took the first bus back to Ft Custer. A few days later, we were issued warm weather gear and Italy as a possible destination seemed possible. I never found out.

I was playing football and got behind the defensive back and the quarterback threw a perfect rainbow. The pass was at my fingertips when my world went black. When I woke up I was in a hospital and an Asian doctor was looking down at me. My mind went crazy. I thought I had been captured by the Japs and he was going to torture me. Seeing I was awake he said, "You through, you through, you finished in the military." Then he walked away.

I was released to a building called the casualty area filled with returned vets missing arms, legs, faces and blind. I really felt like a freak looking like a picture of perfect health. Every morning a captain had me in his office urging me to sign a paper that said the Army was not responsible for my physical condition. When I asked what was wrong with me they refused to answer. Just sign and I could go home with an honorable discharge. I was told if I didn't sign they could keep me there forever. I could send no letters or make a phone call. What I had to eat a dog wouldn't eat. The great Army food had vanished. I lived on three meals of Coke and potato chips out of the canteen machines. I held out for over a week, and then signed the paper. Got my travel pay and my Honorable Discharge which had written across the second page "CONSULT DISCHARGE."

I arrived home my mother was eating breakfast and turned pale when she saw me in grey slacks and a plaid jacket. My uniform was in my shipping bag. She cried, read the discharge and insisted I see a doctor. He took X-rays of my lungs, then asked, "How long have you smoked four packs of cigarettes a day." He couldn't believe me. My lungs were black. In less than six months my lungs had turned black and the only answer was the gasses we used for balloons. In hindsight, I should have gone to my cousin Ken Agee, a powerful attorney who would have loved to sue the Government. Later when I tried to obtain my medical records, I was told they burned up when the records at the Army headquarters were destroyed by fire. Mother asked me to remember my father's wish that I get an education, so I returned to West High.

My class had graduated and I felt strange when weekly there was news of members of my class dying in combat. I worked from nine to one playing piano and singing to help Mother, who was working at a cleaners to pay the mortgage and my dad's medical and funeral bills. My first class of the day was English and I sat behind a very pretty girl with dark blond hair who wore sweaters, plaid skirts and bobby sox. It was a week before I discovered this lovely young woman had once been the little girl that told Wanda Deaton that I looked like a toy soldier. Her name was Rosemary Reed and the family now resided on Binns Boulevard. Not as far from school as Wanda but still a good walk. I asked if I could walk her home and she said yes. On the way, I asked if we could date and she said no. She had to be home every day at 4:30 PM to give her mother, Dolly, dinner and relieve the housekeeper. Her mother was a paraplegic in very bad shape.

"How about Saturday or Sunday?" The answer was still no. She had to replace the housekeeper those days and her dad was gone in the evenings. Not much future here, but she was special. Something kept me involved. I walked her home every night after school, she fed her mom, and then we would play records until her father came home around six. His name was Paul. A big man who always smelled of whiskey. When introduced, he failed to shake my hand. I never asked but I would bet a million dollars that his wife's injury came at his hands. In the four months I walked her home, we only had one date. We ditched school and spent the day at the Palace seeing Vaugh Monroe and his orchestra. Rosemary had hopes he would sing her favorite song, "I Cover the Waterfront," but that didn't happen.

Every so often Rosemary would come to school with bruises on her arms or face and when I asked her what happened, she would say, "Dad was unhappy with me." Rosemary had a kid brother who was a nice kid but seemed to have zero rules.

In mid-fall my mom got a great paying job in the office of the Brotherhood of Railroad Trainmen in downtown Columbus. She had been very active with the Trainmen when dad was alive and this made her happy.

The more I saw of Paul Reed, who had a big job with the State but treated his daughter like a slave, the more I knew this had to end.

I loved her and I was going to save her. I quit my entertainment job thinking her father would come for her where I worked. On December 23, 1942, Wally Connel, who had been a choir boy with me, and with his wife Bonny drove to Cincinnati where we were married by a Justice of the Peace. After dinner, Wally and his wife drove back to Columbus. I called my mom and there we were in a new city alone together.

CHAPTER TWENTY-SIX

It was a quiet New Year's. Rosemary loved the wide gold wedding band I had placed on her fourth finger, left hand. Inside it was inscribed from RMC to RR 12/23/42. She loved that ring and kept it until she died.

We had little money and we needed to find a place to live. A roomy, one-bedroom apartment in Walnut Hills worked perfectly. It was up above beautiful Eden Park a short walk from our door. We had less than twenty dollars left for food.

Leaving Rosemary at the apartment, I started walking the joints along Redding Road looking for work. I got a night here, two nights there, but I needed something steady. Leaving the suburbs, I took the trolley downtown and started hitting the nightspots near Fountain Square, the very heart of Cincinnati. Two blocks north I saw the famous Barn Club in Gano Alley. In my searching for work, several bar managers had told me I should work an upscale room like that. I walked halfway down the alley to the door where the Marque read "In the Barn the Bobby

Gaston Trio." In the Stable (a solo artist) and in the Hangover Room (another soloist).

In the early afternoon the place was quiet. Maybe four men drinking at the bar. A hand touched my arm and I turned to face a gorgeous woman. "Can I help you?"

"I'm a pianist/singer looking for work. Could I meet the boss and maybe audition?"

"The club is owned by the Shavel Brothers, Al and Tick. Al is out but I'll get Tick for you."

Tick was about 5'9, and maybe 150 pounds in prime condition. He smiled as we shook hands then led me upstairs to the Hangover Room where an upright piano occupied a wall. "Let's hear a couple of numbers."

I don't remember what I played or sang. When I finished he told me the man who had worked this room had left to take care of his sick mother in Florida. Would I be interested in this job? Of course, I was interested. He told me they had never hired a white musician. Did I have a problem working in a club featuring Negros? No problem.

"You can start tonight. Nine PM until one AM, 10-minute breaks each hour and one free drink each break."

It was Wednesday and they paid the entertainers in cash each Saturday. All you had to do was sign a pay sheet. Miss Angie, the beauty whom I had met, would have my pay. He stood and handed me a twenty-dollar bill. "I don't know if you're driving or riding the trolley. Either way a guy needs a little 'whip out.'"

I thanked him, grabbed a trolley to our apartment in Walnut Hills, and kissed away Rosemary's tears as we laughed and danced. We were saved! The rent could be paid; we could buy a few extras.

"See, honey, the old music biz will see us through." I never saw the long-range question behind those lovely blue eyes.

The Barn was paradise. First night, I made $35 in tips. The room was packed from nine to closing every night. I met Bobby Gaston and his trio Elmer Warner, all 100 pounds, was in the Jazz Hall of Fame for his guitar work on Louis Armstrong's "Back Of Town Blues." Eighteen-year-old Wendell Wilkins was a genius with his solos on the doghouse bass. Bobby and Warner sang and the three were a terrific musical unit. I met and enjoyed the pianist who worked the Stable. Beautiful Angie was Tick's mistress. I met Al Shavel my first night. About two years older than his brother he told me they had been welterweight prize fighters and he felt Tick made a good move in hiring me.

On Sunday after my first partial week, I took my bride to a store where she selected a table radio that she could enjoy during the nights when I worked. We had a nice dinner out and we passed a movie to take a long walk through Eden Park. The walk in the park on Sundays became a tradition.

We were young and in love. No more would her drunken father hit her when she had done nothing wrong. He had been forced to hire a second housekeeper. They never stayed long. For us, it was honeymoon time. Once in a while we would eat Sunday dinner out, see a movie or go to the club where the fabulous Al Morgan entertained but most of the time it was long walks and just being together was enough.

Two months later a tragic event would change my

life. It was Saturday night and the place was packed to the rafters. Tick Shavel raced up the stairs and grabbed my arm shouting, "Come on, come on!"

I was in the middle of a song. He pulled me off the piano bench and down the stairs. What waited was bedlam; waiters were using thick towels soaked with hot water scrubbing the piano keys that were covered with blood. Soon as they were clean they dried them and Tick was in my face yelling, "Play something!" Elmer Warner was sitting calmly on his stool, guitar in his lap while Wendell Wilkins leaned against the back wall of the stage.

I looked wild-eyed at Elmer who said, "What do you want to play?" I knew over two thousand songs but only one title came out. "Rose Room in F." We were off and running while Tick and Al had the waiters deliver drinks for all the clients in the main room and comped dinner for guests seated by the stage. Warner sang his big hit "Street of Dreams." Wendell set the audience on fire with a mind-blowing full chorus bass solo of "The One O'clock Jump," and I did my imitation of the Ink Spots on "We Three," plus some fancy work on the keyboard.

At intermission the guys told me what had happened. Bobby Gaston, who was just twenty-three, had been having lung problems the last couple of years but never revealed how serious it was, although he had a pianist/singer sub for him on several occasions. Tonight he was playing and singing when he leaned way back on the piano bench, then came forward with blood coming out of his mouth in waves as his head hit the keys. It was panic as Tick and Al pulled him off the bench and laid him on the side of the stage. Angie called the police and an ambulance. Al got the waiters busy cleaning things up as Tick raced upstairs to get me. Tick and Al got rid of their bloody clothes and, in fresh duds, handled the crowds as the star hosts they always were.

We were going on for the last set when Angie, who had gone with Bobby in the ambulance, came back and told us that Bobby Gaston was dead from a lung hemorrhage.

At the end of the evening, Tick had the three of us in his office to have a drink. He told us how much he had admired Bobby and that he and Al were going to Bobby's home to be with his mother and offer any financial support she might need through this trying time.

"You guys know the old show biz saying, the show must go on, so starting Monday you will be my headliner. Bob Cawley here will head the trio. Is there any problem with this arrangement?" The answer was no. When we left the club Elmer pointed to the marquee which read "Appearing in the Barn The Bob Cawley Trio."

The group bonded very fast. The guys were a joy to work with. South of the Barn about three blocks was the Albee Theater where the big bands who played Columbus on Monday, Tuesday and Wednesday, played the Albee Thursday, Friday and Saturday. The Barn had long been a hangout for both leaders and sidemen. The very first to sit in was Woody Herman who played his clarinet on several jazz numbers, then sang "Blues in the Night," bringing the clients to their feet with cheers and applause. The list of "Guest Artists" – Georgie Auld, Vido Musso, Stan Kenton, Charlie Barnet, Eddy Howard, Claude

Thornhill, Charlie Spivak... and the list goes on and on.

The guys introduced me to Cincinnati's Cotton Club, a black and tan club not too far from our work. There were guys selling sticks of marijuana on the front steps three for a dollar. I was never into drugs. I never wanted to lose control of my body and mind and have never understood why people want them. We all passed, went inside and found a table for three. As always, local groups filled the place. There was a stage with a grand piano and throughout the wee hours of the morning groups would be invited to perform. There were always members of various hit radio shows at the Cotton Club. For example, they showcased the super-talented Cyclone Sisters, Rosemary and Betty. I would catch a trolley around 3:00 AM and be on the road to dreamland by 3:40 AM. Get up around 10:00 AM, have breakfast with Rosemary and we would have the entire day together until 7:45 PM when I would dress for work.

It was another great year for music with songs like "Tonight We Love," "Miss You," "Don't Sit under the Apple Tree," "Tangerine" and "String of Pearls" which led the way.

We were going full steam into the holiday season when, just prior to Thanksgiving, I came to work Monday to find a new bassist. Nineteen-year-old Wendell Wilkins had died of an overdose of heroin. Elmer, having no way to reach me since we did not have a telephone, had asked the nice-looking gentleman, standing with his doghouse bass, looking as if he should run out the door, to come and perform with us tonight. Knowing we needed a bassist, he had asked Lee Anderson to do an audition. Lee and I shook hands and I asked where he had been working. He had been on tour with Duke Ellington, but he was the father of eight and his wife told him they needed an at-home father, and if he didn't come back to Cincinnati, his wife and kids would be gone. I realized leaving the Duke had to be a rough deal but I was certain his family was happy and I would be happy if he liked working with us. He told me he had worked with Elmer and had great respect for his musical talent. We got on the stage and went to work. I had only heard the legend that was Jimmy Balaton on records and I'm certain that Lee could play not only as well, but better.

Tick told me that he and Al had bought the building behind the Barn and now the club would run a full block and the new entity would be The Hanger Theater Lounge located next to the Palace Hotel and my trio would have the new room. We would do cocktail time 5:00 PM to 7:00 PM. They have a free dinner at the Barn, and then do our normal 9:00 PM to 1:00 AM shift in the Hanger Theater Lounge. This was not good news at home. I would be away from 2:00 PM until I woke up the next day giving my bride and me about four hours a day together. This became a real bone of contention. She talked about getting a daytime job then we would never be together except on Sunday's. I vetoed the idea. She wondered when I would quit this routine and take a straight 9:00 AM to 5:00 PM job. I kept the answer to this question under my breath and braced for New Year's Eve when we opened The Hanger.

As an entertainer I have always hated working New Year's Eve. People who never get drunk and make fools of themselves do so on New Year's Eve. They wear stupid paper hats, blow noisemakers, are very loud and pushy, spill drinks and act as if they are demented. They drive leaving clubs and kill people, usually not themselves with their cars. Hairbrained owners want the entertainers to wear "funny hats" and blow noisemakers, and that's where I draw the line. People who work with me do not wear funny hats or blow noisemakers. There were no hats or noisemakers at the opening of the Hanger. The place was packed, and as usual we were in our black tuxes.

1943 had to be one of the worst years I can remember. Thank the good Lord that the new songs were good starting with "Paper Doll," and surrounded by such songs as "There Are Such Things," "That Old Black Magic," "You'll Never Know," "People Will Say We're In Love," the crazy "Maisie Doats," and the haunting "I'll Be Seeing You."

The war claimed thousands upon thousands of lives. *Casablanca* starring Humphrey Bogart and Ingrid Bergman won the Academy Award. The song, "As Time Goes By," from that film becomes an instant hit.

The New York Yankees won the World Series.

It was late in the cocktail hour when the beautiful brunette wearing a full-length mink coat slipped into a booth. Later she gave a waiter a napkin asking me to come to her booth at intermission. I did and she was even better looking close up than from the stage. After introducing herself, she asked if I would have a late dinner with her at her home after work. I said I guess so. She told me it would be just this one time and never again. Her husband was in South America and there would be a maid who would serve food. And then we would be alone.

She handed me a card with her address and a twenty-dollar bill for cab fare. I went back to work and she left a few minutes later. The rest of my working hours, I wrestled with *should I*, or *should I forget it*. *Should I* won out?

I grabbed a cab and gave the driver the address. It was a huge house on Mount Washington where the wealthy lived. The home had an elevator and she and I rode up. The maid indicated a door at the end of the hall. As I neared the door opened and the lady was wearing a black robe over what proved to be a see-through lace nightgown over a white, voluminous body. She said she was glad I came, put her arms around me and gave me a kiss that sent my blood pressure sky-high. She told me to be calm, enjoy a nice dinner, then followed hours of making love.

We rode up to a third-floor dining room that was 100% Oriental with low tables and pillows to sit on. She explained that the dining room was her husband's idea. He had the entire room including many expensive pieces of artwork and vases shipped from Japan. He was very interested in the Far East and had business there and in South America. She rang a bell and the maid arrived with the first of four courses. What I had to eat and drink I never had before or since. Following dinner we took the elevator down to the second floor bedroom. She removed her robe, followed by her nightgown, revealing a perfect body, and the games began. For the next three hours, it was a graduate course in how to sexually please a woman. Riding the cab home, I was elated and tired and I was getting home a little late. My bride was in the kitchen.

She said I was very late getting home from downtown and did I want breakfast. I wasn't hungry but I said yes, took a quick shower, and sat down to eat. Nothing more was ever said, but I knew that she knew and I was ashamed. Over the months that followed I bought flowers, candy and little gifts. But it never erased the pain.

In early spring we were offered a three-hour gig at the Flamingo Casino in Covington, Kentucky across the Ohio River from Cincinnati. The hours were 2:00 AM to 5 AM and the money offered was attractive. The guys were for it and Lee with a wife and eight kids was really upbeat that he could have extra cash. Okay, so now we played music ten hours a day. We were young, no problem, but it was a big problem at my house. Rosemary wanted us to move back to Columbus and for me to find a straight job. I asked her to give this a little time and we would save all the money for the move home.

In the Flamingo the stage was right by a crap table. We had made friends with the stick man whose name was Sammy. One night a customer lost all his money, pulled out a gun and killed Sammy and wounded the pit boss. Yes, we kept playing. Security got the shooter and held him for the police.

A happy memory of the Flamingo was the night a drunken customer asked if he could share the taxi we took to the Dixie Showboat, an old paddle wheeler that was docked on the Kentucky side of the river. The old dining room had a piano and we would often have a jam session while our chicken and biscuits were being prepared. The drunk, who was a winner, had requested the song "An Irish Lullaby." Now he wanted me to sing the song but only sing

"Toralouraly" over and over again and forget the rest of the lyrics. If I would do that he would give me a dollar for every time I sang those words. We gave our driver the sign and we took a very long route to the Showboat. I had made enough to buy breakfast for us and give the cabbie a nice tip. The cab headed across the bridge to Ohio with a soused customer still singing the song.

At home the pressure was really on to go back to Columbus. With great regret I gave two weeks' notice to Tick and Al as well as the manager of the Flamingo, both places would keep the trio employed with someone new at the keyboard.

Rosemary was delighted we would be home for Christmas, three months away. My mother was delighted that her son and the daughter-in-law she had never met would be living at her home. However, the trip was going to be delayed. While in the final week with the trio, bandleader Barney Rapp stopped in and told me he was interested in my becoming the pianist with his band. He offered good money and, of course, I would be home more except when the band went on short road trips. Barney owned a nightclub called The Sign of the Drum in Cincinnati which had a radio wire and was heard on a regular basis. The band also had a recording contract. Barney's brother, Mark Warnow was a featured vocalist on a national radio show from New York *Your Hit Parade*, which featured the ten top national favorite songs of that week. The band was called Barney Rapp and the New Englanders. I never asked Barney if his original home was in New England or how his name was Rapp and his brother's name was Warnow. I did know the band was very popular, paid top dollar, and his former girl vocalist, Doris Kapplehoff, now known as Doris Day, was headed for big things as the girl singer with Les Brown and his Orchestra. Rapp's girl singer was Ruby Wright, a very talented lady, who was Barney's wife.

I have two vivid memories of my time with the band. On my first date with the organization was Castle Farms Ballroom outside Cincinnati. Winter had started, and the snow fell. The wind blew and the place was filled with dancers, but the heat in this huge ballroom had been out for three days and had not been repaired. The bandstand was right by the front doors and every time the doors opened, we got a blast of cold air and snow. Dancers went in and out to take drinks out of their flasks in their cars. Ruby wore an overcoat over her black low-cut dress and soon the entire band including the leader had their warm coats on. That didn't help the piano keys which were like ice cubes. I tried to play with gloves on but that didn't work. Every half hour we had to stop dance music while the band retuned the piano which would slip out of tune about every thirty minutes. Oh, I really love show business.

My other memory with the Rapp orchestra was also connected with snow. The Fireman's Ball in Charleston, West Virginia was a very big event and also a big payday for the band. We went by rail in a private car that held all sixteen band members, the instruments, and our cleaned and pressed white band uniforms, all the musical arrangements, and Ruby's cocktail dress and makeup. It was a great trip down and the dancers loved the band. While we worked, a blizzard blew in. When we made our way to the station we were looking forward to the warm surroundings of our private railway car. Halfway home, the train was forced to halt because the snow had blocked the tracks and the train did not have power for heat. With the temperature dropping as gusts of snow kept whipping the car, plus the wind chill, we soon drank our share of hot coffee. The car was below freezing so we ran up and down the aisle; Barney conducted exercises to keep us moving and sane. It was over three hours until the tracks were cleared, then the train could move and heat was restored.

We were happy but tired campers when at last we crossed the Ohio River and were home. I left the band in mid-December and, with Rosemary happier than I had seen her in months, boarded the Greyhound Bus for Columbus.

The holiday season was a lovely time. Rosemary and my mother bonded instantly. I think she was the daughter my mother had lost after only a couple of days and she in turn was the mother that Rosemary had never known due to her injury.

I remember we shared gifts, the two ladies fixed wonderful meals, family came around to meet the bride, and for several evenings, with the fireplace glowing, I entertained with piano and songs that always contained the song that Rosemary and I claimed as our song. "I Surrender Dear" and Mom's favorite the "Chopin Nocturne in E Flat."

Soon the New Year came in and the "new life" was scheduled to start.

CHAPTER TWENTY-SEVEN

In 1944 World War II was raging. This was the year that Anzio entered the American vocabulary and a Texas sharecropper's son named Audie Murphy would become America's most decorated hero. In the Pacific, US Marines would take conquest of the Solomon and Marshall Islands while our fortresses dropped 2,000 bombs on Berlin. On June 6th at D-Day our nation would hold its breath as US forces landed in Normandy.

On the music scene the entire world knew Doris Kapplehoff, now Doris Day as her recording of "Sentimental Journey" with the Les Brown Band was released. Bing Crosby made "Swinging On A Star" a hit and "Spring Will Be a Little Late This Year," "Twilight Time" and "I'm Making Believe" were all big, but why worry? I'm out of show biz. I'm working for the IRS. You read it right, 9:00 AM to 5:00 PM with the IRS. Rosemary, who had landed an office job, was so proud of me she bought us matching reindeer sweaters. Now we would ride the bus together to and from work. I had never seen her so happy. You had to love her. She was so pretty and such a nice, loving person and so good the majority of men would have given anything to be her husband.

I spent the day riding streetcars and buses all over Columbus delivering hand-carried notices to bar and restaurant owners that they had tax problems and should contact the IRS at once. Needless to say, my customers were not happy to see me.

Mother's office was downtown, and once in a while we would ride in together. She started a half-hour later and got off a half-hour later so she never made the trip home with us, so Rosemary and I would start dinner. The two ladies would then listen to their favorite radio show. I joined sometimes but mostly listened to records. Mom was very afraid of storms and would close all the blinds and she and Rosemary would hold hands until the storm was over. I love those big Midwest storms, seeing lightning strike in the middle of a field and hearing the thunder roll. I used to laugh at their terror of the storms. My personal storm was raging inside.

After a couple of months, I'd had it with the IRS, so I found a 9:00 AM to 5:00 PM job with Brinks as an armed guard for bank money and big manufacturing companies.

Shortly after I took the job, Mom came to the Huntington Bank downtown. We were picking up cash for a plant payroll. Most of the time I rode in back. The man riding with the driver would get out and stand at the front of the bank to cover me, and then I would get out of the truck to take cash in or out. Today, I was riding with the driver, so I was at the front of the bank. My mother came up the steps to the bank when she looked up and saw me carrying a gun. I thought she was going to have a heart attack as I waved her to the side so I could cover our man coming out of the bank in case a robbery was in progress. He came out carrying the plant payroll and I moved at the required distance until he got in the back and closed the door.

Passing Mother, I smiled and said, "Just working 9:00 AM to 5:00 PM." She had seen me in my uniform many times but never saw the gun because it remained at work.

Rosemary was convinced I would be shot on the job and I told her she was wound more tightly than Mr. Fink who ran the Brinks' office. He had been transferred to quiet Columbus after heading the Pittsburgh office where one of his trucks was robbed, where men had placed a bomb in a road to a factory Brink's serviced. The bottoms of the trucks did not have armor and the truck exploded killing all three workers while the robbers calmly collected the money, got in their car and vanished. Every delivery or pickup was timed to the second and if a truck was late at the next stop, you could believe Fink was red-faced and sweating. I thought we would lose him the evening we were all checking our then-unloaded guns. Driver Jack Ward had forgotten he had a round in the shotgun he was handing in butt first when it discharged taking a piece of his hand. Mr. Fink, the manager, became unglued.

Almost as much as when I was delivering payroll to the workers at Wright Patterson Aircraft in Dayton. Remember, there were no cell phones in those days, so I was paged to the Plant front office. Fink was on the line. He ordered me to tell the driver to return to the office at once. A different worker had been in the back of our truck this morning and had stolen

$5,000 dollars from a pickup at the Union Station. They had the thief and the police were all over the office and wanted to talk to the driver. I gave the driver the message, got in the back, and settled down for a long ride to Columbus.

Comfortable, I leaned back, and for only a reason that destiny ordained, I let my right hand go between the bench and the wall of the truck. Umm, there seemed to be something wrapped. I pulled it out and there it was the missing $5,000. Your mind has to think that they have the thief that stole the money, so I could take it and no one would know. Then I thought of my co-worker a nice guy with a wife and two kids who had just made a down payment on a small home on the South side. I'd make my own $5,000 and now I had to save him. I said nothing to the guys I was with but wrapped the money in my jacket, turned my gun in, and went into the room where it looked as though half the police force was gathered around my friend with a couple of cops trying to calm a purple-faced Fink who kept calling him a dirty thief. I spotted the detective in charge, took the pack of money out of the folded jacket, and told him this was the missing $5,000 dollars. You could have heard a pin drop when I related my story and then told the officers I had many times been the pickup at the Union Station and they always gave you the cash in packages. You counted the stacks and signed for them. There was no sack or bag to put them in. I always carried a few large rubber bands to secure them on the bench. With all the driving we did, it's a wonder it had not happened before. They took the cuffs off my friend who thanked me and begged Fink to forgive him, but after what had happened in Pittsburgh he was a bundle of nerves. The man stayed with the company, which I would never have done, but he thought of his family and I guess this was the right decision.

As he was leaving, the lead detective asked me if I was related to the Robert Cawley who won the National Championship in Piano and whom he had followed on radio. When I told him I was one and the same, he was amazed. "I thought you would have a great career in entertainment."

"Yea. So did I."

Rosemary and I had been saving the major portions of our money to get an apartment or rent a house close to Mother's. As we went along we gave mom some money and bought a lot of groceries. What the cop had said to me about my career in show biz burned inside of me. I told Rosemary I just couldn't work in Columbus anymore when so many thought I had thrown my career away. I needed to go elsewhere to get a new start. She cried and reminded me that for the first time we were living a normal life. I told her I was going to quit my job after Christmas and we were going to California where the climate was warm and the streets were paved with gold.

Mother wasn't happy and I knew she was aware Rosemary wasn't happy but said it was our decision. It was a Christmas where everyone acted happy but I knew that wasn't the case.

We drew our savings out of the bank the day before, and on New Year's morning 1945 we kissed Mom goodbye, told my dogs, Nip and Tuck, farewell, and caught the Greyhound west. I was happy; my bride was fearful of the future. My bride was right.

CHAPTER TWENTY-EIGHT

Rosemary and I had given our notice to the landlord two weeks ago and had made our final decision. She would leave for Columbus at noon on Friday. Stop and visit my mom, with the news the marriage was over, and find a rental room and let Mom know where she was if I needed to reach her. I would leave for home Tuesday morning, since our rent at the hotel was paid through Monday. It all sounds clean and neat, but that's not the way it went. I realized I had failed her and I didn't want to fail this lovely girl. I offered to go home, get a nine-to-five job and we would save money and buy a house and raise a family. Her answer was no and the reason was simple.

To do this would destroy both of us. In time I would hate her for killing my ambitions and she would hate both me and herself for the person she would have made me become. She told me that I had saved her from a brutal father, and in a part of her heart she would always love me. After all, don't forget I had been her first real beau and her only lover. I got the picture. She did ask for one favor. If I could grant it, it would be wonderful, if not, she would understand. I said I would certainly grant her wish if I could. What was it? She asked if she could keep her wide gold wedding band that was inscribed inside "RMC-RR 12/22/42." I said yes, and she kept the ring until she died. It was one of the saddest moments of my life. She had given her heart, soul and love to me and all she got was a band of gold. I carried her little suitcase to the bus station and she kissed my cheek and told me she loved me. Watching her wave to me as the bus pulled out would be the last time I saw her until a year later when we made things final at the divorce hearing. I noticed she was still wearing the wide gold band. She was right. We would have destroyed each other. She was such a pretty, really nice person. It wasn't easy but it was over.

Tomorrow was Saturday in Los Angeles. I had a great idea. I had told Mickey three years ago I would come back, so I decided to call. Next morning, I waited until 9:00 AM before I called and a strange female voice answered and told me Mickey was very busy. I told her to tell her that the guy whose life she had saved was calling and she would take the call. There was a long wait and then I hear that sweet Irish voice say, "Bob, is that you?"

"Of course, it's me. I told you I'd be back and call for you." I heard a deep inhale then.

"Bob, it's been three years and not a phone call, a letter or even a postcard. I thought you might be dead."

"Honey, I can be there, I returned like I promised. Let's celebrate. We'll have dinner and go dancing, just like old times. Okay?"

There was a sigh. "It's been three years and no word."

"I'm sorry, but I can be there now and we can be together."

"No, we can't. I waited a long time."

I cut over her lines. "But, I said I'd be back."

"You're back on a very important day. I'm getting married this afternoon. You can read about it in today's LA Times. Anyway, thanks for a lot of nice memories."

The line went dead. I went out and bought an LA Times. It was all there with a beautiful picture of that lovable Irish mug and she was marrying an executive of the Defense Company where she worked in a high wedding mass at the Cathedral. Irish eyes were not smiling, but then who desires a life of corned beef and cabbage?

Let's start the music playing. Home, Mother, my old room, and a call to my pal Bill Rundles and we picked up a journeyman drummer, Toddy Best. (We would introduce him as "Hot Toddy") and a swinging trio was born. Todd gave flashy drum solos and did excellent brushwork behind the many vocals Bill and I sang, and we worked steady. I knew Mom and Rosemary kept in touch. Once in a while they would visit when I was at work, but my mother and I never discussed the failed marriage. During this period my cousin, Ken Agee, was gaining a national reputation as an attorney winning case after case for his clients against huge companies for workers compensation. He asked me to get a high school diploma. He would pay for all my costs to attend law school at Ohio State and give me a job in his law offices as a runner while attending school.

It was almost an offer I couldn't refuse. I had considered a career in criminal law as a defense attorney, just like New York's William Fallon "The Great Mouthpiece" who never lost a case, or maybe be an attorney for the Mob, where the big bucks and the high life went hand in hand. As a young man, I spent a lot of time at the courthouse watching murder trials and observing defense lawyers. The only fear I had was that after I passed the Bar, Ken would offer me a legal post with him and I only wanted to do criminal law. In later years, I found out he didn't care what kind of law I wanted to practice. By that time show biz was my world. It did turn my thoughts to high school. It was my father's and mother's dream that I get an education to have a better life than they had. The big problem was that if I went to school I would only have weekend club dates to help her with needed finances. The big thing that made everything possible was the GI Bill which would pay for schooling.

So while the trio was playing tunes like Johnny Mercer's "Accentuate the Positive," and winners such as "Don't Fence Me In," "Rum and Coca Cola," and "Swinging on a Star," I was thinking about school.

On August 6th the US dropped the Atomic bomb on Hiroshima, and on the 9th we repeated by hitting Nagasaki. On August 14th Japan surrendered and V-J Day brought wild celebrations nationwide. *Going My Way* starring Bing Crosby won the Academy Award and Alfred Hitchcock's film *Life Boat* starring Tallulah Bankhead won international acclaim. I made a decision about high school; I would not go back to West High. Too many memories of those who were gone. Also, I knew I needed a fine private school to get the most out of the education process. I boiled it down to Columbus Academy and the University

School located on the north end of the Ohio State University campus.

Both were long street car rides from the west side. I visited the Academy and liked what I saw. On the way home I stopped at the Planter's Peanut shop at Broad and High managed by my old choirboy pal Ernie Nuzzo and told him what I had seen on the East side. Ernie had raved for years about being an alumnus of the University school and asked me to visit the school before making a final decision. It was one of the greatest pieces of advice ever given and the l945/46 school was one of the best years of my entire life. I visited the school the next day and met Mr. John Ramsire, the headman, and told him I was a discharged vet with the GI Bill to pay for my tuition. After he took me on a tour and introduced me to several faculty members, you couldn't pull me away with a team of wild horses.

A veteran had never attended the school, so this was going to be a test of faith on both of us. The University school was a "Progressive Education" school and educators from all over the world came to study the results. The faculty were all members of the Ohio State University staff which gave all students a positive start. Some of the students had been at the school since they enrolled in the elementary division and stayed through high school. The school produced a huge list of grads that made national and international achievements in all different fields. The school was modern with great facilities and a fabulous high school class. I only regret that I wasn't one of the lucky ones who could have gone from grade one to high school graduation. There were two other regrets. I got there too late to try out for football. I might have spent the season on the bench but I would have been a small part of the only undefeated, untied football team the school ever had. The other regret was that I didn't go out for basketball.

All the students were so friendly that I felt like I have been there forever. When I first arrived there were banners advertising the "Ice Breaker Dance" to start the social year. But what to do? I didn't really know anyone. I was coming downstairs from class as a very good-looking girl wearing a cheerleader sweater ran up. We came breathless to the landing at the same time.

She had a beautiful smile and said, "Hi."

I said, "Hi," and added, "My name is Bob Cawley."

"I'm Suzy Oliver."

"Suzy, I would be very pleased if you would be my date for the 'Ice Breaker.'"

Another big smile. "I think that would be great, let's work out the details later."

She dashed up the stairs and I floated down to my first-floor locker feeling like a million dollars. A student a locker away asked me if I was coming to the "Ice Breaker" and I said yes.

"Are you bringing a girl from your school?"

"No, I'm bringing a U-High girl. May I ask who you are bringing?"

"Yea, I'm bringing Suzy Oliver."

"That's funny" the guy said.

"What's so funny about my dating Suzy Oliver?"

"You're new here so you don't know. Suzy and Milt Van Schoik, the center on our football team and the captain of our basketball team, have been going 'steady' the last two years and have won a lot of dance contests together. Someone is just putting you on." He slammed his locker door and headed for class.

My head was spinning. She had said she was Suzy Oliver and I believed her. She said she was going with me, but this clown tells me she is going steady with this guy Van Schoik who I have never met and who is certainly a big man on campus.

Relax...she was Suzy Oliver and we did go to the "Ice Breaker" and many other events together. Milt Van Schoik and I became close friends until he died years later. He is a man I have always admired in every way.

Seventy years later, Suzy and I still exchange Christmas and birthday cards.

CHAPTER TWENTY-NINE

It didn't take long before I was into music, playing and singing at pep rallies, dances and parties and having a wonderful time.

The school had so many neat things that other schools never had and a major one was the lunch room where we ate from tables with white tablecloths, ordered from menus and were served by waiters. Food was fabulous and so were the desserts. We had it all. The library had over ten thousand books and periodicals, several well-equipped science rooms, a great gym, small playrooms for the young students plus excellent industrial, fine arts and home arts labs. Facilities for physical education. Super playing fields, tennis courts, swimming pools and a large music room for group and individuals working instruments and vocals and don't forget theater and psychodrama also.

The faculty made every class an exciting, learning experience; exciting to start each day. We listened to the national and local news, then had a half-hour discussion of the most important items. Each class during the school day had a brilliant teacher who made learning a pure joy. Classes were small and you would be called on at least three times during a class period. I always got a lot of kidding over second period. I had no class this period and could go to the library, gym or sit in a rec room and just relax. Because I was an adult I could leave the campus which no other student could do and this rule worked for me. Across the street at Woodruff and High streets was Larry's Bar and Grill. I soon found out that many members of the Ohio State football team visited Larry's before class. I got kidded about my Bloody Mary "fix" but I never had a drink of anything except strong coffee and would eat one or two of the hard-boiled eggs from the bar while joining the jocks who thought I was a college student. When the U-High yearbook came out some wag on the student press predicted that someday I would buy Larry's and put in a band and a floor show. I formed a trio with Russ Hill on trumpet and Billy Graham on drums that made a few recordings for a small local company.

U-High not only had a great football team led by super running back Forrest "Fogie" Allen and quarterback Whitney Dillion, but also a very light line with only the really big guys being Captain Martin Vory's, whose dad was a US Congressman and my pal Milt Van Schoik. However, out-sized or not, they outplayed every team they met. School members were also involved outside. One of the big things for Columbus High School kids was the Lazarus "Hi-Jinx" show presented each Saturday morning by WCOL radio from the Lazarus assembly center before an all-teenage audience. There were talent auditions available to all students in Franklin County. Lazarus, the largest department store in central Ohio had a reputation for being behind teenage events.

The first show had an all-star lineup. Eddie Metzger of Bexley High was the MC, the Grandview High Choral Group, Bexley String Ensemble, Judy Forney, a great little Blues singer from Lincoln McKinley High and U-High was represented by announcer Gene Satchel and yours truly. Gene had a network announcer voice and radio lost a great talent when he followed his dad into business with the Auto Club. Forrest Allen who made amazing touchdown runs had a smooth singing voice and was U-High's rep on other Hi-Jinx programs. The one person who should have been on the show but never made it was pretty Sunny Modes, a young lady who has had years as a top pianist appearing in major restaurants and has made many beautiful CDs. The show was a winner and we had the chance to work with bandleader Charlie Spivak who played the sweetest trumpet in the world. A delightful man and talented musician who made us feel like members of his band. Happy to say, I did the show several times. It was a great showcase for Franklin County school kids. At midyear my mom got the well-paying job she had aimed for with an office in mid-town with the Brotherhood of Railroad Trainmen. Too late for me for basketball but I was very happy for her.

Suzy and I were dating. I didn't have a car so Suzy had to pick me up and bring me home. In the winter she would also stop at the end of the evening for coffee and either homemade cookies or cake. It wasn't until years later Mom told she sat on the stairs and would see us kiss goodnight in front of the fireplace. Very romantic. Reminded her of her dating days with dad.

The Oliver family always treated me well and I

really liked her mom and dad. Her brother, Glenn "Newie" Oliver, was the greatest athlete U-High ever had, winning sixteen letters during his career. In 1945 he was a freshman at Ohio State where he was first-team fullback for the Buckeyes. In his first varsity game against Pittsburgh, he scored four touchdowns. After college he had an outstanding career as a dentist.

U-High did a very good thing that was different. When you entered high school your class put on plays, bake sales, and other events to raise money. Then your senior year your class did something special. One class had made so much money that they sailed to Great Britain and back and spent a week in London. Our class never banked that much but we did have the cash for a wonderful trip on the train and a full week in New York. We had great fun going up and back and when we arrived the good times really started. We stayed at the famous Hotel New Yorker and really did the town. We saw "Carousel" with the original cast at the Majestic Theater with music by Richard Rogers and book and lyrics by Oscar Hammerstein.

April 18, 1946, it was off to America's only Ice Theater, The Center Theater at Rockefeller Center, to enjoy "Hats Off to Ice" presented by Sonja Henie and Arthur Wirtz. Our theater going ended when we saw *Oklahoma*. Of course, we had to have dinner at Jack Dempsey's at the Great Northern Hotel. We ate at the famous Rice Bowl in Chinatown, and the Automat. We had coffee at one of the many Chock Full of Nuts shops that seemed to be on every corner and went to the Radio City Music Hall for a movie and the fabulous Rocket's. One day, the girls did the stores and the guys visited the New York Yankees. I got to meet my idol, Joe DiMaggio. I was really out of touch. I thought major league players took good care of their bodies. That all went out the window as I watched Joe smoke one Camel after the other. The next day, we met the Dodgers and I was shaking hands with Dixie Walker and Gil Hodges. Then we came to the last night in the city. I can't explain it but during high school and junior college I never went to the Graduation Dance or Final Ball with the girl I should have been with and NYC was going to be the same. Suzy and I went out with a group for early dinner. We were going to dance at the hotel later. Somewhere in between a female classmate, one I had hardly looked at all year suggested we go to 52nd Street to hear pianist Eddy Heywood whose recording of "Begin the Beguine" was sweeping the country. We went. I don't think we said ten words to each other. Eddy was great but Suzy and I were finished. On June 5th, the forty-eight members of the class of 1946 were at the Browning Amphitheater at Mirror Lake on the campus of Ohio State University for graduation.

On the evening of June 7, 1946, the Junior/Senior Prom called The Crystal Ball took place from 9 PM to 12 AM at the school. I think Suzy went with a basketball player from Notre Dame University. I went with a number from Pee Wee Valley, Kentucky whose first words to me were "I've always wanted to get laid on the fifty-yard line in Ohio Stadium in the moonlight." During the dance the orchestra leader announced that someone wanted to dedicate the next song to me. The song was "I'll Remember April."

CHAPTER THIRTY

My agent had set a string of Saturday and Sunday musical dates that would keep me in "whip out" cash. This was perfect because Forrest Allen and I were going to spend the bulk of the summer playing basketball. We had hoped to get the varsity from U-High but they all had plans. I talked to Milt Van Schoik about him and I playing guards and putting Fogie in the center post. Van liked the idea but I was a little late. He had joined the Navy. With the exception of Allen, there was no U-High varsity players on the team called "U-High grads" but every member was a grad. We got several gym rats from school and entered a Columbus Independent league playing former high school stars and some college players. We didn't win a championship but the team played pretty well and Fogie and I got some nice press. We were awarded miniature gold basketballs to hang on our key chains. The end of summer found Forrest headed back to U-High for his senior year of high school while I had a list of play dates for me through the holidays.

When I saw the headlines right after Labor Day, I was jolted down to my toes. Dick Houk, twenty-four years of age, a good friend and fantastic musician I had worked with many times drowned in the Scioto River which runs through downtown Columbus. He was riding in a sailboat that capsized 120 feet from shore. The other occupant of the boat made it. Dick was about forty feet from the shore when he went under. Dick was a wizard with the tenor sax who could have played with any name band in the country.

During the last game of the summer league, I had been run into the bleachers, injuring my right knee. I thought in time it would get better. I was wrong. Although loaded with bookings, I spent a lot of time hanging out at the Ionian Room in the basement of the famous home of the name bands with a radio wire that allowed both tea dances and nighttime performances on a National network. What a line. There was Elliot Lawrence, Charlie Barnett, Blue Baron, Eddie Howard, Gene Krupa, Ray Anthony, Jimmy Dorsey, Frankie Carle, Ray McKinley, Tex Beneke, Count Basie, and more. As a fellow musician I was able to bond with several stars.

Frankie Carle was a friend of Cousin Ken Agee and we had lunch. After the Tea Dance, Eddy Howard changed out of his work clothes and we crossed Broad Street for an early dinner at Dorsams. We got talking music and the time went by until Eddy looked at his watch to find out he had a coast-to-coast broadcast just minutes away. Eddy always carried a roll of 500-dollar bills and the cashier couldn't make change. I had the cash and paid, then we raced across Broad Street, up to his hotel room where he set a record changing clothes. When we got on the down elevator, I had his jacket and he was stuffing his shirt into his pants. I held his jacket and we both ran into the packed Ionian Room as the radio announcer said, "And now coast to coast it's the music of Eddy Howard, his songs and his Orchestra." Lou Quadling, Eddy's pianist made his usual run and Eddy, who had just fought his way through the crowd, jumped to the stage, grabbed the mic from the announcer's hand and in a breathless voice hit the first note of his famous theme, "Careless." After the broadcast, he repaid me for the dinner plus an extra $20 for helping him dress. Over the years, whenever our paths would cross we would remember that day.

The fall and the holiday seasons slipped by very fast. I had my manager cancel dates after I joined the orchestra of Bill "Ziggy" Coyle, a hot trumpet player I knew back at West High. "Zig" was a good guy to work with and knew his way around having been featured with the major territory bands of Chuck Selby and Don Crawford. Swinging Judy Forney and Bill Hagans handled the vocals. I got many showcases but no matter how you sliced it, I still played a lot of rhythm piano. I loved listing to dance bands. I just didn't want to be in one. I called Johnny and he booked me as a single at a major hotel on Lake Erie from January until the end of August. I loved the hotel, the clients, the lake and jogging on the beach working my knee in shape plus the money was very good. I called mom at least once a week and sometimes, but not often, she mentioned how proud my father would have been if I had gone to college. I never gave a thought to education until a certain night in July.

It had been a big night. My pockets were filled with tips and it had been an evening of great songs including "I Still Get Jealous," "Moonlight Serenade," "That Old Black Magic," "Mademoiselle, and "Maybe You'll Be There." The bartender treated me to a cold coke and I took the elevator to my room. The hotel was quiet. I opened the door, closed it behind me then looked up. My father was sitting in the chair by the bed. He smiled and indicated I should sit on the bed. I was not surprised or afraid although I knew he had been dead since December of 1941. We talked of many things both current and past. Then he told me he had been allowed to return to earth to help me plan my college education. Not for his and my mother's desires but for my life when show business was over. I loved my dad and having him there dressed like I had seen him a million times when he was leaving for a railroad call made my heart almost beat out of my chest. At last, he stood. Asked me to think about it. He put his warm hand on my arm, then kissed my forehead. He did not open the door, he walked through it.

I was shaken down to my very core. I knew my dad, as always, was right so I set at my desk and stewed trying to think who I could write. I had the GI Bill but would need additional jingle in my pocket to toward things the Bill didn't cover. Maybe I could get something for basketball. I had just read that tiny Cedarville College in Ohio had lost 99 games. That should be a good target so I wrote and sealed my letter. Stamped it and dropped it in the mail chute in the hotel hallway. Going back to my room, I sat down at the desk and asked myself where I really wanted to go. The answer was like a bucket of cold water in the face. Greenbrier. I wanted to go back but would they have me after the results of my prep year? If they would have me what could be worked out to give me pocket cash? It was 5:00 AM when I finished the letter to my old faculty advisor, Major Benjamin. I sealed and stamped the envelope and with a prayer dropped it in the box. I heard back from Cedarville almost at once. They were interested. The days dragged on.

Then with two weeks left in August the letter came. Welcome home to Greenbrier. They would not give me a regular athletic scholarship, but spending money would be available and they sincerely hoped I could help the basketball team. I was flying at fifty thousand feet. The impossible had happened. I was getting a second chance. The music on my brain was "Nature Boy," "But Beautiful," "It's Magic," "Judaline," "Slow Boat to China," "How Are Things in Gloccamore," "Aip-a-odee-doo-dah," "Shoo-Fly Pie and Apple Pan Dowdy," and "The Dickey Bird Song."

CHAPTER THIRTY-ONE

The summer of 1948 I worked at a nice club owned by Cleveland Indian outfielder, Hank Edwards, in Norwalk, Ohio just a short drive from Cedar Point on Lake Erie. This was the summer that a hit single by husband-wife duo, Jon and Sandra Steele called "My Happiness" was the rage. I got requests to sing and play this tune at least every two minutes. I did manage to squeeze in great songs like "Heartaches," "Ballerina," "Slow Boat to China," and "Beg your Pardon." Come September I boarded the Sportsman for the hills of West Virginia and the click-clack of the train's wheels lulled me to sleep as I went back to my final year at Greenbrier.

I spent a wonderful week with my new Greenbrier College for Women date, Judith Wilson's family. Her mother and father along with her brothers, Gary and Harlan. We had great times gathering around the piano, laughing and singing with either Harland or I at the keyboard.

Judith's dad designed the tunnel that ran under the river from Detroit to Windsor, Canada. They took me to dinner at the famous Russian Bear in Detroit. Harlan would be entering GMS at mid-year as a member of C company. I spent the final week with mom and worked New Year's Eve at the Broad Lincoln Hotel's theater bar in Columbus, just a few steps from Trinity Church where I had spent so many happy years of my childhood. The hotel had put together a dazzling group of performers to greet the New Year. I was doing songs at the piano and Solovox.

Singer/pianist Marla Makay, a red-headed Irish bombshell, was cashing in on the success of the record album "Knockers Up" by Rusty Warren singing sophisticated risqué songs. Marla had been set as the headliner for the spring of 1949. Vocalist/pianist Helen Gray who did cocktail hours at the theater bar was also on hand. Come the first week in January of l949, I returned to GMS.

Johnny Moore had set me for a summer engagement at the theater bar of the Broad Lincoln Hotel. A week into my opening, I was on intermission walking between the guest tables when a very good-looking young lady invited me to join her for a drink. There was something familiar about her and she was a beauty so, of course, I took her up on her offer. Our drinks arrived. She smiled and said, "You don't remember me do you?" How could I not remember someone as lovely as this but I had to admit she was right. Then when I really took a close-up look I realized she was a classmate from University High, but she had never looked like this at school. Wow, what a change. At school I had danced with her a couple of times but never gave her another thought, but now she was a walking dream. She managed a very upscale boutique near the hotel and had an apartment down the street. It wasn't love, but it was high-octane passion, and at closing we went to her upscale residence and my first and only love affair started.

Years later, I found where she had signed my U-High yearbook. "To the sweetest boy I have ever gone with. Best of luck all your life. All my love." Then I remembered I had taken her to a dance and we wound up having sodas at Dorsams. Where was I when she turned into a beauty? I moved my clothes in and we became an "item." During the affair, there was never a harsh word or a disagreement.

Mort Figenbaum of WOSU Radio set me up with my own show, "Piano Reveries" that we pre-taped and it aired on Saturdays. U-High classmates Milt Van Schoik, Whitney Dillon and Bob Hamilton were members of Phi Kappa Psi Fraternity and they made certain I pledged to Phi Psi on September 25, 1949. The Phi Kappa Psi Fraternity house was the old Governor's mansion located on Fourteenth Avenue. In addition to my former high school friends, I spent quality time with All-American basketball star, Dick Schnittker, who owned every Ohio State University scoring record of that era. Dick also started on the Buckeyes 1949-50 Big Ten Champion Football team. Another Phi Psi I would have a long-term relationship with was Fred "Curly" Morrison the fullback and punter on the OSU Champs. Fred scored the game-winning touchdown in the 1950 Rose Bowl then went on to an eleven-year career in pro football with the Chicago Bears and Cleveland Browns before we hooked up in the TV industry.

The year was packed with music. "Crusin Down

the River," "Mule Train," "Again," "Powder Your Face With Sunshine," and "Faraway Places."

Between school, my radio show, spinning records with Bill Hineman on *Glass Door Melodies* sponsored by Kay Jewelers (It's Okay To Owe Kay Till Payday) on WCOL radio, playing the Theater Bar and the affair, I was a busy young man, but my career was at a standstill.

Dick Shelton from the McConkey Agency in Chicago wanted to book me in larger venues for more cash. My lover had dropped hints about homes, long-range plans and babies all at the end of entertainment and her career as well. In the early fall my girl seemed sad and when I asked why, she said she knew I was going to leave her, and if I did, please leave while she was sleeping. No long farewells as it would create a scene and she would beg me not to go. She loved me. I loved her too but if I took her away what would her life be? Shelton called saying I could follow my idol, Jess Stacy, who would be closing Jean's Lounge in Lansing, Michigan, in three weeks and also to bring a bass and guitar with me. To follow Stacy was out of sight. I had to go. I gave my notice to the Broad Lincoln and asked them not to announce I was leaving. I pre-taped a final WOSU show to be played after school and closed all the other accounts. On a snowy day, I packed my clothes and took them to the bus station. When my girl came home we went out to dinner. I went to work and came home to have a coffee by the fireplace. Later, holding her close as she went to sleep I had deep thoughts about not leaving, but after 2 AM she was fast asleep, I dressed and left for the last time. The snow was like a mini blizzard. I went into the deserted Catholic Cathedral, lit a candle for her and asked God to protect her and help her find a man worthy of her love.

I met Norm Khunheim, guitarist and Tommy Whiteman, bass at the Greyhound station and with swirling snow all around we headed for Lansing and what would be a life-changing event.

CHAPTER THIRTY-TWO

When you follow an icon, who has thrilled customers for six weeks, it is not easy, but from opening night, we were accepted. Despite the brutal weather, the fans kept coming and praise for our efforts went back to Shelton in Chicago. He was talking about future dates at Detroit's "Wonder Bar," Pittsburgh's "Twin Coaches" and the "Stevens Hotel" in Chicago when a man came into Jean's with an offer that would change my future, alter my dreams and enable me to make lots of money. On the second Tuesday, we were working Jean's when a man came out of the snow wearing a white cowboy hat. I saw him and passed the word to Norm and Tommy that the Lone Ranger had arrived.

When he discarded his overcoat, he was dressed in formal Western attire including fancy boots. Toward the end of our second set, he sent a message on a napkin that he wanted me to join him. We ordered drinks and the sun-tanned stranger said his name was Kelly Rodgers and that he had been traveling the United States to find a man to star on his own TV show five days a week on KPHO-TV in Phoenix, Arizona.

To this date I had only glanced at TV sets in store windows. Although I had written a twelve-minute skit for an OSU co-ed that she had performed on WLWC-TV in Columbus, I had not seen the show. I laughed. I told him I was not interested, that nightclubs were the future of entertainment and that TV was just a fad that would soon vanish. Rogers showed me a contract signed by John Mullins, Station Manager of KPHO-TV, for one year with my own one-hour-a-day TV show for more money than I had ever earned plus additional fees for any work on KPHO Radio. All he needed was for me to sign. I thanked Kelly and went back to work. He came back every night and I said NO every night. Jean's was talking about extending our stay when fate, kismet, destiny or whatever you want to call it, moved things along. I got a cold. A local doctor told me I was on the verge of pneumonia and needed rest, go home, and have medical treatment. Shelton got a replacement with the understanding we would come back to Jean's when I was well.

Our family doctor was worried about my health. I was sent to bed under Mother's supervision with all kinds of medicines and bowls of Mother's chicken soup. Outside the weather was cold with rain and snow. At night, snuggled warm in my bed I would hear the evening whistle of the Super Chief heading west. Four or five weeks later, almost fully recovered I told Mom that I was going to call Norm and Tommy, set up rehearsal, and call Shelton to let me know when we would go back to Lansing. Mother told me if I did that she would go to jail. I was really alarmed.

My mother in jail? Why? She explained that while I was real sick a very nice man named Kelly Rodgers came to the house and told her about the TV deal in Arizona. He explained how the warm climate would be a tonic for my health and that TV would be the greatest showcase of my talents, where thousands would see and hear me rather than hundreds like in clubs.

"Yeah, mom, this guy wanted me to sign a contract when I was at Jean's and I told him no. You're not in trouble, he's out of our lives."

"Not quite. You were too sick to see him. I just feel you need the warm weather and the chance to be on TV, so I asked to review the contract and when he returned, I gave him a signed contract. I signed your name so if you don't go to Arizona, Mother goes to jail."

"I told Norm and Tommy I would return in six months. I hope they are not still waiting."

Johnny Mullins sent me a check for my plane fare plus a couple of hundred for spending money. On a bitter cold day, I kissed Mom goodbye and cousins Ken Agree and Bob Shumaker drove me to the airport. I had never flown and I loved it. The good food and drinks plus those cute stewardesses serving. I didn't have a definite date to be in Phoenix. I came in on a Sunday evening and loved the warm breeze. A cab took me to a tiny motel near the famous Westward Ho Hotel. I knew that KPHO was right beside the hotel and that John Mills owned both the hotel and KPHO. Next morning, after breakfast, I was walking to the station when a car passed with Johnny Mullins and his Sales Manager, Gil Lee, inside. John saw me and told Gil that I was

Bob Cawley. Gil said, "No way." They made a $100 bet.

Minutes later when I arrived at the KPHO Radio/TV facility I was ushered into Mullins office. He didn't say anything, but called for Gil Lee whose office was next to his to come in and bring his hundred dollars. When Gil came in, I was introduced as Bob Cawley.

"You must have seen a photo of him." Gil said.

"No photo but he's the palest guy in Arizona, so it had to be him."

Gil paid the bet, then Johnny and I set down to talk. Johnny said Kelly Rodgers said I would be dynamite with my own show. KPHO was the only TV station in the state. In radio they were an affiliate of ABC but had the best of all the networks' shows for TV. However, they needed a strong local show and that's why I was here. "We are slowly going to introduce you on radio, then guest shots on TV, and then when we are ready for your show, we will hit them with a big kick-off. But first things first. I guess you got in last night."

I told him I had and where I had checked in.

"I'll have your things picked up and have you checked into the Westward Ho next door. For the next three weeks, I want you to enjoy the pool and get some tan. Take advantage of the great food and add some weight. As of today you are on the payroll and everything at the hotel is covered. Just sign for it." He gave me a roll of bills for personal expenses, then took me on a tour of the facilities. I had never been in a TV studio and was impressed by the size of the cameras and the cable they drug behind them. They were not doing TV at this hour of the morning so we visited dressing rooms, workshops and set storage. The radio side of the station was well-outfitted, and DJs, news and personality shows were either in rehearsal or on the air.

From the get-go I really liked Johnny Mullins. The big Irishman, who had played pro baseball, sold oil leases and owned a traveling carnival among other things was just a great person to work for and his word was his bond. My three weeks at the Westward Ho went by fast, although I did leave the pool long enough to join #586 of the American Federation of Musicians after turning in my Columbus membership. I was to stay in Local #586 for the remainder of my professional life in music. I also made a deposit on a neat little second-floor apartment just one block north of the studio. A small kitchen with eating area. Living room and bedroom that led to my balcony. The building was on a corner lot so had nice views. Since I did not have a car, it was perfect. Johnny Mullins was pleased with my tan and a few added pounds and said it was time to start work.

He had dinner with a lovely lady who has a fifteen-minute daily show on ABC Radio that would like to work with you if you are interested in being her music director. Was I interested? What kind of songs does she sing? John laughed. No songs, she tells stories illustrated with music. When she had her show back East she had live music. Since she came West she has used recorded stings and it just doesn't work. The lady's name is Kathy Godfrey, I'm sure you have heard her brother, Arthur. The world knows Arthur from radio, TV and records. What is she doing in Phoenix? It's a health problem. Kathy and her doctor husband moved here for her health. The next day I worked with Kathy for the first of our five-day-a-week shows. I was really shocked when she made her way into the studio on metal crutches that were around her forearms. I stood and with my best Arthur Godfrey imitation said, "How are ya, how are ya, how are ya" like he did on his shows. It cracked her up and she laughed telling me she could do that too. She was a lovely lady. Slender, well dressed and always ready with a smile or laugh. You knew she was a Godfrey, a very feminine version whose talented body had been wracked with Polio.

I made fees for her shows but would have done them for free just to work with this smart, intelligent woman. It was pure joy. In time Kathy's health declined and the series ended. I just wish I had recordings of those shows just to hear her voice again.

At 11 AM I had my fifteen minutes of radio time with *The Bob Cawley Show* on KPHO Radio. As promised Mullins brought me slowly into TV. Ginny Greer, a super vocalist who had fifteen minutes of shows at 6:30 Monday, Wednesday and Friday evenings called *A Date With Ginny* was also the headliner at the Green Gables local dinner club where her husband, a drummer, Chuck Greerson, led the orchestra. Johnny was introducing me to the TV audience as Ginny's mythical boyfriend. Ginny told Mullins that no guy was going to sing on her show let alone pretend to be her boyfriend. When John made it clear that it was his way or the highway, we went on together smiling and with a kiss at the end of the show. Ginny had been told it is for ten weeks at the most.

I would be moved to the five-day-a-week *At Home With Jack Canaday Show* as the "boy next door."

Ginny, who was pretty and a top singer had the attitude and personality of a sore-headed rattlesnake. I would almost break out laughing when I was singing love words to her smiling face when behind her clenched teeth she would mutter, "I hate you, you son-of-a-bitch." And at the end of each show as soon as the stage manager called "Clear" she would jerk out of our embrace with another oath. At the end of eight weeks, I moved to the *At Home Show*. Several weeks later the *A Date With Ginny* was history.

CHAPTER THIRTY-THREE

From the fantasy boyfriend on *A Date With Ginny*, I became the "boy next door" on Jack Canady's popular *At Home Show*. Three days a week my body was sprayed with water. "Hey, watch the hair." Wet and in my bathing trunks with a towel around my neck I would wander into Jack's living room. Here I would exchange scripted lines where Jack would discuss my first car, a green 1929 Ford coupe I had named "The Green Hornet. After Jack ribbed the "Hornet" I would move to his grand piano and sing a couple of tunes before returning to the pool.

Working with Jack, a very classy mature man who had been an officer in the US Navy and was a top host, was a real pleasure. Jack and his wife Pat made me feel welcome. Jack had a live audience and I would meet them after the show. One fan made me her fan. When we met sparks flew. Her parents were from Central Europe. She was 5'7" wearing an expensive burnt orange silk dress. She had coal-black shoulder-length hair, beautiful face, sparkling white teeth set off by her smooth olive skin. And had green eyes that held unspoken promises and a drop-dead figure. You know how it is. You're young and both of you know you're on a fast track. I walked her to where her new Cadillac Deville was parked and she gave me her address - an upscale bungalow apartment on North Central, and her phone number. I pointed out my apartment, just north of the studio with the "Green Hornet" parked in front. She was a legal secretary for the major law firm in town that handled big cases. Her name was Mary and our hands were reluctant to let go, but at last her black Caddy pulled away into traffic. I should have asked Mary to have dinner but a beauty like this was sure to have a date on Friday evening. I would call her the first of the week.

After a shower I went to Green Gables where Ginny Greer was the headliner. The Gables was very posh with a guy dressed in a suit of armor on a white horse guarding the drawbridge leading into the restaurant. The maitre d' recognized me from TV and said he would let Ginny know I was in the audience. I pressed a five-dollar bill into his hand not to let her know I was dining and to give me a table where I wouldn't be caught by the spotlight. The food and service were excellent and Ginny put on a good show. I always knew she was a fine singer but her attitude was a killer. I got out and she never knew I was there.

The Hornet and I stopped at Joe Hunt's Steakhouse on North Central to have a drink and listen to some cool jazz by the Rocky Constanzo Trio that featured the sensational guitarist, Howard Roberts. I could have closed the night with this great group but I wanted to hit the Sundown Club on Camelback Road to catch the final show of the evening with my new friend, Jack LaDelle. Jack was under contract to KPHO and when I arrived with no car Jack let me borrow one of his two 1950 Ford sedans. When I first saw him I knew I had seen him somewhere before. Then I had it! The movies! With his former wife they were a major dance team that appeared in feature films, movie shorts and the finest hotels, supper clubs and theaters in the world. After the breakup, he didn't want another dance partner and returned to the world of music. What a musician, singer, songwriter and entertainer he was. Truly one of a kind. First of all, he played thirty-two musical instruments and played them as good or better than other musicians played one or two. Jack made a number of record albums during his career and on several of them he played every instrument plus did the polished vocals. If that wasn't enough he was a versatile entertainer. He did an imitation of Bing Crosby that made you think Bing was in the room. When he recorded, he would sing three-part harmony with himself and played three-part harmony on the clarinet. I came through the door of the Sundown as the MC announced "Ladies and Gentlemen, it's gonna be swell with our star, Jack LaDelle," as the follow spot hit Jack and he was opening the show with a song he had written, "On A Little Bamboo Bridge." The show was on and it played to one standing ovation after the over.

After the show, I went home. Took off my clothes and slipped under the sheet as the breeze through the open windows brought sweet slumber. I had drifted off about 1:30 AM to come half awake about 2 AM when I realized that a warm lush naked body with a light perfume was under the sheet and warm lips were kissing mine. I thought I had died and gone to heaven but heaven was in bed and in my arms. Mary had come down the upstairs hall, onto the balcony then stepped over the rail to my balcony, through my unhooked screen door and there we were. Just like in the movies. It was the start of a beautiful relationship, and we managed to keep it under the radar. We went to dinners outside of Phoenix and were very careful slipping into movies. TV was brand new in Arizona and I was getting the big buildup.

The week before I met Mary, two teenage girls stole my pants while I was being fitted for a summer suit at Haney's. Police caught the girls; I got my pants back and would not press charges. Mothers wanted kisses or for me to kiss babies, and it seemed everyone wanted an autograph. It was impossible to eat a meal while it was warm. My show was shaping up and taking no chances, Johnny Mullins hired Ronnie Oxford as my producer. For years Ron had been a major radio producer for the NBC Radio Network handling big shows and even bigger stars. With the advent of TV, Ron made the decision to semi-retire away from the pressures of Hollywood. Mullins convinced him that Phoenix would be just right for both Ronnie and his wife as *The Bob Cawley Show* producer. In all the world I could not have had a better producer than Ronnie. I know there were times I drove him crazy, and Ron, I'm sorry, but I really loved this guy and learned so much about producing from him. Ronnie always reminded me of a miniature David Niven, the great movie actor. He was always dressed as though he had stepped off the fashion pages of Esquire. He was 5'7" tall, salt-and-pepper hair and had a small mustache. He had a California tan and a well-modulated speaking voice. He was also a bundle of energy. Phoenix radio had two super DJs. One was Frank Pollock on KOOL Radio owned by cowboy movie star Gene Autry. Frank played all the good commercial stuff. The other DJ was Al "Sleepy" Stein who spun cool jazz discs on FM Radio. Sleepy later became a Los Angeles icon with his FM Jazz Show in the City of the Angels. "Sleepy" also managed a few good musical acts with the prize being a vocal group that also did major league instrumental backing of their vocals. Ron Oxford snapped up the group for my show and their recording contract with Capital Records hyped a lot of publicity. The Four Deals were out of Baton Rouge, Louisiana. They had won Peter Potter's song contest with "It's Too Late Now" written by The Deal's leader guitarist Lloyd Ellis. The male quartet was signed by Capital Records. The flip side of the recording features a novelty song written by the Deal's pianist Glenn Brewton. (In addition to Ellis who went on to be considered the fastest guitar in the world" in later years and piano man Brewton the other members of the quartet were tasty trumpeter Benny Wilson and blind bassist Travis Anderson.) Another plus was the appearance of "The Four Deals" as guest stars on the *Smiley Burnette Radio Show* doing "Too Late Now."

The Bob Cawley Show started off the first couple of weeks with a Chapter of the Movies Serial "The Adventures of Ace Drummond" plus a few guests for interviews like John Carrol actor/singer. Combining good looks and a good singing voice he was a leading man in action films in the 40s and early 50s when he retired a very wealthy man. One of my all-time favorite guests was bestselling author, screenplay and TV writer Stephen Longstreet. I became a fan when I read his bestselling non-fiction *The Canvas Falcons* about World War I fighter pilots. I knew that Longstreet had written the 1948 sensational Broadway musical *High Button Shoes* based on his semi-autobiographical novel *The Sisters Liked Them Handsome*. While under contract to Warner Brothers he wrote *The Jolson Story*, *Stallion Road* based on his novel of the same title that starred Ronald Reagan and *The Helen Morgan Story*.

Turning to the new medium of television in the 50s and 60s, he wrote for multi-award-winning *Playhouse 90*. The world of jazz was a constant Longstreet theme throughout his life and this plus our mutual interest in writing made for close bonding. A number of his books dealt with jazz including *Jazz From A to Z: A Graphic Dictionary*, his 100th book published. Stephen appeared on my show four times and I never tired of seeing him or reading his work. All the guests were interesting but two others who really stood out were silver-voiced Tommy Duncan who sang "San Antonio Rose" with Bob Willis and the Texas Cowboys band. Bob was a real entertainer with a great musical group but it was Tommy who was invited back several times. There is no doubt that Tommy's version of "San Antonio Rose" is a country music classic. There were several really great Duncan vocals through the years and a favorite of mine was "Walking In The Shadow Of The Blues." Tommy had a great personality and loads of talent.

One show was devoted to songwriter/actor Hoagie Carmichael who wrote the melody to the most recorded song of all time, the immortal "Star Dust" with lyrics by Mitchell Parish. Hoagie was a true delight. The slow-talking native of Indiana not only told stories of his early days in the music business but also performed "Star Dust" along with several of his other hits. Of all the stories he told I liked the one about a tune he wrote that was titled "Bix Lix" named after trumpet player Bix Beiderbecke whom he had worked with. For three years the tune gathered dust until Johnny Mercer added a cool set of lyrics and "Bix Lix" became the hit song "Skylark." "Star Dust" has a beautiful verse but over the years top vocalists from opera stars to Willie Nelson have found the verse difficult to sing. I have never heard anyone except Nat "King" Cole sing it in the relaxed, perfect style it deserves.

My show was shot with three pedestal cameras. They could be raised or lowered plus travel right, left, forward or backward on wheels. Cameras were heavy and required muscle power to move them smoothly. We had two excellent cameramen, Carl Yost and Marshall Faber, with photographic backgrounds. They shot ninety-nine percent of the show. The stationary wide shots were done by a "never was," a camera operator named Leon Black. The son of a Phoenix merchant was a legend in his own mind but knew zero about entertainment.

Like the rest of the staff, I had little to say or do with Black although he was constantly telling me I should get married to a girl who had been his wife's roommate at Arizona State College. The girl's name was Mae Shamblee. I had seen this girl's photo on billboards around Phoenix as she was Revlon's "Miss Fashion Plate of 1950" and the billboards asked, "How much lovelier can a girl look?" A natural blond, good-looking in a college girl fashion but I was not interested in marrying her or anyone else. My love life with Mary was secure. I will never really know why

Black and his wife made me the target but in time I went to dinner with them and Miss Shamblee. She was pleasant but not up to the standards of the girls I had dated at Greenbrier or Mary who at that time was involved with her firm in a major trial.

I learned Miss Shamblee had been accepted by American Airlines for stewardess training. I wished her luck in her new job. She told me she was more interested in getting married and having children. I also learned she lived with the Jack McElroy family on their ranch in Black Canyon. McElroy owned Cal-Vita Produce Company, which sold produce on a national basis. The family was very wealthy and owned a stable of race horses and the family spent each summer at Rancho Santa Fe to watch their horses run at the Del Mar track. From that night on, Miss Shamblee not only attended every single show and the rehearsals, we dined and danced with the Blacks.

Soon I was getting the whole routine about wedding bells, houses, kids, etc. Looking back, my brains were mush, and the last of August I proposed. This was a really stupid thing to do. I didn't love the girl. I didn't want to get married. I just wanted to work and live my life. Once I gave a commitment, Miss Shamblee told me to call her "Dixie." (She was from Aniston, Alabama.) She also wanted me to announce our engagement on my show. I told Mary the night before the announcement and she was shocked and asked how well I knew this girl. I mumbled something and she said it was a mistake but wished me the best. The next day, I announced the coming marriage, and after the show Johnny Mullins called me into his office and told me I was making a big mistake.

The Blacks and Dixie were pushing for a quick

wedding. I had called my mother with the news and found out she would be unable to get away until October. I wanted to wait until then, but Dixie and her friends would not hear of it so we were married in an informal wedding at 6:30 PM September 16, 1950, in the Chapel of the Resurrection of Trinity Cathedral just a block from my apartment. Sue Black was Dixie's only attendant and Lt. Shelby Dale Scott, a Greenbrier grad was my Best Man. Waiting in the church I told Shelby that I was going to bolt. I didn't love this girl. I didn't want to get married. Shelby pointed to my GMS ring which read, "Duty, Honor, Truth" and said, "I couldn't do that."

Ok, it was a mistake but I was committed. Looking back I should have walked and saved fifteen years but destiny had dealt the cards. The station had wanted to film the entire wedding but thank God the Bishop said, "No cameras inside of the church," but when we came out they were there and kept rolling through the beautiful reception at the home of Mr. and Mrs. Robert Bohannan former Columbus residents now living in Phoenix. Both were grads of Ohio State University and Bob was a Phi Psi.

After the reception, Dixie and I stopped at Joe Hunt's Steakhouse. We had a drink and a dance then off to our suite at the Westward Ho Hotel. She went to the bedroom. I sat in a big easy chair and gazed at the lights of the city until I fell asleep cursing the mistake I had made. She never asked why I didn't come to her and I never mentioned it. We stayed two nights at the hotel then returned to my apartment.

On Monday, I introduced my wife on TV and on September 18th the marriage was consummated after I told myself that I had to live with and make the best of it. Johnny Mullins and I had almost a father/son relationship. He did not come to the wedding although all the staff now working came. Life went on but things were never the same between Johnny and I. Dixie informed me my apartment would never do and we moved to upscale Winter Garden Manor on North Central. Our unit was by the deep end of the pool and I could dive in and swim a few laps before having breakfast at the awning-covered table by the water. Dixie wasn't going to be caught dead in the "Green Hornet", so I traded my beloved old car for a repossessed 1949 Ford convertible with low mileage. The car was black and the rear license plate was held by a frame that advertised the Gila Monster Races at Glendale, Arizona. If you haven't seen Gila Monsters race, you haven't missed a thing.

First day I drove my new wheels to work, the station had a concrete light pole placed in the center of the parking lot. The light was not connected and it was night when I left the studio. I backed out, then gunned the engine and leaped forward as I switched on my headlights to see the light pole which I hit full force breaking the pole which destroyed the canvas top and missed my head by inches. I sat there thinking what a hell of a year this had been.

Despite everything it had been a wonderful year for music with great songs for every taste: "Music, Music, Music," "Nature Boy." "Mule Train," "Mona Lisa," Tzena, Tzena, Tzena," "Ghost Riders In the Sky," "Rag Mop," "Tennessee Waltz," "My Foolish Heart," and "Goodnight Irene." What a musical year it was.

My mother came out for a week and during this time we took a flying trip to Los Angeles and saw some of the sights. Soon Dixie talked about leaving Winter Garden and moving out to the McElroy ranch. Jack had been out of town during our wedding but his wife, Millie and her mother, Nana, had been present. I hated to leave the manor because we had made friends with Harold and his wife Ruth who spent every winter in Arizona then returned to their home in Mankato, Minnesota, in the late spring and returned to the Valley of the Sun next September. Although we moved to the ranch my friendship with the Severson's continued into the 90s when they died.

I really liked Jack McElroy and he gave me a chance to get back to the nightlife. He was opening a restaurant to be called "Durant's" (Jack's name was never advertised on things that he owned) and this steakhouse bore the name of Jack Durant who had worked for McElroy as a pit boss at the Flamingo Hotel and Casino in Las Vegas, Nevada where Jack McElroy was one of several owners at that time. McElroy wanted a duo. The Musicians Union recommends a guitarist/vocalist Marty Martell who had been featured with the great Chuy Reyes Orchestra. It was a pairing made in heaven. Marty was a top-five guitarist and his pleasing voice embraced great Latin tunes in Spanish. We opened Durant's and the place did fabulous business and is still doing the same today. Best steaks I have ever enjoyed thanks to Chef Jim Yancy and the world's greatest Caesar salads made at your table by Harry Wolf. We had a swinging holiday season and went into 1951 at full steam. I couldn't believe how fortune had smiled.

CHAPTER THIRTY-FOUR

KPHO knew many groups in Phoenix and Tucson were anxious to obtain TV licenses and we built a strong show lineup that would keep a firm fan base after other stations came on. As competition in Ken Kennedy we had a valuable talent who as the brother of a major motion picture director/screenwriter, Bert Kennedy, who had started his career as a screenwriter for John Wayne's Batjac Productions. The Kennedy brothers had worked in vaudeville with the family act "The Dancing Kennedys." Ken often appeared at the Sundown Club with a nightclub act but for KPHO he created a TV character called "Gold Dust Charlie" that thrilled kid viewers for several years. Also in demand by juvenile viewers was the *Wallace and Limo Show* created by two young Phoenix actors which ran for many years setting all sorts of records for years on the tube. Lew King, a local producer had a Saturday half-hour series *Lew King's First Federal Rangers* that featured the preteen Newton brothers. As an adult, brother Wayne Newton became the sensational "Midnight Idol" of Las Vegas showrooms and hit the record charts with several hit songs. His live show was second to Frank Sinatra and the Rat Pack with a thirty-year run before he lost his voice. His live shows were top-drawer but he failed in TV and movies and no one ever figured out why. Jack Murphy was out front as a newscaster and a good-looking announcer, later became an actor and did several films including *Dirty Harry* with Clint Eastwood.

In January 1951, *Country Song Roundup*, the number-one magazine covering country music, did a full-page story about my show. Yes, I did some crossover country like Eddy Arnold and Ray Price tunes but never got into the groove of Hank Williams, Rose Maddox or Kitty Wells. At night, I did at least twenty vocal numbers plus five or six on my TV show plus my opening and closing theme, "Everywhere You Go", and my throat was getting tired.

I went to Johnny Mullins and told him I wanted to hire a real country artist to do a twelve-minute daily segment on my show. John reminded me that I wouldn't be having throat problems if I quit the nightclub scene but go ahead and find who I wanted. Ron Oxford and I ran an ad in the newspaper and on the given Saturday morning over two hundred men and women carrying guitar cases lined the street in front of the studio. I told Ronnie we would let each person sing one chorus. Ron held his head and told me eight bars would be enough. I held to the one-chorus format and one by one the contestants came in, gave their name, address and phone numbers to the girl who was taking their facts.

The first seven were awful. Number eight came in. He looked to be seventeen or eighteen. Wore a clean but patched denim pants and jacket with a white shirt. He set down on the stool that was offered. After eight bars, I jumped out of my chair and turned to Ron in the control room. "That's it! This is the guy I want! I don't care if every major country star in the world is available, this kid is going to be the best."

I pulled the switch on the intercom and told the kid to stay where he was, I would be right out. Ron was in deep shock. "What the hell are you doing? We have over 200 people outside."

"Ron, you're a big-time producer, you'll know what to say." With that I raced out to the studio where the young talent waited. I introduced myself and told him he would have a twelve-minute segment on my daily show with a special set built for him and he would play and sing real country music. The young man had a winning smile and just beamed. He told me he lived with his family in Glendale, Arizona, and that he name was Marty Robbins. I took him to the office of our Program Director to get him signed to a contract.

Our Program Director at that time was Harry Stone, who had been one of the founders of the famous Grand Old Opera in Nashville. No one realized it but that was the day an American legend was born. Marty was to become one of the greatest songwriter/performers of all time. We had a great time working together.

As I promised, Marty had his own set and soon became very popular. I wrote a country song for him titled "Raindrops on My Window, Teardrops in My Heart" that he recorded with Sheldon Gibbs and his Arizona Ranch Boys, an excellent country band. We had sponsors standing in line for my show and I was doing several of the on-camera pitches for Hoffman Television. The guest list proved to be a current who's who of national interest. Female bullfighter Patricia McCormick was getting a lot of press being an American lady in a Hispanic sport. Patricia, a native of Texas, fought bulls on foot just like the famous male matadors. A quiet, calm lady she had no fear of the bulls although she had been gored twice and was gored a couple of times later. A very interesting interview with the inside story of a sport that American's know little about.

Eddy Howard was most welcome and sang his theme "Careless," which he wrote and one of his super hits "To Each His Own." Eddy was a big favorite with the studio audience as well as the TV viewers who wrote many cards and letters wanting him back.

Irish actor Dan O'Herlihy proved to an extremely pleasant visitor. Tall and distinguished looking, he had started his career as a stage set designer but soon begin acting with Dublin's Abbey Players and on Irish radio. He appeared in many films and on TV. In 1952 he would be nominated for an Academy Award as best actor for his work in the film "The Adventurers of Robinson Crusoe." Dan's younger brother was a prolific film director of features, TV movies and series. Most famous as director of the feature film classic *Odd Man Out* starring James Mason.

Vocalist band leader Vaughn Monroe was in Phoenix's Riverside Park ballroom for a one-nighter and we managed to get him for a guest appearance. We had hoped he would bring his female vocal group The Moonmaids but we had Vaughn and he did his hit "Ballerina" and his theme "Racing with the Moon."

I have no idea what went wrong between our studio and Riverside Park but that night he did the entire four hours including his network radio show for Camel Cigarettes with his back to the audience. I had a feeling during our show that Vaughn might be tough to deal with.

Dixie wanted to be on camera as part of the show. What could she do? Unable to sing, play an instrument or dance and the guests wanted to be interviewed by the host of the show. When I told John he was very unhappy. When I told Ron he considered retirement. We were going to present an award to the winner of the pre-teen talent search the station had conducted and planned to take a segment of my show and have an on-the-air party for the winner with Dixie as the hostess. Ron conducted the rehearsals and I held my head. I have a still photo from that show and that's all I need. Dixie then wanted me to sing love songs to her like I had done with Ginny Greer. We tried that a couple of times but when the female doesn't sing back it's pretty dead. Johnny said enough was enough and Dixie told me I should quit show business and sell real estate. This is something she would repeat many times during the next fifteen years. She had it in her head that people selling real estate make tons of money, and some do, but not me. I do what I know how to do.

Jack McElroy flew Marty Martell and me to audition for a spot at the Flamingo Hotel and Casino in Las Vegas as well as the Desert Inn Casino. We did a couple of sets at the Flamingo plus two more sets at what was called the Sky Room of the Desert Inn which was a lounge two stories high that overlooked their swimming pool. Afterwards, we told Jack that although both spots would have openings for us in the future we were not impressed with Las Vegas and wanted to return to Durant's. We did and a couple of weeks later I got three speeding tickets in one day, two in the city and one in the country. I was very upset. Not to worry, I gave the tickets to Jack and the citations vanished.

Dixie wanted to move to the McElroy ranch. I really liked Winter Garden but didn't want to set up problems. At the McElroy estate we had our own private rooms. The ranch was a working ranch, and each morning I would shake a scorpion or two out of my shoes and always checked for them in the shower curtain before turning on the water. Jack's wife Millie had been "Miss Georgia" when they met. She was still a good-looking woman with a nice personality. I would have breakfast with Mille and Nana, the mother and Dixie, and then most days be off for the studio followed by dinner and four hours of work at Durant's. The McElroys had two adopted children, cute little Marta, about ten, and her younger brother, Jackie, a blond-headed live wire about eight. Some days I left later for the studio as I was teaching little Jack to play tennis.

The racehorses had their stables in an area away from the main house where their trainer could work with them. Each spring, the family would pack up and move to a leased house in expensive and deluxe Rancho Santa Fe, California. This was close to the Del Mar Racetrack "Where the Turf Meets the Surf," where most racing days you would see Bing Crosby and many celebrities in attendance.

There were parties in La Jolla, at the world-famous hotels, the Del Coronado and the Valencia. Dixie had always been a part of this prior to our marriage. I never got the real story of why she lived with the McElroys. One story was that Jack had met her brother, Jep, 6'5", 245 pounds in Alabama and recruited him for the Arizona State College football team of which he was a star end who led them to victory in a Sun Bowl encounter on New Year's Day. Dixie had another brother, Woodrow, who was a chef, and an older married sister in Alabama. Her mother and father were dead so she came to live with the McElroys, who paid her way through college.

After Jep's college days were over McElroy set him up in the real estate business. Jep loved to fight, drink, gamble and meet the ladies. He always dressed like KFC's Colonel Sanders. In a white suit, big white planter's hat, white shirt and a black string tie. He liked to use his southern drawl and if he smiled that meant he was going to hit someone in the next second.

Dixie liked men like her big brother and was always trying to get me into a fight when she would say a man had insulted her, which was always a lie. I first saw this work a week after our wedding when we met Jep for a drink. We were in a booth and the bar was across the aisle. She and I talked, and then Jep went to the restroom. When he came back, before he resumed his seat, she said, "Jep 'darlin', that man (indicating a man sitting at the bar with his back to us and never knew we were in the place) insulted me and my husband won't defend my honor."

I couldn't believe what I was hearing. I started to tell Jep that nothing had happened but I was too late.

Jep grabbed the man off the stool, knocked the drink out his hand, broke his nose, and beat him backward and out the front door. After knocking him down, he grabbed him by the hair and smashed his face again and again into the grill of a parked car. After kicking him in the ribs he dropped the bloody body in the parking lot. He was smiling.

I tried to tell him that man had done nothing, but he brushed me aside saying his lovely sister had been insulted and I had failed to protect her honor. He also announced to the patrons that anyone who insulted his sister would get the same thing. Dixie was so happy. She had gone outside to watch him destroy the man's face on the grill and told me if I were a real man I would defend my wife. I would fight and had always fought when I was in the right, but I was never going to fight over a woman's lies. This same scene happened three or four more times and I would not go out with her brother. I always hoped he would pick on a guy with a gun who would fill him full of lead, but of course, that never happened.

Halfway through my second successful season at KPHO: I got a call to have dinner with some TV people from out of town. The deal was this: double my current salary to do *The Bob Cawley Show"* five days a week. There would be separate fees for any other show I was a part of. I would have the chance to direct some local programs. I could work nightclubs if I desired. If the first year's profits from my show either equaled the profits that it had made in Arizona or exceeded those profits, they would do something for me that would boost my future career. I would be a major player in the future of KOTV in Tulsa, Oklahoma. I would be working for TV icon Helen Alvarez, the "only" woman in America to own her own TV station.

We worked out the generous moving expense and the deal was completed. The only stipulation was I was not to tell Johnny Mullins that I was going to another TV station, but back on the road as an entertainer, and to cement this I would be booked into the exclusive Bachelor Club in Dallas, Texas, for one month before joining KOTV.

In the distant past Miss Alvarez had dated Johnny Mullins and didn't want him to feel she had stolen his star. The following Monday I gave my one-month notice. I had done very well in Phoenix and Johnny Mullins gave me my start in TV, and for that I will be eternally grateful. I would miss Durant's and my musical partner Marty Martell. I would miss Jack McElroy and always remember our many drives to tiny Scottsdale, Arizona, where he urged me time and again to buy land at five dollars an acre. Jack knew it would be a wealthy hot spot but I had no foresight. I could have been a millionaire. I was going to miss KPHO, Kathy Godfrey, and Ron Oxford a truly great producer with all his caring and skill. I would miss Marty Robbins, so super talented and fun to work with and of course my pal Jack LaDelle and the fabulous Four Deals and their leader, Lloyd Ellis.

As always, money talks plus the chance to direct was so tempting to say nothing of the chance to work with and for Helen Alvarez. After leaving KPHO we had two weeks before I opened at the Bachelor Club in Dallas. We went to Los Angeles so I could sound out the TV operations to see what the future might hold, I was really interested in landing with a network but would have considered a local station in the nation's number one market but from the start my hopes were aimed at NBC. The answer everywhere was "No" and I stood on Vine Street gazing at the NBC studios across their big parking lot watching all the stars that would hang out on their loading dock. After an hour of gazing and wishing I went into Coffee Dan's across the street from NBC for a cup of java. I was slowly drinking my coffee when a young man in the uniform of an NBC page boy sat down on the stool next to me. We got to talking and I told him I was in TV but really wanted a career at NBC. Could I get on the page staff and work up? My new friend, Jim Damon, laughed and explained that all the guys on the page staff were top grads from Ivy League colleges and were being trained for executive positions within the network. Jim had graduated with honors from Yale. Once in a while, they would bring in a director from an NBC affiliate but they had to start as Stage Managers and work up. However, that had never happened during his watch but if someday it did happen and if he could help me he would. We agreed to stay in touch.

The Seversons came over for a few days before going back to Minnesota and we took in the Hollywood nightlife. We danced and dined at Ciro's, the Trocadero and Macombo, and got to see the radio network show *Breakfast in Hollywood* with Jack McElroy and Tom Brenaman and had tickets for NBC's TV's *You Bet Your Life* with Groucho Marx. April 10, 1951, was the last night in Hollywood and the best. We had dinner at The Coconut Gove at the Ambassador Hotel and danced and enjoyed Phil Harris and his orchestra. I made a mental note to tell my mom that his theme was our old favorite "The Rose Room."

We stayed until the place closed and joined the rush to the valet to reclaim our wheels. The area was packed and I was shoved up against a couple who had their backs to the wall. I took a good look and saw the couple was All-American Heisman Trophy winner Glenn "Mr. Outside" Davis and his date was screen star Elizabeth Taylor. Glenn was one my football heroes, so I had to say "Hello." He was quite friendly and we both wished his Army backfield mate, Felix "Doc" Blanchard "Mr. Inside," also an All-American Heisman trophy winner was there to blast a hole through the crowd. Glenn introduced me to Miss Taylor who said, "Hi" as we shook hands. I thought Elizabeth had a beautiful face with violet eyes but was "dumpy" from her breasts down. I felt Glenn could do much better. I had no idea that I would get to know Glenn and have business dealings with Elizabeth in the years ahead.

I had a music date in Dallas. The day before we arrived in Dallas, a grasshopper plague hit Dallas and covered every square inch of sidewalk. They clung to window screens and doors, landed in your hair and made life miserable. There were no grasshoppers in the Bachelor Club; it was in a high rise and grasshoppers can't fly that high. They may have covered Dallas with dark, low-flying clouds but never up in the clear sky around the club which was extremely plush with a super sound system, a Steinway grand and many wealthy clients. The hoppers hung around for five or six days, then one morning they were gone, leaving thousands of dead bugs that were quickly picked up. Dallas was clean and neat and back to being one of our country's finest cities.

There were many nice things about "Big D" but

the most amazing thing was lunch hour. When this hit hundreds of the most beautiful women in the world would pour out of the offices and you would see one beauty after the other. Beautiful to look at wearing the latest fashions and million dollar smiles. I have always wondered why the powers in Hollywood which has few truly beautiful women don't go to Dallas where there are thousands to choose from.

The Bachelor Club wanted to extend my engagement, but at the end of the month, we were off to Tulsa and KOTV. There may be another city somewhere as clean as Tulsa, Oklahoma but I have yet see it. No trash, everything sparkling, and loads of friendly folks who say "Good morning" or afternoon or evening. We leased a lovely high-rise apartment with a park area around it. We soon found out that we were right down the hall from movie star Peggy Dow an attractive leading lady (*Harvey*, *Bright Victory*, and many other films) who was giving up her acting career and had just moved in with her husband an Oklahoma oil millionaire. Johnny Swenski a major name in professional wrestling and his wife Freda were also neighbors. I checked in at KOTV found that Texas did not have all the beautiful women. Helen Maria Alveraz, owner of KOTV would have to be in anyone's top ten. Jet black hair and eyes, flawless skin and a perfect figure PLUS she was very smart and a master of the games that "The old boy's network" liked to call their own. When they dealt with Helen they soon found out they were over matched. Helen was a very lovely lady, always the same, it wasn't long before she would come to our place for dinner or dessert and she always insisted that she wash and dry the dishes. You had to love her and you gave one hundred and fifty percent all the time. She had come up with two top musicians to form my trio. Jack Musick owned a drug store but had been a bassist with major-name bands including Jimmy Dorsey. Guitarist Howard Stanley was brilliant and was later featured with the CBS Staff Orchestra in Chicago. We were a perfect fit.

CHAPTER THIRTY-FIVE

The fragment of my life in the KOTV period was full of laughter, music and good times. The lone exception, married life.

My show got off to a very positive viewer response. Howard and Jack were great musicians and we mixed the old songs and the top new tunes that included "Hello Young Lovers," "Shrimp Boats," "Getting to Know You," "In The Cool, Cool, Cool of The Evening" and "Kisses Sweeter Than Wine." My show had a very talented director in Fred Komo, and Jimmy Harmon (Helen Alvarez's brother) was my number one cameraman. He and his wife Jasmine built a lifetime friendship. The entire staff was fun to work with.

Soon after the show opened Jack, Howard and I were booked into the swank Southern Hills Country Club to provide dance music and entertainment. At the station, I became a feature player on *Matinee at Noon* with host Perry Ward, a Tulsa favorite who was also a first-class play-by-play sports announcer, plus Miss Oklahoma Louise O'Brien, who would later star on Broadway.

Louise was a super beauty and had talent to burn. Blessed with a great singing voice, a warm personality and a natural actress we had some memorable TV moments together. In addition to our solo acts Louise and I did duets and some clever boy/girl skits that included a scene in a boat on a lake in the studio moonlight in a romantic duet on *Moonlight Bay*. We played off each other with lightning-fast ad libs, and with Perry Ward, that show was hit from day one. Louise was married to Luke Lane, who had been an athletic legend in Oklahoma. Luke, a very personable guy, was someone I would have liked to know better but Dixie was very jealous of Louise's talents and my wishes to invite the Lanes to dinner went nowhere.

The third week of *Matinee*, a guest on the show referred to Louise and I as "cute couple." That night when I came home Dixie had vanished. This was a Friday. On Saturday, I called Arizona to see if she was at McElroys. I bit the bullet and called Sue Black, but no one had seen her. When I came home from work on Monday she was there. She said she had visited "friends," although we had no "friends" in the area. When I pushed things farther, she wouldn't talk about it. Avoiding a scene that could escalate into something that could hurt KOTV and my career, I let it drop.

Helen had promised me I could learn directing, and I started under the calm and steady teaching of Fred Komo to direct *Bill Shiels on Sports*. Bill was a young talent who resembled movie actor Robert Wagner. As a sports reporter he was a phenom. Seated at his desk he would, launch into sports news including stats for baseball without a single note. No looking at papers or cue cards he had the full fifteen minutes memorized and NEVER made a mistake. This is something that doesn't happen too often in anyone's lifetime and I had to see how he did it. An hour before each show he started reading the wire service and by show time the entire fifteen minutes was in his memory like it was written in stone. I would go with him in prep every evening and started the memory process when he did and discovered that I had memorized it as well. I also directed the *Martin Weisdoner Show*. Martin was a big game hunter and guide who took hunters on safaris to Africa and India and also collected rare birds and animals for zoos and circuses.

This wasn't my pick of the pictures to direct, but if you are going to learn the craft you take every assignment. On a whole the show went well although wild animals often miss the cues Martin would give them but the show gained a solid audience. Then one day we featured a performer with his pet parrot, a high bird perched on a stool in the center of the jungle set. As anyone knows wild animals go to the bathroom on their time, not yours, and it seems some birds go constantly. For the show, there was a soft and absorbent floor covering that was disposed of after each show, and by cleverly directing, the TV audience did not see or hear the animal's movements. Remember all these shows were live and there were no retakes.

We had a new stage hand on the show named Manuel Roudesaks. I had recommended him for this job. I had known Manuel when I was a student at Greenbrier Military Junior College. His family owned the Court Restaurant in Lewisburg, West Virginia, where the cadets and the college girls hung out. In a fashion Manuel played the piano and wanted to get into the TV business. When a stage hand position opened up, I informed him about the opening and he got it.

Knowing the parrot was the featured performer, he spread tin-foil under the perch. With a little bit of luck, we might have got away with it, but luck was nowhere near. Coming out of the middle commercial, which was on film, the last fifteen minutes would be Martin and the bird. I came out of black onto a close-up of the bird. While Martin was introducing the parrot, a blast like a machine gun drowned out this audio. I was on the audio engineer's case asking what was wrong with his equipment when Jimmy Harmon gave me the word that the audio was fine. The machine gun sounds I heard were the parrot having diarrhea on the tin foil.

I was trapped. If I went to wide shots, the TV audience, who by then was overloading the studio switchboard wanting to know what was wrong with the audio, would see the bird going like Niagara Falls. I had to stay with a close-up. Out on the stage Manuel had crawled under the perch and tried to pull the tin foil lose. After fourteen of the longest moments of my life, the machine gun blasts were going into soft cloth. I relaxed and got all three cameras into motion. Then came into a two-shot close-up of Martin and his parrot. Martin told the audience what gentle pets parrots are when all of a sudden the bird grabbed his nose in his big beak and wouldn't let go. We played the closing theme while Martin fought the bird and spoke what I know were curse words in some foreign language.

Dick Campbell the announcer in the booth was choking with laughter as he reminded the audience that the big game hunter would be back next week. The bird let go of Martin's bloody nose and first aid was applied. We never had another show like that one.

Meanwhile, Manuel was not doing too well as a stage hand. The sets were heavy and took at least two men to carry them. A man would take the front and Manuel would take the rear. As they went through the studio, if they passed a piano Manuel would drop his end of the set and play a few bars on the piano. Sometimes Manuel would come to work with his pet monkey on his shoulder. He was requested not to bring the monkey to work. He was fired. After being fired, he got a job playing and singing at a local piano bar. The monkey would sit on his shoulder and eat peanuts given to him by the bar's patrons. The monkey would walk around the top of the piano with a cup to collect tips. Manuel and his monkey were fired after the monkey peed on several patrons who failed to put money in his cup. So Manuel and his monkey left Tulsa for greener pastures.

I was named Musical Director and got to work with Irish tenor Eddie Jones and pretty Zula Belle Linder as we headed into the fall. That's when I went to Helen to pitch the idea of KOTV having a basketball team in an AAU League. My motivation was three-fold. I wanted to play basketball, a team would bring additional publicity, and most of all I wanted to play on a team with Denver University's All-American Jack Hauser, who held the All-Time College Scoring record for Madison Square Garden in New York. Handsome Jack was a product of Columbus, Ohio's North High School, who reached the heights in Denver and just happened to be our TV-time salesman. Helen saw to it that our green and white uniforms were ready. Sales chief, Leo Howard, who had played college ball at Kansas, was named coach and we had a season of fun. We won games because of Jack Houser, who could make a basket from anywhere on the floor and was a rebounding tiger. We lost games Jack could have won with players near his equal but we did have a good time and people came out to "see the TV gang" play ball. Bill Shields was called for the draft and I asked Helen if I could have a shot at the sports desk, something I had always wanted to do so I took over Bill's two ten-minute slots with News Director Cy Tuma doing news, J. Kreiger weather, and I closed the news block that kicked off each evening at 6 PM and returned at 10 PM. I assumed Bill's format and never used notes or cue cards for sports reporting, I also worked specials covering University of Tulsa football with Perry Ward. Spare time was spent with the Harmons playing endless games of Rook.

There are many fine eating establishments in the Tulsa area but the only spot for lunch was a small kitchen called Phil's Grill located in the alley behind the studio. The back door to the Police Station was on the other side of the alley from Phil's so many of the cops ate there. The specialty was the soup of the day, which Phil always served with his thumb in the bowl, and the best ham sandwiches ever made. The smoked hams hung by cords and Phil would shoo the flies off the ham and make one of his fabulous creations. Don't tell me about the flies. Phil's little place did not have screens and never in history did a cop or TV worker get sick from Phil's food. In fact, we seemed to thrive on it.

The famous Cimarron Ballroom was close to the station, and once in a while, a group of us would walk down to hear Leon McAlliuf, master of the steel guitar and his great western swing band.

Helen threw a beautiful Christmas party at her ranch-style home that was all done in black and white. Very attractive. As l952 came in we were ready for a banner year.

1952 was truly a year to remember. The shows all built audiences and my plate was filled with interesting assignments. Although our football interests were focused on the University of Tulsa's "Golden Hurricane" we did get to Norman, Oklahoma to see Buzz Wilkinson's national football power at the University of Oklahoma in spring practice and had quality time with All-American backs Billy Vessels, Buck McPhailcheck (and one of the greatest college quarterbacks), Eddie Crowder, plus coach Wilkinson. Baseball season found me involved with the Tulsa Oilers processional baseball team. What a great bunch of guys they were. The big attraction was pitcher Johnny Vander Meeric (the only man to pitch consecutive no-hit games in the major leagues as he did for the Cincinnati Reds.)

The club was stacked with men who would make baseball history. Alex Grammas, Hobie Landrith, Johnny Temple, Jack Wiesenberger who had been an All-American running back at the University of Michigan and team manager Joe Schultz. (Just one memorable event was "Tulsa Oiler Family Night" when the players, their wives and kids were honored and as KOTV's Sports Director, I was proud to be the MC of that evening when the stands were packed to honor the players and their families.) Toward the end of the baseball season, Governor Johnston Murray presented me with a citation for my efforts in furthering sports for the youth of Oklahoma. I promoted baseball and all sports for kids and the information was so effective that over 1000 boys went to St. Louis as guests of the St. Louis Cardinal Baseball Club. Later I was given the rank of Commodore in the Honorary Oklahoma Navy by Governor Murray. This rank is given only to those who have done great service for the State of Oklahoma.

Then came the blockbuster. Helen Maria Alveraz was named TV's National Woman of the Year. If ever an award was deserved it was this one. *LIFE* magazine descended on the studio and took a portrait of Helen for the cover. Then their writing team did a three-page centerfold layout for that issue of Life. To top it off, they took a group photo of the entire staff that was used in the center of the story. In the middle of the picture, I am sitting on top of the piano and Helen is leaning against my leg.

Helen Maria Alvarez, who was called Helen, had an impossible climb to success. A young, single mom deserted by her husband, she didn't fall apart, but with drive, hard work and a never say defeated attitude she became a millionaire by her 29th birthday. With a child to support without any sort of assistance, she got a job at a Tulsa radio station as a secretary. When a popular newscaster at the station failed to show up for work Helen took to the airways with such success that the job became hers.

Television was just emerging when she met oil man George Cameron, brother of movie and TV actor Rod Cameron. George was bemoaning the fact that although he was a millionaire, he could not be a member of the swank Southern Hills Country Club because he was not from "old money" and he wished he could do something to make the members realize he was a powerful figure. Helen laughed and told him that was easy. Apply and get a license to build a TV station, call it Cameron Television, and put a neon sign on his TV tower and everyone would be forced to see and know Cameron Television since it would be the only TV station in this part of Oklahoma.

Since Tulsa was known as "the oil capital of the world" and the majority of the members of Southern Hills had made their fortunes in oil, this would be salt in the wounds. Cameron liked the idea and asked Helen if he got a license would she run the station for him. Of course, her answer was yes. The rest is history. While Cameron's lawyers pursued a license, Helen went to technical and management schools and excelled in her studies. Keeping her radio job, she read everything she could find about TV. She took correspondence courses in electronic engineering. When Cameron got the license Helen was just twenty-seven years old, and with his financing, she converted a former tractor sales space into the modern design that became KOTV. The largest broadcast center of its time and the sign Cameron Television sparkled on the KOTV tower on the roof of the bank building, the highest rooftop in the city and could be seen for miles. The studio had twenty-two feet high ceilings and doors wide enough to enable parade floats and elephants to enter. After force-feeding Cameron Television for a little over a year, George was ready to return to his home in Palm Springs, California, and his Texas oil wells and sold his interests to Helen who became the first female CEO in television. No wonder *LIFE* magazine dubbed her "Helen of Tulsa."

Later when Walt Disney needed cash for the construction of the Disneyland Hotel, Helen came to his rescue. In 1955 she cut the ribbon at the hotel opening. Helen Alvarez crashed through the glass ceiling to be a high roller, top player in what is considered a man's world.

She knew the ethic of hard work. She was a wonderful boss and friend. One of a kind. I have always missed her.

It was mid-October when Helen called me into her office and we sat in chairs by her coffee table. She reminded me that she had promised to do something to boost my career if my work at KOTV was top quality. She felt I had gone above and beyond in every way and then she handed me a document. It was a contract to have an on-camera interview followed by eight minutes of vocal and piano music that would be seen coast to coast on the number one show on daytime television, *The Kate Smith Show* from NBC TV in New York. My adrenaline raced and it was hard to speak I was so happy. Helen told me I would have airline tickets for Dixie and myself, or if I desired to drive, NBC would pay the cost of the trip. In the Big Apple we would have a suite at the hotel New Yorker with the network picking up the tab plus I would be paid for my rehearsal time plus $100 dollars a minute for the time I would perform.

I signed, hugged Helen, thanked her, and danced out on a cloud. I decided I wanted to drive over the famous Pennsylvania Turnpike and on the way home stopped at the Buick agency and traded my Nash sedan for a brand new two-door grey Skylark with a slash of chrome down both doors. Those wheels could fly, and we passed everything on the Turnpike except the gas pumps. I was getting about eight miles to the gallon. Louise O'Brien took over my show while I was away.

We arrived the morning of November 3rd, and after breakfast I walked over to the NBC offices at Rockefeller Center to let the network know I had arrived. I was told an employee of the network would see that everything would be taken care of. I sat down in the waiting room, and in a few seconds George Rogers came through the door. We were both shocked. We were doubles in every way, looking like twins. We shook hands and laughed and I told him my dad had never been to New York. His mother had never been to Ohio, but no matter how you sliced it we were exact copies.

George and I went to lunch and went over the game plan. The show was telecast from the Hudson Playhouse Broadway which at night was the venue of the Steve Allen Tonight Show then converted back to the *Kate Smith Show*. The songs I had submitted for clearance, "Everywhere You Go," "Till the End of Time" and "September in the Rain," had been cleared. George said I could use the entire orchestra or any group of musicians from the orchestra. It was a great temptation. I had worked with Frankie Master's entire group and it came off very well but in the end, I chose to use the same instrumentation that I used on my daily show. From the Kate Smith orchestra, I selected guitarist Mundell Lowe, who had just been selected by Downbeat as the number one jazz guitarist in the United States and bassist, Harry Goodman, Benny's brother. They would not be on camera yet still very close. The following day I would meet Producer Ted Collins, Associate Producer Barry Wood and Director Herb Susan plus Mundell and Harry. I would meet George at 9:30 AM and we would walk to the Hudson Playhouse.

That evening Dixie and I had dinner at The Aquarium which was right across the street from The Hudson Playhouse. Gene Krupa and his orchestra provided the music. After dinner we returned to the New Yorker to catch Bernie Cummins' orchestra which featured his wife as vocalist. A very good singer with the same smooth delivery she had when we worked together as kids in pioneer radio back in Columbus, Ohio where we dreamed of big-time show biz in New York and Hollywood and she was Ethel Mae Thompson.

Ted Collins was a hands-on producer handling the rehearsal in a warm, personal way while staying on top of the endless problems inherent with a major production. His assistant, Barry Wood, had been the singing star on *Your Hit Parade* prior to turning to producing and understood every aspect of performing. Director Herb Susan, a master of variety shows, was relaxed and easy to work with. Mundell talked about the ranch he would one day buy and retire to in Louisiana (he later found a permanent home in San Diego) and Harry was funny and both were superb musicians.

We had the musical numbers down pat when Kate Smith arrived with that great smile and a warm greeting, I thought of the many times I had joined my folks by the radio listing to "The Songbird of the South" as Kate was called, and here we were chatting like old friends. I was surprised how tall she was. The stagehands had to provide two stuffed pillows for me to sit on during our interview session so we would be the same height. I had always realized Kate was heavy from the waist up but she really had great legs. I would work on a white Steinway on the left of the interview area and just walk over to that area when the interview was over and do eight minutes. The Hudson Playhouse had a large audience area and it would be filled. It had to be the easiest rehearsal I was ever part of. I would work the third segment of her one-hour show. George Rogers hung around listing to Kate's wonderful voice as she rehearsed with the full orchestra.

George and I discovered it was pouring down rain when we reached the front doors of the Hudson Theater. It had been misting that morning so we were both wearing raincoats and we walked the short distance to NBC headquarters. The rain was coming down in cold sheets, the afternoon had turned dark and all the cars had their headlights on and the scene was a huge traffic jam moving very slowly. George had an idea that he thought would be fun. Since we were exact look-a-likes, I would wear his hat and coat, and when his wife arrived to pick him up, I would get in the car with her and we would see how long it would take before she realized she was not with her husband.

I donned George's hat and coat and we waited. When her car pulled up I dashed through the downpour, said, "Hi, Honey," like George always said as she pulled away from the curb. Driving in that rainstorm took all her attention and we drove several blocks with her intent on the road as I answered her question about the guest star George had taken to rehearsal.

I'll never know what pulled the trigger when all at once she said, "You're not my husband!" I confessed the whole joke to her as she skillfully drove back through the rain where George ran out. I gave him his hat and coat, put my coat on, thanked Mrs. Rogers for the nice drive, then took the short walk to the hotel, although Mrs. Rogers had offered to drive me. I would have loved to hear a recording of their talk going home. I had forgotten this was Election Day in the United States. During dinner in our room, we watched TV as Dwight Eisenhower became the thirty-fourth President of the United States of America. The rain was gone by morning.

Dixie would resume her shopping that had been interrupted by the rain. She had her ticket for *The Kate Smith Show* which ran from four to five PM New York time. I would see her back at the hotel. There was no doubt that appearing with Kate would provide a career boost that would continue giving for TV, hotels, supper clubs and casinos. Kate had started her brilliant career on radio and then on records became an American legend when she sang Irving Berlin's "God Bless America." She was already one of show business' most durable stars when she debuted on TV in 1950 in *The Kate Smith Hour* for NBC, a late afternoon entry.

In 1951 Kate moved to prime time with *The Kate Smith Evening Hour*, a variety format. Kate was also featured in motion pictures and TV dramas.

November 5, 1952, I was the guest star on *The Kate Smith Show*. Kate opened our segment by singing the popular hit, "Wish You Were Here," did a commercial for Ballard Oven Ready Biscuits, then the camera found us seated, yours truly on two big pillows, behind her desk where we had the interview session. Then off to the piano to play and sing "Everywhere You Go" and introduce and play "Till the End of Time." The interview portion had run long and the Stage Manager gave me the sign to short-end my version of "September in the Rain.". The audience applause indicated that everything had been well received.

Kate thanked me, asked God to protect Dwight Eisenhower, our new President, then went into filmed commercials before coming back to the fourth portion of her show which featured Ted Collins famous "Cracker Barrel" segment. I watched the final fifteen minutes backstage, then said thanks and goodbye to Mundell and Harry, Barry Wood, Ted Collins and Kate. My segment got reviews of excellence/sensational and I knew Helen would be happy.

The next morning I picked up my check at NBC, thanked my look-alike for his help, then headed for the Turnpike and Tulsa with a quick stop to see Mom and pick up my old dog, Nippy (her sister Tuck had passed away), and took her home with me to live out the short life span left. I was anxious to get back to work at KOTV and also Fridays and Saturdays with my trio at the Town House Restaurant to play more swinging jazz and give our rendition of current pop tunes "Kiss of Fire," "You Belong to Me," "Tell Me Why" and "Lover." I was intent on perfecting my directing skills which were a long way from what I had observed in Herb Susan in New York.

Helen had opened talks with millionaire oil tycoon and entrepreneur, Jack Wrather, about a possible partnership. Jack was married to movie star Bonita Granville who had been nominated for an Academy Award as a child actress in the motion picture *These Three*. She played the title role of a girl detective in the popular *Nancy Drew* film series before graduating into major leading lady roles. Although she had done many movies, she was intrigued by TV and used to sit in the control room with me when I was directing. Bonita and I became friends. A pretty and charming lady, she later became producer of her husband's "Lassie" TV series and held executive positions in his business empire that included holdings in oil wells, real estate, hotels and entertainment enterprises that included The Muzak Company and TV Programs. When Jack died in 1984, Bonita became Chairman of the Board of Wrather Enterprises. She also served as Chairman of the America Film Institute and as a trustee of the John F. Kennedy Center.

Helen was also considering the purchase of KFMB TV in San Diego and I expressed the desire to make the move with her, and there was interest on her part but this never happened.

In late December, Dixie informed me we were expecting a child and we had to move back to Arizona where she could be near friends including Sue Black with whom she had been in contact. She had also contacted Bob Bohannon who had staged our wedding reception and told him I wanted out of the crazy entertainment business and could Bob find a job for me in insurance with The National Casualty Company. She had canceled the lease on our high-rise apartment without my knowledge, so with great regret I left the company that had done so well by me and had been so much a pleasure to work for just being a part of the team and to dump the thoughts of San Diego. It was mind-blowing and I was not a happy camper. Before leaving Tulsa I bought a tiny little Fox Terrier puppy recently born that I named Cactus to be pal to my old dog Nippy. That's a purchase I never regretted. Cactus brought great joy to me and to my children in the long years ahead.

CHAPTER THIRTY-SIX

Maryvale, Arizona, was a brand-new subdivision with large lots and roomy ranch-style homes. We found one we liked and paid $7,500 and moved in. Gave the house a real tropical feel by furnishing it with colorful rattan furniture. There were large bedrooms, large kitchen, living room, and two baths. A carport that included a storage unit, big back and front yards with grass lawn. Next purchase was a lawn mower. There was no TV. During the months prior to baby's arrival, a nice stroller and baby supplies were purchased. I checked into the National Casualty Company and Bob Bohannon gave me a crash course in selling insurance. Then I was given a list of possible clients and I was on my own.

Depression is a word that had never been attached to me, but I was really depressed by this job. My would-be clients were young married couples who either had a child or were expecting. They were struggling to make ends meet and one glance at their homes told me they were on the edge of loosing what little they had and needing to pay an insurance payment every month was a luxury they couldn't afford. I told them to wait a few years until they had some kind of financial security. You don't sell a lot of insurance, but by not selling you may have saved some nice folks a world full of heartache.

Bob saw this was not my area and we parted. I had not asked for the job and I felt I gave it my best shot, but I could not sell something to people who didn't need it and couldn't afford it. KPHO found out I was back in town and they wanted *The Bob Cawley Show* for an hour five days a week. I snapped at the job, and although it caused more than a little ripple at home, Dixie was happy to see a regular paycheck. I was so elated I bought a small TV set for our house and TV became a staple in our home life. KPHO was a brand-new game. Johnny Mullins and the majority of people who had opened the station including Jack LaDelle, Marty Robbins, and Ron Oxford were gone. Ken Kennedy as Gold Dust Charlie and Ladmoe and Wallace still entertained kids but otherwise the Meredith Broadcasting Company broom had swept pretty clean. The viewing public was happy I was back and the new show was a success.

I thought of pitching to Jack McElroy about bringing Marty Martell and I back to Durant's, but before I got around to it I had an offer I couldn't refuse. A beautiful new hotel and bungalow apartments had been built at the key intersection of Camelback Road and 24th Street. Financed out of Chicago the Clown's Den cocktail lounge inside the hotel would soon be the "in" place in Phoenix with popular bartender Harvey mixing the drinks while Marty and I provided the entertainment. The ads made it quite clear that I had been a guest on *The Kate Smith Show*. Arizona Manor honchos Jack

Kogen and Maury Green signed Marty and me as the resident artists then informed us we would share the opening weekend with one of the first modern pop stars of the teen idol type. He was singer, actor, bandleader and entertainer who thrilled millions, Rudy Vallee. We had heard rumors that Rudy was difficult to work with. I anxiously awaited his arrival a day before opening.

That day never happened. Blizzard conditions hit the southwest and flights were grounded. Rudy and his wife, Eleanor, made the decision to drive. Arizona's White Mountains were packed with snow and there was delay after delay. They arrived exhausted and hungry shortly after 6 PM on opening night to find that Rudy's music had not been packed. They wanted to eat and rest in his bungalow for a couple of hours before the first of his two shows, Rudy met with Marty and me with a list of songs he hoped to perform. He sat down on the piano bench with me and started by asking me if I happened to know "My Time Is Your Time," "The Main Stein Song," "Viennu, Vienna," which Rudy would sing in three different languages, "Life Is Just a Bowl of Cherries," "The Whiffenpoof Song," "The Sweetheart of Sigma Chi," "Down By The Sycamore Tree" and his super hit, "As Time Goes By," which closed each show. What key was each song to be played in, I asked.

"Play it in any key that is comfortable for you, I can sing it," Rudy said. So much for being hard to work with. That's what we did, and Rudy was happy and would later want me to back him on a round-the-world cruise. Those first two nights with Rudy as the headliner at the Clown's Den overflowed as middle-aged women whose screaming and wild antics once brought him to fame and fortune, as young girls would do later for Perry Como, Sinatra, Dean Martin, Andy Williams and today's rock stars relived, for forty minutes their loyalty for the still handsome idol of their youth. It was a great honor to work with Rudy and we kept in touch until his death in 1986.

The Clown's Den became the place to see or be seen. Almost every weekend America's favorite gossip columnist Walter Winchell would be at our piano bar with a striking young lady. With him would be his pal Groucho Marx with a couple of blond sex pot twins who should have been in moving pictures. From time to time we had young men from Chicago in tailored suits who once in a while would brush their jackets back and we could see the butt of their guns in shoulder holsters.

One evening, soon after the hotel opened, I came to work to find the unflappable manager very nervous. He was afraid I might be late and he had a very important guest staying in a bungalow who wanted live piano music in his bungalow when his dinner was served that evening. A spinet piano had been rented, put in the bungalow, and tuned, awaiting my arrival. I reminded Jack it was time for Marty and I to start our nightly gig. Jack said Marty would do a solo song and guitar act until I was available. Given the bungalow number, I followed the walk bordered by green grass until I arrived at my destination. Upon knocking, I told the tall well-dressed young man who answered that I was the music man and was led in to the piano where I was instructed to play soft romantic ballads until I was dismissed. My fingers caressed the keys with "Serenade in Blue." A white tablecloth covered a candlelit table set for two with sparkling silver. I did several pretty ballads and then the couple entered from the bungalow interior.

The man was billionaire oil man, film producer, aviator, entrepreneur, and playboy of the western world, Howard Hughes. The willowy young lady he seated was movie actress, Janis Paige, who at that time was on the cover of several national movie fan magazines as "the girl who has never been kissed." So much for the truth in magazines. I played my tunes as the couple were served and they ate and talked. As they finished dessert, I was told by the young man that my job was completed. Hughes stood up and handed me a folded $100-dollar bill and thanked me for the nice songs. That was the largest single tip ever.

Arriving back at the Clown's Den Jack Kogen was all smiles. Thanked me for a job well done and slipped a new $20-dollar bill into my jacket pocket. I wished Hughes and his lady would stick around but they were gone by the next morning. The Clown's Den was the Phoenix hot spot. Comic Jerry Lewis built a big club across the street that had a splash opening but within a couple of years had faded into memory.

At KPHO the Meredith people pulled out all the stops in getting movie stars and others of interest as my guests. To list them all would require a thick "Who's Who" book but the most remembered are: A man known to the world as Major Speed Chandler, a man whose real-life adventures were greater than any work of fiction. A motorcycle and auto racer, military flier, and top Hollywood stunt pilot. He hung out with movie star John Wayne before Speed himself became a celebrity. During World War II he served in the US Air Force. Flew the "Hump" in India, Burma and China. Was chief test pilot at Rome Air Force Base, New York. For three seasons Major Speed Chandler and his International Flyers Air Show dazzled the citizens of Chicago before he moved to Beverly Hills, California, for movie stunt flying and a position in the automobile business. His true tales of stunt flying kept viewers glued to their sets. What movies these tales would have made. Before leaving the show he invited me to his Beverly Hills home when I came to California. It took me a couple of years to make it but in time I did.

In 1954, Mickey Spillane did two guest spots on my show and if he could have been on the show for a month he would never have run out of interesting stories. Mickey was in Phoenix working as an actor. He was playing himself as a detective in the feature film "Ring of Fear" for John Wayne's and Robert Fellows', Wayne-Fellows Productions. Mickey rewrote the screenplay of the film without credit. Mickey said he had written for a variety of publishers of comic books creating adventures for Captain Marvel, Batman, Superman, and Captain America. Needing an influx of cash to buy a house, he took a shot with a novel he wrote in nineteen days titled *I, the Jury*, sent it to a publisher, and it sold sixteen and half million books in the United States and millions more worldwide. He built the story around a fictional hard-boiled detective Mike Hammer. It was to be the most famous character he would ever create and it proved to be a gold mine with more Hammer books to follow plus seven motion pictures and two long-running TV series plus TV movies. Actor Darren McGavin, Stacy Keach (who I would later work with on a major film) became Mike

Hammer in the series produced for CBS-TV with elements of classic film noir and the haunting theme song, "Harlem Nocturne" played by a blues-tinted saxophone.

Versions of the Hammer series would first run until the end of the 90s with a spin-off titled *Mike Hammer: Murder Takes All* that featured Lynda Carter (Wonder Woman), Michelle Phillips and Jim Carrey. Mickey played the role of Hammer in the motion picture of his novel *The Girl Hunters* filmed in England. His is one of the few times in history where the author of a literary hero portrays his character.

Publicity proclaimed that "Mickey Spillane" sold more books than the Bible. I know he wrote many books that gave all of us endless hours of exciting reading. The movie *Ring of Fear* provided another excellent interview in the person of Irish actor Sean McClory who was playing the role of the demented killer in *Ring*. Sean's career ran for six decades working in over one hundred feature films and TV series. Movie credits included *The Quiet Man*, *Cheyenne Autumn*, *The Long Grey Line*, and John Houston's *The Dead*. Sean a native of County Galway, Ireland bewitched viewers with his lyrical Irish brogue and his fascinating tales of his years in film and TV.

We reserved an entire hour to stage a TV party for bandleader Ralph Flanagan who had the most popular dance band in America. Ralph had started his professional career as pianist/arranger with the Sammy Kaye Orchestra and also provided arrangements for Gene Krupa, Tony Pastor, Charlie Barnett and Alvino Rey and many top bands. His manager, Herb Handler, convinced Ralph to write Glenn

Miller-type arrangements for his own orchestra and the rest is show business history.

Now the Flanagan Orchestra was featuring outstanding male vocalist Harry Prime and a singing group called The Singing Winds were currently the top crowd-pleasing band in the land and were the favorites of the college crowd from coast to coast. Our studio audience and TV viewers were thrilled when Ralph took to the piano keyboard to play his theme "Ginnina Mia" followed by his super hit "Hot Toddy". Harry Prime delivered two beautiful ballads, "People Will Say We're In Love" and "The Sweetheart of Sigma Chi." Ralph and Harry mingled with the audience and we all enjoyed ice cream and the special white cake made for this occasion.

On Tuesday, August 18, 1953, at 8:01 PM our son was born at St. Joseph's Hospital in Phoenix. We named him Robert Kim. The joy of holding your little son for the first time is a thrill like no other. Kimbo, with blond hair, blue eyes, and a perfect body would bring many hours of happiness in the years ahead.

One of my many sponsors was beautiful and scenic Mt. Lemon Lodge at the top of Mt. Lemon near Tucson. They wanted me to film a commercial at the Lodge which also acted as a ski Lodge during the winter snow season. For the commercial, they wanted to highlight their many riding trails through the tall and fragrant pines that graced the mountain. No problem. Bundling up baby Kim we went down to the Lodge where we were guests for the weekend.

Saturday morning the film crew was ready to roll and there was my horse in front of the Lodge. Someone forgot I was a city guy and the only horses I ever saw were at the racetrack. I went out to my horse and got upon the right side and my horse bucked me off into the street. This got lots of laughs from the onlookers until a cowhand whispered, "Always mount on the left." With some hesitation, I swung into the saddle from the left and my horse seemed happy and I know I was happy to be in the saddle and not sitting in the street. Later my steed and I cantered, galloped, and had a nice ride through the forest. I took a couple more rides during the weekend. When I saw the film on TV, I was thankful that the editor knew how to cut the film and the viewers thought I was tall in the saddle.

1953 had its share of pop music hits including "You, You, You," "I'm Walking Behind You," "Vaya Con Dios," "P.S. I Love You," "That's Amore," and novelty tune "How Much Is That Doggie in the Window." My directing dreams had been side tracked but that was about to change.

CHAPTER THIRTY-SEVEN

I had to get my career as a director moving and started reading the ads in Broadcast magazine. My initial move was to WCHS-TV in Charleston, West Virginia. It was a natural. Close to my old school in Lewisburg and to mom and the old home place in Columbus plus the fact that the Oakes family lived just a few miles from the station. I signed on as Announcer/Director. Everyone at the station was nice to work with, but the station was new and there was little announcing and even less directing to do.

I had left the family in Arizona. I advised them to meet me in Great Bend, Kansas, where I had signed on as Sports Director and Live Show Director with station CALL, an NBC affiliate. We had the highest TV tower in that section of the Sunflower State and Les Ware was an aggressive station manager. We had three live shows. Gil Canfield with News; Howard Morgan and his clever animated helper "Thermo" doing weather, and I had sports covered.

The oil boom was on in Great Bend and the only living quarters was a basement apartment. It only took a few weeks to realize I was building a good viewing audience for sports, but directing time was zero. Dixie and Kim returned to the McElroy ranch in Arizona and I headed for WUSN-TV in Charleston, South Carolina, to do another version of *The Bob Cawley Show* plus directing assignments. The change was radical, to say the least. At Great Bend, there was a very modern, specially-built for TV facility. WUSN-TV was a gigantic Quonset hut the size the Army used for aircraft and it was set in a swamp, and you reached the studio via a wood walkway floated on the green water of the swamp.

The owner and CEO was a fiftyish gentleman who still wore his college-type clothes complete with his USC necktie. His family was very prominent and historically correct in the city. I found out he didn't care for Yankees when he threw a party for the staff at his home. Four other Yankees and I were not allowed to go to the second floor but were served on the first floor. I thought that all the Yankees might be sent to slave cabins, since it was obvious that the Civil War was still going on and the south would rise again. The huge metal studio was a disaster. For my evening show with two local musicians, we had to put soundproof baffles around the set and it still sounded as if were in an echo chamber. The station tower was directly over the studio and a few days after my arrival a tower worker dropped a bucket of bolts that tore through the studio roof like a bomb.

Looking for a residence, I leased a wonderful house on Sullivan Island just north of the famous Charleston Bridge. It had a glassed-in front porch and I spent many happy hours gazing at the ocean and the big ships that went by. Dixie and Kim came out. Kim enjoyed playing in the surf and the two of us would build sand castles. They stayed until a hurricane warning was put up then flew back to Arizona. So much of the studio was jury-rigged as was brought to light after the hurricane missed Charleston but destroyed a great deal of Myrtle Beach.

The hurricane was pounding the east coast. NBC wanted to do news coverage of Myrtle Beach, but with the weather the network was unable to send a crew from New York. Not to worry, we could cover it on a coast-to-coast hookup. I took a camera crew to Myrtle Beach and shot film. My most remembered moment from that trip was an ocean front home with all four walls destroyed but the front porch was still intact and sitting in a rocking chair slowly moving with the gentle sea breeze was a dead elderly lady. The film was developed on a priority basis and was excellent. Our news director managed to get the Admiral of the Atlantic Fleet as a guest and we were ready to roll with our NBC News Special.

Hurricane Hazel, the deadliest, costliest hurricane of the 1954 Atlantic hurricane season, was headed for the United States, and NBC – TV in New York had requested that WUSN in Charleston, South Carolina, put together a TV special after the storm hit the Carolinas and created a path of destruction all the way up to Toronto, Canada.

Hazel had formed on October 5th with tropical rain and storm-force winds as it approached the Lesser Antilles. It made landfall on the Island of Grenada on October 6th with winds clocked at 75 miles per hour. The winds had reached 80 miles per hour when Hazel hit the northern coast of Venezuela. October 9th found Hazel elevated to the status of a major hurricane with 115-mile-an-hour winds. On

October 12th the hurricane tore into Haiti, leaving 1000 dead. It touched Cuba and bypassed the Bahamas, then headed for the South Carolina coast. It was impossible to fly a crew and equipment from New York, so we had the assignment to be ready with a hurricane special as soon as possible after the hurricane passed. I wondered why they thought Charleston would still be standing once Hazel made land. Thanks, New York, for your support.

Drayton Hastie, WUSN's owner, said I would direct the special since I had survived Hemingway's hurricane in the 1930s that had destroyed the railroad from Miami to Key West and taken hundreds of lives. I think Drayton was hoping I would be swept out to sea and this Yankee would be out of his life.

Charleston was bracing for Hazel to rip in from the ocean and prayed it would not destroy much of this historic city. Charleston got lucky as the storm veered slightly northeast and on October 15th Hazel unleashed her full fury including winds as high as 130 miles an hour on Myrtle Beach where eighty percent of the waterfront homes were destroyed and a three-story hotel and an 800-foot pier were washed out to sea. Hazel would end her run on October 18th in Toronto, Canada where she would cause 81 deaths and over $100 million dollars in damages. On October 16th my crew and I were at Myrtle Beach. The name Hazel has been retired from use for North Atlantic hurricanes. In Charleston, she left 1,191 dead and damages of $382 million and an untold number of injuries.

I called my mother in Columbus to watch this special as I would be directing it. She called several lady friends who did not have TV and served cup cakes and coffee as they watched the telecast. The show was in the last third when all of a sudden a voice came booming out of her TV "God damn you, I said take two" and Mama announced "That's Robert!" Mama, of course, was right. The WUSN control room from which I was directing was not sound proofed and only had a slab of beaver board between the control room and the announcing booth. The announcer had failed to turn off his mike. I had told the technical director twice to switch to camera two and he sat in front of his board like he was deaf. When I yelled "God damn you, take two," he made the switch like he had been hit by an electric shock and almost at once the hot line phone from New York started to ring. Broadcast Operations had thought they had heard profanity on the line but I assured them there was no profanity here but to check the Chicago hookup. Outside of the news event, there was little to direct and no sign of anything in the future.

A few days later, I was reading the New York Times, when I saw an article of great interest that said Sean Dillon a major network producer was leaving the Big Apple to become a General Manager of a fourth TV station to be built in Phoenix, Arizona. Dillon's name hit me like a thunderbolt. About a month ago I had read a story titled "Screaming Genius in a Soundproof Booth." The story had been in a major publication. It told the story of the rise of Alex Siegel, a Russian immigrant from nothing to the finest director in television thanks to the teaching of Producer Sean Dillon who had been with the Abbey Theater in Ireland before coming to the United States. I thought I might get Dillon to teach me and it was worth a try. I called KTVK which had offices in a former private home on North Central Avenue in Phoenix and Dillon answered the phone. I told him who I was and that I was working in TV but my ambition was to become a first-class director and after reading the magazine story about Alex Siegel he could teach me. In his Irish brogue he told me he was only hiring old friends from New York but if I ever passed through Phoenix, stop by the office and he would see me. I hung up and something told me that this man was involved in my destiny.

I went to the station, met with the owner and got my instant release. Went back to my house on Sullivan Island and called the owners telling them I was leaving at once for Arizona. My current lease was paid up for another week and I didn't want a refund. I called Dixie and told her I was on the way home and had enough money to rent a house, but no job. Packed everything I had in my Nash station wagon, put the keys to the beach house under the front door as agreed and started driving straight through from South Carolina to Arizona.

Four days later I was in Sean Dillon's office and I was the first production person he hired. If I wanted to be a director it would be a rugged work schedule six days a week. In addition, I would star in a new *Bob Cawley Show* from 10 PM to 11 PM five nights a week with a format similar to "The Tonight Show" with a live studio audience, band, comic, girl singer and a side kick announcer. We were the fourth station in a four-station market and the other stations had bought up all the syndicated shows so we would be "live" from sign-on till sign-off with all types of programs and sports events to direct.

Art Brock who had been with me at KPHO defected to KTVK as Sports Director and the sidekick on my nightly show. When he had been brought to KPHO from Washington State he was a Sports Director but he never saw the sports desk. Some would-be production executive put him on the air as weather man wasting one of the best play men in the business. We would not make that mistake. Jim Silvus, a talented office manager, who was a friend, left KPHO for the new venture.

I rented a nice home on Orange Drive and now the Cawley family was back together. Father had a job and Dixie was "expecting." The major stockholder in KTVK was former US Senator Ernest McFarland who was to become Governor of Arizona shortly after the station began broadcasting. I had a chance to observe the Governor close-up and he was never the sharpest knife in the drawer. On nights that he would do his address to the state, I would have to start fifteen minutes prior to airtime to wake the Governor who would be asleep on the toilet and would have to give him three calls to get him in the studio. We never shot a full body shot of the Governor as his boots were caked with mud and manure from his ranch. It was obvious that he could be controlled and was another Kemper Marley selection to run the State. Kemper who liked to say he was just a rancher was the power behind politics in the state. Ralph Watkins, a car dealer from Glendale who was a pal of the Governor also had a block of stock and was around the station a lot of hours during the early days. The studios and permanent offices of KTVK were completed and we had shows ready to roll. "Moods in Food" a five day a week cooking show hosted by cook and nutritional expert Bee Pine was a favorite with the ladies from day one. Alan Franklin, who had been a fixture in New York radio and TV, brought his daily poetry show to our studio. Marylou Hosford Whitney brought a touch of class to her daily talk show. Don Tuckwood our newscaster of choice was well received. Art Brock's sports had a huge following and he was kept busy with play-by-play remotes of major league spring training games. (National Women's Softball, calling horse and dog racing plus my nightly show and a relaxed half hour called *Overture* 2 PM to 2:30 PM daily.) I was there as announcer, interviewer and piano player/singer. Art Brock delivered news capsules; Helen Coddson gave a weather update and also modeled what she was wearing.

We pulled out all the stops on my show with a western swing band, my pal Marty Martell on guitar and vocals, Rita McCann, girl vocalist, Lloyd Steincamp, with zany skits plus star imitations, and the swinging clarinet styling's of Al Overend, leader of his orchestra, "The Musical Blend of Al Overend." He played great sax and clarinet plus handled backing the vocalists. His band also worked the fabulous Flame Restaurant in downtown Phoenix every winter season. He and the band played a top resort in Wyoming during the summers.

The days and nights at KTVK left many memories. I remember sitting in Dillon's office at 1 AM or later as Sean consulted his notebook and reeled off mistakes I had made as a director. He kept tabs on every show I worked and we went over it in detail, the good and the bad. I can still hear him saying, "You want to be an Alex Siegel and do big productions, you have to clean up your style."

Then there were the days I turned in almost flawless performances in the director's chair and the praise was warm and I was certain it had been earned. We televised horse racing from Turf Paradise and I was in the remote truck. We had done the races many times, but today, well one of my top cameramen was a small man, Steve Miles. Maybe 5'7" who had come from Canada looking for a job. The Chief Engineer told Steve Miles he was too small to handle the heavy camera. I liked what I saw. This little guy had done a great audition and I told Sean I wanted him as part of my crew. I was right. I can picture Steve with his work gloves in his hip pocket ready to do his job. We had a little problem today. The engineers had forgotten the sticks for Steve's camera. They had only brought a camera pedestal with wheels like we used in the studio. Steve's camera position was on the roof of the grandstand which was slanted and the missing sticks fit behind a one-inch strip on the high end of the grandstand which provided shelter for fans below. There was no time to return to the station for the missing sticks the first race would start in a few minutes. Now it was the director's decision. I told the engineers to put the camera with a rolling pedestal on the roof with the back wheels hooked over the tiny strip, then, to tie Steve to the camera.

By leaning back his weight, Steve would hold the camera in place and he could get me great shots on the back stretch. Three other cameras were in place plus the camera on top of the remote truck where my number one cameraman, Rick Benewitz, had the finish line. I put my headset on, checked Art Brock in the announce booth and all five camera positions. We were one minute to air when Rick called in and told me he was going to offer some sizzling shots of the winners. His camera was doing some different angles. Then all at once the camera was just swinging around and around and I heard groans form outside the truck. I stood up and looked out to see Rick on the ground with two broken legs. He had stepped backwards off the truck. I called for the stage crew to get one of the ambulances that were at the track to get Rick to a hospital and for the engineers to send a backup to take the camera on top of the truck.

My technical director yelled that in ten seconds we were going live. I got to my seat in time to cue Art Brock and racing at Turf Paradise was on the air as I heard the ambulance leave the area. Years later I would work again with Rick Benewitz when he was one of the top soap opera directors in the business. We laughed about our days at KTVK. Rick had been taken away and the cameraman who replaced him was doing a journeyman's job on the winners. I settled down to the races.

When we were coming up to the fifth race when I heard Steve Miles' voice in my ear. "Mr. Cawley, I'm slipping off the roof. The wheels have gone over the strip."

"Hold on, Steve, keep giving me those great shots, help is coming." I called the chief engineer bringing him up to speed. He and three assistants had to go to the entrance and through the crowd before reaching the ladder to the roof. Steve was tied to that camera and he and that heavy equipment would fall on the unsuspecting crowd and many would be killed or injured including Steve. I looked outside the truck and saw Steve and the camera were almost a third of the way down the roof. I have never prayed any harder than I did that day for God to save the little guy.

The fifth race was on when the chief's voice told me they had Steve and were pulling him with his camera to the top of the roof, and the four of them would stay with him till the races were over. While all this was going on, Steve stayed in focus and got great shots of the back stretch. We televised the horse races many times after that, and with the correct equipment it was just another day at the races.

As the fourth station in a four-station market, without the ability to buy syndicated product or network shows, every second we were on the air we were live with the exception of filmed commercials. We covered the races at the dog track, did shows in super markets, any place that offered excitement and entertainment. Then came the day of the snake show.

We were covering an expert in milking rattle snakes for their venom for medical purposes. I was directing this epic with my new head cameraman, Steve Miles, leading the way. The expert had several glass cases of rattlers containing about twenty snakes per case when one of his assistants tripped over a camera cable and fell into a case which fell into two other cases and all the humans were racing for the exits as snakes slithered around the studio floor with fangs bared ready to strike. Did I say everyone ran? That's incorrect. One person remained, Steve Miles with his legs wrapped around his camera pedestal as rattlers struck just underneath his legs.

"Just stay focused, Steve, and zoom in for some nice close-ups. We'll scare the hell out of the viewers."

"But, Mr. Cawley, the snakes are after me."

"Not to worry, the expert and his assistants are on their way with snake bags and they will pick them up."

The assistants armed with snake bags and batons with a loop attached calmly picked the reptiles out of the smashed glass, the other cameramen returned along with the stage manager and the expert continued milking the snakes until the show ended. Steve told me he liked working with me but I always seemed to bring danger. I told him that was just an accident that would never happen again.

I meant what I told him, but destiny was laughing in the wings. We had just seen nine innings of Women's Professional Softball with Dot Wilkinson, one of the greatest pitchers in the game, throwing another masterpiece. Art Brock had come down from the announcer's booth to interview Dot before she headed for the showers. A film commercial was playing from the studio before we did the live sign-off. During the commercial Dillon called to tell me that due to an engineering problem they couldn't switch back to the studio and we would have to fill until the problem could be corrected.

"Great, Sean, the game is over, the crowd is leaving and what can we do?"

"You have forty minutes to fill."

I asked with what and he reminded me that Alex Siegel would do something and hung up. Alex Siegel never saw a moment like this. Then I had a flash. I had the stage manager give Art his headset and told Art we had to fill for forty minutes and I wanted him to move to first base, tell the story of major league baseball as he moved from position to position with stories of the greats who had played that position. He said "Okay" and gave the headset back to the stage manager and we were on the air. I sent the stage manager to tell the head of the ball park to leave the lights on as we had an emergency.

For the next forty-two minutes I was mesmerized as Art moved around that vacant field telling stories of the men who played the national pastime. It was the greatest ad-lib performance I have ever seen. Art was on the mound talking about great pitchers when the station called. They could make the switch. Art did the closing, and at last we were off the air. We got 500 pieces of mail regarding Art doing the glory talk again. Dillon was on the phone for both of us with congratulations for the most remarkable fill he had ever seen. I asked Art what would have happened had we not been able to switch. He laughed and said, "He could do another thirty minutes on baseball managers, then he would have introduced me to sing, dance and tell show biz stories." Art Brock was a special talent but KTVK under Dillon was the only station to make use of this great talent.

We had a wide variety of programs and one of my favorites to direct was *Open Your Eyes* hosted by world-famous artist, author and anthropologist Paul Coze who for decades was French Consul for Phoenix. The subject of his TV show was art and he was a master. In 1954, he was awarded the Chevalier de la Legion d'honneur. Paul was a warm friendly man and I enjoyed visiting Paul and his wife at their home where he would always open a bottle of fine French wine with a slash of saber that took off the neck of the bottle yet never left a shard of glass in the spirits. He assured me this is the way wine is opened in the French Foreign Legion.

Paul was famous for nine pieces of public art in the city of Phoenix including the very large multimedia installation at Phoenix Sky Harbor International Airport, the Veterans Memorial Coliseum and other civic landmarks, most with native themes. He had great interest in Native American Culture. He spent two years producing major educational murals at Mesa Verde National Park. Paul had an art school and still found time to paint wonderful paintings that were on exhibit and sold in the USA and in Europe. The only oil painting I ever wanted to own was Paul's painting called "The River of Life" which depicted the life of a woman in every major change of her life from birth to death. I tried to purchase it years after Paul had passed away, but I was too late. It had been sold.

One can still see Paul's work in his fabulous murals and in a variety of paintings for museums and art galleries. Hundreds of his collected artifacts now reside at the Royal Alberta Museum.

When I visited Paul we use to talk and not always about art. In fact, one subject was the amount of gambling that went on despite the fact the city fathers said the city was clean. How could that be when the largest betting wire in the southwest, The Trans-America Race wire, was located in the Lures Tower in downtown Phoenix? It was managed by Phoenix native, Gus Greenbaum, a member of the Chicago outfit and former head of gambling operations at the Flamingo and Tropicana Hotel casinos in Las Vegas. I knew there were games of chance at the top of The Westward Ho Hotel because I had gone several Sunday mornings with Jack McElroy who had a financial interest in the Flamingo in Las Vegas. Also, major mobsters had permanent homes in Phoenix, including Willie Bioff, Tony Arcardo, who lived across the street from Senator Barry Goldwater and Greenbaum in the upscale Encanto area. Neither Paul nor I gambled but it was something to think about.

Sean Dillon wanted me to become a producer/director. He said there was an investigative reporter in Phoenix whose crime stories were syndicated in newspapers all over the USA. His name was Gene McLain and he worked for *The Arizona Republic*. What separated this guy from everyone writing crime stories was that he, McLain, solved the crimes, not the police. This is the stuff great network TV series are made of and if this works it can shoot you to the top in the TV industry. It almost did!

I called the newspaper and asked for McLain. I was told he was on a case. I asked the young lady who had answered where he was. As I later learned she was new on the job. She gave me the address of the crime scene which was a private home in an upscale area of town. Upon arrival, I saw the parked police cars and the crime scene tape around the area. A young police officer stood by the walk to the front door. He must have been new on the job for when I told him I was here to see McLain he told me Gene was inside. When I opened the door the foul odor almost floored me. The house had been closed for a week without air conditioning and body parts and dried blood were everywhere including the walls. A wealthy doctor had gone on a rampage and killed his mother-in-law, his wife, and their three small children with an ax before blowing his head off with a shotgun. I looked at the sofa and saw McLain sitting there eating half of a tuna sandwich. He smiled and spoke. "What do you think, kid, murder one? Would you like half of a good tuna sandwich?"

I'm trying to keep from barfing and he's talking about eating. In a strangled voice, I asked, "Mr. McLain, could we go outside and talk?"

He said, "Okay," and we moved out into the fresh air.

As I tried to get my breath, I asked McLain for a thumbnail sketch of his career. He was born in a tent on a mountain near Bisbee, Arizona, and by the age of five, this tough Irish kid was selling newspapers on the streets of Phoenix. He never wanted to be anything but an investigative reporter and had done that job his entire working years except for the time spent in the Navy during World War II. He worked for *The Arizona Republic* where an older brother worked as photographer and took the only picture ever taken of the entire Dillinger gang when they were captured in Tucson. Gene felt the news game had done well by him. He had won seventeen "Story of the Year" awards; his work had been profiled on the popular network show *The Big Story* five times and he had been nominated for the Pulitzer Prize. He had married "Blondie," his childhood sweetheart. They had two preteen sons and Blondie was a cop. As I watched this compact 5'7" man who you wouldn't want to meet in a dark alley, because only he would walk out, the big smile and the raspy voice was TV star quality.

I learned from the start he was not interested in fame or money. He was only interested in justice. If you were guilty he would never rest until you were behind bars, but if you were innocent he would do everything possible to set you free. I told him I wanted to produce and direct a TV series about some of his famous cases to be called *Special Assignment*. Gene said although the idea was good he wouldn't wear a suit, jacket or tie like the guys on the popular TV series *Dragnet*. He was in his work clothes now. A Hawaiian print Aloha shirt over his slacks. The shirt concealed the holstered 38 he carried clipped on his belt. I solved this objection by telling him he would only have to wear the jacket and tie once; we would film an open and close in one session that would be used on all shows. He could throw away the dress-up clothes and do the rest of the show in his work clothes.

Special Assignment owned its Tuesday night time slot no matter what the competition threw against us and it was the most remarkable series in the United States. The open and close were filmed but ninety-nine percent of each show was live. We did stories on the actual scene of the crimes with the 'real' criminals acting out the crimes. We used the 'real' detectives who made the arrest. The only actor was the victim. I urged McLain to write a book about his cases but he insisted I write a book or a series of books. Gene, Blondie and I recorded ninety hours of audio tape concerning his work then they gave me the file to me. It would be years before I wrote *Components of Murder*, a case McLain solved where there were no bodies, motives or clues.

It looked as if Dillon's prediction would come true that this series would shoot us to the top of the TV business. ABC-TV wanted this series which pulled over a thousand pieces of fan mail a week. But although the series had the cooperation of the Phoenix Police, the Maricopa County Sheriff's Office and the Arizona Attorney General, the ABC legal department could never come to grips with the 'real criminals' and lost what would have been a historic event in the world of network TV. Gene and Blondie became the brother and sister I never had. We've had high times and hard times but the friendship and loyalty never wavered. As if my plate wasn't full, early Wednesday nights I became Mr. Marco, as my assistant pretty blond Maryann Corn, who doubled as the station receptionist, played Marko with a studio audience and hundreds of viewers. Marko, which was played just like bingo, was played on Marko cards obtained at our sponsor, Booster Rooster gasoline service stations. We had a bank of telephones, hooked up for our answer crew so TV viewers could win if they had the correct numbers. Later they would have to bring their cards to the station for verification and pick up their prizes while the studio winners took their prizes home with them. I would say the magic words, "Let's play Marco." Maryann would turn on the glass case with the numbered ping pong balls shooting around. Maryann would pull the balls with the numbers and I would do all the dialogue for TV and the studio audience.

When you are involved with production sign-on to sign-off schedule, you have zero time for station politics. There is great relief when you have a union contract that politics doesn't touch. I was hearing talk about excellent experienced employees who were being replaced by relatives of the Governor who had no idea which end of a camera we shot out of. Of course, some of the owners didn't have a clue. An incident that became a laughing legend happened one day, when I was directing the races from Turf Paradise. Ralph Watkins, a major stockholder, happened to be in the station's master control room when I put a superimposition on the air.

"How did he do that?" Watkins asked the engineers.

"Oh he just put the picture of one camera over the other" was the answer.

"You're telling me he has two cameras running at once?"

"That's right, Mr. Watkins. In fact, he has all five cameras running."

"He's bankrupting the stockholders," and he gets on the phone to the remote truck and tells them to turn the power off to four of the cameras and just use one at a time. The engineer doubled over with laughter when Dillon walked into the control room and explained that in TV all cameras are on every show, be it two cameras or sixteen, they run all the time. He didn't grasp it and thought the cost would put the station out of business. I got a lot of ribbing from the technical guys that I had expensive tastes that were going to break the bank. This of course was all in fun.

Something that was not fun was a Program Director the Governor hired named Roger Van Duzer with the build of a pulling guard in big-time college football and a lousy attitude critical of all that Sean had accomplished. Van Duzer and I were on a collision course.

A major moment in my life happened on April 11, 1955, when my beautiful daughter Sharon was born at St. Joseph's Hospital where her brother Kim was born. I announced Sharon's arrival on my show that night. Kim's birth had been uncomplicated but Sharon's birth had been complicated and the Nuns had told me if it became a choice between the mother and the baby they would save the baby's life. Thank God everything had worked out and mother and daughter were both doing well.

After I joined KTVK, our expenses started to rise. There seemed to be more cash going out than was coming in, and I didn't know why. To help the cash flow I got a music job weekends at the famous Flame Restaurant whose fine food and the Jungle Bar with exotic birds and monkeys were the talk of the town. I alternated with Al Overend's orchestra.

One night I told Gene McLain we would open the show this night without the film opening. We were doing the story of a wanted criminal who had been captured during a stakeout at a pharmacy he planned to rob. The real arrest had been a blood bath. The criminal had pistol-whipped the owner so bad he became a paraplegic and had sold the store. There had been some cuts and black and blue lumps with the police officers, but all that was to be toned down.

As always, uniformed officers armed with shotguns were stationed on the perimeter of the set and our four cameras concealed them. The store was large with many aisles of merchandise plus six large glass display cases and a soda fountain. The cops who had been involved in the original stakeout were in place. One was in the men's department. One was in the pain medicine area, and two had sandwiches and milkshakes at the fountain. The cops and the criminal needed little rehearsing since they had done it.

My work was with the actor playing the victim, who in most shows already is dead, but tonight I have the new owner of the store who wants to play the role of the former owner. I had made my point that I wanted a professional actor in the role. The owner made it plain he played the role or we didn't use his store. There I was just minutes away from air time standing by the cash register with the owner who will play his role in this spot and the criminal who will rob him. The owner, nervous as a mother hen said, "I'm not sure what to do," although we had gone over his couple of lines for fifteen minutes. He repeated his statement looking at the criminal who would rob him who in turn looked back at him with his cold eyes and said, "I know what to do!" Little Steve, who would get the entire close-ups of the robbery, shook his head and I started toward the remote truck. There was no theme, no open announcement. Just a wide shot outside the store and Art Brock's voice just above a whisper telling the viewers we were outside this store on a police stakeout where we believed a wanted criminal was going to rob.

A young woman and her daughter (actors) came in picked up a prescription and left. In his quiet voice pointed out the undercover cops in a variety of work and sport clothes. Then a car pulled up by the store and the criminal got out and entered the store. He looked at a couple of magazines from the rack then moved to the cash register area where the owner was stacking packages of cigarettes in the area designed for them. Owner, "Can I help you?" Criminal, "Yea, you can help me" (draws a pistol from his jacket and jabs it at the owner) (pistol is really unloaded) "Give me all the bills you have in your cash register?"

Owner starts to pull bills out of the register. Criminal grabs owner by his shirt and jerks him toward him. "Show me some speed before I kill you." Owner pulls all the bills out of the cash drawer hands them to the criminal. Criminal pulls owner to him and opens the side of his cheek as he whips him with his gun barrel. The blood spurts in every direction and all hell breaks loose as the cops spring into action. The battle that follows destroyed a great deal of the store. All the glass cases were smashed and aisles of merchandise dumped over. The owner has his forehead split open after another whip from the criminal's weapon and the fight is on that will end with one cop with a broken arm, one with broken fingers and everyone else covered with cuts and black and blue areas.

I am hanging in the wind. I can't get off the air and back to the two-minute film commercial since they don't come until the middle of the program. I just covered the fight that went on all over the store until the criminal was subdued and cuffed and an ambulance arrived to take the owner away and medics treated the cops and the criminal. I had shaped this show with the surprise opening as a copy of Orson Welles' radio blockbuster *War of the Worlds*, which panicked Americans to believe the nation was being attacked by people from another planet. However, I panicked 900 viewers in Arizona who believed they were seeing a real stakeout and called the Sheriff's office begging him to send help to the embattled cops. I knew this for a fact. I had a phone call on the set from the High Sheriff who wanted to see McLain and me in his office at 7 AM. We were there on time. Gene had a long-time relationship with High Sheriff Cal Boies, an icon in Arizona law enforcement.

Many national publications had done stories about Boise and the Ford Times had him on the cover plus a super story called "The Last of the Cowboy

Sheriffs," a lawman in the tradition of the great lawmen of the old west who liked to track criminals on horseback across the vast Arizona desert and mountains. The Sheriff always got his man and he brought them back dead. It seems they always resisted arrest. There was never a scandal about the High Sheriff or his deputies. I had never met the Sheriff and when I did I knew this was the one man in the world I never wanted after me. Tall, slim with a tough wiry build the man was graying at the temples and he is the only person I ever met with eyes like a diamondback rattlesnake. These were the eyes of death. The message was brief. We would never open *Special Assignment* without the film opening or he would see that the series, which he liked, would be taken off the air. His office had almost 1,000 calls asking for him to send law enforcement to the store. We got the message.

In the heyday of radio, there were tramp announcers, guys usually single who moved from town to town after they tired of their current location or had met all the ladies in the neighborhood. Whatever the reason they moved around cities in the United States because there were always jobs for good speaking voices. There were a few in the early days of TV and one of these was Larry Nayland who landed at KTVK. Larry was a guy with a lot of personality both on and off camera. Alan Franklin had a large group of fans who enjoyed the way he read poetry and short stories by such top authors as Jim Bishop in his deep voice while relaxing in his big leather recliner with soft organ music in the background. This was Alan's "Dreamy Den." The show was sponsored by a local funeral home and next to Alan's set was the replica of a funeral home slumber room where various caskets were displayed for "when the time comes." Larry Nayland did the live commercial.

On this day one of the caskets had a divided top and was red, white and blue. In solemn tones he pitched the other two caskets then turning to the red, white and blue model bursting into laughter that almost doubled him over, he flipped the split lids open and through gales of uncontrollable laughter asked the TV audience if "Isn't this a hell of an interesting box?" He then leaned on it and laughed with tears running down his cheeks. Dip to black cutting Larry's mike and coming up on Alan who continued as if nothing had happened. When the show ended Larry was long gone and Larry's employment at KTVK was history.

Larry still had one more chance to be infamous in the history of Phoenix broadcasting. He was hired as a late DJ by KOOL Radio owned by movie and recording star Gene Autry. There was a major commercial disk that he played at the wrong speed two nights in a row and no doubt management said something to him about this error. I was listening to his record show when he played the commercial once again at the wrong speed. He slid the needle over the disk, then opened his mike. "Mr. Gene Autry. I am putting on a long play transcription. I am now leaving the station but this will give you time to get down here and keep the music playing." Larry Nayland vanished but I would have bet he landed at another radio or TV facility.

Our first year at KTVK ended on the highest note possible. We had beaten the other three stations and our all-live format designed by Sean Dillon had attracted solid sponsors and excellent financial returns. A big victory breakfast was thrown by the station with everyone employed plus stockholders. Sean was given a trophy and the Governor made a speech thanking him for the year we had just completed. When the gala broke up, I hugged Sean and thanked him for all he had taught me and we both looked forward to the year ahead. I had to leave to scout a remote location for an upcoming special but would return before 1 PM.

Arriving back, I asked Maryann at the reception desk if Sean was back from lunch and she told me that Sean was no longer with the station. Coming back from lunch he found the lock changed on his office, his personal belongings dumped in the hall and his final check thumb-tacked to his office door. He was going to be replaced by another relative. I couldn't believe what I was hearing. I had just attended our big victory breakfast. I stormed into Van Duzer's office.

He was coming around his desk.

"What the hell is going on?" I yelled.

"The company has made changes and from now on you will answer to me."

"You've got to be kidding, I answered to Sean Dillon, the guy who made this operation a first-class TV station."

"That no good, shanty Irish son-of-a-bitch is out of here."

I will never throw a right hand harder than the one I rocked his jaw with. Rocky Marciano would have been proud when I put all 185 pounds into the punch that sent him flying across his desk into a far corner where they could have counted a hundred over his prostrate form.

Leaving his office I stopped for a second at Maryann's desk. "Tell them to mail my check to me. I'm out of here." I called Sean, but he had checked out of his hotel. I would never see or talk to him again but the lessons he had taught me would live on and I will always love the man who made me a director.

CHAPTER THIRTY-EIGHT

No station, radio or TV, would touch me, and what little savings we had was almost gone. I contacted Jack McElroy at the Flamingo Hotel in Las Vegas about a music job but even with his clout it would take two months and I needed to earn a payday now. Melon season had just started and I could go to work packing melons for Jack's Cal Vita Company. Next morning I was in the produce shed by the railroad tracks packing crates of cantaloupes. The shed was filled with workers who could only speak Spanish. The only other worker who spoke English was the former world champion Welterweight, the great Lou Ambers.

Lou, who had tons of scar tissue around the bright eyes in his beaten face, had been an idol of mine on the Friday Night Fights on TV. Lou never ducked an opponent, fighting the best men of his era. When I was a choir boy I used to admire his photo in the window of the Adams Hat Store at Broad and High in Columbus. A majority of the great fighters then wore Adam hats. We became instant friends and Lou who worked the sheds during shipping seasons for various crops taught me how to pack melons. You lift the melon to shoulder height then slap it down into the crate so all melons are tight. The outer covering of the melons does a number on the skin covering the palm of your hand but you grit your teeth and live with the pain. Your week is seven days because fresh fruit has to get to market.

A great many former boxing champions earned millions of dollars, but when their careers are over, they became broke, homeless and disabled. Lou was one of the few exceptions. He had been lucky to have one of the few honest and caring managers in the fight game in Al Wile, who also managed the greatest heavyweight champ, Rocky Marciano. Al had banked Lou's winnings and bought annuities that left him financially secure. His home was paid for. He could buy a new car every three years and could afford steak and lobster when he desired. Lou didn't need to work but he needed to keep busy and he was a valued worker.

From sunrise to sunset we packed melons as they came in from the fields and Lou took me round by round, punch by punch, at least fifty times through his greatest fights. He also spoke of his two encounters with the pride of Texas, Lou Jenkins, who took his title and the rematch when Lou failed to regain his title. In telling how Jenkins broke his nose with the first punch of their last fight. Lou would put down his melon, get into his fighting stance and move around the way he had when Jenkins caught him. Lou made life bearable in a work place where nobody spoke your language.

One day the shed boss came up and with motions let me know I had a phone call in the office. This could only mean the kids had an accident. Breathless I raced to the office and picked up the phone to hear a voice ask what I was doing in a produce shed. I asked who this was and the answer was my NBC page, Jim Damon, who had moved up the executive line and was offering me a job with NBC in Hollywood if I was interested.

"What are you doing in a produce shed?"

Thinking fast, I told him I was purchasing fresh melons just brought from the fields, and yes, I was interested in the job. He was sending me a Western Union money gram with money to fly to Los Angeles plus cash to live on for three or four weeks while looking for a home for the family and NBC would pay moving expenses. I told him I would fly into LA within two days and would call him with my arrival time so he could meet me. I ran back down the shed to let Lou know I had a new job. He hated to see me go, but we were heading for a future in Mecca, the entertainment capital of the world with NBC.

CHAPTER THIRTY-NINE

Hollywood! This is the way I imagined it would be only more so. Smog had not taken over the city yet as it would in the next few years. The sky was blue and the sun was shining. Jim took me to the Re Tan Hotel on Wilcox Avenue just off Hollywood Boulevard where he had arranged a room for me. It was just a few blocks away from the studio. We then went to the Director's Guild of America where I paid my initial dues and got an employment card clearing me to work for NBC as a Stage Manager. The next stop was fabled Sunset and Vine the very heart of the film capital. We drove the chain link fence on Vine Street into the NBC parking lot and I thought back when I stood there and peered through the fence at the celebrities. The parking lot was very large and I was surprised and delighted when he pulled into a space that had my name on it.

The NBC property covered an entire city block running from Sunset Boulevard to Argyle Street which was north. The studios faced Sunset Boulevard. The offices were across the parking lot facing Argyle and across the street from the offices was

Nickodell's Restaurant. We went up to the second floor of the office building where I was introduced to the man in charge of all NBC Western operations, Thomas C. McCray. He was a tall slender bald man with a pleasing speaking voice. He had started with NBC years ago back east as a vocalist on his own radio show.

After a brief meeting we went to the office of Andrew Greeley, whom I would only meet this one time, but Mr. Greeley made a deep impression on me with three different issues. First of all, he presented me with my NBC employment ID. Second, he handed back to me the resume of my efforts in the minor leagues and told me to look at what was behind a black curtain that hung behind his desk. He pushed a button and revealed a big sign that said "There were no yesterdays." He said I want you to remember this because your life in television started as of today. In closing our brief meeting, he said also, remember this, if you every have to make a choice between NBC and your family, the company comes first. He wished me luck and we departed.

Jim took me down to the ground floor to where I had a private office and introduced me to the lady who was to be my secretary. Blond and buxom Margaret Marshall, who was a native of Australia. Next we walked across the lot to tour the studios which were very plush with their theater seating arrangements, the big stages, the sets, the lights and all the things that go with great theater. He then took me out to the loading dock where the shoe shine stand was. The same dock that I had looked at so longing three years ago that then seemed a million light years away. There was a group on the dock of members of the

NBC family, and the first one Jim introduced me to was a comedic icon, Jimmy Durante. I will never forget he hugged me and welcomed me to NBC. Also in the group that welcomed me was Dinah Shore, Gordon McRae, director Tom Belcher, John Storm, the famed announcer of the series hit *One Man's Family*, and also handsome Alfred Apaka, the golden voice of Hawaii. I was really in a daze meeting them but in the years ahead I would spend a lot of time meeting many other luminaries on that same dock.

Being at Sunset and Vine really put you in the center of things. If you went a block down Sunset to the east you would be at the famous Hollywood Palladium where in later years I would direct two outstanding television specials. If you went past the Palladium for another block you would arrive at CBS and I would have the privilege of meeting many of their people at Nicodell's for a toddy and for lunch. Looking west on Sunset there was the famous RCA recording studios and looking south from Sunset was the famous Hangover room where you could see and listen to great solo piano like Joe Sullivan, Jess Stacey and Bob Zurke, the old tom cat of the keys. Across from NBC were the studios of ABC and also on the other side of the street was the headquarters of Cy Devore, the tailor to the stars. There was also the Spotlight bar which was the home away from home of the NBC announcing staff and a large Coffee Dan's Restaurant. Looking north of Vine Street there was Hatton's Restaurant and the famous Brown Derby. On the west side of the street was the Plaza Hotel and on the corner the famous Broadway Department store. It faced Hollywood Boulevard, and right beyond Hollywood Boulevard was the Pantages Theater, where for many years the Academy Awards were held and the famous Capital Record Tower. On the west side of the street was Clifton's Cafeteria and the Palace Theater, which was used for a TV series by NBC.

After going back to my hotel, the night was still young. I called the telephone number that had been given to me by Major Speed Chandler when he was a guest on my TV show. He had told me call him if ever I came to Hollywood. Well, I was here now. The man who answered the phone said that Speed would love to see me. He was having a party that night and I was invited. He told me I didn't have to dress up but to come casual. He gave me the address in Beverly Hills and I caught a cab and arrived at his palatial residence.

As I went up to the door to ring the bell, I noticed there were many cars parked there. A man in a tuxedo answered the door and told me Speed was looking forward to seeing me and I would find him in the master bedroom upstairs where he was recouping from a broken leg in a stunt accident. He pointed to the stairs and told me which way to turn.

As I made my way through the crowd, I couldn't help but notice that many of the women were nude and so were some of the men. Everyone was eating and drinking and seemed to know each other. I got to Speed's room and there he was on this big bed with two lovely starlets, one on each side, and his leg in a cast. He seemed glad to see me and asked how things were going in Phoenix and I told him I had just joined NBC and would be headquartered at the studio. A lady serving cocktails came in with a tray and asked me what I would like, and I told her a bourbon and water and she was back in just a few seconds with a tall one. Speed and I chatted about his accident and he told me we would have to get together later once he was up and walking.

Other people dropped by and I decided to excuse myself and slowly went down the stairs. A couple of the nude women wanted to be assured that I wasn't leaving early and they would see me later. I got down to the living room and realized I was in over my head. I finished my drink and left telling the man at the door that I had to go to work that night at NBC but tell Speed I would be looking forward to hearing from him. I never did but it was probably best for both of us. I had just seen my first Hollywood party and I wasn't sure that I was cut out for the party game. I just wanted to get to work in the industry.

CHAPTER FORTY

My first assignment as a Stage Manager took me into the world of professional golf at the celebrated PGA Los Angeles Golf tournament, a three-day event with top players involved. Dynamic and demanding Director Marc Breslow would be the artist covering the event for NBC-TV while veteran sports announcer, Cleve Herman, was on deck to give viewers the standings, statistics and some interviews. My job was to keep all interviews to five minutes and to keep all talent aware of time left for those interviews. I wore a silver stopwatch with the NBC logo engraved on the back around my neck.

However, my most important duty was to take care of the rising female movie star who was the tournament hostess. This is what Director Breslow told me as I reported just after sun up to the remote truck. "You are responsible for getting our hostess form green to green on my cue. There is one small problem her long dress, which has nothing under it, is so tight she can only take baby steps, so you will have the job that most men would do for free. You're going to carry her."

I was about to ask how many tons this person weighed when Marc's face broke into a smile so many women loved. "Here's our beautiful star. Turn around and say hello." I did and I looked into the face millions of men dreamed of.

There stood the voluptuous Jayne Mansfield. She stood 5'6" with a 40-21-35 figure, a thick mane of blonde hair wearing a green sequined dress that fit like her skin that was low cut and barely covered her famous breasts.

"You must be Bob Cawley. Marc told me that we'll be close together the next three days. It sounds like fun." She spoke in a breathy kind of baby talk voice, but who cared about the voice it was those D-cupped breasts that kept one's eyes straining. Jayne and I shook hands and she reminded me I would have to take her around in a Fireman's carry so I put her over my shoulder and carried her to the spot where she and Cleve would do the tournament opening. Cleve Herman had lost his left eye and wore a black eye patch. I wasn't sure his good eye would survive after he sees Jayne's cleavage.

Walking out of the shot, Breslow's voice came over my headset. "Don't fuck this up or you will be back in Arizona." This was a major factor that made the Golden Years of live television so exciting. Each day you slide down the razor blade of life and one mistake could end your career. This was the reality of the business. The pressure was on every working hour and a lot of the off-work hours as well. One mistake and it was over. Home, kids, school, income, job, everything gone and either back to the minor leagues or out of the business altogether. If you got fired in Hollywood, you had no friends. When they saw you coming they would cross the street. No one wants to be associated with failure. Some people crumbled. Some just could not take the strain and stress. I loved it and so did Marc.

The tournament was on hand for three days I heard dozens of cat calls and guys offering to pay me and let them do my job. I carried Jayne for eighteen holes for three days, threw all the correct cues and had a ball. I love the television biz.

Not everything went perfect during the tournament. In the middle of the second day, Marc told me to give Cleve the signal that he wanted to cut back to an important shot coming up. I gave Cleve the cue but he kept on giving current standings of the players. In a split second, I heard Breslow's temper almost break my ear drum, "That one-eyed son-of-a-bitch, I'm going to kill him," as he gave his technical director the shot he wanted of the player and kept on calling shots of the current play. I thought the outburst was over but I was wrong. When Marc cut back to the studio for a film commercial, the voice of doom came into my ear. "I want your complete attention. Tell Cleve that if he ever fails to take my cue at once, I will come out of this truck and punch his good eye out on the green grass of this golf course. You tell him what I said and leave your mouthpiece on so I can be certain you deliver my message, as I want it delivered." For an instant I wanted to plead Cleve's case then I remembered that Marc had put the cord of his headset around the neck of the audio engineer during *The Curt Massey Show*, which he directed and started to strangle him for being a sixteenth of a second late in opening a singer's mike.

I gave Cleve the message and Marc told me I was

going to do ok. I realized the director and stage manager's job was on the line every second you worked. At the end of that Cleve handed me his headset and vanished into the crowd. He was not going near the remote truck until air-time tomorrow. Jayne and I had a great three days together. She did first-class interviews and I had the distinct feeling many of the players would have liked to stay and talk with the sex kitten rather than go back to hitting the little round ball. Jayne and I bonded over music. She was an outstanding violinist and singer and also played piano and viola. She would later make single records and albums both in English and German and sing in movies and become a top nightclub and hotel/casino act. She would win the theater World Award for her acting on Broadway and a Golden Globe for "New Star of the Year" in 1957. Jane was smart with a winning personality. Working with her was fun and I'm sorry we never did it again.

Marc Breslow was the star of the directing staff. Standing about six feet tall with close-cropped, black, curly hair and olive skin, he would have been my first selection to play a Roman Centurion if I were producing a biblical epic. He would have looked perfect driving a chariot in ancient Rome instead of his MG sports car. Marc could be charming, yet he had an explosive temper. He strove for perfection in his work and expected perfection in others. I learned a great deal from Marc and felt he had many traits of the great Alex Segal. Marc and I became good friends until I replaced him as producer/director of *The Curt Massey Show*. When his career at NBC was over Marc became a legend as the ultimate director of game shows for game show giants Mark Goodson Productions. He directed the popular *Match Game* show on CBS-TV as well as *Card Sharks, Classic Concentration,* and in 1972 he was the original director of *The Price is Right*. When he retired to his beautiful home atop Mulholland Drive he left Goodson Productions with a one million dollar severance check.

The house in Arizona sold, recouping our investment. We now had a mortgage and a more expensive brand-new home in Sepulveda, California, just a block away from where Kim would go to kindergarten. A very modern ranch home with attached garage on a knoll of a tree-shaded street. New furniture was required, and during the moving process I discovered my wife slept with a very sharp butcher knife under her pillow. When I asked why, she said it was to kill intruders who would never expect a woman would be armed. At that time there were no intruders in the vicinity of this nice quiet development of modern homes.

We had a nice front lawn and a large fenced backyard that got my attention with my electric lawn mower. We had hardly moved in when Dixie told me she hated the neighbors across the street. Like everyone in the development, they were young and had two young and very well-behaved children. I soon deducted it was not the family that had this feeling going but the lady of the house.

She was blonde with a figure like Marilyn Monroe that was usually clad in short shorts and a halter top or a form-hugging bathing suit. They had a swimming pool that we were invited to use but never did. My wife liked to be attractive to the men in the neighborhood; after all, wasn't she "Miss Fashion Plate?" In short, she didn't like competition.

I liked all the folks in our area, although I saw little of them. I was at the studio. This screwed-up emotion was festering and arose the night we had a little get-together with all the neighbors on our short block with a variety of sandwiches, mai tais, coffee and cake. Very popular then was the game of charades which we played. A guy played his guitar and conducted a sing-along. A very relaxing evening with my main duty going through the guest with trays of drinks and coffee.

After the happy group departed, we cleaned up and I volunteered to wash dishes while Dixie dried. We chatted about the evening and I turned to hand her a plate to dry, she lunged at me driving a steak knife deep into my left shoulder. Her eyes blazed with an insane light as she screamed, "I saw you looking at that bitch (the woman across the street) when you served drinks!" I had looked at everyone as I carried the tray around. Just like nothing had happened she touched my left arm telling me I had to drive to Van Nuys to a Quick Care Medical Center to get some stitches. She pulled the knife out and wrapped a towel around my shoulder. I got to the Quick Care and the doctor just couldn't come to grips with how I had stuck myself with a steak knife. This was the first time I realized I was married to someone with different personalities. I tried to make believe this was an isolated incident. I would be proven wrong. Most of all I was concerned about our children.

I was moved into Studio F to stage manage for celebrated Director Alan Armer and the *Dick Contino Show*. Always dressed as though he had stepped off the pages of Esquire, Alan Armer a Stanford University graduate with a B.A. in Speech and Drama and an M.A. in Theater from UCLA, started at NBC as a stage manager who rose to be one of the finest directors and producers the TV industry has ever known. I had observed the "take no prisoners" style of directing and I was now exposed to Armer's gentle handling of a difficult star and the patience to make each second of a show as good as it could possibly be. He was very calm with no temper and a quiet voice in my headset. Alan would move to 20th Century Fox where he would write, produce and direct several TV series including *My Friend Flicka*. He was later the executive producer of *The Untouchables* starring Robert Stack with Quinn Martin Productions. He won an Emmy award as the producer of the gigantic hit series *The Fugitive* starring David Jansen. Alan also won an Edgar Award from the Mystery Writers of America for his writing on the show. I was a careful observer of both the Breslow-and-Armer-style of directing and mixed a bit of each with my own style.

Dick Cantino had flashed onto the American music scene on December 7, 1947, when he took first place on the national radio broadcast of Horace Heidt's Philip Morris talent show when it played his hometown of Fresno, California. He dazzled the listening world as an accordion virtuoso playing what was to become his signature song, "Lady of Spain." He won the final round of the contest December 12, 1948. He toured with the Heidt Orchestra and was billed as "The World's Greatest Accordion Player." He did guest appearances on the major variety shows of that era including *The Ed Sullivan Show* a record forty-eight times. Unfortunately, he was jailed as a "draft dodger" during the Korean War for several months before he served in the Armed Forces and was honorably discharged as a Staff Sergeant and was given a Presidential Pardon. He had been making $4,000 a night prior to this trouble and it did serious damage to his career.

After his NBC show he became a hit with a new generation of listeners thanks to movie and TV work. Alan's major problem with Dick is that he wanted to play piano and sing. He's the king of the accordion but was never a threat as a pianist to Nat "King" Cole or Joe Buskin. His vocals were okay, but the advent of TV singing stars like Eddie Fisher and Gordon McRae (both with shows on NBC), he was doomed. The project like all Alan Armer productions was well-produced and directed. There is no doubt that Dick Cantino is the all-time great accordion artist just as Tommy Dorsey was on trombone but the accordion was never an instrument that millions of kids played. In future years the vast majority of kids never learned more than three chords on the guitar. Everyone can play three chords but there are only a few really good accordion players. The instrument is bulky and takes a great deal of practice to play plus girls were not interested in playing the instrument because of its size. The window when the accordion sound was popular was very short. Styles in music change with every generation.

Days became weeks and weeks became months and my schedule as a stage manager grew. I enjoyed working *George Fisher's Hollywood* thanks to guests like Sammy Davis, Jr. who always brought his gun belt that held twin Colts (unloaded) with him and worked his fast draw. Sammy was always fun and his impersonations of other famous artists was jaw-dropping. Sammy worked the show several times as did actor Vincent Price, a collector and critic of fine art. We had time to talk and get to know each other and I found him to be very interesting. I worked shows with fat Jack McElroy who had co-starred with Tom Brennan on the historic *Breakfast in Hollywood* pioneer radio show. Jack covered a variety of subjects including a deep sea fishing segment off the coast of Mexico with me operating a 16mm camera in a violent storm that convinced me I never wanted to be in the Navy. Jack had a spread in the San Fernando Valley where he had burros that my young son loved to ride wearing his black cowboy hat with the silver band, playing the role of a real caballero.

The last time I worked with director Alan Armer was the *Mary Macado Show*, a very popular show with guest and film clips of Mary's travels. Mary knew, as did all artists appearing on NBC, that any film brought in by talent or their managers had to be screened by the film department before it aired for content approval. Pretty Mary had come direct from the LA airport after a trip to Paris telling Alan this film had to be a part of her half-hour show. The film would run for exactly ten minutes. The pressure was on, we were just minutes from air and this was a popular show. He gave the film to me to run to the film room and have it loaded on the projector that could feed Studio F where the show was being produced.

I got back to the stage as the theme started and on Alan's call cued Mary who was sexy and charming as usual. About seven minutes in, the film would be played and Mary and her guest could relax for about nine minutes. The film rolled, Alan took it, the mics in the studio were cut off and I announced a nine-minute break and pulled my headset down around my neck when I heard a strangled cry from Alan. He was halfway out of the control room to talk to Mary when the engineers were screaming for his return. There on the screen was a French porno film, dubbed in English screening for our audience. Alan took the screen to black while calling over the intercom for Mary to do her guest interview. All hell broke loose when the show was over. Mary and her sponsored show were finished. NBC client and viewer control spent endless hours answering viewer and sponsor calls and Alan had a long meeting with the head honcho, Thomas C. McCray. I doubt if ever a single foot of film was played at NBC without the film room okay after that.

I worked a dramatic show with actor Edward Arnold one of Hollywood's most versatile and convincing character actors as well as leading man. Best remembered for his starring roles in the motion pictures *Diamond Jim* and Frank Capra's *You Can't Take it With You* and *Mr. Deeds Goes to Washington*. The TV show I worked with him would be his final appearance. He died two days later.

Between the studios and the loading dock, I was meeting the Who's Who of the industry. Then I was upgraded to director and assigned to Film Studio 5. I was surprised by the quick promotion as I felt the next promotion would go to the best stage manager at NBC or anywhere else had ever seen Darol McAlister. He was the ultimate at his craft. As a director, I loved to work with him as I never had a seconds worry about control of the stage. He was never given a chance to direct. Film Studio 5 wasn't where I had hoped to be. I wanted to direct lives shows. Little did

I imagine that I was headed into the busiest place in the entire network and now I had to rise at 2 AM to get to work on time as we would be feeding the *Today Show* in New York which was three hours ahead of Pacific Coast time.

CHAPTER FORTY-ONE

On the home front everything was quiet. My mother came out for Christmas and the kids had loads of fun with Grandma, who read and told them endless stories. She loved them and they loved her and there were tears when she left. Son Kim had told his kindergarten teacher his dad had appeared with Kate Smith and the teacher wondered if his dad would entertain. So, one morning, before the routine Studio 5 started, Kim and I walked down to Gledhill School and I gave a thirty-minute performance of songs kids loved except for the closing tune they had never heard, "The Little Red Caboose Behind the Train." They picked up the melody, lyrics and train sounds and on request did it over and over until I had to beg off. The little musical was a success and son Kim was very proud of his dad.

Starting life in Studio 5 was far from the artists. I now only saw them and mingled with them on the loading dock in the early afternoon when I was through work. Studio 5 was the money machine for NBC where we fed all film and later videotape commercials for both the east and west coasts.

The technical directors, Jim Thornbury and Ed Burnhiem were NBC vets from radio who had learned the technical requirements and were in daytime Studio 5 until they retired. They were good men and we worked well together. Young Ed Siebenthal was the tech who with his aides kept the many projectors loaded and knew the number of the machines each film was loaded on. Sounds easy? It was bedlam. The technical director made the setting, but you, the director, was responsible that the settings were correct. In the darkened room to my right sat one of the finest announcers in the world waiting to read from his "Daily Book" what he is to say about the film we are showing but only on my cue. This is not a place for anyone with heart problems or someone who can't stand constant stress. You always know that in a dark room on another floor a member of BOC (Broadcast Operations Control) is sitting, stopwatch in hand to make a report if you are a 16th of a second early or late in getting a film on or off. Get on the BOC report and you can put your house up for sale and start packing.

The race starts at 2:30 AM when we use the hotline to New York to see if the associate director of the *Today Show* has any changes that are not on the show format he sent us yesterday. If I have a hot news story breaking in the west that has to run, I give him the film time, or if it is live from Hollywood, how much time our announcer will need. Any changes from New York I pass along to Ed in the film room. There are duplicate rolls of film for every single foot of film projected. Should something happen to the main projector the backup will come on at the exact spot where the trouble happened and the viewer will never know we had a mechanical or electric failure.

For every film a backup is loaded. The film crew works on a show from start to finish. Loading projects and giving the technical director the number of the machines every film is on. They will be busy loading and unloading film throughout the show plus being ready to handle any film not on our sheet that NBC might want to run. Fun-loving but dead serious about his work, Bill Celello is getting ready for video control.

Then at 2:59 our time we get braced for the action ahead. 3:00 AM and there is Dave Garroway, Helen O'Connell, Jack Lescoulie and the *Today Show* gang. When the show is over we're ready for the rebroadcast of the show for the West with many new commercials and updated news clips. When this rat race is over, it's breakfast time and that means great eats at the famous Brown Derby on Vine Street.

Studio 5 was not the only new thing in my life. Some dim wit at the University of Southern California thought it would be a great idea if people currently in the new TV industry would teach the final term to seniors who were considering careers in this new media. A great thought but four years late. It should have started when they were freshmen. By the time we reached them, they had four years of information from instructors who had never worked a single day of their lives in TV and taught from books written by men who also had never worked in the media. Top lighting directors, writers, set designers, make-up and wardrobe people were sent to the school. Mr. McCray sent me to teach producing and directing for TV. It was a disaster.

I had twenty-seven seniors with three very good students and one genius. The others didn't know where the lens was on a camera. Having been taught for four years they knew zero about the industry making them ready for a career that was the impossible dream. Betsy Simon could have been another Ida Lupino as a female director but love and marriage killed that. Gene Lilly became a news anchor and later a producer in the mid-west. Hadda D. was a CBS award-winning newscaster and was on the path for a career with that network. The genius was Lou Steinberg; a former Golden Glove boxer out of North Carolina who was married with a wife and child who showed from the first class that he was ready for a Hollywood career. Lou saw the big picture, while three other good students only saw the area they were focused on like a horse wearing blinders. The first night I told Lou he had all the tools to be special in the industry. He informed me that he could not afford to take the low starting pay that didn't come close to what he made selling used adding machines. I wasn't about to let this talent go down the drain. He had the needed desire and drives to make it in a very tough industry so I kept in touch after graduation and in time he made it and made it big.

In a few years we would go together to attempt to buy Columbia Pictures Studios at Sunset and Gower, but that's another story. At the end of the term, I met with Dean Harwood and told him that twenty-three members of the class failed and would not be graduating. For a moment I thought he would have a heart attack.

"Why are you failing them?" he asked in a strangled voice.

"Because it is better to fail in college than in life. College you can take over. You can't take your life over. Not a single one of these failed students can get a job in the TV industry, not even sweeping the floor in a station in Monnahan, Texas, or anywhere else in the United States." One student's father offered me one thousand dollars to pass his daughter. No sale. I wasn't invited back to USC nor were any other of the NBC instructors. However, the college learned and today they have a top-rated film school.

As you drive into LA on Route 10 you will see the home of Metro Media Studios. Lou Steinberg, one of my students, was one of the far-sighted executives that brought a TV series called "All in the Family" through the door and made Producer Norman Lear and the shows stars a "must see" for viewers from coast to coast.

I went back to Studio 5 without the added stress of USC where my first concern was breakfast after the *Today Show* was over for the day.

CHAPTER FORTY-TWO

The original Brown Derby restaurant was owned by entrepreneur Wilson Mizner located on Wilshire Boulevard near the Ambassador Hotel. During my years in Los Angeles, I may have eaten there four times at the most. For me the Brown Derby would always be the one located at 1628 North Vine Street in a building designed for movie legend Cecil B. DeMille just a block north of NBC and close to the intersection of Hollywood Boulevard and Vine St. in the heart of the film capital. I could write a book about the fabulous times I enjoyed there and the famous people who shared its wonderful food and décor. This was a place to live Hollywood history.

"The Derby" was owned by Robert H. Cobb and Herbest Somborg, an ex-husband of film star Gloria Swanson. It was here Clark Gable proposed to Carole Lombard and where multi-million dollar deals were made. Waiters connected telephones at your table while you munched on their exclusive thin slices of rye bread toasted with a topping of crisp cheese. On any given day you could be having lunch or dinner in the same room with studio moguls, famous producers, agents, directors and stars like Jack Lemon, Tyrone Power, Lana Turner, William Holden, Lucille Ball, Desi Arnez, Burt Lancaster or Lee Marvin. People like these were "regulars." The walls of the main dining room were decorated with caricatures of famous clients under the huge crystal chandeliers. As you entered the restaurant to the right was the Hall of Fame Record Room, for intimate dining that contained oil paintings of the top 200 recording artists painted by Nicholas Volpe, whose paintings of Academy Award-winning actors were displayed in the restaurant's "Academy Room."

Today, in most first-class restaurants you can enjoy a delicious "Cobb Salad" which was first made at "The Derby" by owner Bo Cobb. He created it from "leftovers" that he made for Sid Grauman, the owner of the famous Grauman's Chinese Theatre, where the great stars' handprints and footprints decorate the cement.

The Derby was the goal of engineer Hal Fransblau and myself every weekday morning after our early hours with the *Today Show*. Each day we walked up sun-drenched Vine Street. Out of the NBC lot, across Argyle with the bank on the corner, then Hatton's Grille, home of Hollywood's greatest ham sandwiches and the favorite watering hole for the Capital Records gang from their famous tower which was located on Vine Street north of Hollywood Boulevard. There was an upscale jewelry store, then The Derby, my all-time favorite restaurant.

Of all those mornings there are two I will never forget. One was the day Hal and I were on our way to breakfast and were passing the parking lot of the Hotel Plaza which was on the west side of Vine

Street. I grabbed Hal's arm and yelled "look." A young girl had just stepped into a window of a room on the 14th top floor of the Plaza. "She's going to jump!" The words were still leaving my mouth as she launched herself into thin air. I told Hal to stay where he was as her body crashed through the canvas top of a big Chrysler convertible parked in the lot.

I raced into the jewelry store, grabbed the phone on the counter and called the newsroom so they could get an exclusive, then dialed the police to report an apparent suicide. As I left the store, the manager looked like a fish gasping for air. I got Hal and we ran to the Chrysler to have a first look at the gruesome mess. There was no mess!

The young lady pressed into the soft leather seats of the car was crying and kept saying she didn't want to die. We assured her she was not going to die and kept her from trying to move until medical help arrived. In a couple of minutes, an ambulance and police car were on the scene to join the gathering crowd. Oh yes, NBC news with film cameras rolling had the exclusive. After carefully removing the young lady from the car, the medics found the only injury was a broken left wrist caused when she hit the center support that holds the convertible top. She was taken to the hospital to be checked out but before leaving we heard why she had rented the room and wanted to die. She put on her prettiest dress and jumped. She was just twenty years old and her twenty-four-year-old boyfriend had jilted her. Just unbelievable someone would try to end their life over something like this. Hal and I had a delayed breakfast.

The other morning I remember started at the guard's room that controlled who drove onto the

NBC lot. The guards had copies of the two major trade papers The *Hollywood Reporter* and *Daily Variety*. I was running late when I drove in that morning and passed on the papers. When I got them later, I read the headlines: "Director Alan Armer Leaves NBC for Contract with 20th Century Fox."

I was in Studio 5 and didn't see Alan to ask him about it, but this news was a real shock. Hal and I were talking about this as we reached the Derby door. I looked up to the corner of Hollywood Boulevard and saw Alan at the newsstand buying the trades. Telling Hal to go ahead, I set a track record getting to the newsstand and caught Alan as he was leaving. Out of breath I congratulated him on his great fortune and told him what a great motivation this news gave that perhaps one day I could make a jump like he had.

Somewhere along the line I realized he was giving me a very strange look and when I ran out of breath he said, "You really don't know do you?"

"Know what?" I asked.

"My uncle is a top executive at Fox. You know Walter Grauman don't you?"

"Sure, I know Walter. He's an NBC director but I have only met him a couple of times."

"Walter is my brother-in-law and he will be leaving for 20th Century Fox in three weeks. We worked at NBC to polish our crafts. We have always known we would go to 20th. I gotta run." He flagged a cab and was gone.

I had just had my first lesson in nepotism which is rampant in Hollywood. In this case these men rated at the top in their professions but in most cases this is not true. With a heavy heart, I joined Hal for breakfast.

Dixie was expecting again with an August date scheduled. The homefront was rocking along but always on eggshells. There was no way of knowing what would set her off. You could remark it was a lovely day and dishes would be flying and lamps overturned. You walked softy and always knew where the exits were. The only sure thing was that Kim was doing well in kindergarten; Sharon was growing into a beautiful little girl, and whenever Dixie might desire a toddy at dinner, the Vodka supply had dwindled or had been overstocked. There were always parcels from I. Magnin's or Neiman Marcus. Dixie had charge cards and would drive her Chevy convertible to Wilshire Boulevard to shop in Beverly Hills, leaving Sharon with a babysitter. She had made friends with a lady named Lois on another street in our development and they palled around. I realized we were on the fast track when the bills started coming in. It made me remember the great Studio One drama written by the supreme talent of Reginald Rose. In it an old man explained to a young writer how Hollywood works. "They pay you $5,000 a week and pretty soon you're spending $6,000 a week. Then they have you."

I never forgot music. It was a constant on my car radio, Elvis – "Heartbreak Hotel," Patti Page – "Allegheny Moon," Dean Martin – "Memories Are Made of This," Doris Day – "Que Sara, Sara," Guy Mitchell – "Singing the Blues," Vic Damone – "On The Street Where You Live," and Bing Crosby and Grace Kelly's duet of Cole Porter's "True Love." However, I was more impressed with the music that came from the NBC stages. The magnificent theme of Gordon McRae's show *Face to Face* in my book is one of the greatest love songs ever written. Coming from Dinah Shore's stage was the golden voice of Hawaii, Alfred Apaka, with the haunting "Legend of the Rain" and of course the theme "Anytime" was being belted out by Eddy Fisher on "Coke Time."

CHAPTER FORTY-THREE

Sunday morning, mid-March, sun shining in a blue sky and the four of us, Dixie, Kim, Baby Sharon and I, are having breakfast and gazing over the living room through the big glass window to the brand new Nash station wagon. Maroon exterior with tan interior and all the "bells and whistles" of that era was parked in our driveway. I had picked it up from the dealership late yesterday and the family had piled in and we had taken a drive to Thousand Oaks with a stop at an ice cream parlor for treats. After the drive, the kids were put to bed and Dixie and I caught a couple of hours of TV. She had a couple of Vodkas while I settled for a pastry and coffee.

We finished breakfast and everyone headed for the showers to get ready to go to church. The kids were dressed. I was ending my shower when Dixie jerked the shower door open yelling like a mad woman that she was going to kill me. With an insane gleam in her eyes and a broken milk bottle in one hand, she started slashing at my groin. Trying to get out of the shower, I put out my left arm to defend myself. The glass caught me high on my inner arm and then ripped the flesh down to my wrist. Blood spurted like a fountain, some of it on her.

As I staggered out of the shower she stepped back and in a little girl voice said, "You're hurt." I grabbed the dark jogging shorts I had worn the evening before and managed to get into them, wrapped a bath towel around my arm, and dashed barefoot out the door to my new car. The keys were in my shorts. I got the car started and headed for Emergency at the Van Nuys Hospital. The blood soaked the towel and ran over my seats and floor covering. Two blocks from the hospital I was blacking out and so dizzy I was unable to drive. There was a service station open and a couple of men working on a car. I pulled into the drive and got out of the car and called, "Help me." I collapsed on the pavement and didn't come to until I was on a table in Emergency and doctors were working on me. When I got out of my car I was holding my cut arm in the towel across my belly and blood was running down my legs. The men thought I had been shot and called the police who rushed me to the hospital. I had lost a lot of blood and needed a lot of stitches in my arm. Two uniformed cops wanted to know if I knew the person who had cut me. I couldn't turn in the mother of my children so I said, "I fell on a milk bottle and it broke."

I needed a blood transfusion, and while that was being done I went to sleep. When I awoke I was on a gurney and a plain-clothes detective was sitting beside me. He kept telling me I had never fallen on a milk bottle and that I knew who cut me. We went round and round over this subject. I had one hell of a headache. It was late afternoon. I wanted to get my car and go home. At last the doctor said I could leave. The credit card paid the hospital bill and the detective drove me back to the service station where my car was parked.

As he let me out he said, "I know you never fell on a bottle, and by not reporting who did it they will try again and next time it may be fatal."

I slowly drove home with the windows open as the smell of hot blood from the seat and the floor mats made me ill. The kids in play clothes ran to meet me asking how I hurt my bandaged arm. I forget what I told them but it wasn't the truth. Mama had told them I had been called into work and our friends at church had missed me.

I got to the bedroom and pulled the drapes and fell into bed and went out like a light. It was late when Dixie came in and asked if wanted a sandwich. Her friend Lois was there and they were going to have a bite. My arm was throbbing but I was hungry. Lois asked me what had happened to my bandaged arm and I looked at Dixie as I gave Lois my "fell on a milk bottle" yarn and Dixie smiled.

With the windows open I drove to work at 2 AM, then when I was through, I dropped the car off at the dealership and took a "loner." They worked long and hard but could never clean up the odor of blood, and by fall I took the loss and bought a new set of wheels. At last the stitches were removed leaving a long white scar that diminished with age.

Sean Patrick Cawley was born 8:02 PM on Thursday, August 23, l956, at St. Joseph's Hospital, Burbank, California. Dixie said her labor had started and I tried to rush her to the hospital but not until she stopped for a chocolate soda on the way. We did and exactly seven minutes after we walked through the hospital doors Sean was delivered. Healthy laughing and a little bundle of joy named for my TV mentor Sean Dillon.

A few days later, I had a new assignment. No, not live studio which I wanted, but Studio 5 during prime time. All those big shows with super expensive commercials as it was explained that NBC was losing $5,000 a week in mistakes made by the film studio and Thomas C. McCray was going to put a stop to the loss by moving me into the director's chair and young Bob Reis, who was considered to have the fastest hands of any technical director, would do the switching. Bob and I had never met but we became a great team in nothing flat. Our first week together we cut the loss from $5,000 to $1,000, and after the second week the losses were cut to zero and stayed that way. Although I was pleased with our success, I was afraid we would be in Studio 5 forever.

Despite my fear there was one great pleasure that I am certainly glad I had and that was working with the world's greatest announcing talents, and what a crew it was. Just look who was on the greatest announcer staff ever assembled. There was Don Stanley, John Storm, Frank Barton, Arch Presby and Vince Pelletier. I worked many times with all of them. Some I was really close to. Friends for life, such as Eddy King. Eddy had intended to be a concert pianist; instead, he enjoyed a fifty-six-year career as a radio and TV announcer. He started in radio in Portland, Oregon. He took his talents to San Francisco where he met and became friends with another young man trying to carve out a career named Jack Webb. Eddy was the sign-on announcer for NBC's, KPO. Jack was the sign-on announcer for ABC's KGO. NBC and ABC shared the same studios in the same building where the announce booths were back to back. It seems that Jack Webb, then married to singer Julie London, was always late so Eddy signed on for both stations and held the fort until Jack arrived.

When the famous radio and later TV series *Dragnet* hit the airways, it was the voice of Eddy King saying the opening lines. "The story you are about to hear is true. Only the names have been changed, to protect the innocent." *Dragnet* was just one of the many major productions Eddy was associated with. He was the only actor I ever worked with who could read a script through just once and then deliver it without a single error. Jimmy Wallington was the Dean of the announcing staff.

More than just a great announcer he was also an on-screen personality in such major shows as *The Alan Young Show*, *Fred Allen Show*, *The Martin and Lewis Show*, *The Colgate Comedy Hour* and *Texaco Town with Eddie Cantor*. He always announced the "Fireside Chats" of United States President Franklin Roosevelt. Jimmy found time to appear in several motion pictures. Jimmy and I became good friends. Jimmy was married four times and all four times he took his new brides to the same hotel suite at the Royal Hawaiian Hotel on the beach at Waikiki. When I would ask him why the same hotel, he would say, "Every woman's beauty fades in time but the beautiful view of Diamond Head from my suite's window stays the same." Jimmy has a star on the Hollywood Walk of Fame.

As a family we were very close to Don Rickles (not the comic), his wife Bernie and son Jay. At one time Don was the host of Ford News. Both Don and his lovely wife had great personalities and we shared many good times together. Their family suffered when their son Jay became a suicide.

Handsome John Lang had been in movies and it was said he had worked in a couple of films with Joan Crawford. Be that as it may, I worked with John when he was a part of the super NBC announcing staff. John was a great talker and we had many chats on every subject. John had a ranch near Lancaster, California. His hobby was collecting spiders and scorpions and he would bring them to work and play with them on the desk in the announce booth that was only lit by a pin spot on the Daily Book on his desk. I would watch him play with the varmints while he read from the Daily Book while on the air, stopping spiders and scorpions before they fell off the desk. The other announcers hated to go into the booth after John had been there for fear he had lost a black widow or a scorpion. Not to fear, John always got his little friends back in their jars to take home. Many times John was the sign-off man when the broadcast day ended and he informed viewers they had been watching "The National Broadcasting Company" just as it was written in his Daily Book.

It had been a long movie, and during the last reel he closed the book, turned off his pin spot, and informed me he was going to take a nap. This was nothing new and I would wake him when the film started its final five minutes. He went to sleep and I called him over the intercom that we were five minutes from touchdown so be ready. I was not alarmed his light was off and book closed. John had been doing sign-offs for almost thirty years, so he could do it in his sleep. I gave him a one-minute, then a thirty-second and a ten-second standby, cued the soft music that followed the film then hit the red button and John launched into his goodnight spiel and all went well until it was time to tell the world who they were watching.

John: "You have been watching..." (Pause)

John: "You have been watching...."

John cut his mike off and yelled on the intercom "What in the hell network are we watching?" Almost thirty years and he doesn't remember who pays him?

Bob: "The National Broadcasting Company."

John: "You have been watching the National Broadcasting Company."

Maybe that was the longest sign-off in network history. I can assure you that we never turned off the pin spot or closed the Daily Book until we were off the air. Not on my watch.

Many times the announcers had fifty-five minutes between announcements. If the booth was empty, we knew where to find them. Across from the entrance to NBC parking area was a dark little bar called "The Spotlight." The walls were decorated with 8 x 10 publicity pictures of our announcer staff. We had a hotline to the bar so we could give ten-minute warnings to get back and in the booth. God must love these guys because it was a miracle that no one ever got hit as they zig-zagged across a very busy Vine Street.

We bought a new house. A rambling ranch-style home in Van Nuys that had a big tree that Sharon and

Kim loved to climb. Our new neighbors had a swimming pool where the kids learned to swim. At first little Sean would run out on the diving board and go off head-first right to the bottom of the pool. It kept me busy diving in and pulling him out. In time, he developed into an excellent swimmer. The kids called this residence "Papa's House" and it is here that Sharon's cute little Siamese kitten, Moon Flower, became part of the family.

Just across the street was Panorama City, a place where I was to make a good and valued friend. This good friend was an actor that millions of people have seen in movies and TV around the world. He is best remembered in the role of "Master Kan" in the hit TV series *Kung Fu*. His name, Philip Ahn, and we didn't meet on a stage but at his beautiful Moongate Restaurant which he owned in Panorama City that served the best Chinese food in Southern California. Philip was a Korean-American who was the first Asian American actor to receive a star on the Hollywood Walk of Fame. Philip was highly educated and very bright. A delightful man to know. In the 1930's he had worked in films starring Bing Crosby, Shirley Temple and Anna Mae Wong. During World War II he played many Japanese villains often informing actors playing captured US troops, "I was educated at UCLA." In the real world, he was a graduate of USC. Philip and his two siblings served in the armed services during the war. Back to films he worked in a variety of good pictures including "Love Is A Many Splendored Thing" with William Holden and Jennifer Jones, "Around The World in Eighty Days," "Paradise Hawaiian Style" with Elvis Presley, and "Battle Hymn" with Rock Hudson. TV guest appearances included *M.A.S.H.*, *Hawaii Five-O*, *Bonanza*, and *Hawaiian Eye*, plus TV movies. The kids loved the Moongate menu so we ate dinner there many, many times and I remember quiet afternoons when the two of us would talk. Philip Ahn was a very special man.

CHAPTER FORTY-FOUR

Sunday evening January 22, 1956, we were very busy feeding inserts into the *Steve Allen Show* in New York from film Studio 5 in Hollywood. The Red Hotline phone rang. Jimmy Wallington had been on his way home from a weekend trip in San Diego when he saw there had been a train wreck on the Santa Fe Railroad. As soon as he could find a phone booth he had called to give me the location which was just southwest of Boyle Heights in South Los Angeles. There were deaths and many injuries and this would be a major story for the *Today Show* in the morning if we could get some video. If I could reach network news on a Sunday which was very slim with all the executives out of town every weekend.

Studio 5 was at max pressure with all the commercials, station breaks and regional feeds. We resembled the deck of a battleship in combat. I didn't want to lose a major news story and I was not about to interrupt the *Allen Show* with a news bulletin.

At that moment, one of our two landline phones rang and a voice was screaming. "What the hell is going on, you stupid SOB. There's a major train wreck and you don't have NBC news on it." A wave of profanity followed and I hung up and started working the phones in an attempt to find someone from network news. The phone rang again and the same screaming voice was demanding I get a news crew to the scene of the wreck. Screaming more profanity and once again I hung up. We were coming up to more commercials and the station break and about to go into action when I reached a news executive just back from Palms Springs who rolled remote gear and crew just as we started into the mid program break. When it was over we set back in our leather chairs and breathed deeply.

Then the Red phone rang and the screaming voice followed. "This is Gordon Wyle and I want your name."

I held the phone from my ear and spoke to Jim Thornberry my technical director. "The crazy SOB is back. Say's he's Gordon Wyle and he wants my name."

Jim turned pale and he motioned me to cover the mouthpiece. "He's an NBC Vice President," he whispered.

I resumed my conversation. "Mr. Wyle, what can I do for you?"

His voice was ice cold. "I want your name." He got it plus the fact a crew was now gathering the full story of the *Today Show* that would air in six hours. He told me he would see me and I was sure he would.

After the *Allen Show*, I managed to reach Jim Damon who had brought me into the company and gave him the whole story. Jim chuckled and told me to stay calm. Easy to say but not so easy to do.

After work I went down to the wreck site to see

the grisly scene and catch up with the news crew. The site was Redondo Junction near Washington Boulevard and the Los Angeles river. Thirty people were killed and more than 117 were injured. It turned out to be the worst train wreck in the city's history. After months of investigation, it was determined that the train went into the curve at Redondo Junction at a high speed, well above the posted speed limit, with deadly results.

I had crawled into one of the overturned passenger cars when I heard the voice of doom ask, "Which one is Cawley?" Jim Damon then introduced me to VP Gordon Wyle whose burning eyes measured me like a funeral director would measure a corpse for a coffin. I did not sleep well and the Studio 5 crew had a pool going as to what day I would be fired.

One afternoon, nine days after the train wreck, I drove into the parking lot and a smiling security guard handed me that day's trade papers. On both the *Hollywood Reporter* and *Daily Variety* the headlines exploded: "NBC VP Gordon Wyle Fired." I forget why he was fired but he was gone. The crew in Studio 5 had made a slight addition to the trades. There the headlines had been changed to read "Cawley got Wyle fired at NBC. You may be next."

Although a great Brown Derby fan, I spent a lot of time enjoying meals and libations at the famous Nickodell's Restaurant located at the junction of Argyle and Selma Avenues just a few short steps from the front door of NBC's offices. This was the only watering hole where I ran a tab. Just sign for anything and the bill would arrive the first of each month. CBS-TV was just a couple of blocks south of

NBC and there were always CBS personnel around. It was there I was introduced to a man who became a friend. One of the most remarkable men I have ever known. Graduate of Princeton where he was a football star who rose to the rank of Major in the Army Air Force in World War II and taught actor Jimmy Stewart how to fly military aircraft. James T. Aubrey was a handsome six-foot-two with a million-dollar smile and flashing blue eyes. Always dressed as though he had just stepped off the pages of Esquire he was CBS-TV's number-one salesman on the west coast. Within a short space of time he was promoted to manager of all CBS television network programs based in California. This opened the gates for Jim to become the greatest management executive in the history of the entertainment industry. Later Jim would become president of CBS Television Network and brought TV programs that would dominate the industry. He would later save Kirk Kerkorian's MGM movie studio when he erased their heavy debts and created huge profits. Author Jacqueline Susann used Aubrey as the model for her bestselling novel *The Love Machine*. Years later, I would have the pleasure of working with Jim on a motion picture project.

At last I was moving to live production but before leaving Studio 5 there would be one more tragic event burned into my memory.

Sunday, June 30, 1956, I was reading the teletype and saw that a TWA Super Constellation and a United Airlines DC7 had both failed to fly over their checkpoints and were considered missing. Was NBC News aware of this? I doubted it as no news people worked on Sunday, but before I would try to locate a news person, I wanted to check this report with someone who had been an airline pilot.

I called the home number of Robert "Doc" Livingston, an NBC director who had flown for Flying Tigers Airlines as a Captain. Doc was home and after I read the message to him he said they were both down in Grand Canyon. Calling the newsroom I got a lucky break when Dexter Alley picked up. Dexter Alley was a superb news cameraman. His father was the world-renowned cameraman who for years had thrilled millions with Fox Movietone News and Dexter was looking to set new records. I brought him up to speed on the teletype and Doc's report and reminded him we could scoop all the other networks by having film to feed to the *Today Show*. He gave me the home number of Rafe Newhouse and said to tell Rafe what we had and to meet him in the newsroom in about four hours ready to develop film, edit it so it would be ready to feed New York at 3 AM Pacific Standard Time for *Today*. He told me he was headed for Grand Canyon. I called Rafe and gave him Dexter's message. I asked Eddy King, our booth announcer, to stay over to do the voice on what would be our network feed. After sign-off, we trudged to the newsroom. Rafe was there with some techs. The film had been developed, printed, and they were editing. Rafe had newsmen on their way to LAX to get the back story.

As I got it in bits and pieces from Dexter, he had hired a helicopter pilot, his aircraft and an assistant paying out of his own pocket, and flew to Grand Canyon. After spotting the wreckage of both planes a little more than a mile apart Dexter, with a rope tied around his waist shot fantastic footage. The light was starting to cause shadows deep in the canyon where the remains of the crashed and burned wreckage of the TWA aircraft rested, so Dexter filmed this first, then the smashed remains of the United DC7, which crashed into a high butte. There were no survivors. 128 people had lost their lives.

It didn't take long to figure out how this tragic event had happened. Both aircraft departed Los Angeles International Airport within three minutes of each other. The TWA Super Constellation, the "Star of the Seine" carried a crew of six and sixty-four passengers. Veteran pilot Captain Jack Gandy at the controls, destination Kansas City. The flight was to fly at 19,000 feet with a speed of 310 MPH. United Airlines DC7 "City of Vancouver" with a crew of five and fifty-three passengers had veteran pilot Captain Robert Shirley, whose flight plan was to fly at an altitude of 21,000 feet at a speed of 330 MPH. destination was Chicago.

It didn't take a rocket scientist to see that the two flight plans allowed for very little change. Somewhere over Grand Canyon the United flight flying at a faster speed would fly over the TWV plane. Flight control should have kept sharper notice of both flights until they had safely passed their checkpoints. The controller was aware that if everything went as planned the two flights would cross paths with only 2,000 feet difference as they flew over the Painted Desert. Thunder clouds were building up over Northern Arizona as the TWA flight drew near. Captain Gandy requested ground control to be allowed to change his altitude from 19,000 to 21,000 feet. The controller refused the change and told him "You have United Flight 718 crossing and his altitude is 21,000 feet."

Then two decisions that would prove fatal were made. Captain Gandy requested the controller for permission to fly 1,000 feet on top of the bad weather on a seen-or-be-seen basis. Knowing the United flight was in the area, the controller should have refused the request. Airliners fly through turbulence every day. Yes, it's a little bumpy for passengers but no big thing. TWA should have held its altitude until the United flight passed its checkpoint. The controller gave the okay to change altitude and TWA came up out of the clouds right under the path of the United flight, who never saw them.

The United DC7's left wing struck the TWA tail as the United DC7 slid along the fuselage of the TWA plane. The DC7's propellers ripped open the rear cabin of the Super Constellation and severed the tail section sending the TWA plane into a four-mile vertical dive to the floor of the canyon in a fiery crash. The United DC7's Captain Robert Shirley still hoped for a safe landing. His outer left wing panel was gone and he still had lift but not enough. The Salt Lake Control Tower heard him say, "We're going in," prior to the plane crashing at the top of an 800 sheer cliff called Chuar Butte. Most of the wreckage remains on the rocky crags.

It is interesting to note that a Salt Lake City controller knew both planes were at 21,000 feet and would cross each other's path over the Painted Desert at the same moment, but he did not advise either plane. One hundred twenty-eight lives were lost in an accident that didn't have to happen. In those years airliners did not have black boxes like they carry today. Someone from NBC news got copies of the two pilot's final communications and I went with "Doc"

Livingston to hear the replay. It was horrific. The screams of passengers as they went on the four-mile drop to death. The two Captains who never lost their cool control and tried to fly their aircraft at the end told their families goodbye. That tape vanished but I will never forget it.

There are two memorial sites created for the crews and passengers. TWA arranged a burial site at the Citizens Cemetery at Flagstaff, Arizona. Many of the victims of the United Airliner are buried in Grand Canyon National Park.

CHAPTER FORTY-FIVE

At last! Live studio shows and my first director's assignment was NBC's best children's program *Faith of Our Children* hosted by super film star, Eleanor Powell. I would direct 156 shows in the series before it ended its run. The show aired on Sundays and we videotaped the show during the week. We would win seven Emmy Awards before the series had its final curtain. Eleanor was a pure joy to work with and we established a friendship that lasted until her death in 1982. Ellie was the world's greatest female tap dancer and her tap dance with Fred Astaire to Cole Porter's "Begin the Beguine" in the film *Broadway Melody of 1940* is the greatest tap dance ever filmed. You can still get it on DVD and be amazed!

Fred Astaire told the world that Ellie was his equal as a tap dancer. Although she appeared tall on the screen Eleanor was only 5'5¼". She had starred on Broadway before coming to Hollywood at the age of eighteen as a leggy, shapely dancer with exuberance for her work. She shot to stardom during the golden years of MGM musicals. Ellie retired from films following her 1943 marriage to actor Glenn Ford. She made a highly successful tour of Las Vegas and New York nightclubs and showrooms before going into complete retirement. Later she was asked to host the TV series *Faith of Our Children,* a non-denominational religious program that featured guest stars from sports and films plus around eight to ten young children each episode. The series was produced by Clifton Moore one of the nicest guys in the business. The kids on the show were not actors but just regular kids. Ellie's son Peter, a very well-mannered young man was often one of the kids.

With all children, you never know what will become of them as teenagers or adults. One cute little boy who appeared on several shows was a little curly-headed guy from Beverly Hills named Jackie Wrangler. Bright and funny he often sat by my daughter Sharon who was part of several shows. We would never have guessed that Jackie would grow up to be a superstar and producer of porn movies known as Jack "Heavy Equipment" Wrangler. He was the star of the porn blockbuster *The Devil in Miss Jones*. I used to cringe when during an interview Jack would always say he got his start on NBC's *Faith of Our Children*.

I felt very sorry for Ellie because of her home life. According to the fan magazines, her marriage was made in heaven. Not so, Glenn Ford was a very sadistic husband. They had an intercom in their home and when Glenn would call Ellie she had seconds to get where he was or be beaten. Her arms were always black and blue and her body ached from his punches. I asked her why she didn't divorce him and her reply was, "Every boy needs his father, but once Peter is eighteen I'm gone." She stuck it out and Peter grew up to be a fine singer and actor. Despite her home life, we really enjoyed working together.

My next major contract was with Fred Rice, a VP at Capitol Records, who produced a half-hour musical series called *Hollywood Record Room,* which was a great promotional tool for the record company as it used only Capitol artists. Fred, a super creative guy who always came up with the next great thing before anyone else thought about it had laid-back rehearsals. It was like a big family get-together with lots of laughs and hijinks. I remember one show had Ernie Ford, Ray Anthony and other artists when Nat Cole arrived wearing the most beautiful seersucker jacket I had ever seen. There was not a single wrinkle in it.

I said, "Wow, Nat, what a great jacket, where did you get the threads in town." I realized he was talking about Cy Devore, the tailor to the stars whose shop on Vine was across the street from NBC. I had a couple of sports jackets, slacks and suits that Cy had done for me. Nat's jacket was lined and was the ultimate. The next day I had Cy measure me for a jacket like Nat's.

The next week when Nat arrives at rehearsal he saw me wearing a jacket like his. "Hey man, you've got my jacket."

"I had to see Cy, I love the lining."

Nat growled through rehearsal. Next week he arrived to see that both Ray Anthony and I were in seersucker. That did it. Nat never wore his jacket again.

The remaining years at NBC would evolve into a whirling kaleidoscope of colors making memories that would last forever. I met Fran Scott who had been a key member of the famous vocal group The Modernaires who sang "Chattanooga Choo Choo" with Tex Beneke on the Glenn Miller recording of this song which was the very first to be certified gold! Good-looking and a talented trombonist, singer and arranger he had formed a vocal group called The Fran Scott Singers to record musical jingles which were very much in style in that era. Fran lived close to me and we would kick around ideas of things we might do to build our careers upward and onward. I said I would speak to the powers and see if we could get the backing for a TV special. Just when I thought all my nights would be free, Tom McCray informed me that I would be teaching producing, directing, and writing from 7pm to 9pm on Mondays at Columbia College on West Seventh Street. At least all the instructors would be professionals from CBS, ABC, and major advertising agencies. NBC would be represented by Allan Hanson, director credits included *Matinee Theater* and *Ellery Queen*, lighting director Boris Issacson and myself. The school Dean Ernie Baumeister was very pleasant and their equipment in both studios and control rooms was first rate. The class was large with many foreign students.

By the third class I knew that few if any of them would have a career in the industry. There was one exception and that one exception is what makes instructing worthwhile. This dedicated young man was native of Medford, Oregon, where he had been a major league prospect in baseball but an auto accident ended that dream. He was married with a couple of kids pumping gas for a living and wanted to be a TV director more than anything in the world. Watching him work, I knew that at the very best he would wind up as a one-camera director at a tiny TV operation eating his heart out for what might have been. I realized that he was a creative genius and had every talent a truly great producer needs and most of all, he saw the big picture, not with the blunders that so many directors wear.

He worked so hard and wanted it so bad I stepped in to be a dream maker. I asked Conrad Holzgang to stay after class. I don't sugarcoat things. If you're bad you're bad. If you have very little talent, there's the door. He was very nervous when I told him I was going to fail him. Panic set in. He told me he had to pass. I told him he was a one-camera director and that's all he would ever be, however, if he gave me his word he would forget about directing and concentrate on producing I would give him a passing grade and would find a job for him at NBC. Instead of looking through the fence, he would be inside where the sky was the limit. I also told him I felt he could be the best TV producer this town had ever seen. He had the drive and the smarts to make it. So, I asked him to think over my offer. It's tough when you kill someone's dream but better to kill it than let them slowly die. A week later, Conrad told me he would accept my offer and a short while later he moved into his new job in the NBC mail room where he would meet every producer on the lot. I arranged for him to have a gold card so he could visit even closed sets to observe producers at work.

Weekends with the kids at Zuma beach were special. They loved the ocean. Son Kim entered the All San Fernando Valley Track meet and won more ribbons than any other trackman in the meet. Kim was also a choir boy at Saint Marks and Sharon and Sean were wearing out the tree at "Papa's House." We got word that my mother would spend the holidays with us and that she was having my piano shipped to Sharon as part of her Christmas gift.

Once in a while, I would find a matchbook cover from a place I had never been. I asked Dixie about it and she said the owners of these places put their matches all over town for the publicity. Really? I discovered the oldest restaurant in Hollywood right on Hollywood Boulevard near Vine. Musso & Frank Grill where once two young men, Clark Gable and Gilbert Roland, who dreamed of being movie actors, stood outside gazing at chickens roasting on the revolving spits in the window. They had no money, ah, but one day when they were famous...and their dreams would come true. Musso & Frank always served fabulous brains and eggs, a dish I had not had since leaving home. Through the years they got a great deal of my business.

I noticed that when directors would hang their jackets up, they left the label out that read "Tailored by Cy Devote." I also was clued in that well-dressed directors had their hair cut by "Little Joe" in his shop in a high rise on Wilshire Boulevard in Beverly Hills. This was before stylists came on the scene and a haircut was a thing of beauty. I became a client of "Little Joe" and was sold when I visited his shop and found Tony Curtis, Kirk Douglas and Burt Lancaster in the waiting room and in nothing flat we were talking like old friends. A haircut was $75.00 dollars plus tip. Worth every penny and a lot cheaper than what my wife paid at her hair salon.

Being based in Studio F, I was near the loading dock hangout and closer still to the large marble rotunda that led to the audience studios that fronted on Sunset Boulevard. Every once in a while Eddie Fisher would join the group outside but his hectic non-aired performances came after his *Coke Time* show and would involve his wife Debbie Reynolds. I know the media called them America's sweethearts but the media didn't see or hear them after Eddie's shows. The makeup room serving Studio F was just a few steps from the rotunda that led to the studio where Eddie worked his magic on teenage girls.

The Fisher/Reynolds scene was always about the same thing. Debbie in no uncertain terms wanted Eddie to come home and he wasn't coming. He would tell her he was going to see some girls at the beach and relax and for her to go home. All of us had heard profanity but nothing like what came out of Debbie's mouth. What a collection of four-letter words she would scream. The results were always the same. Eddie pushed her away and went to a car on the lot with some of his musicians inside and they went to the beach and the girls. Debbie went home alone. So much for "America's sweethearts." Eddie and Debbie were not alone for using the rotunda for private matters. There was the night a security officer had to pull a screaming June Allyson off her husband, actor singer/director, Dick Powell, before she destroyed his face with her long fingernails.

Cleve Herman may have had only one eye but he was a top-level interviewer, but on this evening fate/destiny or whatever you want to call it stepped in to create a once-in-a-lifetime TV memory. We were one of several NBC production units covering famous movie stars prior to the telecast of an Academy Awards show. The men doing the interviews drew lots. Cleve Herman was the lucky guy who would do his thing with the breathtaking star, Kim Novak, at

Mike Romanoff's famous dining establishment. The setting was perfect. Kim was a beautiful vision in her designer strapless dress and Cleve in his dark suit and tie. They chatted like old friends as we waited for the cue for this interview to start. Just remember, this was live television.

At last we were on the air and the dialogue between Kim and Cleve was sparkling. All too soon we were down to the final minute of our segment. Cleve led into his close-up, as he turned away from Kim and faced the audience, with his bad eye covered by his now famous black patch and his good eye twinkling and big smile lighting up his features. After a few short words he quickly turned back to face Kim. At that instant, she lost the top of her dress and one of her now naked full white breasts with its pink nipple was in Cleve's good eye. Cleve came unglued and his few mumbled remarks were lost. The camera was close up on Kim as she smiled, adjusted the top of her dress and thanked Cleve for the lovely interview. Alas, being live TV there are no copies of that moment.

Helen O'Connell, one of two superstar musical acts presented to the world from Lima, Ohio (the other being the fabulous Mills Brothers) left her talk assignment with the *Today Show* to return to her musical roots with a twice-weekly *Helen O'Connell Show* on NBC from Sunset and Vine. She had joined the Jimmy Dorsey orchestra during the 40s, made musical recording history paired with Bob Eberly on such tunes as "Green Eyes," "Tangerine," "Yours" and "Amapola." Bob would sing the first chorus in his romantic baritone, and then a short instrumental break and Helen would do the last chorus up-tempo and swinging. Their recordings sold in the millions. She was the darling of the GIs during World War II. She retired in 1943 after her first marriage.

When it ended in 1951 she returned to show biz with several solo hit records in addition to many TV guest appearances. She teamed with Bob Eberly, plus Ray Anthony's orchestra on *TV's Top Tunes* on CBS-TV. She was also the featured vocalist on *The Russ Morgan Show* on CBS-TV. Helen's dressing room was just four doors down from the makeup room by Studio F where we used to have coffee and chat. It was there I met her best friend, movie star, Joanne Dru. Her real name was Joan LaCock. She was from Logan, West Virginia and had a brother named Peter Marshall, a fine singer, actor and host who was slowly making a climb to TV stardom. Joanne started her career in New York as a model. She was selected by Al Jolson for the cast of his Broadway show *Hold on to Your Hats*. Hollywood saw her, and as they say the rest is history. Sometimes I wonder what it is with cameras. You saw her beauty in such top grossing films as Howard Hawks' *Red River* with John Wayne and Montgomery Clift, John Ford's *She Wore a Yellow Ribbon* again with John Wayne, the Academy Award Winner, *All The King's Men* with Broderick Crawford and John Ireland, *The Pride of St. Louis* co-starring with Dan Dailey, *Thunder Bay* with Jimmy Stewart, and *3 Ring Circus* with Dean Martin and Jerry Lewis. She was very pretty in all these films and on TV, but in-person her beauty was 500% more than on films or video. For example, years later I would see Raquel Welch every day and in-person, you wouldn't look at her twice, but on the screen... that was something else. I'm glad

I got to spend some time with Joanne. She had a great personality and was fun.

Color came to NBC and the large RCA cameras arrived. It was love at first sight for the cameramen. An hour before telecasting started, four beautiful, long-legged redheads wearing shorts in various colors of the rainbow, would sit on high stools and the engineers would line up the color components in all four cameras in the various studios. These guys were really happy. Then of course the techies ruined it when they figured out how to line the cameras up electronically. These guys preferred robots to real live girls.

I had been hot to direct and I got my wish. Some programs I directed on a full-time basis just for short periods and a variety of commercials. Guys left NBC to work as directors for advertising agencies and packagers of game shows for a great deal of money and I had offers but had no interest. I was "the" director of *World News Tonight* with a real icon in news broadcasting, Elmer Peterson. As a very young news hawk, he made radio history during the Spanish Civil War lying on a raft in a river when he did a "play by play" of the fighting between the Nationalists and Republican forces as the bullets from both sides whistled over his prostrate form. As a mature young man, he was a key part of the team of NBC war correspondents during World War II, and what a team it was. In addition to Elmer, there were Merrill Mueller, John MacVain and Morgan Beatty. You can still hear many of "Elmer Peterson's Comments from London" on historical CDs. Elmer was from the old school. He studied the reports, then wrote his own news show. No "managed" news like we saw creeping into newscasts from various channels. "World News Tonight" was the real thing and for me a great honor to direct such a legend.

As members of the Director's Guild of America, we were young and the majority with families. We sought to obtain life insurance as a group but were rejected by all the insurance companies. We felt Lloyd's of London was the answer so we asked them to do some research into our profession then send a rep to meet with us and enable us to obtain life insurance. The rep came and delivered the shock of our young lives. Lloyd's would not insure us under any circumstances. Research showed that the life span expectancy of anyone who directed "live" television was twenty-eight years old. The pressure of a job where one small error could end your career and your earning power, the overall stress of the job made us uninsurable. Like the rest of my fellow directors, I laughed and told the Lloyd's rep he was crazy. I wasn't laughing when a week later an LA-based director who worked for another company died of a heart attack in the control room while directing a prime-time show. He was twenty-four years old. Two weeks later a director dropped dead of a heart attack. He was twenty-eight and left a wife and four children. It puzzled me. I always liked the pressure. All the elements stretched to the maximum like a rubber band pulled to the breaking point. I liked crisis and did my best work under these conditions. I was aware that people were leaving the industry due to stress. Others stayed in the business but with advertising agencies, where doing commercials was a long drawn out and boring process. I liked being where the action was.

My work caught the eye of Cal Phillips of J.

Walter Thompson, the fourth-largest advertising agency network in the world. They bought lots of air time for their clients on NBC and they shot commercials for Alka Seltzer and Allstate at NBC. Cal Phillips requested that I direct their spots. The top talent for both commercials was Ed Rhymers. Cal would arrive with four or five young associates and hold a production meeting with the technical director and audio and video engineers scheduled for that day; Lonnie Stucky, our lighting director, cool and calm Fred Heglund who had won a Peabody Award with NBC Radio, as our stage manager, plus two stage hands, and the set director, Curt Nations, to discuss the position and the lighting for the lone bottle of Alka Seltzer. One thing was a certainty. It would be on a five-foot high pedestal that would be draped in black velvet. The lighting and the camera used on the bottle, its angles and the needed light of same was always open for discussion. Ed would stand close to the bottle and toward the end of the spot, as written, I would start a five-second roll of the film provided by the agency. Then take it showing the figure of "Speedy Alka Seltzer" flying over the bottle while Ed, now off camera ended his pitch. Sounds simple, right?

It would take at least six to eight hours to get it to the standards the agency and the client demanded. Turn the bottle a sixteenth of an inch right, relight it. All the agency suits would debate. Then we would turn the bottle left, relight and another long debate, over and over staging it. The arrival of video tape recording had replaced the filming of many commercials. This would go on until lunch break then we'd come back and do it all over again. After all parties were happy, we started the blending of "Speedy Alka

Seltzer" and the bottle. Once the videotape engineer was ready to work with us and the film was ready to roll, we entered our final phase. Drop the film over the bottle. Too high, too low, late coming in, leaving too early, Ed not in sync with "Speedy" and lots of debates.

At last it was declared that we had a winner. The technical director was ready to cry. The audio engineer was pulling out his hair and the lighting director wondered if he could kill the agency guys and beat the rap with a plea of temporary insanity. I was just bored. Although Ed Rhymers was getting a big fee for his efforts, he needed a handful of pain pills for his aching head. When we finished the agency people glowed with happiness and I needed a Jack and Water at Nickodells. The following day we were all back together for the Allstate session. Ed Rhymers was the talent and he always was perfect with his lines but it was the closing that made for a long day. You know the close. "You're in good hands with Allstate." When the pitchman utters that phrase he puts his hands together. We would repeat this over and over. No one could agree if the hands were together the way the client liked. Did Ed rush or was he late with his hands? We would break for lunch then come back and repeat, and repeat, and repeat, and hours later, frazzled and worn, we would receive the blessing of the agency for the great job we had done. Those evenings in LA there were some unhappy wives when their beloved husbands snapped at them, the children, the dog and even the cat. It was just the end of a day making commercials. I liked Cal, he was a special guy and so were his disciples.

Several times he told me I had a job waiting for

me at J. Walter far from the stress and tension of doing shows. If I would have taken that offer I would have needed a padded cell within a month. Another agency wanted my tender touch doing commercials, for Pabst Blue Ribbon Beer. The stage crew loved doing this spot because we threw out gallons of cold beer that they could drink. The longer we shot the happier they became. Once again it looked simple but you're wrong. The closing was the mountain to be climbed. The pitch about this wonderful drink was perfect, then in close-up a delicate female hand with a perfect manicure took a tall bottle of Pabst off the table. With the label front and center, slowly pouring the beer into the stein until it overflowed and the beer and foam ran down the side of the stein and onto the red and white tablecloth.

Trying to get beer to spill out and onto the cloth like the client wanted could require a hundred or more takes. The unused cold beer goes into a big tub. The tablecloth tossed into a big laundry bag. The wet stein is removed and the table cleaned. The empty bottle thrown in a large container, a fresh cloth and glass, (they have brought over one hundred cloths and polished steins) sat on a new table with a cold bottle and we are ready for another take. This spot was always taped late in the evening which was lucky for the stage crew.

I let it be known I had all the commercials I wanted. I had these three major clients, then one day I was notified that we had an emergency and the director who did this client's work was on vacation. The Borax people were unhappy with the way a box of Borax had been shot and they needed it replaced, a five-second freeze frame of just the box and it would be used on a prime-time show this evening. It would require a stand with a blue velvet cover to sit on. I would have a lighting director, one stagehand, a videotape engineer, and a technical director. I would not need a stage manager as this required no audio and would be shot in an insert studio with one camera, and I let the agency man know when the tape was rolling as I would be beside the camera and not in the control room. A monitor would be provided so the agency man could see what we shot. Bob Jones, the technical director, was good but he had never been assigned to work commercials so he had no idea how agencies worked but this was only a five-second spot.

The agency guy arrived with the Borax box and it took a half hour to get it lit to his satisfaction as he kept changing the box position. At last we were ready to tape the five seconds freeze frame. We did a dry run for the agent and he loved what he saw on the monitor. I told Bob to roll tape and get speed. He told me when we were ready and I called for the take. Five seconds later, we had it and I told the client we had it. Bob was standing up in the control room taking off his headset when this agency clown told me to take the box at a different angle. I told Bob to sit down to keep the first take and keep the tape engineer on standby until I released him. We would take one more. The box was turned, re-lit and we took take number two.

For the next half hour this jerk had us re-lighting and re-shooting until we had eleven five-second takes of the box. The agency guy said he needed another take. The lighting director was up on the ladder changing the lights when Bob came roaring out of the control room. He hit the agency guy with a bone-crushing right hand and left the studio. The agency guy was in a bad way. I got him seated and a couple paper cups of water. After a while he went to see Tom McCray and I got a call to hold the tape with all the takes for another agency guy on his way to the studio. The new guy showed up and viewed all the takes. You guessed it, he selected take number one. Although NABET, the engineers union is very strong they were unable to save Bob's job. No matter what, the client or their agency is always right.

Back to work I was the director of a new show. *Feitelson on Art* hosted by noted art critic scholar, teacher, lecturer, collector and pioneer of modern art, Lorser Feitelson. This brilliant, brilliant man was one of the founding fathers of "Hard Edge" painting. His paintings, exhibited worldwide were dazzling exhibitions. He made a profound contribution to the development of American abstract painting. Lorser had the skills to make painting interesting to non-painters or collectors. I enjoyed directing his series and from the fan mail received I know it was a favorite of the general public.

CHAPTER FORTY-SIX

The powers gave me the needed backing, studio crew and limited sets to see what I could do as a producer-director-writer of a half-hour musical special. I could select a small number of musicians from the NBC payroll. That was great by me and the first one selected was Hall of Fame jazz trumpeter Ziggy Elman. I dreamed of Ziggy doing his world-famous "An the Angels Sing" in Fralich style just as he had done on his recording with Benny Goodman's orchestra. Overjoyed I told the family I had landed Ziggy for my show. Fate had other ideas.

The following morning I was coming up to the intersection of Victory and Van Nuys Boulevards when I heard a blazing rendition of "An the Angels Sing" being played Fralich style. Like everyone I slowed in traffic to see what was going on. There was Ziggy Elman, stark naked except for his shoes blowing a chorus that Gabriel could hear up in heaven. The police took him away. He had suffered a mental breakdown. In a few months, he recovered and rejoined the NBC orchestra but much too late for my show. Ray Lynn who had been a trumpet star of the Artie Shaw orchestra was my replacement for Ziggy.

This incident was one of many headaches given to Ralph Armbruster the director of the NBC orchestra but the one that became a legend was the one that concerned another trumpet player, Wingy Manone. Although he had only one arm he had become an icon as a jazz player and Ralph admired his work. He called Wingy at his Chicago home and offered him the jazz chair with NBC. Wingy was delighted and received a check for his flight and other expenses to come to Hollywood plus a two-week union salary should things not work out plus airfare back to Chicago. Wingy skipped the plane ride and took a bus arriving later than expected. A rehearsal was set, all the music passed out and the downbeat given. The full orchestra responded then dropped out for Wingy's solo. Not a sound came out. Ralph asked Wingy what was going on and Wingy told him he couldn't read music. Pretty tough when you can't read music in a band.

There are exceptions, of course. Buddy Rich, a Hall of Fame drummer, couldn't read a note. Neither could Frank Sinatra and many members of Duke Ellington's famous orchestra have this problem but this was NBC and you had to read. Ralph was really broken up. He loved Wingy's style of playing so he sent him home with financing to get a teacher, learn how to read, call him, and the jazz chair would be his. About seven months later Wingy called Ralph telling him he knew how to read and was ready to join the NBC orchestra. Once again Ralph sent the money for the flight and expenses plus the same contract as before. Wingy took the bus. Although put out by the late arrival, a rehearsal was called, again the band came on full and then dropped out for Wingy's solo. The orchestra members leaned forward, Ralph cued his trumpet player but nothing came out. Frustrated and out of sorts Ralph asked Wingy what was the problem since he had said he had learned to read.

Wingy's answer became a standard joke in the music business. "You know Ralph it's amazing what you forget on a bus ride from Chicago." You can be sure we never mentioned Wingy's name anywhere near Ralph who helped me put an all-star group together for my show. Jack Sperling, drums; Ray Lynn, trumpet; Tony Rizzi, guitar; and musical director and pianist Al Pelligrini.

Everything would be played with "head" arrangements, no music, and these cool cats could handle anything. The show would be called *Hollywood Backstage* and for the majority of the show we would have a *Chorus Line* look backstage with two sets for production numbers. Fran Scott was the host and we co-produced the show. Our guest stars included a fabulous jazz vocalist, Mavis Rivers, a Fred Rice discovery new to Capitol Records. Also Trumpeter Dick Cathcart whose horn was featured in the motion picture *Pete Kelly's Blues*. Dick was an alumnus of the Modernaires vocal group.

We managed to get Marilyn Lovell from the Jack Parr Show to fly out from New York and Johnny Drake, formerly of the Modernaires, for a show-stopping alto sax solo plus the dynamic Fran Scott Singers. Fran and I invited the founder of The Modernaires, Hal Dickinson, to help write the show. I worked overtime to get the best engineers for a musical. Bob Finch technical director; Bob Johnson audio;

Gene Reed lighting director while the art direction was handled by the talented Ted Rich. Our announcer was "Mr. First Nighter" Vince Pelletier. Fran opened the show with a swinging "Hello Everybody" backed by his vocal group. Mavis lit up the stage with her jazzy hit "One Minute to One" and Dick Cathcart did a slick trumpet number using a hand puppet on "In a Little Spanish Town." We dropped to a ballad that was brand new but would soon become a classic. When Marilyn Lovell arrived at the studio she was almost in tears she had left her music on the plane and she had a new song she wanted to do. A song that none of us had ever heard. No problem. Just hum the melody to Al Pelligrini. She did and this version of "I Wish You Love" was magic. If recorded it would have been a million seller. Marilyn had a slight overbite and I got close-ups of her pretty face saying the word "love." It made all the guys want to marry her on the spot. With a set that included an airplane, Frank and Marilyn did a nice turn on the Matt Dennis standard, "Let's Get Away From it All." Fran, Hal and I had written updated lyrics for the second chorus that brought new sparkle to that old chestnut.

Mavis Rivers provided a change of pace singing a bluesy lament to love, "It's Four AM." Then came a sizzling, knock-out version of "So Rare." Johnny Drake led the way with his sensational alto sax plus the blended voices of the Scott Singers and great solo efforts by our musical group. Following the final commercial we found Fran and his singers in front of a little country church where they delivered a melodic version of Steve Allen's "Lets Go to Church." Near the close with the singers humming the melody Fran did his closing, and then joined the group for the final chorus. The critics liked the show, the performers, the musical group, the writing and the direction. That was the frosting on the cake.

The following Monday I was back to harsh reality. Due to health problems Eleanor Powell was leaving as host of "Faith of our Children" the long-running series that had won seven Emmy Awards. I didn't envy producer Clifton Moore who had to find an actress to fill Eleanor's unfillable shoes. She was the series and how do you replace a legend? First replacement was actress Marie Windsor a 5'9" dark-haired beauty whose hometown was Marysville, Utah. Marie had studied for a career in films, stage and TV with famed drama coach Maria Ouspenskaya while working as a model for glamour photographer Paul Hesser. She made extra cash by selling jokes to Jack Benny as M.E. Windsor, no female gag writers accepted at that time. When at last she met Benny and he saw her beauty he had a producer sign her to a contract which led to MGM who put her into two small roles which was the start of a long career. As a leading lady, Marie worked well with film personalities and extra well with people from the world of sports. Marie was an accomplished athlete at swimming, dancing, horsewoman, tennis, golf and a top skier. She has a star on the Hollywood Walk of Fame. She told Clifton that she would only be able to serve as hostess for a few weeks on *Faith of our Children* because of heavy film, stage and TV commitments. I enjoyed directing Marie. She was easygoing, friendly and 100% professional. My daughter, Sharon, worked several episodes with Marie and I asked her what, as a member of the cast was her take on the change. "She's not Eleanor but I like her and I think she works well with the kids and the guests." Sharon was right and if we could have gone a full season together we would have had a nice rhythm.

Fred Rice and I were co-producers and I directed a Christmas special titled "Stars of Sound." The host was America's number-one dance band leader. He was a trumpet virtuoso and a pint-sized "look-alike" of Cary Grant or Ray Anthony. One of the key segments would be a three and half minute animated film of Santa's reindeer, "Dancer, Prancer and Nervous." The film was based on a Christmas recording that Capitol Records hoped would create many sales to small fries and their parents and grandparents.

There were several memorable moments. Gordon McRae sang his romantic theme, "Face to Face." Lorenda Almeida, with his guitar, played a breathtaking classical number. At that time he was rated among the five best guitarists in the world. Any would-be guitarists, and there were well over three million in the United States watching, should have considered selling shoes or insurance because music would never be their occupation.

Through the years, I have wondered why so many female vocalists are so bad. They scream and shake but sing they do not. A real how-to-sing education was on display by Mavis Rivers with a beautiful arrangement of Johnny Mercer's "Fools Rush In." Ray did two of his many hits with the full tone and style that made him famous. The special was in color and each performer would have their own set. I had art director, Curt Nations, put the sets in a horseshoe configuration with Ray on a high stool, forward and in the center of the sets. Our three cameras worked in and out of the sets while camera four was exclusively on Ray. At rehearsal, I asked everyone to stay in their sets until I completed my shot selection and Ray was to stay on his stool for the entire time. We started rehearsal with Ray. We would only have a half hour between rehearsal and time to record. Ray and his horn followed by his opening remarks then the cue for Mavis' song. I was busy getting shots of Mavis and at the end came back to Ray, but there was no Ray, just an empty stool.

I let my stage manager have it. "Where is that little Italian SOB? He's supposed to be on the stool!"

There was a tap on my shoulder. I turned and saw a grinning Ray kneeling by my chair and he said, "The little Italian SOB will get back on his stool and stay there." We both burst out laughing as Ray headed to the studio and his stool. The entire show went like a fine-tuned watch. The critics loved it and the animated film worked to perfection. If my kids, who watched the show on TV, remarks were very typical, it worked. We had to buy the recording of "Dancer, Prancer and Nervous."

NBC's Christmas party was always an event held at a major hotel. There would be fabulous food, desserts, drinks and a present for everyone. I loved the parties but had to leave early as Dixie got drunk and out of control. I had always been able to leave before an incident occurred but not this year. Les Brown and his orchestra played for dancing. Bob Hope, Eddie Fisher and Dinah Shore entertained. Before the dancing started, I suggested we leave. "I'm not ready to leave this gang of fagot show business idiots," she said in a loud voice that drew many looks. Waving her arms, she managed to spill the majority of her drink over her new Neiman Marcus cocktail dress. She yelled for another drink and got quick service. I urged that we leave and at last got her up on wobbly legs. I started her toward the check room for our coats when she spied Tom McCray, my boss and Vice President of NBC West Coast Operations. She pulled out of my grasp and staggered toward McCray saying, "I want to give that SOB a piece of my mind." When she stood in front of McCray she really turned up the volume. "I don't know why you hired my husband, that SOB can't direct his way through the front door." I tried to apologize to Tom as I turned her to leave. He said he understood and wished me Merry Christmas. I wasn't sure I still worked for The National Broadcasting Company.

Next afternoon, when she sobered up she hoped she hadn't killed the golden goose that supplied the money for Neiman's and the fancy boutique shops where she dropped the bulk of my paycheck. I got the old speech that if I would quit show business and sell real estate she wouldn't drink. "Oh, and by the way we need to buy a home with a swimming pool. All our friends have pools." That stumped me. I didn't know we had friends except Don and Bernie Rickle and they didn't have a pool. "Also, since all your shows are in daytime why not see what might be open for you to play and sing to make us more money and you have to get Kim into private school." This was her statement with not a word about her performance at the NBC party.

Next year she would get drunk at the party and I refused to ever attend another one. I pulled the Christmas Eve Midnight Mass an NBC tradition.

Cal Phillips and the gang from J. Walter

Thompson sent us twenty-four quarts of eggnog and eight bottles of top-of-the-line whiskey and brandy. I let the guys draw lots for the goodies and I took two quarts of eggnog. No booze for Dixie.

My mother was with us for the holidays and she brought the boys Ohio State football sweatshirts and Sharon a pretty silk robe among the presents for everyone.

At the first of the year, I directed several episodes of *General Electric Presents Dr. Frank Baxter*. The good doctor was a pleasant man with a wry sense of humor. He was a University of Southern California professor of English who brought a dimension and substance to TV it had never known. During his TV career, he would win seven Emmys, a Peabody Award, and would be honored by a star on the Hollywood Walk of Fame. The next year, he gained millions of fans as the star of the Bell System Science series. The good doctor was an ultimate showman and educator who changed many lives and inspired thousands. Dr. Baxter truly was a very special man.

A restaurant on Vine Street by the Plaza Hotel was a place the kids loved to visit. The motif, including Shamrocks, was 100% Irish as was the food but the big attraction was the serving staff. All were midgets dressed as Leprechauns. Asked where they wanted to go for dinner this was their choice.

Bob Crosby hired Fran Scott, Hal Dickson and I to write special material for a promotion Pillsbury was doing for Mother's Day that included a white cake with white icing plus a recording for "Mom" that Bob sang. Fran and Hal with the Modernaires had worked with Bob and his orchestra on CBS Radio's *Club Fifteen*, a show that might have run forever had Bob, after a few too many drinks, not beat his wife. This bought unwanted national headlines and the sponsorship of the *Club Fifteen* show vanished. Now Bob, a very likable and talented guy was on the comeback trail and we were there to help. We worked at his lavish home in Trousdale Estates with a panoramic view of Los Angeles and the Pacific Ocean. We laughed a lot and ate endless samples of the Pillsbury cake accompanied by cups of hot coffee. My favorite memory of that time was created by Bob's mother. This little lady with a strong Irish brogue split her years living three months at Bing's home, three months with Bob, then back with Bing so that each son had Mother six months of the year.

The morning of her arrival Bob answered the doorbell and his mother entered. Frank, Hal and I were putting our morning snack of cake and coffee on the big dining room table. "And what are all these lads doing?" his mother asked.

"These gentlemen are writers working on a project I have been hired by the Pillsbury people to do." Mother Crosby adjusted her glasses and looked at her son. "It's good to know you have a job. Your brother Bing works all the time."

We cracked up with gales of laughter. Bob took his mother's coat and she joined us for cake and coffee. The Pillsbury promotion with Bob's record went very well and I hope our writing was a part of that success. Bob was never blessed with a voice like brother, Bing, but then who was? Bob was likable with humor and a good personality and his vocals went well when the Modernaires were included. Bob has two stars on the Hollywood Walk of Fame. One for radio and the second for television. For those who love jazz Bob will always be remembered as the leader of what may have been the greatest jazz band ever, "Bob Crosby and the Bobcats." Every member of that band was a star in his own right but I was amazed by the great jazz pianists who at one time were members. They included my idol Jess Stacy, Joe Sullivan and "The Old Tomcat on the Keys," Bob Zurke.

Bob Woods, a super talented writer and I became co-producers, and I, the director of the *Lee Giroux Show* a talk, interview afternoon showcase. Lee Giroux, "The Fabulous Frenchman" could do it all. A native of O'Neil, Nebraska he lived across the street from Frank Leahy, later to be Notre Dame Immortal and one of the greatest football coaches of all time. Everyday Lee and Frank would run to school tossing a football back and forth. Lee went to college at Northwestern where he was a football star and Frank to Notre Dame where he was an All-American. While Frank followed sports Lee concentrated on radio and television. He was first noted for his excellence as a play-by-play announcer, then played dramatic roles, did newscasts and became an on air personality.

We had a wide variety of guests, past and present headliners from many professions. A select guest spent a week on the show. Among the most outstanding was one of the queens of silent films, Mae Murray. Prior to movies, Mae worked on Broadway as a dancer and was Vernon Castle's partner in *About Town* plus several starring roles in editions of *Ziegfeld's Follies*. With a beautiful face, Mae, was an instant star in silent films. Billed as "The Girl with the Bee Stung Lips" Mae had a vibrant personality and a graceful dancer's body. She played glamorous blondes and co-starred with Rudolph Valentino and John Gilbert. She became one of Hollywood's highest-paid stars. Her greatest screen performance was in the *The Merry Widow* directed by Eri Von Stroheim. A couple of forgotten talkies ended her film career. On the Giroux show she discussed her just-written autobiography *The Self-Enchanted* and told wonderful stories about the early days of the film industry. Although much time had passed since her days as a leading lady, and she was older, Mae still had star quality.

Gene Krupa "The King of the Drums" spent a week with us and we heard many tales of life with Benny Goodman and Tommy Dorsey. Gene, who as a young man had planned to be Catholic priest, was a delightful addition who also gave us drum lessons.

I must admit my favorite one-week guest was one of the two greatest comic actors who ever lived. We missed Charlie Chaplin but we got Buster Keaton and what a delight he was. I remember when the little guy with the tone face, the pork-pie hat, black string tie, too-large jacket and the baggy pants walked into our studio. What a gem, what a man! We would have loved him as a permanent member of the show. On the last day of his stay, Buster gave me a copy of his memoir *My Wonderful World of Slapstick* and our stage manager took a photo of Lee, Bob Woods, Buster and I. It is one of my most prized possessions. Buster's book is a great read about the little kid who joined his parent's vaudeville act at age four and reached career heights that will never be equaled.

Wanting to get their clients on the show, agents were on the phone every day. One agent was willing to give her all for her client. One day after the show I walked across the lot to my office. It was late and everyone was gone. I opened my office door to find a good-looking young woman laying spread eagle naked on top of my desk.

She had moved my working materials off the desk and was using my seat cushion as her pillow. "Shut the door and remove your pants so we can talk," she said with a smile.

"What do you want to talk about?"

"I'm going to convince you to book my clients on your show."

"Your clients will never be on our show, get dressed and out of here before I call security." I went out in the hall and in a few minutes, she was dressed and left through the door to the parking lot. Going back into my office I found her panties hanging on my desk lamp with her business card. She had scribbled that I should call her when I had a change of heart.

I went back across the lot to find Lee and Bob Woods to see if they were interested in a libation at Nickodells. I found them in the newsroom and we headed towards Nicks. We heard a cry of delight as the makeup artist in his sports car was driving off the lot at high speed. The agency girl was performing oral sex. He screamed as he climaxed and his car shot through both lines of traffic, with screaming brakes. He made a wild turn through the red light at Sunset and Vine then vanished in traffic going south. Just another day at the office. I love show biz.

CHAPTER FORTY-SEVEN

After several temper tantrums by Dixie that included throwing expensive china and a vase or two I bit the bullet. I needed the money a night time music job would provide. I took my film clip from the Kate Smith Show and hit the agents. They had lots of great jobs in Los Angeles, but I wanted something out of town where I wouldn't see anyone from NBC. They came up with a location and the answer was a gorgeous restaurant that could have been the pride of Beverly Hills. Interior was of dark polished wood and field stone with a Steinway concert grand piano and a state of the art sound system. The room was large and featured a fireplace where clients could enjoy cocktails in easy chairs before partaking of the delicious food prepared by an award-winning chef and his assistants. The service was impeccable; the soft lighting gave a warm romantic glow. The clientele was wealthy and the tips were large. This kind of room you could enjoy years if TV wasn't your prime employment.

This was the Somerset Restaurant on the Old Coast Highway and Butterfly Lane in ritzy Montecito just a couple of miles from historic Santa Barbara, where a Japanese submarine had shelled during World War II. Just ninety-five miles from Los Angeles. I would drive 190 miles a day, six days a week round trip to work. Driving the posted speed limit the trip took one hour and fifty-three minutes each way. I had asked for a class job out of town. I had it! Closing at 1 AM I should be home a little after 3 AM. Hit the bed until 7 AM then up for breakfast and drive Kim to St. Martins in the Fields, a wonderful private school which Sharon and Sean would also attend when they got older. With a little luck I could be back in bed by 9:30AM and sleep until noon, have lunch and report for work at NBC. Kim's mother would pick him up when school was over. Coming back to bed was a great idea but it rarely happened. Real Estate people were taking us to see houses with swimming pools. Being young, strong and out of your mind was a plus. I loved the Somerset Restaurant and it loved me. The owner said he would extend my eight week contract for an indefinite period of time. After a couple of near misses on the highway coming home even the young, the strong, and the mindless started to realize this wasn't the smartest way to stay alive.

I was into my seventh week at the Somerset when NBC made the decision for all of us. Vacations were coming and I had to be available to take over directing shows at night. Dixie gave the studio a good cursing for cutting off the extra money. I got a little more sleep but I still had to drive my son to school and the constant search for the right house with a pool was on a seven-day-a-week basis.

I directed Chick Hearn, the voice of the Los Angeles Lakers basketball team on his daily sports show.

It won an Emmy. Chick was a very intense person 100% dedicated to his career. We worked together as a smooth team but would never be close as friends.

There was a new guy in town with a new show that would be a prelude to his becoming an American news icon. Chet Huntley from the Big Sky Country of Montana had stardust sprinkled over him from the get-go. *Chet Huntley Reports* was a winner. Chet was old school, writing his own news script and gave the viewers an unsugared and unmanaged report by telling facts as the way it really happened with all the bad tidings along with bumps of happiness. Working with Chet was pure joy and although he deserved the finite showcase the network could give, I was sad when he departed to New York for the soon-to-be-famous Huntley-Brinkley show a high point in broadcast journalism.

I had a habit of tagging friends with nicknames. Not to be mean but with a kind of affection. During college there had been "Crow," "Volley," "The Skull" and "Captain Pear Shape" to name a few that had stuck. Tom McCray was a man I always admired. He was bald and I would call Tom "Curley" to the crew but, of course, never to his face. My technical directors kept telling me that someday I would slip and address our boss as "Curley." That prediction came true.

I was on my two week vacation when I was notified of a special directors meeting and although I was on vacation Mr. McCray was hoping I would attend. I did. There we were in a room on the second floor. My colleagues in their dark suits were seated at the long table and I was seated at the back. Being on vacation, I wore a gold shirt and slacks and was working on a double dip ice cream cone I had brought with me. The meeting started as it always did. A male aide brought in a fancy French phone and plugged it in by the head of the table where Mr. McCray would sit. Seconds later Tom took his seat and the meeting started. I really wasn't listening but was watching the traffic on Vine Street while busy with my ice cream when I heard Tom shoot the question, "Cawley, what do you think of that?"

Think of what? I had no idea what he was talking about. With a mouth full of ice cream I replied, "Well, Curley I...." One look at my peers faces and I realized what I had said.

Tom barked in a hostile voice, "What did you say?"

The fact that I choked on my ice cream saved me and I replied in a stammering and choked whisper. "Mr. McCray, what I was trying to say is that I agree with your point of view." I had no idea what his view point was on anything. I didn't know what he was talking about. My answer must have made sense as the meeting continued as I junked what remained of my cone into the nearest trash basket.

My cousin, Ken Agee, had not only won national acclaim as an attorney by winning huge amounts for his clients for compensation due them from labor related injuries suffered while working for industrial giants like Bethlehem Steel, his law offices took up two floors in the AIU Tower in Columbus, Ohio. Ken owned a private plane and was associated with famed San Francisco lawyer, Melvin Belli but in addition, he had become a movie producer with offices on Las Palmas Avenue in Hollywood, California. Ken produced a series of "B" pictures, biker films that were in vogue. Our cousin, James Agee was the film critic for the New York Times and had moved to Hollywood in 1948. In 1951 he co-wrote the classic screenplay for *The African Queen* with John Huston that starred Humphrey Bogart, who won an Academy Award for his performance, and Kathryn Hepburn. In 1955 James wrote the acclaimed *The Night of the Hunter* which starred Robert Mitchum. James was always interested in cinema as an art form; Ken was interested in film to make money. Ken met with James and urged me to see him. Sorry I didn't get around to doing that. In 1958 James was posthumously awarded the Pulitzer Prize for his novel *A Death in the Family* which in 1963 was turned into a film titled *All the Way Home*.

Vacations were in full swing and I subbed for the regular director of a very, very popular one hour series, *Juke Box Jury* hosted by the show's creator disc jockey deluxe, Peter Potter. Peter, who was married to song bird Berle Davis, had actor and writer credits in addition to his disc jockey hosting on his long running radio show of the same name. Peter with his relaxed and friendly style was a person that viewers felt they would like to know. *Juke Box Jury* was fun for everyone watching as well as the revolving celebrity panel that made the decision if a recording was "A Hit or a Miss." The celebrity panels were a who's who in show business and a partial list included Johnny Mercer, Anthony Perkins, Mamie Van Doren, Robert Wagner, Tab Hunter, Natalie Wood, Sal Mineo, Debbie Reynolds, Jane Meadows, Steve Allen, Walter Brennen, Steve McQueen, Zsa Zsa Gabor, Polly Bergen, Dean Martin and Gloria De Haven. Of the many guests who served on the "Juke Box" panel was the talented actress, singer Polly Bergen. She is the only person I ever saw that you could start with a shot of either eye filling the screen, and then painfully slow widen out the shot until her entire beautiful face filled the screen and every inch of that face and neck had 100% perfect skin. Not even a whisper of a blemish.

Juke Box only had two glitches while on my watch. One evening a male TV personality arrived with Jayne Mansfield after they had dinner at the Brown Derby. Before air time a "Lady of the Evening" I had seen with this guy, and Jayne got into a screaming, hair pulling fight over this clown and I had to call security to separate the two women. The male personality was thrilled women were fighting over him. The "Lady of the Evening" was escorted out of NBC. Jayne's hairdo was ruined and her silk blouse was torn. She waited for Mr. Personality until he completed his appearance on *Juke Box*, and when they left he was promising to get her a new blouse.

The second incident happened while the show was on. A beautiful movie and TV star whose name we won't mention since she is still coming into your living room on a regular basis was the next star Peter Potter was going to introduce. Darrel McAlister, my stage manager, told me to send another star out before the camera since the star scheduled was "involved."

"What the hell is the problem?" I asked. He chuckled and told me to stand up and look out the control room window and at the back of the set facing it. I did and saw my star making out with a stage hand. I brought her on later and America loved this jewel. A survey showed that *Juke Box Jury* had in excess of twelve million fans.

We signed papers to buy a home on Leonora

Drive in Woodland Hills right around the corner from pianist, singer, composer and friend Matt Dennis and his lovely wife Virginia Maxie who had sang with the Tony Pastor Orchestra. Did we have a pool? You bet. Twenty-two by forty-four and fifteen feet deep under the diving board with a big area for entertaining.

I directed the final cook-off contest of the Mrs. America Pageant held in a ballroom of the Ambassador Hotel in Los Angeles. The room was filled with stoves and soon the contestants would be cooking or baking their favorite dishes. It wasn't the show coverage that made the nations newspapers the following morning but this incident. People were dining in the hotel garden. From the side of the hotel unseen by the guests, our engineers were stringing camera cables across the roof and dropping them down into the ballroom.

The diners were enjoying lunch when our technical director came into the center of the diners and yelled in a loud voice, "Saint Peter, are you up there?" The startled diners thought a demented religious man was in their midst. When there was no answer, he called again, "Saint Peter, are you up there?"

They were really shocked when from far away they heard an answer. "Yea, I'm up here." Had they just witnessed a holy miracle? Not quite. Jim was calling NBC engineer Lionel St. Peter to see if he was on the roof with the camera cables. The story was on all the news shows and in every newspaper across the United States.

Marie Windsor was leaving *Faith of Our Children* and actress Nancy Gates stepped in on a short-term basis. Nancy had entered movies when she was fifteen and had been screen tested by Orson Welles. She got her first credited role in the film *The Great Gildersleeve*. Nancy was very active on TV yet found time to act in such films as *Some Came Running*, *Death of a Scoundrel*, and *Suddenly* co-starring with Frank Sinatra.

It was kind of hello, goodbye as she was followed by Dale Evans, a star in her own right and the wife of cowboy super star, Roy Rogers. Dale was so talented in so many areas. She had been a pianist-singer on radio; a top big band singer playing major supper clubs; and a composer. "Happy Trails" is one of her hit compositions and also, of course she was a movie star who made twenty-eight features with her husband, Roy Rogers and pictures with other stars including John Wayne. A deeply religious person, Dale authored the classic *Angel Unaware*. I found her funny and very pleasant and very good with children. We had hoped we could have Dale for the long run but her heavy commitments with Roy and the family business made this impossible. Producer Clifton Moore was exhausted and told NBC he was pulling the show after one final season and that was too bad because for that season we had the hostess that came very close to what Eleanor had been to the show. This lady was Beverly Garland remembered by millions as the star of the film *Where the Red Fern Grows* and the classic noir thriller, *D.O.A.* In television she is remembered as the wife of Fred MacMurray in the beloved sitcom *My Three Sons*. I think everyone in our crew was a little bit in love with Beverly. She was patient, kind, a real pro you could trust and a truly wonderful person.

On a Saturday night when all the executives should have been in Palm Springs or Las Vegas we had an incident to remember. I was directing *World News Tonight* and wandered into the makeup room to chat with my star, Elmer Peterson, who was laid back in the makeup chair while the makeup artist did his magic. I saw we had female visitors in the room. One with brown hair was seated by the mirror on the makeup table with her skirt around her waist and she was not wearing panties. The brunet primping in the far side of the mirror was naked from the waist up with her full breasts on display. No one had to tell me how they got in. Mr. Personality of the Jayne Mansfield affair had been in taping a commercial and they came with him then he ditched them. Elmer Peterson in the makeup chair was Mister Straight Arrow and the makeup artist was gay. I sized up the situation and was starting to go to the control room and call security when from the doorway came the voice of doom. It was none other than Thomas C. McCray, NBC Vice President of West Coast Operations. What the hell was he doing here on Saturday night and why were two half naked women doing here?

With his deep, Orson Welles voice, Tom spoke. "What is going on here?"

With her skirt around her waist and no panties, the brown haired female slipped off the makeup table and wiggled her way to where Tom was standing. From the moment McCray spoke, the gay makeup artist panicked as he saw his career going up in smoke and without realizing what he was doing he tightened his grip on Elmer's throat, choking him. The woman with no pants got directly in front of Tom and announced, "I'm a guest of the National Broadcasting Company."

Tom drew himself up to his full six-foot-three and

in that great baritone said, "Madam, I am the National Broadcasting Company."

I'm trying to get the makeup artist's hands from Elmer's throat before he dies and the second woman with her naked breasts bouncing says, "Baldy, you're cute. I think you'd be a great lay."

That did it for Tom who stepped into the hall calling for security. There happened to be two security guards in the rotunda who came running. Tom told the guards to take the two "Ladies" to the exit then return. I watched the naked buttocks and bare back wiggle down the hall and vanish. By this time a choking Elmer was sitting up drinking a cup of water. Tom wanted to know how such women had invaded the sacred halls of NBC, but I wasn't telling and neither was the shaking makeup man. I reminded Tom that Elmer and I were going on the air in about twelve minutes with *World News Tonight*. We were sent on our way but Tom and the security guards continued their investigation. The results were not too good. The stage crew not working the news was caught in the prop room watching a porn movie. A member of the stage crew was found in the client's booth over the studio having intercourse with another "Lady of the Evening." The next morning the doors of the NBC studios all had new locks and new security devices.

Vacations were almost over when I subbed for Marc Breslow as director of *The Curt Massey Show* with Liltin' Martha Tilton and Country Washburn.

CHAPTER FORTY-EIGHT

Pure gold, *The Curt Massey Show*: fifteen minutes a day, five days a week that delivered high ratings that led into *Shell News*. In fact, the contract with Shell had a short paragraph that read, "If for any reason *The Curt Massey Show* which precedes the *Shell News* is ever canceled or replaced, this contract with NBC will be null and void." This was a secure job. My friend Marc Breslow was the director and I would cover for him during his vacation. To say I was delighted is putting it mildly. I had been a fan of the show during its nine years on CBS Radio for Alka Seltzer. When I was a kid, my father and I would be by our radio to listen to the WLS Barn Dance whose star was Curt's older sister Louise Massey a fine singer who had penned the hit song, "My Adobe Hacienda." Curt had played fiddle in her band. Martha Tilton had been a favorite when she sang "And the Angels Sing" and "Loch Lomond" with Benny Goodman and who could forget Country Washburn's fantastic arrangement of the hit "Heartaches" for the Ted Weems Recording. This was a director's dream. I arrived at my office at 11 AM, read my mail, returned calls, went to lunch. At 2 PM I was at rehearsal across from Studio F where the show was produced. Curt did not work on Fridays. On weekends he took his wife Edith and their sons, David and Stevie, to his 9,000 acre spread near Julian in San Diego County or his 5,000 acre ranch on the Feather River where he returned to his Texas roots as a real cowboy and taught his sons to rope and ride. The rest of the time the family lived in a large paid for home in Beverly Hills. On Wednesdays, we would do that day's show live and tape the show to be aired on Friday.

Wednesday was always special. We taped Friday's show around 12:30 PM then took a lunch break until rehearsal time at 2 PM. Curt, Country and the musicians would go up Vine Street to eat at Clifton's Cafeteria while Martha and I would take my car to Fairfax Avenue to enjoy Mexican food at the famous Farmer's Market. The first day I did the show, Curt introduced me to everyone. Frank Leightner, the pianist had broken into music as the pianist for Rudy Vallee's first band. The guitarist was a wizened little fellow with a contagious laugh and a great disposition. His name was Luther "Red" Roundtree and he had been the original guitarist with the famed Memphis Five. He could really play guitar and banjo. Gene Estes, a top flight drummer who also excelled on Vibes, had played with several name bands. Musical Director Joe "Country" Washburn was a master of the "dog house" string bass, piano and tuba. He sang and wrote hit songs including "One Dozen Roses" which reached the top of the Hit Parade. He had been a major arranger for big bands and he had been featured performer for fourteen years on the popular

Fibber McGee and Molly. "Country" was easy going, fun and he loved music.

What can I say that hasn't been said about Curt? He not only had a fabulous voice but he also could play thirty-two musical instruments and on the show would take turns at the piano, trumpet, violin, trombone, clarinet or clavaetta. He was a recording artist, song writer, "The Honey Song," "Draggin The Bow," and the theme of *The Curt Massey Show* "We'll Sing the Old Songs" among others. Curt would later be Musical Director for two TV series that would be huge hits, *The Beverly Hillbillies* and *Petticoat Junction*, for which he would write the themes. Relaxed and easy going, he expected perfection from his musicians, performers and his director.

The show seldom had a guest star but today we did. A man I had admired as long as I could remember. The world's greatest jazz trombonist vocalist, recording star and band leader, Jack Teagarden. Rehearsal was a blast. Teagarden, Curt, Country and the musicians blew up a jazz storm which I wish I could have recorded. It was classic. I also wish I had a copy of the show. Jack played and sang "I Got a Right to Sing the Blues," and with Curt on trumpet and the musicians in fine form tore things up with "South Rampart Street Parade."

Before the show I asked Country for a copy of his conductor's score. He asked why I needed it and I told him I made my camera cuts on the music.

"You can read music?" he asked.

"Sure thing, Country. I've been reading music since I was five."

He got the copy for me and the rest is history. After the show we all told Jack goodbye. Then members of the show went to a private screening room to see a playback of the show. Something that would never happened again. I watched Curt, Country and Martha during the playback as they would nod their heads at each other. When the lights came up Curt shook my hand, then Country, Martha and the band saying "great job." This was a Friday show we had taped on Wednesday.

When I arrived at my office on Monday, I had a note from Tom McCray that he wanted to see me. Tom told me that Curt wanted me as his permanent director starting at once. He knew that Breslow and I were close friends but Massey was a star they could not afford to lose. Tom said he would contact Marc when he came home from vacation, take him to lunch and explain the situation. He did, but for Marc the friendship was over. He got an agent and in a short time was signed as the director of all Goodman Todsen game shows which made him a small fortune. Marc always thought I had lobbied for the *Massey Show*. The only reason Curt wanted me is because I read music and cuts and camera movements should be cued to what is going on musically.

Working four days a week while being paid for five, gave me time to find the right agent for my next career move but you know all about the best laid plans. Mister Sid Casaloff called and wanted to know if I would be interested in directing a musical feature film with the working title of *Hollywood Beauty* Of course, if I can do it around *The Curt Massey Show*. Sidney said this would not be a problem.

The movie had complete financing. The music had been recorded; the movie cast and the locations selected so come in and pick up a copy of the screenplay. Sid was overweight, wore an ascot and considered himself a comedian. Out of the side of his mouth he said that he couldn't afford one of those expensive guys like Busby Berkley but liked what I did on the Massey Show so why not give a new kid a break? He chuckled at this bit of wisdom and I took the screenplay home. It was a story that's been done a thousand times. Beauty pageant winner from a small town comes to Hollywood for fame and fortune as a singer, dancer meets a nice young man, falls in love and they work as a team. They win an audition for a part in a big studio production. Son of mogul comes between them and offers her solo stardom if she dumps her lover. After soul searching she returns to lover and they sing and dance to cinema greatness. I've seen this before but I tell Sid to count me in as he sets shooting for early days and nights. We agree on my fee and he orders his attorney to write my contract.

Two days later I go to his office on Hollywood Boulevard a little after 9 AM to sign on the dotted line. Sid is wearing a lime green jacket and a blue and pink ascot. We shake hands and Sid offers me a chocolate from a five pound box of Belgium's finest chocolates that someone sent him. I decline his offer as I just had breakfast. I sit down. Sid pats my shoulder and as he starts around his desk, he pops a chocolate in his mouth. Reaching for his swivel chair he makes a strange sound, gurgles, then falls like a sack of cement behind his desk. As he falls, his left hand claws my contract and takes it with him. I yell for his secretary, who rushed into the room as his chair hits the wall, to get an ambulance and she races to the phone on her desk. I kneel by Sid who has the chocolate drop mashed with the cream running out of his lips and is bug eyed. I check his neck. DOA. There was no truth to the rumor that I tried to force his dead hand to sign my contract. So much for my debut as a film director.

Dixie's sister was coming out from Alabama and could I get her on a game show so the folks down south can see her on the tube. I checked in with Bill Leyden hosting a series called *It Could Be You* that came from our new NBC studios in Burbank, California in living color. Bill got all the information and on July 3rd he selected Sis out of the audience. She got several nice prizes and became a celebrity in Anniston, Alabama. She was a real nice lady, not like her sister. I never saw or heard from her again.

NBC had opened new studios at 3200 Olive Avenue in Burbank September of 1957. Just a stone's throw from Warner Brothers Studios. The NBC ads said this was the "Place Where Dreams Work." Nice phrase, but not always by a long shot.

It would be three years before *The Curt Massey Show* would move there. We visited the new plant. It was huge, like standing in a series of Yankee Stadiums. Whoever designed it had never been a director. The control rooms were two floors above the stage. If talent needed to talk to you, you had to run down two flights of stairs or try to make contact through the stage manager's headset, instead of just stepping into the control room as you did in Hollywood to set shots up. The needed close contact between talent and director had been destroyed. We hoped we would never move there. Huge tape machines were in Burbank and the not-so-smart technicians had fast speed erase buttons on their fronts which sometimes caused serious problems.

At Christmas, in New York untold amounts of money was being spent to produce a biblical epic *Amhal and the Night Visitors,* to be taped in Burbank. Major actors were cast. The show ended and the actors left New York for holiday destinations around the world. Executives asked to have the tape played back from Burbank. There was no tape! After the show was completed a tape engineer in Burbank took a long personal phone call during which he leaned against the tape machine activating the high speed erase on both copies of the show since the two machines were interlocked. Imagine the cost to fly the actors back to New York, house them, pay them, and finance their flights back to their holiday destinations. Now add to that the cost of re-setting and lighting the sets, getting the costumes back from the cleaners, the same crew and director, etc, etc... No wonder it became a staple for yearly Christmas airing.

The *Massey Show* was rolling in high gear in late 1958. I was still looking for the agent I wanted to spend my professional life with. I had reached a decision. I wanted a divorce with reasonable child visitation. I moved to an apartment in Studio City. I had just made the move when I had a call from Lee Worman.

Lee had sold TV time when I was in Arizona. Now he was a producer getting ready to produce a syndicated films series of twelve half hours for children, with a firm offer for an additional twelve shows if the first twelve were successful. The financing for twelve half hours was in place. The series was about wild animals and a man who captured them for various zoos. He had a long term rental for a crane camera and a second "stick" camera, animal handlers, a full working crew plus private security. Talent had been signed. I was paid an inflated fee to write the script, direct and write and record the music that would be a part of this series. The series would film Friday, Saturday and Sunday and I would return to LA Sunday night. Filming would take up eight weekends.

This series was for kids and the accent was on animals and would use a minimum of dialogue except when Jungle Jack who had captured the animal would in the last part of the show, filmed in his office with the animal, would give the kids the story of the animal, and their lifestyle with lots of close-ups, a nice educational touch to a thrilling adventure. His sidekick who with a sixteen millimeter camera was filming his adventures during the animal hunt portion of the series. Of course, there was no film in the camera, and the sidekick's girlfriend tagged along. The later was a mystery to me but this was what the investors had bankrolled.

Lee and I agreed to call the series *Danger Wild Cargo*. I would write the initial script in a format and since we would be live at the same motel the cast could have their pages for the following day. The only thing that really changed was the animals and the method of capture. Kind of like writing a "B" Western. Same story with only the horses changed.

The first week of filming locked in our future schedule. We would film one show on Friday, one show on Saturday then film the interiors of both shows on Sunday at the studios of KOOL-TV in Phoenix. I would take the film of both shows back to LA to have the film developed. Then the developing lab shipped the film to Phoenix for editing. I was able to keep the editing costs low by editing in the camera, cutting scenes to dovetail. We would complete all filming in six weekends. With the shows competed, I would record the music and after the editing was finished I would dub it and the sound effects, add the title and end credits over weekends and *Danger Wild Cargo* would be ready for distribution. We would wrap the project on time and on budget, which in the end we did but now it was time to go to work.

I flew out of LA shortly after 5 AM on TWA. I was devouring a good breakfast and hot coffee. I looked out the window to see the right wing was on fire. We were nearing the San Bernadino Mountains as the calm voice of the Captain announced we have a problem and we're returning to LA where we would be put on another flight. The power on the right wing was dead but we made the return. There is something about flying in a plane that's on fire that gets your adrenalin pumping. The aftermath flight got me to Phoenix forty-eight minutes late where a nervous Lee waited. I threw my bag in his car and we made the eighty mile trip to our African location. I had never been to Africa but what I saw could have been the location of a vintage "Tarzan" movie.

There I met the cast and workers. My star, "Jungle Jack," was a laid back, gentle, nice guy who would probably have good communication with the animals. It was then I discovered Jack owned an alligator farm that included a motel and restaurant where the cast, handlers, Lee and I would stay. Jack's sidekick in the series was called Bob which was his real name. Bob Corrigan in time became my best friend. Vicki, the girlfriend of Jungle Jack's sidekick was Vel Ritchie a very lovely and sensuous lady who wore the shortest shorts I ever saw topping lovely long legs. I could see why she was "Miss Canada." I had a feeling that both handlers, Buddy and Rocky had elevators that did not go all the way up.

My cinematographer was a grizzled vet of many RKO movies. Now retired his name was not to appear in the credits and he was paid in cash. I figured he didn't want the healthy fee he was getting to flag interest of the folks at the IRS or Social Security. He was a gaunt man with a long grey ponytail not a mark of fashion in the late fifties. He told me to call him Mitch. I met his son Rick, a forties replica of his dad. They both were responsible for the shots and knew their craft and did top quality work. The four black pygmies had worked in a carnival, spoke no English but smiled a lot. They carried their spears everywhere and were happy campers. The security guys were highway patrol officers, past or present, moonlighting with their shotguns and side arms just in case that an animal attacked. The company they worked for provided patrol cars complete with blue and red lights and a siren. The slate boy was a junior college kid with show biz dreams. His name was Mel. Archie and Bedford the sound men were in position. Margie our makeup lady was finished with the cast and we were ready to roll. I got on the crane with Mitch. Slated the scene and up we went.

I could see the gorilla lying on a big branch. I didn't know Buddy and Rocky had an unseen wire with small electrical charges under him that they would set off when Jungle Jack spotted him. Coming across the land we had Jack, Bob and Vel with the four pygmies in the lead with their spears at the ready as they approached the tree. When they were about six feet away, Lee called out something and all at once the pygmies get excited, wave their spears and call out the words I had written in the script and Jack had worked long hours to get them to speak. "Ugga, ugga, bwana, bwana." This would be their lines repeated in all in twelve episodes. I know that when my kids saw the series they loved those lines and would imitate the pygmies. You're thinking my kids elevators didn't go all the way up. They were kids and they found this funny. For years Bob Corrigan and I would do a pygmy imitation. We were big kids.

After the pygmies had alerted Jungle Jack who was utterly fearless (that's what the script said) he told everyone to step back he would handle things. Bob had his filmless camera at the ready with lovely Vel clutching one arm for protection. I was getting ready for the close-ups.

Evidently no one had included the gorilla in the script meetings. He leaped out of the tree but not at Jack but to the side. He looked at everyone, scratched his head, and made two gorilla sounds then took off like a world class runner and headed for Phoenix, eighty miles away.

The security guys jumped into their patrol cars with lights flashing and sirens blaring. As Rocky and Buddy got their truck started I came down and ran to a jeep carrying workers and we were off. Why I joined the charge I have no idea.

Ahead of us there were three deep dips, then straight desert all the way to Phoenix. I saw the patrol cars go into the dips then come up hot on the trail of the racing gorilla. Our jeep went down and up out of the first two dips. As we went into the third dip, we went by a lone Palm tree and there posed against the tree a mature naked blond woman with her arms above her head and a horrified look on her face. A few feet away, a man in a Panama hat, gripping a speed graphic camera and his mouth open in a silent scream stood as if he were a statue.

When we returned a half-hour later with the gorilla safe in the handlers truck the model and her photographer had vanished. I bet he sold her on going to where it was isolated to take nude photos then from nowhere a gorilla comes into their hideaway followed by cops, a jeep full of guys then a big truck. Have a nice day!

We got back to location had lunch and then made the gorilla capture as scripted. I only had to change early morning to late afternoon in Jack's dialogue. We got our rooms at the motel and I eyeballed the many alligators whose evil eyes watched my every move. We returned from location at their feeding time. A crowd of tourists watched as hunks of meat were thrown at those hungry mouths filled with ugly teeth. Occasionally two gators would want the same morsel and a fight would ensure.

After dinner, I went to my room and knocked out the script for tomorrow's shoot. This should be fun. Jack was going to capture a deadly cobra bare handed. I made copies and gave them to the people involved. I joined everyone for a cocktail then headed for my room and a good nights sleep.

What a day. Plane on fire, the gorilla chase, the gators feeding and once in bed I was thinking what would happen if a gator got out of the pool, came to my room door, stood on his hind legs and opened it. I got out of bed, tested the lock, then slid a chair under the door knob. Back in bed, I went to sleep wondering if this was the way Cecil B. DeMille started. Gators or not, I slept like a rock.

My wake up call got me moving for a fast shower and shave. Stepping out of my room, I realized I was by the alligator pool while the restaurant was on the far side. I looked at the reptiles laying like logs in the water than remembered how they looked at feeding time. I was about to start the long walk when Jack stepped up beside me. "Ready for breakfast?" he asked.

"Yes, I'm going to walk to the restaurant."

"That walk is too far, let's take the shortcut."

"What shortcut?"

"Just follow me."

With that he stepped on the back of a gator and started to breakfast. I must admit it took some coaxing but every morning after I walked over the backs of gators, Jack explained that in the cool morning gators sleep and don't let a little weight on their backs bother them. It could be another gator moving to a new position. I watched Corrigan and the handlers running over the gators backs throwing a ball back and forth and Vel in her short shorts dancing as she moved gracefully over the reptiles. Just don't try that after 10 AM or you'll be gator bait. After my first morning over and back we took off for the India location and the cobra capture. Could it top yesterday with a burning plane, a gorilla chase and walking on alligators? It could!

I was told this location was just like cobra country in India, Pampas grass at least six feet tall and semi-clear spaces where cobras like to sunbathe. I have definite dislike of snakes unless they are essential to a movie plot. I remember my dad killing rattlesnakes in

West Virginia. Rattlers can strike the length of their bodies when lying straight out but straight or coiled made no difference to my father. Rattlers have poor eye sight and strike at heat. Dad would put his left hand in front of the snake. It would sense the heat and strike like a bolt of lightning. Dad's right hand had it behind the head and would snap its spine. I have no idea how well cobra's see and I don't want to find out.

Mitch and I go up on the crane. Jack, Bob and Vel and the pygmies do their rehearsal. Rocky lays the cobra in the clearing and I call "action." The cobra in the clearing has its mouth sewed shut. Jack will capture it in a close up. We will stop. Buddy will have the second cobra and while he wears Jack's shirt, I will take a close-up of his hand and wrist with cobra number two shooting his forked tongue in and out and kids will be thrilled how fearless Jungle Jack is. I call "action" and my cast advances to the edge of the clearing. The pygmies do their "Uga, uga, bwana, bwana" and Vel screams as she sees the cobra with hood spread and she grabs Bob who yells for Jack who lets everyone know he will make the capture. Jack dances around the snake then in a flash grabs it with his bare right hand and lifts it toward his face. I have the action in close-up. Horror fills Jack's face as the cobra flicks out its forked tongue. Rocky had put out the wrong snake.

Jack screams, "Jesus Christ, it's a hot snake!" and he throws it into the tall grass. The results are twofold. First our star is still alive and second the rest of us spend the next six hours gingerly hunting the cobra in the tall grass. These snakes have to be on their way home to India Sunday night. The "hot" snake was located, captured and after lunch I got the "hot" snake with tongue shooting in and out in Buddy's hand for the edit then completed the outdoor portion of this episode. The cobra with the sewed mouth had the stitches removed and both would be ready for indoor action that went without a hitch.

I had my bag packed and with the exposed film went direct to the airport for my return TWA flight. The gorilla and the cobras in their shipping crates rode in the truck with Buddy and Rocky for their flights to Africa and India.

On Monday, I delivered their film to the lab, wrote the scripts for the next week's shows. "Capture of the Giant Boa Constricter" and "Capture of Hugh Parrots and Macaws." On Friday, I was back on the early TWA flight. Breakfast was served and we crossed the San Bernardino Mountains. So far, so good. Finishing my coffee, I glanced out the window. The right wing was ablaze. How can this be? Two weeks in a row my plane was on fire. The Captain told us we had a small problem but would continue to Phoenix which we did only a little late. I knew my destiny was to die in the crash of a TWA flight. I got the message and from now on I would fly American.

I was more than a little shook up when I arrived at the so called South American location for the capture of a giant boa. Big trees, small creek about four feet deep running by. The pygmies and the rest of the cast and crew seemed happy to see me. The boa, very long with the thickness of an inflated fire hose, was lying in the tree on a wire with electric charges. Jack was going to wrestle this beast until Bob could give him a shot of some kind of sedative prepared by Buddy and Rocky. He would be loaded into their truck and when next seen would be in the studio. The crane was up on a flat bed truck so Mitch and I could go over the top of the tree, after the establishing shot of the boa, to see Jungle Jack and his disciples on route to the stand of trees lining the creek and be able to give our viewers a pan shot of this huge snake before the action started. Same story, little band comes across the plains. Pygmies spot the boa and they "Uga, uga, bwana, bwana" as Jack tells everyone to step back and uses a pygmy's spear to get the boa's attention.

Buddy and Rocky throw the heat to the charges and that huge snake comes out of the tree as if shot from a canon. His impact hits Jack like a middle linebacker and they both go into the creek. It's perfect for our camera set on the far side of the creek. We ride down so we are just over the struggle in the water. Mitch who's really up for this fight tells me his money is on the snake. He may have something for the boa was getting his huge body coiled around Jack who has the snake under his mouth. They are up and down, thrashing in the water as we take the camera for some really close work. They come up out of the water and I see Jack is turning blue. I yell for the handlers and everyone else to get the boa unwound. Buddy shoots the snake with a sedative. Mitch and I jump off the camera into the water to join the fifteen other men trying to save Jack. A second sedative shot, plus seventeen of us, using all our strength gets Jack free and he and the snake are out lying on the bank of the creek. Jack comes around first. He is scared as he well should be and is pretty badly beaten up. It seems there are no broken ribs which is a miracle. He takes a well deserved nap in the van, and then joins us for lunch. Afterwards, he and a much sedated boa get back in the creek and we complete a wild capture.

The following day is a piece of cake with parrots and a couple of macaws. I see the film from the first week's work and the pictures are major studio quality. Tuesday Lee calls with the news that Jack has some problems with his ribs and is taped up. Lee met with the investors and the decision has been made to only film one episode each week so more care can be made with safety preparation.

It doesn't affect me since I am only doing the *Massey Show*. I don't mention to Lee that this will increase the number of my round trips in the air. I'm having nightly dreams of being in a plane that's on fire and crashing.

When I depart Phoenix on Friday, I'm aboard a 707 American Airlines jet. I took a seat in the tail section of the plane. I hope it would prove to be a survival factor when we crashed. I was in bad shape and when the jets roared prior to take off I gripped the arms of the seat with white knuckles. I had not noticed that a stewardess was sitting beside me until her soft hand closed over mine. With an angel's smile she told me everything was fine.

We were airborne before she left to help serve breakfast. I relaxed and she returned and sat with me. Her name was Argie and she was from Animas Valley, New Mexico where she had been raised on a ranch. Kind, patient, brunette and lovely, I had to see her again. She gave me her phone number. The flight we were on terminated in Chicago and at present was her regular run. All at once I loved flying and hoped the filming would go on forever.

Jack wasn't moving so well but we managed to

film the "Monkey Capture" without incident. Some very risky episodes were ahead. Pythons, snapping turtles, lions, caimans, rattlesnakes and tigers. Back in Los Angeles, I called Argie and we started dating. She lived with a group of stewardesses in a house in Fox Hills. I met Argie's brother, a young Gary Cooper type, a real cowboy who hoped to break into movies. Argie is Mormon and spent some of her time off helping out at the Los Angeles Temple. We drank lots of hot chocolate, laughed a lot and enjoyed being together.

In the mean time, Curt had asked me to see if we could get some good songs that would lend themselves to become production numbers. The mail received indicated fans really looked forward to the two productions we did on each show. I think the NBC Music Library has every song ever written and I came up with winners and set designer Curt Nations made them come alive. A couple of my favorites were "When the Sun Comes Out." Martha sang the song in an "attic," with a batch of love letters as rain beating on the window until the sun would break through.

Another was "Snow Country," a Russ Morgan tune I had never heard. I called Russ and he sent us a complete arrangement. We used this during the holidays complete with falling snow, at train stations, during sleigh rides or riding a Greyhound Bus. Of course, it always snowed, fake snow. The "snow" was on a huge rubber sheet that had perforations so it would fall like the real thing. Each end of the sheet had a spring attached to a pole and when "snowing" the sheet was gently vibrated by an electric motor. One day, taping our Friday show, the sheet broke and

Curt was buried in a "snowdrift." We got Curt out and cleaned him up. Then the "snow" on the stage had to be cleaned. With a new sheet with new "snow" we were in business.

Our rehearsals were always open. Curt would walk around singing with a lariat in hand roping the lights, Martha, Country or maybe a guest. Lawrence Welk used to attend our rehearsals until we realized he took our production ideas back to his show and used them on the air. Lawrence was banned from our rehearsals. He told Curt he didn't understand why he wasn't welcome. He said, "But, Curt, what's good for you is good for me." Goodbye, Lawrence. Wonderful, wonderful.

On the *Wild Cargo* set we had some dicey moments ahead with the python and the snapping turtle got our attention when he crushed a policeman's nightstick in his powerful jaws and anxious moments with a lion. I used the extra time we now had to spend a day with my old friend Marty Martel recording the musical score for a series. The score included a pretty piece played when Bob and Vel would watch a sunrise, sunset or share a chaste kiss. This bit of music was named "Argie's Theme." I selected the sound effects including African drums, bells and gongs of India, background jungle noise, waterfalls and other needed items.

We had a big problem coming up with the caiman episode. The reptile, from South America, was as long as an extra large moving van. It had the mouth of a crocodile, the body of a huge alligator and a thick, scaled tail that could smash all your bones with one swing. It had to be captured in water.

There is very little public water in Phoenix except for swimming pools and the caiman was not the pool type. There was only one body of water we could use and that was the lake in Encanto Park. Lee and I visited the city fathers to get a permit to film in Encanto and the answer was a resounding "NO." The caiman was being shipped and we could only keep him for three days then he had to be shipped by air express back to his South American home. I told Lee not to worry, we would film in Encanto Park.

The following week's shoot was called off and Bob Corrigan and I spent Friday and Saturday at Encanto. The lake had a single security guard and on both Friday and Saturday he left for lunch at 12 noon and returned promptly at 1 PM. We would film the caiman on Friday when he arrived. Do the studio portion on Saturday and ship him out. On Friday we were ready, Buddy and Rocky had wired the caiman's mouth and he was in a large rental moving van. All seventeen men were in Buddy's truck to help handle the giant reptile. No crane was required for this capture. The cameras on sticks. The cast had been rehearsed. We would have an hour to film and make our escape. The park was very quiet with the big lake sparkling in the sunshine. Corrigan and I watched the guard. When he left at noon, we signaled the trucks. The moving van with the caiman backed up to a lagoon and the men dragged the caiman out with at least ten men holding the tail that had already smashed parts of the van's walls. They hauled it into the water. We rolled the film. The pygmies did their "Uga, uga, bwana, bwana," Jack ordered everyone back and jumped into the lake. He had to stay clear of the deadly tail while wrestling the caiman. We were getting wild action when a kid about eight, eating an ice cream cone, walked out on a little spit of land behind the lagoon right in the middle of my shot. "You guys shooting a movie?" The little brat asks licking his cone. I would have liked to have thrown him to the caiman's jaws. Instead, I get Lee to lead him away and give him a dollar for another cone.

Meanwhile, the clock is running, the guard will be back and we'll all go to jail. Jack is losing the battle with the caiman, who keeps dragging him underwater. I have enough good footage of the capture and I add a couple of reaction shots of Bob and Vel and the pygmies. We have twelve minutes before the guard returns. The moving van backs up and the loading of the caiman begins. It didn't want to get into the water, now it doesn't want to get out. All of us were in the water trying to hold the tail and get it back into the van. With three minutes left we close the van, get the seventeen men working in Buddy's truck and they leave out the far end of the lake. Waterlogged Bob and I leap in his car and we wave to the guard as we pass him coming in the front entrance. I joked with Bob telling him we should have unwired the caiman's mouth and left him to enjoy the lake. One night when a young man was taking his squeeze on a moonlight canoe ride, which was very popular, the caiman would take, boy, girl, and canoe and we would have the start of a great horror film.

My life was turning into a horror story. I met Dixie asking her to see our attorney, and file the divorce papers. She refused, then made endless calls to my secretary and made threats to call McCray which I knew she would never do because she wanted the money to keep rolling in. The only relief was the hours with Argie or when I was working.

The *Wild Cargo* film, the lion capture, went well. Thinking about big publicity the handlers let a very old and toothless lion free in the suburbs. The stunt hit the national press when a drunken Phoenix resident, staggering home at 3 AM, swore off drinking after seeing a lion lying on his lawn enjoying the sprinklers. Buddy and Rocky retrieved the animal. The story became national news.

Argie was flying the Los Angeles to New York run so I took the Thursday night American flight to Phoenix. It was booked to capacity. I had a window seat and beside me was a recent double amputee with legs removed almost to his torso. He was rolled onto the plane in wheelchair and was lifted into his seat by medical personnel. The bottom of the seat belt was fastened just above the amputation. He told me the loss of his legs was the result of an accident at sea. He had been hospitalized at a Navy facility for a long time but now was going to Phoenix and a home the Navy had built for him complete with ramps.

It was raining when we left LA but it turned to a major storm somewhere over the Painted Desert and continued to build. Lots of turbulence, crying and praying throughout the trip. The captain attempted to land. All of a sudden he pulled the nose of the plane up and we flew over the airport. Then gained altitude. The soft voice of the captain came over the speaker. "We're having a little turbulence and we will try another landing. It should not be a problem."

A man seated behind me gave the stewardess two 500-dollar bills to have the captain land in Tucson. The money went up to the flight deck and once again the captain spoke. "Folks we cannot land in Tucson as we do not have enough fuel to fly there. We will land in Phoenix as scheduled." The thousand dollars was returned.

We had seemed to have reached a considerable altitude when the lights in the plane went out and it dived toward earth. In the blackness there were screams, prayers and curses. Then, some way the captain pulled the nose of the plane up and we headed for altitude. My seatmate had been thrown out of his seat, his body hit a stewardess standing in the aisle and both of them were against the door to the flight deck. She had a broken leg and my seatmate's stumps were bleeding. There was a doctor on board. With the help of other passengers the stewardess was carried to the rear and made as comfortable as possible. The doctor stopped the bleeding in my seatmate's legs and he was placed back in his seat. He seemed to be okay but was worried that the Navy personnel that were meeting him would take him to a hospital and he wanted to be at his new home to greet his wife and daughter when they arrived from the east the next day.

The captain apologized for the turbulence and announced we were preparing to land. We dropped low and I could see the runway ahead. Between us and the landing strip was a high chain link fence. In flashes of lighting I could see we were banked left with our left wing below the top of the fence. Only God knows how he did it but at the last second the wing came up and we cleared the fence. Soon the sound of landing gear on the rain swept tarmac was the sweetest sound in the whole world. I was the last person off and I waited at the bottom of the steps until the captain came down. I shook his hand and told him that was fabulous flying and I was going to write

American and tell them that he, Captain Jack Mounts, was the world's best pilot. The captain thanked me and told me it was really nothing just a little turbulence. Of course captain, it was just a little bad weather with the tops of palm trees touching the ground, gale force wind and rain. I wrote the letter and Captain Mounts is my hero.

The next to last episode in *Wild Cargo* was filmed at Jungle Land located in Thousand Oaks, California, which was under the supervision of a Mel Kunz, and internationally known wild animal trainer. When I arrived, two lion cubs were playing on the grass by the parking lot. I got out of my car and started to walk up to where Lee and the cast and crew were standing. One of the cubs ran to meet me, stood on his hind legs and he was my height. He put his big paws on my shoulders and the two of us went down in a heap with him on top. He felt as though he weighted a ton and his big tongue was licking my face. Kunz broke out of the crowd, and came to where I was pinned. He spoke to the lion that rolled off of me and Mel helped me up. He laughed telling me the cub was welcoming me to Jungle Land.

After my heart returned to normal, I looked at Jack and noticed how much he had changed. No longer happy and laid back but a man full of fear. Why did I expect anything else? He was a warm hearted really good person who had taken on a very dangerous movie roll job for fame as an actor but to make a nice bundle of cash for his family. I know Lee had made it sound easy. Jack had received several close calls and now he was being asked to step inside a steel cage filled with a mixture of wild lions and tigers who don't like each other and who like humans less.

SILENTS TO DIGITALS

The world was enthralled by Clyde Beatty who performed in the steel cage with lions and tigers and who ended his act alone with a huge tiger named "Satan" who had twice attacked him tearing off pieces of his flesh. Now millions packed the circus when Clyde performed with the tiger who had twice tried to kill him. Beatty would throw away his whip and chair and at the acts climax the snarling beast would spring for Clyde who grabbed the escape door which would be closed behind him by the lunging tiger and the audiences would roar approval. I read the fear in Jack's eyes and took Mel Kunz aside. Mel would go through his act in his white trainer's suit. Then with the cage empty Jack would go inside and perform with the whip and chair and when we edited the film the audience would never know the difference. It worked.

CHAPTER FORTY-NINE

The final episode of *Danger Wild Cargo* was "Rattlesnakes," reptiles that Jack had worked with and had a great deal of information to relate. On my arrival, Lee had a telegram from Dixie stating that she and the children would arrive in the afternoon and she had accepted an invitation from friends for all of us to stay at their large home. Damn, these "friends" were friends of mine since I first came to Phoenix. What the wife of the "friends" didn't know is that Dixie had eyes for her husband and a million times told me she wished she had married him. She never realized the attraction was never a two way situation. The husband had been a very close friend of mine, so there was nothing to do but report after work and use what little acting skills available to pretend a happy marriage. It almost blew up when I told Dixie I would not be on the Sunday plane with her but would fly back Monday. She made threats to yell, scream and have me arrested for abuse unless I went with her and the children. Rather than have a scene in my friend's home I gave in.

At the alligator farm, I shot promotional film of

Jack and the cast as well as the final episode and made arrangements to do the final music and sound effects scoring at the lab in Los Angeles. Jack had told Lee he would not be playing in future editions of the series. As it turned out this would be it for *Danger Wild Cargo* which enjoyed success in the United States and the rest of the world. I would not be surprised if in some far flung outpost kids are being thrilled by Jungle Jack and are giving out cries of "Uga, uga, bwana, bwana." Jack Adam sold the alligator farm and in later years became an Episcopal priest and did outstanding work at St. Jude's Ranch for Children in Nevada. I would never see Lee, Mitch, Vel or the pygmies or my friends again but Bob Corrigan would play a major role in the years ahead.

The trip back to LA was quiet. I sat with Kim and Sharon while Sean was with his mother. All hell broke loose after we picked up our luggage. It may have been the biggest meltdown in the history of the airport. Screaming, profanity, throwing things until under threats of arrest, we were escorted to a taxi and went home. As I was leaving, I looked up into the balcony. Argie and her brother were waiting for me. I knew that after what had gone on, Argie and I would never date again. Who knows what might have been.

When a marriage has gone sour the children always know no matter that parents work overtime to pretend life is normal. The old mantra "we will stay together until the kids are out of high school" means that both children and parents lives will be twisted. It is far better to divorce and as much as it breaks your heart not to be with your kids every day, kids will grow up and in time, will make their own decisions and your relationship will be strong. I wish I would have followed that advice.

I found the agent I needed. Mitchell Gertz whose brother, Irving, was a respected talent composing and writing scores for major motion pictures. Mitch took the high road. Every Thursday we lunched at his reserved center table at the Brown Derby. Hollywood royalty would come to the table to say hello to Mitch who would introduce me as "the brilliant young director/writer who would be doing big things in TV and movies." One had to feel that a great future was ahead as you met Henry Fonda, Loretta Young, Jimmy Stewart and TV producers Bernie Barron, David Suskin and Norman Lear. Mitch was looking to make a major deal and I was his boy. Fred Rice and I had NBC interest in a couple of musical specials we were putting together, one with Bob Eberly and the other with Stan Kenton.

Coffee Dan's which stood at the western corner of Sunset and Vine had been replaced by the world's largest music store, Wallach's Music City which called for a TV special in prime time. With our friend Johnny Mercer as singing host Fred and I made our pitch. NBC was unable to clear time and ABC won the bidding. Fred and I got busy with recording stars to interview plus stars to perform. It was highly advertised and we were assured a large TV audience and a mob of autograph seekers outside the store.

Performers included Johnny Mercer, The Bobby Troup Trio, Nat "King" Cole, Dodie Stevens, Stan Freeburg, Fran Scott playing his number one hit "Calcutta," Shecky Green, Curt Massey and Al Viola. Fred and I wanted Peggy Lee to perform. A couple of weeks before the show we were invited to Peggy's for a party. We went but she was with trumpet player Roy Elridge and we didn't mention the show. Johnny's interviews would be Dorothy Provine, Pat Boone, Mary and Norman Kaye and Frankie Ross, the famous "Mary Kaye Trio," Tex Williams, Lawrence Welk, Stan Kenton, Peter Potter, Meredith Wilson, Billy Vaughn, Fabian, Charlie Barnett, Peter King, Andre Previn, Berle Davis, Al Jarvis, Glen Wallach, June Christy, Henry Mancini and Clyde Wallach. Bob Heiston would direct.

I brought Curt and Al Viola from NBC and they stole the show. Our guitarist "Red" Roundtree had left *The Curt Massey Show* just two weeks earlier due to failing health and we had locked in the fantastic Al Viola who soon became a good friend. Al played club dates with the Troup trio and backed Frank Sinatra on record dates. He had just had his first solo guitar album released by Capitol. Curt performed Johnny Mercer's "Dream" with Al on guitar and it was the hit of the show. Al's solo number, an up-tempo razzle dazzler was a close second. The show was live and super hectic.

Johnny opened the show out on Vine Street singing "I Hear Music" and managed to push through the mob of fans outside by the time he sang the final eight bars. Some unknowing soul had set out an open bar for the entertainers. This almost caused disaster. You never give entertains an open bar. They drink. With the exception of Curt, Al Viola and Pat Boone, who drank milk, even I had a few toddies during the evening.

Stan Freeburg had the green light to ad lib as he ran into Fabian who looked confused with all the activity. Freeburg asked how things were going.

Fabian said, "I'm not sure if they want me to sing."

Stan said, "I hope not."

I was amazed that Shecky Green didn't hold his audience. He did a clever bit where he played a stand-up string base like a guitar and told the fable of little Benny Lipsky. Shecky went into his act and the crowd left him alone with the cameras. The closing of this epic had Pat Boone, with his trusty glass of milk, Lawrence Welk, Stan Kenton and a couple of other guests around Bobby Troup at the piano singing Bobby's hit song "Route 66."

Bobby was out of it. His fingers no longer on the keys but trying to play the wood frame above the keys. Nat "King" Cole was leading the singing and the whites of Nat's eyes were the color of the bourbon he had imbibed but he was in tune and on the beat. Only Nat and Johnny Mercer knew the lyrics although Nat gave everyone a chance to warble a few bars. He turned the mic to the composer, Bobby Troup, who was too far gone to know anything and Nat asked him "Are you sure you wrote this song?" Nat and Johnny closed things out. The mob was then let inside and the place became bedlam.

Fran Scott and I were hired to audition girl singers for the *Rex Allen TV Series*. A sponsor's wife thought Debbie Kaye was just a shade too old for Rex. Debbie, who had just crossed the thirty mark looked good and sang good and was perfect as far as Rex, Fran and I were concerned but we had been hired to find a replacement. Rex was a handsome real cowboy with one of the greatest singing and speaking voices I have ever heard. His album *Under Western Skies* with Victor Young's Orchestra is in my top five album collection. We are going to audition for three days, Friday, Saturday and Sunday from 9 AM until 5 PM, Bring your music, an 8 x 10 photo and your resume. Oh yes, you must be between twenty-two and twenty-eight years old. Be able to sing solo, duets and act. Auditions will be held at the Moro-Landis Studio in Studio City. There's only one guy I want at the eighty-eight keys for these sessions and that's Al Pelligrini. We make a deal with Al and he holds his head to learn each of these girls is to sing an entire chorus. I remembered auditions where I had been stopped after eight bars.

Rex, Fran, Al and I along with Rex's manager, Mickey Gross, arrived at 8:30 AM. The Moro-Landis secretary would send the girls one at a time into the rehearsal hall where Al was seated at the piano, Frank and I were seated at a long table with Rex and Mickey behind us.

The line of potentials stretched a block and a half with the start of auditions still thirty minutes away and it was raining. Girl number one came in. Did I say girl? She had been a girl thirty years ago. The ad had a top age of twenty-eight which was out of sight on her rearview mirror. Pelligrini rolled his eyes. She was carrying her raincoat and wore a black lace see-through dress over her heavy frame. Frank and I put on our best smiles and asked her name. She growled like a sore-headed lion "Scarlett O'Hara."

Fran and I both laughed and said, "Your real name, please."

She growled, "Are you deaf? I'm Scarlett O'Hara."

"Okay, Miss O'Hara, give Mr. Pelligrini your music and what are you going to sing?"

Another growl. "Some of These Days." She growled the song as she did bumps and grinds. I was happy Sophie Tucker was dead and couldn't hear Scarlett slaughter her signature song. We thanked her and took her photo and resume. Peaking at the photo, we all decided it was taken about the time that Al Jolson was a very young man. I asked Rex if he wanted to continue the auditions since I thought Scarlett fit the show. I'll let you guess his answer.

So it went one after the other. Girls with bad voices, singing sharp, singing flat while Pelligrini aged before our eyes. There was the skinny lady whose mother had told her she had a beautiful voice. She croaked "The Last Rose of Summer" holding a rose that had wilted and died in the humidity that followed the rain as she stood in line. Al, Fran and I were taking headache pills when Lisa Kirk came through the door and belted out a great tune. She had sung with Ray Anthony and other name bands. Lisa would have been in the running for she was a beauty as well as a top-flight singer, but just before leaving she gave each of us a key that was supposed to be to her apartment and it had the address. None of us ever tried to use the key and it may have been a promotional gag but Mickey told us to cross her off the list. The sponsor would be turned off by the key bit.

At 6 PM we hung it up and had a drink at Bob Waterfield's pub. Bob, now married to movie actress Jane Russell, had been a great quarterback for the Los Angeles Rams and his club was a very popular spot to dine or drink. The next day, Mickey stayed at Rex's office on Rossmoor across from the high rise where retired movie star, Mae West lived.

The next day it was more of the same. Lots of rain

as we drank lots of coffee and kept smiling. Then at 4 PM a young lady named Sissy Bruce entered our lives. She was an exact look-alike for a young Judy Garland. Her hair was cut like Judy's. She wore black fishnet stockings and a Judy-style raincoat and did a rendition of "The Man that Got Away" that Judy would envy. Even Al was excited. Rex, Fran and I talked with her and learned she was also a dancer. We told her we would be in touch...then Sissy killed it.

She started to go out then faced us and opened her coat. She was stark naked except for her stockings and shoes. She held the pose, then asked, "Do you want me to sing a song or sell it?" Closing her coat, she went out the door. Even the unflappable Mr. Pelligrini was speechless. I still don't know the meaning of her final statement.

Rex didn't make it Sunday and he missed Sue Barber who wowed us, not with her voice but how fast she stripped. Her song was "I Wanna Be Loved By You." Within sixteen bars of music her shoes were the only bit of clothing on her shapely body. Al stopped playing and joined Fran and I picking up her clothes trying to get her dressed, which wasn't easy as she wanted to hug each one of us and give us a big fat kiss. At last, Sue was dressed and had left the building. We had auditioned 231 females with zero results. Debbie Kaye kept her job.

It was late on Christmas Eve in 1959. Fran Scott, Rex and I were spinning stories of our years in show biz regaling each other with tales of high times and hard times. I asked Rex how he happened to be a part of Louise Massey's *WLS Barn Dance* radio show. Rex was born with what in those days was called "crossed eyes" that could only be corrected by surgery. He had read about a doctor in Chicago who corrected this problem, so he took himself and his guitar to the "Windy City" with hopes to be hired for the *Barn Dance* to earn enough money for the operation. He was hired and worked alongside Curt Massey, then a fiddle player, who was Louise Massey's brother. Rex was a real cowboy. Born and raised on a ranch near Wilcox, Arizona. He made his first feature film in l949 at a time when singing cowboys were the rage and made nineteen westerns playing himself. He became a top ten box office draw. This clean cut, God fearing hero of the west, wearing his white Stetson who loved his horse "Koko" was soon a comic book favorite. Rex had several single hit records including "Crying in the Chapel" and "Sparrow in the Treetop." His album *Under Western Skies* is a masterpiece. As a narrator Rex did over 225 Walt Disney nature and wildlife productions and many major commercials. Rex has been honored with a star on the Hollywood Walk of Fame. Blessed with one of the world's greatest voices, he would be the last of the great "Silver Screen Cowboys" that included Roy Rogers and Gene Autry.

Around five, Rex suggested we go down to Nickodells on Melrose order dinner and tell the restaurant to put it on his tab. Mickey, his manager, would be there and Rex would be along later. After all, it was Christmas Eve. We met Mickey, ordered dinner and had completed eating when there was a great disturbance at the front door. It was Rex astride his famous horse "Koko." He rode into the bar and told the bartenders to give everyone in the place their favorite libation and then waving his Stetson wished everyone "a very Merry Christmas," and rode off into the sunset leaving behind a permanent Christmas memory of a warm and sincere man it was a privilege to know.

In January of 1960, J. Edgar Hoover, the Director of the Federal Bureau of Investigation, approached NBC with the desire to make a three-part mini-series regarding the work of the FBI with the closing segment concentrating on the "Betty Grable Extortion Case" and the capture of the extortionist in a Los Angeles cemetery which the FBI had filmed. The series technical advisors would be Agents John Cashell and Web Burke a former University of Mississippi football All-American. This mini-series would be shown on Monday, Wednesday, and Friday as the featured segments of *The Lee Giroux Show*." I was told I would direct this project. A writer had not been selected and I requested the job. They told me they would hire a known writer. I asked to meet Cashell and Burke and get the details and I would write a spec script and would not charge a dime for it. If the script was approved, I would get the job; otherwise, I would just direct and they could hire a writer.

They gave me a chance. I not only got the writing job but was also named producer. My agent Mitch Gertz was delighted as this would be another sales tool in his plan to associate me with a super production. The mini-series titled *This Is Your FBI* was a most enjoyable experience. I learned so much about the inner workings of the FBI. Betty Grable, under contract to 20th Century Fox was the highest-paid star in the movie business and had been very stressed and afraid when the extortion attempt began. The story had been history but with the help of Agents Cashell and Burke the tension built to the breaking point by the time the capture took place. The series played *The Lee Giroux Show* the first week in March. On March 16, 1960, I received a citation thanking me for my efforts from J. Edgar Hoover and the Bureau.

This would be the year *The Curt Massey Show* would win a second Emmy.

During the summer the kids and I saw National League Baseball at Dodger Stadium and the American League daytime games of the Los Angeles Angels and the New York Yankees. The Yankee games were gratis thanks to tickets left for us by Yankee pitcher Jim Bouton. He was related to son Kim's friend Rae Ellen Jensen. Twice we met Jim during pre-game workouts. The young pitcher had loads of personality and would later be the author of *Ball Four* rated as one of the three best sports books ever written. I would have loved for us to go to some night games but that was impossible since 1959 I was back in the music game trying to get us out of debt.

Dixie had maxed out the credit cards and the bank accounts were overdrawn. How could this happen? It was the old Hollywood legend come to haunt me as Reginald Rose had written. "They pay you five thousand a week and pretty soon you're spending six thousand a week, then they have you." Dixie was supposed to manage the money. She managed to spend it. I took away the credit cards and the bank accounts. I let her have one credit card with a low limit and looked for work out of town but closer than Santa Barbara.

I did six weeks at the Hollywood Inn on Hollywood Boulevard. They had a steady clientele and did no advertising still my heart would almost stop when someone entered. The only person that I knew was

Sean McClory, that wonderful actor who had been a guest on my Phoenix TV show but I knew I had to get out of town because sooner or later an NBC face would appear.

I ran into Eddy Brant, a well-known singer/pianist who was ending a long run at The Wagon Wheel in Oxnard, the Ventura area of coastal California. I auditioned and got the job. I would work steady in that area for the next two years.

I'm always asked about women and entertainers. If you're in the public eye be it musician, athlete or movie star having women is no problem. They come to you. Hall of Fame basketball star Wilt Chamberlin, the only pro player to ever score 100 points in a single game, claimed to have bedded 20,000 women during his career. I knew Wilt and I believe him. The gentle 7'2" giant made tons of money, was always in the headlines and had a great smile and a warm personality. Also he kept names and dates of his conquests. The women who make themselves available have husbands who are well educated, and presidents, CEO's or have high positions in major corporations or other big enterprises. They make big salaries, and even larger bonus checks. Their wives are high maintenance. Their women wear expensive clothes, drive expensive cars, and live in expensive homes with maids and housekeepers. They have the money for endless spas, beauty salons and fitness programs to keep their bodies sleek and firm and you can be assured their kids go to private schools. They are in the twenty-five to thirty-eight range and in their physical prime yet only one out of thirty is an accomplished lover. Please, no young girls need apply. Most are dull and boring. The "Bubble Gum" groupies are with

Mick Jagger and the rock crowd who rely on drugs for their "high."

There are nights a woman you have been with comes in with their husband and maybe their children. They have dinner. Comment regarding the nice music, might even make a request. Later the happy family leaves. Her secret is safe. When you date you buy your lady flowers and candy, take her to dinner, movies, and events. Not in this game. You never spend a dime. In the days of the big bands men would fantasize about the girl singer. Forget it. She was either sleeping with or married to the leader. I was at an audition by famed band leader trumpet player Harry James who was looking for a new girl vocalist. Seven girls were in the room and Harry announced "any girl I hire will sleep with the leader. If this is a problem please leave now." Not a single girl left. I have always been amazed that women think movie producers will put them into movies because they are beautiful or have talent. No one ever told the girls they spend a lot of hours on different casting couches and then if they get in front of the cameras they will be giving favors to producers and directors for a long time. The late Marilyn Monroe said, "It was not until I became a bonified star that I could sleep with who I wanted, not someone I had to sleep with to work."

Driving back and forth to Ventura six nights a week I bought a small sports car that got a lot of miles per gallon and only drove my Cadillac to work at NBC. During the magic years that big bands and show groups crisscrossed the nation, there would be many deaths on the highways. Long jumps between engagements with extreme driver fatigue, drinking, boredom and road hazards do many musicians in. The list of accidents is endless.

In the wee hours of the morning, I left work and headed home on I-15 South. The highway was clear except for a drunk driver in a big Chrysler weaving slowly back and forth across the highway laughing like a madman. I was anxious to get home, and grab a couple hours sleep before driving the kids to school. I decided to pass this idiot when he went to the right side of the road. When I got even with him he turned his car into my little sports car. Attempting to avoid an accident, I jerked the wheel. The left front tire hit the median and in a split second I was rolling over as the still laughing driver in the Chrysler sped away. My little car kept rolling. The seat back broke and the small of my back had intense pain. When the rolling stopped, I was upside down in a ditch in the median. The car was so smashed I couldn't get out and the smell of gasoline was overpowering. Big trucks whizzed by heading north. They didn't see me and I prayed they wouldn't flip a cigarette out their window. I would burn to death.

After what seemed like an eternity, a truck hit me with their big spotlight. They slowed, turned south at the next turn around, drove back and walked to the wreck as I yelled not to strike a match or smoke a cigarette. The two men from the truck walked both sides of the highway setting emergency flairs. They got on their radio and called for medical aid, highway patrol, a tow truck and the "jaws of life" to cut me out of what was left of my car. Free of the wreck the medics taped my back and suggested I see a doctor. There was no time for a doctor, I had to get the kids to school, take a short nap, get to rehearsal, do the show then back to Ventura. The tow driver put the scrap metal that had once been a car on his truck and drove me home.

I have always been a great reader and now time for that hobby had been cut drastically. I did my reading by putting the book into the ring horn on my steering wheel and enjoyed books as I flashed down the Hollywood freeway. During those two years, I worked the prime locations in the Ventura/Oxnard area including the Colonial House Hotel with their famous "living sign" a black man dressed like a chef, white uniform and a chef's hat on a high platform waving his towel at tourists.

After being away from performing I had to learn a lot of songs that the public knew but I didn't including "Love is a Many Splendored Thing," "The Yellow Rose of Texas," "Sixteen Tons," "On the Street Where You Live," "Love Letters in the Sand," "76 Trombones," and "Mack the Knife." Current hits I got from the radio as I only had to hear a song once and I knew the melody and lyrics. The two years of performing was ending, debts were paid and we lived within my normal salary. Physically tired I wondered if life was really worth living.

This was my mind set one of the last nights I worked Ventura. I had a heavy foot and I going about 90 MPH when I passed a Highway Patrol car parked off I-15. He hit the lights and siren and was in pursuit. I had a long lead and turned the Cadillac up to 100 and wondered if the trooper was willing to risk death over a speeding ticket. I reached the two lane road that went across the mountains leading to the beach and Malibu. This is a twisty, winding road with shear drop offs and dangerous curves. I kept my speed but turned out my lights. I had driven this road hundreds of times and knew every twist and turn. When the patrol car now farther behind slowed his speed and was having a problem with no tail lights to follow, half way up the mountain, I slowed, turned into a lane leading to a house, cut my engine and let the car stop without using my brakes. Later the trooper drove by using his spotlight. When he vanished, I went back down the mountain with my lights out until I reached the Interstate. The trooper and I both got home alive.

Rehearsal of *The Curt Massey Show* had been closed with the exception of Gordon McRae. Curt and Gordon often played golf at Lakeside in Toluca Lake and they would work out their schedules. Rehearsals had been closed because of disruptions by Jim Parks, an NBC time salesman who would talk to musicians while Country was rehearsing and be a distraction. I had always remembered what Jim Aubrey had said one day when we were talking about time salesmen. Jim stated, "That guy Parks is a weasel. He can't tell time, he's just an order taker." I barred Parks from the set and he told me he would get even.

The kids had a couple of great Christmas thrills when NBC invited all the children of the employees to the studios in Burbank, Santa was there and a huge decorated tree and everyone had a present with their names on it. One year the kid's hosts were the cast from the *Bonanza* series and after gifts were passed out, the kids took stagecoach rides with Loren Green, "Hoss," Little Joe and the whole gang. Another year the host was "Roy Rogers, the King of the Cowboys." Roy and his wife Dale Evans gave the kids their presents. Roy's horse "Trigger" was there and his dog "Bullet." Gaby Hayes was there and the kids talked about those parties all year long. In 1959 there was an afternoon telecast of the employee's kids in New York and Los Angeles Jerry Lewis hosted the New York portion while Lee Giroux hosted the California kids and I was the Los Angeles director. My kids Kim, Sharon and baby Sean were part of the west coast group. The show went back and forth. Going into a station break, Lee had Sean in his arms and announced that when we came back the kids were going to tell what they wanted Santa to bring. All of a sudden Sean said on national television "I want to go to the pot!" As we cut to commercial Jimmy Merrill, my regular technical director on *The Curt Massey Show* and was my technical director on this special, joined the technical crew in the control room in gales of laughter and shouts "just put Cawley's kids on TV if you want a disaster." They had fun for months asking when another one of my kids would be on the tube.

Going into l961 it was no secret that I had an agent and like Arner, Breslow and Belcher, I was looking for a strong career move. Jim Parks tried to move things along by planting a story in the *Hollywood Reporter* that CBS had made an offer to *The Curt Massey Show* to be a prime-time summer replacement program with a possible prime time slot on the CBS fall schedule. Right behind this story was an announcement that Fred Rice and I were working on specials with Bob Eberly and Stan Kenton. The word on the specials was old news. We had presented these ideas to NBC months ago and they had been approved. Parks was trying to indicate I had gone to CBS trying to make a deal. Tom McCray knew that I knew Massey was tied to a Shell contract and that I had never been through the doors of CBS Television City. There was lots of talk by people who didn't know how the contracts were intertwined.

On April 12, 1961 my agent, Mitch Gertz, who at one time had been Clint Eastwood's agent called to set a meeting at his office at 338 North Rodeo Drive in Beverly Hills. I never saw him so happy. All the lunches at the Brown Derby had paid off and on Monday morning we would meet with Bernie Barron at Skelton Studios, 1416 North La Brea to sign a five-year contract to direct *The Red Skelton Show*. Now Mitch could start working on a career in movies for me. I didn't care about the riders on the contract that would require Mitch to provide certain guests for the Skelton Show. These riders were common on all contracts. I knew I would be happy with Red and we were talking big money.

When I broke the news at home Dixie started planning the move to Beverly Hills and the furniture she would buy and of course the complete new wardrobe she would need. I asked her not to start spending until the contract was signed. Mitch called me early Friday to confirm we would meet at eight thirty on Monday morning at his office and drive to Skelton Studios. He also told me he was checking into Cedar Sinai Hospital for a checkup and would be there over the weekend. The night before he had a chest pain and just wanted to be sure he was okay. Mitch had lost his wife two years ago and he had two young children to raise so he wanted to stay healthy. I wished him luck with his test and he said he would call Saturday evening. Meanwhile, I tried to vision how it would be to see Red again and I could hardly wait for that moment. Mitch called Saturday evening.

His heart was fine. The doctors did want him to lose ten pounds which he would do.

"We'll still do the Derby but I'll have salads" he laughed. "I'm staying here until Monday. I'll see you Monday morning. We've waited a long time for this day."

I was hyper the whole weekend. The kids and I swam; saw a ball game and the family went out to dinner. On Monday I showered and shaved and headed for Rodeo Drive. I had my favorite music radio station playing and I sang along. Arriving at Mitch's office I told his receptionist to tell him I was here.

She looked at me as if I were an alien. "Didn't you have your radio on while driving over? It's all over the news."

"I had music on. What's on the news?"

"Mitch is dead. He dropped dead tying his necktie at the hospital. He had a heart attack." I'm surprised I didn't have a heart attack. Mitch had my world, our world ready to go bright and shiny and now it was gone. Long afterwards when sanity returned I realized I should have seen Mr. Barron and talked to Red. After all, we had some great times together when we were both starting out. I didn't do it and by the time I started thinking straight *The Red Skelton Show* had signed a director. Needless to say things were depressed at home. The dreams of a home in Beverly Hills, the new clothes, the money gone like a puff of smoke.

In May my friend Bob Eberly came to town to record an album for Collectors' Choice Music that would reunite him with Helen O'Connell to recreate their hits with the Jimmy Dorsey Orchestra. I was there for one session and got to see Helen and talk about old times. I was able to have Bob out to the house and have two dinners out. Bob was a hit with the kids. Laughing joking and telling funny stories about his son and daughter home in New Rochelle. Bob said he had never eaten Mexican food. Could that be possible after all those Latin songs? I took him to the El Torito where he put away lots of good Mexican dishes. I was also amazed that he had never been in a car with seat belts.

The next day I took Bob to the studio to visit *The Curt Massey Show*. He met Curt, Country and the musicians. Martha was in makeup, lying back in the chair with her eyes closed. Bob leaned down and whispered, "Let's sit in the back of the bus."

Martha screamed "Bob Eberly" and sat straight up. We teased Martha for weeks how she knew it was Bob. Helen and Bob completed recording the following day then went into the control room to hear the playback and for the very first time heard their voices in stereo. Helen was off to host a "Miss Universe Pageant" and Bob back to New York for his radio series *The Bob Eberly Show* with vocalist Monica Lewis.

Stan Kenyon, My World is Music would be the swan song for Fred Rice and me at NBC. Paul Pieratt a recent addition to the staff would get baptized as a producer with two vets to guide him. I would direct. The show had been scheduled for an hour but due to problems with the band it had been cut to a half hour with three guests. They were vocalist Mavis Rivers, the Les McCann Trio, and Music Authority and Critic, John Tyman. An animated film clip by artists John Wilson would tell the story of Kenton's "Cuban Fire." Talented writer Brown Meggs wrote the script and our super set director Curt Nations created a 'future world' set using the award winning abstract paintings of Lorsor Fietelson. We had a top technical crew with technical director Jimmy Merrill, audio engineer Bill Levitsky, Bob Grapperhaus and Joe Williams handling audio and Parker Oliver as lighting director and Troy Workman heading the stage crew.

Stan Kenton was a jazz pianist, band leader, composer and arranger who became famous leading a band that over time featured the world's greatest jazz sidemen. His band was innovative, controversial with his progressive jazz. He first came to national attention when the Capitol recording of his theme, "Artistry in Rhythm" and "Eager Beaver" hit record stores. Later singers Anita O'Day and June Christy propelled the bands fame as well as a raft of super sidemen that included Art Pepper, Stan Getz, Chico Alvarez, Vido Musso, Milt Bernhart and Eddy Safranski. Stan was well over six feet with hands that spanned an octave and a half. Music was his world and he and the band traveled more than fifty weeks a year playing one nighters.

You can imagine my surprise when Stan came to me about a half hour before the show in a panic. "Mavis Rivers wants to sing the standard 'Little Girl Blue' in the key of C and I can't play it in C." I was dumbfounded. The great Stan Kenton was unable to play a song in the key of C? I got on the phone and asked NBC music if they could send Al Pelligrini to handle this emergency. Al was out of town but they sent Vic Peamonty, a fine pianist who did the job. By careful editing, the viewers thought Stan played for Mavis' beautiful vocal. The show got great reviews.

While looking for a new agent I got a call from a

man named Gordon Davis who was a Vice President of Westinghouse Broadcasting who wondered if we could meet for lunch at the Brown Derby. Davis was a fashion plate in his dark suit. Warm, friendly and sincere. He told me his mission was to find a producer-director to take over the western half of their network show *PM* that was sponsored by *PM Magazine*. The *PM* people wanted to add a west coast version to their popular show which would soon be called *PM East – PM West*. They were offering me a five-year contract at more than twice what I was making at NBC and I would produce and direct *PM West* from KPIX the Westinghouse station in San Francisco.

I didn't have an agent and I could use the money. In a couple of years, I could get out of my contract and come back to Hollywood. Being in San Francisco I could make appointments in Los Angeles and fly down and meet with contacts. Mr. Davis needed my contract to start in a month, giving me time to give notice and get ready for a new challenge. I signed the contract and that afternoon saw Tom McCray and gave notice and thanked him for my years with the company. I thanked Jim Damon for getting me through the door in the first place then broke the news to Curt, Martha, Country and the band. I recommended they get Doc Livingston as their new director which proved to be a good fit. The last few weeks leaving Mexican food with Martha was rough. Little did we know we would work together again.

The kids were excited to go to someplace new yet hated to leave their school and old friends. Dixie liked the money and thought we should build a home in San Francisco. Doing this would make things "all right." I mentioned I could fly home on weekends and the kids could stay in St. Martins, but no, she wanted to be close to where the money was paid, so she put the house with the big pool up for sale. I had lunch with my cousin, Ken who thought the move made sense and was happy that it was in San Francisco as he traveled there often for business with Attorney Melvin Belli. At the end of the month I flew to the city with the Golden Gate ready for *PM West*.

CHAPTER FIFTY

My flight to San Francisco arrived in the late afternoon and Gordon Davis waited at the gate. He suggested a drink and we went to the Sky Lounge. After drinks arrived Gordon said he had bad news. "The *PM East/PM West* show had been canceled. I reminded him I had a five year contract with Westinghouse Broadcasting not KPIX the Westinghouse station in San Francisco. He agreed. I would never be a member of the KPIX staff but would I mind directing some shows for the station until the home office back in Pittsburgh could come up with a national show for me? Since I was being paid national money how could I not help out. So I said yes.

The Westinghouse studios were located at 2655 Van Ness Avenue the street that led to the Golden Gate Bridge. Just south of the studio was a very comfortable watering hole called "The Living Room" where leather recliners and soft sofas were available. The KPIX equipment was top of the line black and white. The engineers were not Los Angeles talent but were relaxed and did their best to please. Everyone was happy at KPIX and you got the feeling they would like to stay with the station until they retired. Lou Simon, the general manager of KPIX, was a prince of a fellow and program director Ray Hubbard was very creative and would have been a major player in Hollywood. I was there and yet I wasn't one of them. I did not belong to KPIX but to Westinghouse.

With the city of San Francisco it was love at first sight. The cable cars, Fisherman's Wharf, The Cliff House, fabulous hotels, the 49ers and the Giants, Candlestick Park, the feel of fog on my face, and the lovely ladies with beautiful legs from walking the hills, the white gloves they wore and the little hats on styled hair, it was glorious. How could you not love this city? In town all you needed were the cable cars and street cars to get around. While in Los Angeles I heard guys rave about the city but when they talked homes they were boosters of "Marvelous Marin," Marin County right across the Golden Gate north of San Francisco. Checking things out I quickly saw that you would need a sack of gold if you wanted to build a home in the city. Marin was calling. I had sold my car and I bought a Rambler convertible whose top was never up unless it was raining.

When I firsat arrived I lived at the Mark Hopkins Hotel high atop Nob Hill. At the "Top of the Mark" awaited endless libations and a fantastic view of the city and Alcatraz Prison where Al Capone played banjo in the prison orchestra. Downstairs, I could dine while listening to Anson Weeks "Dancing with Anson" Orchestra or cross the street to the fabulous Fairmont Hotel with its glass elevator and the music of Ernie Heckshire and his orchestra.

I crossed the Golden Gate, which was a never ending thrill, past the Muir Woods with the famous

Redwood Trees on my left, the road to romantic Sausalito on my right. I turned left by Richardson Bay and into the quaint but captivating town of Mill Valley. I knew that somewhere in this area I would find just the right place to build a house. I couldn't spend every hour exploring San Francisco or Mill Valley. I had promised Gordon Davis I would help out at KPIX. I was named director of the series *World of Art* produced by Judith Tattersfield a capable and pleasant young lady. Henry X. Ford, President of the College of California Arts and Crafts introduced the series which started with the basics of drawing and later covered water color, oil painting, woodblock printing, lithography, silk screening, sculpture, ceramics, jewelry, textiles and interior design. Rehearsal at 6 AM, show time 7-7:30 AM every Saturday.

Next I directed the popular *Dick Stewart Dance Party*, hosted by good-looking Dick Stewart who was an excellent host for the bubble gum crowd that danced the hour away. Some guests included short lived recording stars of that era plus an occasional real recording star. Westinghouse had great ambitions as it battled Dick Clark and his *American Bandstand* show. The Stewart show needed name guests and more production money which never arrived. Dick's show aired five days a week and was a winner with the young. When Lou Simon learned I had directed Chet Huntley and Elmer Peterson he asked me to drop everything to direct the lo PM news with Van Amberg and Nancy Clark. This was a serious show. Write your own news show that could have become a national staple. Both Van and Nancy were very good and audiences liked them. Doing this show gave me a friendship I really enjoyed with a man I always admired. The name was Johnny Unitas who played a little pro football for the then Baltimore Colts. John, who may be the greatest quarterback of all time was dating Nancy Clark. They would have dinner then Nancy went to work. That gave John and me better than an hour to go to "The Living Room," have a toddy, and talk football. Johnny had some great tales to tell. Always funny and easy going it was a time I will always value.

I met Mildred Vail considered Mill Valley's top realtor and we got busy hunting land to build on. Mill Valley is surrounded by mountains and I wanted to be on one of them. 55 Rose Avenue was perfect. From the valley you went to Rose Avenue down a dirt road bordered by pine trees on both sides and went up. Across the valley was beautiful Mount Tamilpais and if a house was built high enough from the rear you could see over the Redwoods of Muir to the blue Pacific Ocean. I rented a cottage within walking distance of the building site where the kids, Dixie and I lived, while our house was under construction. Builder Frank Bitz and I worked on the plans. Frank completed a one of a kind home. The parking area was three feet higher than Rose Avenue. The living room was ninety feet higher than the parking area. The front of the living room was all glass with sliding doors that opened on a huge redwood deck. We had the view of the ocean from the kitchen. Everything I asked for Frank delivered.

Years later after we moved this property sold for three million dollars. The land around the house was a steep slope covered with ivy, much of it poison, but that didn't stop the deer, chipmunks and beautiful birds from their daily visits. The chipmunks loved to wash their faces in the bird bath on the rear deck. Carpeting and new teak wood furniture did not come cheap. It was the best place for the kids. They walked through the woods to Old Mill School with their Fox Terrier "Cactus" who returned home when his charges had gone to class. In the afternoon he would go down to the school to meet them and bring them up the mountain home.

I flew to Las Vegas to meet Cousin Ken Agee where we formed A.C. Productions while a female harpist floated on a huge lily pad in a lagoon inside the Dunes Hotel made beautiful music. Our project would be a TV series. Twenty-six half hours of *The Frankie Carle Show*. Offices for A.C Productions were at 2 Pine Street in San Francisco. 2 Pine Street was located across from Pacific Gas and Electric Company's offices on Market Street. Fickle fate never gave me a clue that inside that company's office was the woman who would change my life and be the best thing that ever happened to me.

I asked for and got my Cousin Bobby Chandler from Ken's office to be assistant producer on *The Frankie Carle Show*. I had told Frankie I was going to pitch the show and he was locked in with a deal memo. I packaged the show in a *Curt Massey Show*-format without Curt and Country Washburne. I needed a ten-piece orchestra. One phone call got my friend Al Pelligrini as musical director. Al signed the best musicians available. There was only one girl singer I wanted. Hall of Fame artists Liltin Martha Tilton, who would also be perfect exchanging lines with Frankie. I had to fill the musical hole that had been so effective and did this with the dynamic vocal group "The Lancers." Four very talented guys, masters at performing. Jerry Meacham the lead singer had a monster hit with "Lonely Street." Bob Porter played a mean jazz trumpet. Dick Burr was an invaluable frontman while Corky Lindgren was the best bass singer anywhere. This group was a hit in personal appearances and on recordings.

Frankie and his wife, Edie, Martha, Al and the Lancers would stay at the Mark Hopkins as would our out of town guests. The Mark gave us rehearsal rooms. The Top of the Mark had limited space for cameras, so I rented space at KPIX and used their engineers. The station was happy to get some money back from a director who only did a news show five nights a week while drawing down paychecks for national shows. The engineers were happy to make extra money and they knocked themselves out. I was busy getting my guest list together when Lou Simon called to ask a favor. Would I stand in for him and meet Judy Garland and her present husband Sid Luft who had been out of the Unites States and she requested to see a show in her current CBS-TV series that she had done but had never seen. We carried her show and had a copy. Of course, I would be happy to stand in for Lou. With an engineer to roll the copy I awaited Judy's arrival.

The world would learn the inside story of the CBS-TV *The Judy Garland Show*, in Mel Torme's memoir *The Other Side of the Rainbow*. This evening in early l963 I got a preview of a star whose career was in the rear view mirror. A woman who had world acclaim yet managed to lose it all with the help of drugs, booze, lack of discipline in both her private and professional life, plus tremendous insecurity. Judy and her husband Sid Luft arrived late. Judy was a mess. Wild hair, little makeup and looking old beyond her years and constantly twitching. She had a carry all that had an open bottle. I gathered it was her favorite, Blue Nun. Whatever it was she drank often. Sid Luft, her husband, had been a test pilot for Douglas who had been a pilot in the Royal Canadian Air Force in World War II. He had once been the manager of dancing star, Eleanor Powell. Luft was a business man. He produced Judy's movie *A Star is Born* which failed to recoup its production costs. Now he was her manager who tried to keep her working. I felt that Sid had many attributes of Jim Aubrey, the major one was not sugar coating conditions but telling it like it was. Watching them view the show had me twitching by the time it was over.

Every entertainer, athlete or person on the street knows when they have lost a step or their talent is fading. Joe DiMaggio quit at the top of his game. Johnny Carson hung it up when the fun and the glitter started to fade. After Rocky Marciano destroyed every contender he quit although he could have made millions more. Quitting is hard on the ego but you know before anyone that you are slipping. Be honest, hang it up. Sid was in a lose-lose situation. As a caring husband, he would have suggested a good rehab followed by retirement and a life as wife and mother to their two children. As her manager, he had to point out that the failure in her show was not the other people as she liked to proclaim. It was her. Several times watching the show he told her "she was a has been" and "her career was over." It was one of the longest hours of my life. When it was over, Sid thanked me and sent his regards to Lou. Judy finished her bottle and they vanished into the night.

CHAPTER FIFTY-ONE

Bobby Chandler had locked up a deal for Frankie's wardrobe to be provided for credits on the show by a major men's store and Frankie flew in before rehearsals started to be fitted. We spent most of the day getting this done before we took Frankie to the airport for his trip home. I had asked him to the house for cocktails and to meet the family. I knew Dixie would invite people and I made a point for guests not to ask Frankie to play. As an entertainer, I would not sing or play at people's homes. That was my profession. Would they ask an attorney for legal advice or a minister to give a sermon? All I ever owed the public was the best performance possible when they paid to see me. I had no desire to drink, eat or get to know them. My private life is private.

Everyone had a cocktail, the kids had soft drinks and of course someone asked Frankie to play. Being the gentleman he was he said he would play a medley of his hits. Kim stood by the end of the keyboard watching. When Frankie finished there was polite applause.

Frankie looked up Kim and said, "How did you like it?"

Kim replied, "It was good but you don't play as good as my dad."

Frankie roared with laughter and said, "You're probably right."

We had a wonderful guest list including my old boss, Curt Massey, who brought his twenty-one-year-old son Steve Massey with him to do "The Last Stage Out" which they had recorded on the album *Curt Massey Time* for Capitol.

My Cincinnati friend, Al Morgan, of the flying hands, and the pleasing voice that made his single recording of "Jealous Heart" sell over five million copies for London Records. Al, a 300 dollar a week pianist/singer had, without his wife's knowledge, withdrawn their savings to record Jenny Lou Carson's "Jealous Heart." Then walked all over Chicago, where he was working, asking diner owners to put his record on their juke boxes. A London recording executive stopping for lunch put a handful of coins in the juke box and punched buttons at random. While eating, "Jealous Heart" came up. The executive asked the owner who the performer was. Al had left his card and the next day he was under contract to London and soon was signed by Dumont Network for his own half-hour *Al Morgan Show* on Monday evening. The show was a huge success. One of the stipulations was that although he was backed by an orchestra, he never had to rehearse. Often he came to the program with a song he had just recorded, but the band had never heard. Seated at the piano Al would announce the title, give the band the key and they played. The fans loved Al. One day when a big snow fall made it unable to take off to Chicago his fans dug the snow off the tarmac and he flew in a private plane to Chicago and made the show. A town in Pennsylvania was renamed "Morgan" in his honor. With cash falling like rain he bought three top of the line Cadillac's. One for his wife, one for him and the other to sit parked in the drive at his home to show the world the minister's son from Kentucky had made it. In time, he became a twenty thousand-a-week entertainer playing major theaters, selling records like *The Place Where I Worship.*" Guest television appearances plus, his own television series and world-famous Casino appearances including Las Vegas where he recorded his live performance for the London album *Al Morgan at the Dunes* made him extremely successful.

"Jealous Heart" had been lucky for me. My rendition won my initial television contract for my own show, *Love That Song*.

It was fun seeing and Al recalling old times when he worked WLW with Rosemary and Betty Clooney. The times when both Al and I had shoveled coal off pianos in storage sheds so we could go to work.

A guest we fell in love with and featured on four shows was big, blond handsome Dick Noel who had been the male singer with Ray Anthony. Dick was now featured daily on the *Tennessee Ernie Ford Show* from ABC in San Francisco. One of my all-time favorite records was Tony Bennett's "Green Dolphin Street" until I heard Dick Noel sing it with the Al Pelligrini band. Dick never recorded the song but I have the soundtrack and it's priceless. Speaking of songs, Al composed a pretty waltz titled "Two Kisses" for Martha which drew favorable notice.

The entire production went very smooth with

two exceptions. Dixie had upped her quota of martini's and after dinner would sit in her blue teak wood chair with her big Siamese cat "Fitzsame" wrapped around her shoulders hissing at anyone who came near. Cousin Bobby Chandler lived at our house while we produced Frankie's show. Most nights we would eat at the Iron Horse in Maiden Lane in San Francisco. We didn't eat at home because seven nights a week dinner was steak, salad and French fries. Dixie no longer cooked. Daughter Sharon did dinner and did it well but I don't like ice cream every day of the year.

Bobby and I came home for a song score and were headed for dinner when I told Sharon not to fix anything for us. Bobby was going downstairs when Dixie called, "Bobby." He stopped. She reached beside her chair and threw a hatchet as hard as she could, missing Bobby who dived head first down the stairs and the hatchet was buried in the wall where he had been standing. Going downstairs, I pulled the hatchet out of the wall and later threw it into a trash can in Mill Valley. Bobby checked into the Mark Hopkins. I brought his things to the hotel the following day. We were not out of the woods. I had the wall repaired and repainted.

The second incident came at rehearsal a week later. The Mark Hopkins had provided security outside rehearsals. People heard the music and wanted to enter. This day Edie, Frankie's wife was standing by the keyboard where Frankie and our guitarist were working when Dixie stormed through the door yelling and cursing and drunk. Her voice rose as she yelled, "God damn sleazy wop bastard playing that God damned piano, I don't want to hear." Earlier the guitarist had smoked a cigarette and put it out in a leaded ashtray sitting on a table. Still cursing at the top of her voice she grabbed the ashtray and threw it at Frankie. He ducked, the ashtray almost hit his wife, then took out a window of the hotel. The security guard had heard all hell breaking loose and rushed in, grabbed Dixie, who was fighting, cursing and clawing, and removed her from the room. She was barred from the hotel. I was embarrassed and concerned for Edie who was pale and shaking. I wanted to call off the rehearsal but Frankie just wanted a few minutes to take Edie to their suite then he returned. The next day Edie had a mild heart attack. This made Herb Caen's column. The most-read column in the Bay area. Herb said nice things during the shoot and was kind in not saying what caused Mrs. Carle's heart attack.

Frankie and Martha were on the cover of *Where Magazine*, Frankie had a beautiful new wardrobe, an RCA Victor album *Frankie Carle at the Top of the Mark*, A.C. Productions had thirteen half hours of a wonderful musical TV series *Frankie Carle at the Top of the Mark* and also for syndication, thirty-six fifteen minute radio programs *The Frankie Carle Show*.

My partner, cousin Ken Agee had come to town a couple of weeks before the shoot started. I went with him to see Melvin Belli and to his favorite night club, "Gold Street," which was in a basement and you entered by going down a fast wood slide. "Gold Street" celebrated New Year' Eve every night when at twelve the confetti would fall, noisemakers would blow and everyone would yell "Happy New Year" and kiss. You could lose the blues everyday as you started your own New Year.

On Saturday, I flew to Los Angeles to have Announcer Burt Barer do the opens and closes for the TV shows and the same for the thirty-six radio programs. Then we had the titles and credits put on and sent to our syndicators, Medallion Distribution, headed by John Ettlinger, (a member of the Hertz auto family) who also represented John Wayne's Batjack features package and "Adventure West."

Sunday I had a late lunch at my cousin's hotel. He had great psychic abilities and he told me I was no longer with Westinghouse. I reminded him I had three years on my contract. He knew that but before the night was over, my stay with them would be over. Ken had to be wrong. No one in San Francisco knew where I was. When we landed, I was walking across the tarmac when I saw Gordon Davis waiting by the gate.

Gordon told me that Westinghouse could no longer pay my national show fees when all I was directing was local news. If I would move to the headquarters in Pittsburgh, my pay would remain the same. They were working on national show formats but nothing was set at this time. l told Gordon I had just built an expensive home in Mill Valley and would not move east. He offered me an extremely generous buy-out and I accepted.

I was free to return to the Mecca...Hollywood. With a healthy supply of money in the bank, I could afford a few weeks off. April l7, l963, the Mill Valley Little League Baseball season opened and son Kim was the right fielder for the Mill Valley Eaglets of the American League. It was a memorable day for the 300 boys on the eleven teams making up the two leagues. The teams paraded from Old Mill School through Mill Valley to Boyle Park where Russ

Hodges, the voice of the San Francisco Giants, was the opening day speaker and there would be four games. KRON TV called and I wasn't interested, although my friend Jerry Jensen was their star newscaster. Jerry and I took a couple of trips in his sailboat, under the Golden Gate Bridge out in the blue Pacific to the Farallon Islands. An exciting trip as the wind filled the white sails.

I was getting ready for my return to Los Angeles when I got one of those phone calls that changes your life. The caller, ABC Vice President David Sacks, the head honcho of ABC's owned and operated KGO-TV at 277 Golden Gate Avenue. Mr. Sacks had some things he felt I would be interested in. First he needed a producer for the ten televised games of 1963 High School Football Season. But the plum was producing AFL Pro Football for a brand new venture by Roone Arledge Director of ABC Sports to be called *Wide World of Sports*. I met with David Sacks and the Program Director Cal Thomas both men got my respect as quality people, and I was on board. The High School telecasts went like clockwork.

However, the real high was when my black sport jacket with the *Wide World of Sports* logo arrived. I would be producing a telecast of the AFL Oakland Raiders from Frank Youell Field in Oakland with one of the greatest sport casting teams ever, Paul Christman, George Ratterman and Curt Gowdy. Not only great sportscasters, they were great guys to work with and have good times with. Paul Christman, a member of the College Football Hall of Fame, had been All American for two years at the University of Missouri where he was the starting quarterback for three seasons. His number "44" jersey was retired by the school. Paul played for the Chicago Cardinals and the Green Bay Packers during his Pro career. He and Curt Gowdy called the First Super Bowl. Paul had a game he and I played in the announce booth. We both had a set of numbers each one indicating the play we thought the offensive quarterback should call. Paul hit the call 99% of the time.

George Ratterman was one of the funniest men I ever knew. He had played quarterback at Notre Dame as a backup to Frank "Boley" Dancewicz and Johnny Lujack. George was the last athlete in Notre Dame history to letter in four sports – football, basketball, baseball and tennis. Frank Leahy said, "He was the greatest all around athlete in the history of Notre Dame." George played pro ball in the AFL and Canadian Leagues before he was selected by Coach Paul Brown to replace retiring Otto Graham with the NFL Cleveland Browns. A leg injury ended his football career. He earned his law degree and became general counsel for the AFL Players Union. George wrote a hilarious novel, *Confessions of a Gypsy Quarterback*. George was often paired with Jack Buck and Charlie Jones on broadcast teams.

Curt Gowdy, one of the most beloved sports announcers, was a legend when he arrived at Youell Field for Oakland Raider Football. He had done New York Yankee Baseball with Mel Allen; been the voice of the Boston Red Sox; had called Ted Williams last at bat home run; and with Paul Chrisman had called college football as well as AFL games. What the public didn't know was that Curt had a great deal of pain from a disk injury that happened to his back when he was the star of the University of Wyoming basketball team. It can get cold in the booth. In his briefcase Curt always kept a heavy black shawl. I took care the shawl was removed before Curt was on camera then replaced it when we went to Paul or George.

Prior to games I went to both locker rooms as George did interviews. These huge bodies were black, blue and purple and there were many sets of false teeth placed in lockers. I was always amazed the fans thought the spots on their pants were dirt. They were blood. These men are gladiators.

After the games, we headed for Jack London Square in Oakland and Jackie Jensen's restaurant for top food, drinks and conversation with Jackie, "California's Golden Boy." Jackie, big, blond and rugged had been a legend at Oakland High in both football and baseball. He was an All American halfback at the University of California. A legend as a Rose Bowl hero with a future in pro football but he chose baseball as a profession. He played for The New York Yankees. Sold to the Boston Red Sox, he was the American League's "Most Valuable Player" in 1958. But now the "Golden Boy" was retired and very troubled having given up his career through fear of flying and a wife who was jealous of his professional standing after her career as a diver had faded. Although Jackie always sat with us, talked and laughed we wondered where his story would end.

I produced the one-hour Prime-time TV special *Big Game Fever*, the greatest moments and colorful history of The Annual California Stanford Grid Clash. This event is the Big Game of each year in the Bay area. I planned to use historic game film screened from ninety hours of vintage material. Comments from former stars of the game with two famed alumni as hosts. The honorable Herbert Hoover, Former President of the United States had been water boy for the Stanford football team and a former University of California cheerleader, Ralph Edwards known to every television fan as the host/producer of *This is Your Life* would head the show to air Friday, November 22 the night before the big game.

I knew the director assigned for *Big Game Fever*, Marty Pasetta. This was the Sammy Glick that Bud Shulberg was writing about in his classic novel *What Makes Sammy Run*. I am certain there are male and female Glicks in all types of business but they are prevalent in show business and especially in motion pictures and television. Just watch the film "All About Eve" Sammy Glick's have no love or loyalty for anybody or anything. Their only work is their job and their advancement in that job. If needed, they will destroy other people and those people's careers for their success. I knew that Marty had been written up for violating union rules at least five times by every technical director in the company. The camera and effects were controlled by engineers of NABET. Members of The Director's Guild of America called for what we wanted and the technical director's got it for us. In that nervous little herky jerky way of his, Marty would reach over the control board and punch what he wanted. I always wished I was a technical director. If he had reached across my board I would have broken his arm. Marty was creative but could never work within the rules. He never spoke, he yelled and made no bones about crushing anyone to advance his career.

He also had a mean streak for female performers. Women trade a great deal on their beauty and after thirty, when that beauty starts to slip it is the director's duty to stay off extreme close-ups. Use Vaseline on the lens or diffuse the shot and never do a close up when the lady works with someone younger. Roles as leading ladies fade much faster than leading men.

I have always remembered what James Wong Howe, one of the greatest cinematographers who ever lived said to Marlene Dietrich when she returned to movies after being away ten years. Marlene told Jim she hoped he could make her as beautiful as he had ten years before when they had worked together. James smiled and said, "Miss Dietrich, I'm ten years older." His lighting magic and camera angles gave the viewers an ageless Marlene. I have always taken extra care with female performers to use makeup, lighting and camera movements to hid the "crows feet" mad wrinkles that in time Mother Nature brings to all of us. Marty loved extreme close-ups to disclose an actress. I informed Marty that if he violated union rules, he would be out and I would produce and direct. I certainly would welcome his ideas to benefit the show. We had no problem in pre-production or production. I did have to write filler material for former United States President Herbert Hoover who had to bow out due to health reasons. I had to write material that showed our former President as the Stanford water boy using still photos and old film.

Sportscaster Bud Foster replaced Hoover and Bud and Ralph Edwards, two old pros did a fabulous job as hosts. I had no doubt Pasetta would have a brilliant career in Hollywood and he did. He produced the Elvis Presley television special *Elvis–Aloha From Hawaii*." He later directed seventeen of the Academy Awards shows.

Being Marty, he yelled once too often when he clashed with Broadway legend Michel Kill and Academy President Robert Wise and was let go from the Oscar telecasts. His legacy is the use of technology in television production.

We had the *Big Game* show taped and ready to air two days prior to deadline. The morning of November 22, l963, David Sacks, Cal Thomas, Bud Foster, Marty and myself and a couple of time salesmen screened *Big Game Fever* and there were "high fives" all around for a job well done. We dispersed. I was talking with Ernie Ford when David Sacks ran out of his office and told me not to go away. President John F. Kennedy had been shot in Dallas.

Our nation went upside down with the news and ABC in San Francisco was no exception. I was ordered to stay at the Richelieu Hotel on Van Ness Avenue. I could not leave the hotel for lunch or dinner at Orestes, one of my favorite restaurants right on Golden Gate Avenue just a short walk from the station. I had to remain in my room at all times including meals. If David Sacks needed a director for a remote or studio shoot he knew where to find me. Of course, I could not go home and my call explaining this was met with profanity about ABC, the government and the world in general. David sent a runner with the current magazines. So I settled down with a TV, radio and reading material for the next three days.

The fact there was a Blums Restaurant in the hotel was a delight. If you have ever eaten at Blum's you'll try to find an excuse to stick around.

My mother came out for the holidays and it would be the first and last time in Mill Valley. Coming up the stairs, I heard my mother saying, "No,

No." Walking into the kitchen I found mother on her tip toes and Dixie with a knife under her chin. Talking calmly, I managed to get the knife and mother went to pack her bags. She checked into the Mark and left for home the following day. When I asked what the problem was Dixie told me, "They were just talking." She called my mother at the hotel asking her to, "Come back because I love you." Merry Christmas and Happy New Year.

ABC asked David Sacks why he had not done a major TV special from a night club in San Francisco. David said he would correct that. I had never done the club or entertainment scene in San Francisco with the exception of the Troubadour in North Beach when my friend Matt Dennis and his trio would appear there.

A tall, thin man with should-length blond hair wearing a green pullover sweater over ragged and faded jeans, brown loafers and no socks was the first talent to show up for the auditions. He was speaking in a soft, raspy voice. He had worked at The Purple Onion, a well known San Francisco nightclub and the Hungry I as a folk singer and had recorded a couple of albums for Decca. In fact this young, white man had sung with Lionel Hampton's Band and just returned from New York where he had composed and conducted music for the *The CBS Workshop*. Hampton and CBS really grabbed my interest. I was ready to hear Rod McKuen do his thing. He did, about six minutes, and he had me singing him praises. Neither Rod nor I guessed that in 1966 with the publication of the poem "Stanyan Street and Other Sorrows" he would soon be America's greatest poet whose books would sell over sixty million copies. He would write 1,500 songs that would account for the sale of over 100 million records worldwide. Add to this the returns from his concerts and motion picture soundtracks like *The Prime of Miss Jean Brodie*.

Not only did Rod record his works in that soft raspy voice, his work was also recorded by many of his peers. An entire album of his songs was recorded by Frank Sinatra. McKuen songs were recorded by Duke Ellington, Judy Garland, Robert Goulet, Noel Coward, Mabel Mercer, Dinah Shore, Petula Clark, Perry Como, Madona, Barbra Streisand, Andy Williams, Waylon Jennings, The Boston Pops, Johnny Cash, Pete Fountain, London Philharmonic, Chet Baker, Johnny Mathis, The Kingston Trio, Al Hirt and Anita Kerr. In l969 my kids and viewers of all ages would enjoy *A Boy Named Charlie Brown*, the first feature-length animated movie based on Charles M. Shultz's popular comic strip, *Peanuts* that included Rod singing the title. I gave him a deal memo and we were in business.

If there was to be comedy in the show how could you do better than Ronnie Schell who was a Hungry I staple? I will always be thankful that auditions lasted two days. The next afternoon, I met and hired a man whose compact discs I have worn out over the years. This husky guy with a bright smile said his name was Glenn Yarbrough who had founded and been the lead singer of a very successful group called "The Limelighters." A folk vocal group who enjoyed major record sales, played the nation's top night spots and were in demand for concert dates. I asked why with all this success he wanted to be on my show. The answer was simple. He had left the "Limelighters" to go on his own as a solo performer. I knew nothing of folk music or the "Limelighters" but I was willing to listen. I noticed the staff were very excited as he picked up his guitar. He did a wonderful medley of songs in different tempos. "The Honey Wind Blows," "Time to Move On," and "San Francisco Bay Blues." When he finished he had made me a folk music fan. As Glenn's mellow tenor hit my ears, I knew this voice and singing style was special. He whistled and sang and it made musical sense. I told him of meeting Rod McKuen and discovered they were friends and Glenn planned to do a complete album of McKuen songs in the near future.

The next year, 1965, Glenn would record the title song, "Baby, The Rain Must Fall" for the motion picture with the same title starring Steve McQueen and the song would become a monster hit. Glenn also provided vocals for the animated versions of "The Hobbit." With Rod and Glenn as our two star performers we went into rehearsals. Then I had a call from David Sacks' secretary saying David wanted to see me as soon as possible. David looked worried and serious. The big smile was gone. "Bob, I've watched the tapes of the *Hungry I* show and I feel you're in deep trouble. That guy that reads poems and sings in that raspy voice will kill audiences and the big guy who sings and whistles has got to go."

I knew in a split second that David knew zero about folk music and zero about Rod McKuen. "David, I'm the producer/director of this show and Glenn and Rod are great entertainers and the entire nation will love them."

David shook his head. "I have spent a lot of time building you and this show up to the ABC brass in

New York and if you keep these guys in it you and I will have a failure."

"David, I am not going to change my cast. If the shows fails, it is my failure and I will stand by my decision and take any fallout."

David and I both stood as he said, "It's a bad decision and I wish you would change your mind."

I always had the highest respect for David but I knew he was wrong and it wasn't his fault. His job was not to know musical trends. The show hit the air in prime time and it was a huge success. Mail poured in wanting more of Glenn, Rod and *Hungry I*. The day after the show Ernie Ford stopped by David's office telling him how much he liked the show and ABC, New York had also called David telling him how much they had enjoyed it. David called me in, shook my hand and apologized. I reminded him the show was a success for both of us, for without him green lighting the production, then standing by my decision to go with Glenn and Rod the show would have never happened. Both David and I were all smiles when I left his office.

CHAPTER FIFTY-TWO

David Sacks spent a long time talking about a job opening with KTVI-TV Channel 2 in St. Louis as Program Manager, a major management position, that could in time lead to a top job with ABC network management in New York. The idea made me want to throw up and I told David I was returning to Hollywood to write, direct and produce. David insisted I at least take an interview with their Board of Directors. After all, as David pointed out, this was an ABC affiliate, in a prime market owned by The Newhouse chain. To keep my good relations with David I agreed to take the interview. I met the wise men of the board whose knowledge of the industry was zippo. A big mistake in many ways but destiny was calling the shots.

It was spring and baseball season was ready in Mill Valley. Son Kim's Eaglets had won last year's championship and hoped to win another title on the pitching arm of Scott Palmer. Saturday, April 25 was opening day and the feature attraction was the "Yankee Clipper" Joltin' Joe Di Maggio as the opening day speaker. Joe watched the kids warm up then gave son Kim his greatest athletic compliment when he said, "You have the greatest arm I have ever seen on a young man your age. No one throws from the outfield as well as you do." Joe signed his glove which Kim treasured. Heady stuff from the greatest fielder of them all.

Over the weekend I talked and Dixie raved about management. I made my vision clear. I was a writer/director/producer who loved my work. She said the only job in TV was management. I had to let go of the actors, stage crews, musicians, technical crews; these were low life and scum, but management was the elite and she and the children deserved the upper class. I said suppose this job should lead to New York was she ready to move there? She said, "We could have an apartment in New York for visits but our home would remain Mill Valley." I reminded her that working with the low life provided a beautiful home and money to buy nice things. It was like talking to the wind. I set a date to meet the Board in St. Louis with the muddy Mississippi rolling by.

I met the wise men of the board who may have been successful in their line of business but had zero knowledge of the television industry. They had read there was big money if a local show could be developed for something called syndication with not the least idea of the cost with very long odds for success. They wanted me to create major sports documentaries to sell to Budweiser. This was doable. Also build a strong daily schedule.

That wish would be granted. Of course there were two mistakes that would be impossible to overcome. The wise men had hired a local radio announcer with zero knowledge as a television executive as station manager and we were saddled with an old and out of touch relic of his early days with the Newhouse newspaper group as a production advisor. He was 100% bewitched, bothered and bewildered by the electronic age. The new station slogan was "KTVI." St. Louis is a Brand New Ballgame." Very clever since St. Louis has always been a super baseball town and this fall the World Series would be here. We had an excellent sales department, public relations and quality engineers but with top management's lack of television knowledge, we began a wild ride that for me lasted five months and thirteen days that seemed like a long slice of eternity. The studio located at 5915 Berthold Avenue, St. Louis, was set for black and white telecasting, color television was just coming and networks were showing programs in color so viewers were starting to buy color sets.

The studio was a couple of easy walking blocks from the famed restaurant, "Stan and Biggies." I dined there many times and got to know and enjoy talking with co-owner Stan "The Man" Musial, a national baseball legend. Another block away were the offices of Budweiser for whom I would create sports documentaries. Going to the offices at Budweiser was a real kick. Need a drink from a drinking fountain? You got ice-cold Busch Bavarian beer.

I lived at the Forrest Park Hotel in a room above St. Louis Cardinals Manager, Johnny Keane. We would see each other at breakfast and make small talk.

I moved in as program manager July 27, 1964. August, I had a call from Richard Colbert of Four Star Productions in Hollywood who was in town. We had a most pleasant dinner at the high-rise 300 Restaurant then met the following day at my office.

Dick knew the KTVI full schedule and had a top syndicated product that could give us high ratings, the ratings that TV lives and dies with. I followed his advice and we were off to a good start. Richard and I became friends and he would play vital roles in my future.

My office at KTVI only needed a bed and shower to be home. I had a kitchen, a fridge and monitors to every studio plus on-air monitors as well as separate monitors to view our competition. I also had not one but two of the finest secretaries on this planet. Young, vibrant Nancy Toffont and Carole Wainiger with poise and features a major model would envy.

I managed to get a commitment to add *The Les Crane Show* to our schedule. His talk show was a hot item that year.

Then who should walk through my door but Lloyd Thaxton who was on a station tour promoting his *Lloyd Thaxton Show* packaged by MCA then the number one agency in the land. Lloyd needed new promos for his show and I directed them and he was pleased. *The Lloyd Thaxton Show* quickly became the highest-rated musical entertainment program in the nation for the next eight years. If you were not around for the 60s, 70s and 80s you missed one of the greatest talents television ever produced. Warm, witty, funny Lloyd Thaxton won five Emmys during his career and was nominated fifteen times. A producer/writer/director and host creator of game shows he had no competition and his knowledge of music and the artists who made that music was awesome. Lloyd ended his career as a producer of NBC's the *Today Show*."

Our honorable station manager gave me a list of

eleven employees he wanted fired. I protested I had not evaluated their work. He wanted them to think their firing was my idea. I have no respect for an executive who has someone do his dirty work. You hire them, you fire them. Before I did his bidding, I evaluated their work and every single person was doing a good job in the workplace. This had to be a personal vendetta.

At this time the old relic Curly came to town to "advise" on something he knew nothing about. His most outstanding feature was a glass eye. A Newhouse family member who worked for the station told me Curly's eye had been destroyed by a union organizer in the early days of the newspaper. Since he had lost the eye fighting for management, he had a lifetime job. That was nice gesture but they should have kept him with publication. Our first meeting was to decide on a news set for our to-be-formed news team. I came with a detailed plan for a set I knew would work and I said so. Then Curly did what he would always do when he was lost in the electronic age. He pressed his temple and his glass eye popped onto the table with the pupil spinning as he said, "Cawley, your ideas are irrevocable." I almost laughed as I looked at the spinning eye, then the empty red socket it had came from. I didn't laugh.

Two weeks later, he called a meeting where he revealed the design for the news set. He was using my exact plans calling it his idea. He ordered me to hire a sports man to cover our news/weather/sports block to be anchored by veteran newsman Spencer Allen who was solid and respected. I got four-time Emmy winner, Art Brock from Arizona. As it turned out, Art would never do a word of sports.

The day he arrived Curly and our beloved station manager hired Ed McCauley, a St. Louis University All-American and an all-time great with the Boston Celtics and the St. Louis Hawks as sports director. I had no quarrel with this. "Easy Ed" was qualified. We worked well together and did some good things. But why hire Brock? Art did nothing but station breaks until another ill-advised acquisition of Curly's and the station manager would cost money and fail. Then Art came to the rescue. There was a fever to find a talent to build a show around that could be sold in national syndication. Were talent agents contacted, film clips collected and lengthy auditions scheduled? Of course not. Curly and our station manager went after a local woman whose show on the local NBC station was going off the air for low ratings amid a swirl of rumors of a personal nature. I saw the woman's show and her feeble attempts as a singer and host and asked them to set up a search for real talent. That did not deter our two talent scouts. They proposed a big contract and she accepted. When the official signing was recorded by still photos and video tape, I was seated by this over weight person with hair dyed an unnatural black with the fake smile, as she cursed me behind her teeth. It was evident the talent scouts had told her I was against her hire. They soon found out they had got more than they bargained for, but why worry? It was my problem, not theirs.

We built her a beautiful makeup room with mirrored walls and ceiling. She refused to use it until the floor was mirrored. She was a legend in her own mind, slapping her belly proclaiming she was a star. The talent scouts tried to tell me she was the prototype of St. Louis housewives. If that were true, every man in St. Louis would be leaving town. From early rehearsals, she ate our young directors up. To launch her show with some kind of order, I brought in Fred Heglund who had spent nineteen years with the NBC network as a director/producer/writer. Fred was used to working with insecure ego-driven stars. He had won a Peabody Award and created "The Whistler Series" among his many credits.

Every day, the would be prima dona created a crisis. Then the talent scouts came up with their ultimate conquest. They signed Pat Fontaine, the once weather girl on NBC's *Today Show* to join Spencer Allen and Ed McCauley on the news block. The scouts brought up Pat's name to me and I almost became unglued. It was known that excessive alcohol use had ended her network career along with known personal issues. They didn't listen but gave me another can of worms and another daily crisis. I met Pat at the airport upon her arrival with a bouquet of roses. She was drunk and almost fell down the airliner steps. The only thing that saved my sanity that summer was the fact that the Cardinal organization presented me with a pass to all of the Card's home games and I spent many evenings in old Busch Stadium.

As fall came in the two daily crises were being handled. The prima dona was still a whirlwind of problems but things were somewhat better than the start when she told the TV audience how happy she was in her new TV home with the exception of the program manager, Mr. Cawley who was a barracuda. The talent scouts had to let New York know what they were working on for syndication, so they sent them a copy of the show. New York answered with a demand the prima dona never criticize an executive on the air. When she made the same statement the following week, New York said her show would be cancelled if she did it again. Since we were an ABC affiliate, they had that power. Pat Fontaine was having trouble with booze and would call in "sick" and Art Brock would step in and do weather.

CHAPTER FIFTY-THREE

I was getting a great deal of pressure to bring my family to St. Louis. I called Dixie and told her the situation. She said that if the family moved to St. Louis it would require buying an upscale home but still keep the home in Mill Valley. Another pressure was the last name on the list of eleven that the beloved station manager had ordered fired without cause. Jack Fierben was by far and away the best local director, plus I knew from what the staff had told me that he was the station manager's best friend. When it could no longer be avoided, I took Jack to dinner at the 300 Restaurant in the high-rise. After cocktails, and while waiting for dinner to be served, Jack told me that the station manager wanted to fire him but didn't have the guts to do the job. I told Jack that the staff believed that they were best friends. He said they had been but the station manager knew things about him that he didn't want to go public. Jack never told me or anyone else the station manager's secrets. I later got a letter from Jack saying he was very happy doing a job for a college in Illinois.

The 1964 World Series was between the Cards

and the New York Yankees. The Cards provided me with a reserved seat. Prior to the start of the series I did an "on air" interview with the Card's captain and second basemen, Dick Groat, a delightful guy who had earned All-American honors as the star of a Duke University basketball team. The Cards were depending on the blazing fastball of pitcher Bob Gibson to be a major factor and Bob didn't fail them. The night before the opening game, I was quite late getting back to my hotel. The bar was deserted except for two occupants. Mickey Mantle and Whitey Ford of the Yankees both worse for wear and the series opening just a few hours away. The Cards won the series.

Before leaving for a quick trip to see the kids, I brought Bob Woods from NBC to bring talent and energy to the writing side of TV. Bob had the ability and genius to be one of America's great writers. His work was just phenomenal. Always a fashion plate, Bob was funny, a great idea man and a good friend. At this point, it had not been discovered that a drinking problem was fast stealing his talent. There were no signs. Not in speech or walk or driving. Everything was straight arrow.

The time with the kids who seemed to have grown so much went way too fast. My youngest Sean Patrick had won the National Ford Punt Pass and Kick Championship for Mill Valley and was wearing his Division Grand Prize, a red and grey warm-up jacket just like the ones worn by the San Francisco 49ers Pro Football team. Son Kim and sister Sharon were decked out in their scout uniforms. Nine-year-old Sharon had a group of little chickens and the gang was happy with the St. Louis Cards jackets that I had brought them. Their mother only wanted to know if I would get a Christmas bonus. She agreed to bring the kids to St. Louis during the Christmas season and would look at upscale homes to buy if realtors had something to show.

I arrived back at the station just in time to catch a flight to Dallas. There was a pro football game between the St. Louis football Cards and the Dallas Cowboys and they needed a producer. I arrived at the Cotton Bowl, met my crew, director Tommy Thompson, who did a terrific job, plus the first class announcing team of Jack Drees and Hal Fisher. Jack had been an All-Big center on the Iowa University basketball team. Jack was a sports giant who had called super bowls and many major events. The voice of the Chicago White Sox baseball team, he was also considered the all-time best caller of horse racing. Hal Fisher, doing the color on our telecast had been an All-American lineman at Notre Dame.

Working the Cotton Bowl was fun plus just across the midway from the Bowl was a place that served the best fried chicken this side of heaven. I went with Jack and Hal on the team interviews and "Dandy Don" Meredith. The Cowboys quarterback was a one-man show as he later proved after his playing days were over and he became a TV star. We had the final camera rehearsal the night before the game, then Jack, Hal and I went to a popular club called Nero's Nook that had a long line waiting to enter. A big Texan shoved his way into the front of the line and everyone grumbled but did nothing. Hal left Jack and I, went to the front of the line, picked the big Texan up and carried him to the rear of the line to the cheers and applause of the crowd. An executive of the club recognized Jack and we were ushered in like royal guests. Another thing I will remember about that trip was the Marriott Hotel where we stayed had the largest, round beds I have ever seen. Wilt Chamberlin would have loved them.

Returning to my office Fred Heglund, who had aged ten years since arriving asked for a two-week leave to try and regain his sanity after dealing day in and day out with our prima dona. She had unraveled this kind, gentle man. Having watched this happen I was bringing in my old friend director Fred Komo, from Oklahoma to take over the reins of her show. She could bully and throw tantrums forever but she would never unravel Mr. Komo. Fred Heglund planned to spend a couple of weeks in Hawaii, and when he returned I planned for him to direct the news.

I was invited to attend the Teamsters Joint Council Annual Charity Event at the Chase Park Plaza Hotel. With my credentials, I went backstage to see Bob Hope, who wondered what I was doing there when I should be in Hollywood with NBC. Bob introduced me to Tony Martin and George Jessell who were also entertaining and I shook hands with and exchanged a few bon motts with the President of the International Brotherhood of Teamsters, James R. Hoffa.

On Saturday, Bob Woods and I drove to Champagne Urbana to see a favorite Illinois team play Ohio State. All-American Dick Butkus of Illinois had played havoc with opposing teams but Woody Hayes, the great Ohio State coach, had a simple game plan. The Buckeyes ran every play at Butkus. He was hit by a tackle, a pulling guard, a blocking back and the fullback on every play and by the third quarter he was finished. Ohio won 26-0. After the game, Woody was asked what he thought of Butkus. "Who?" Woody asked.

On Monday I got the terrible news that Fred Heglund had shot himself to death after arriving back in Los Angeles. His daughter, Willow later sent a note that Fred had left for me saying he was sorry he had let me down but after years of working with real stars the actions of prima dona, not taking direction, the tantrums that kept all concerned was just too much. When I informed prima dona of Fred's death her remark was "He didn't know how to handle a real star?" She had caused the death of this kind, talented, gentle man. I wanted to take over the direction of her show but the two talent scouts killed that. Her tantrums continued but Fred Komo directed with a firm hand and despite her daily complaints he stayed in charge.

The pressure was on for our first documentary for Budweiser. Bob Pettit of the St. Louis Hawks would soon be the first player to score 20,000 points in his career. The documentary would be based on his book, *The Drive Within Me* written with Bob Wolff. It traveled his life as a kid in Baton Rouge who had been cut by his church team, who was only a substitute in high school, to All-American at LSU and All-pro with the Hawks. Soon he would do what no other player had done. I gave the writing assignment to Bob Woods. Ed McCauley would host the show with Richie Gurin and Lenny Wilkins. Guests included Bob Pettit, Cliff Hagan Paul Silvas, Jerry Lucas and Hawks' owner Ben Kerner. I produced and directed. We would tape the entire show then follow Bob and the Hawks until he scored the 20,000th point. The day before the taping, I asked Bob Woods for the script of the show so copies could be made. The only thing he had written was the title page. I spent the remainder of the day and most of the night writing the show. I gave Bob Woods writing credit, knowing I had a major problem.

The taping of the show was fine, now Bob Pettit had to reach the 20,000-point mark. We followed the Hawks at home and away and Bob Pettit, who always scored in double figures, was getting double and tripled teamed as no team wanted to give up that historic marker. At last, in Cincinnati Bob reached 20,000 points with a jump over All-Star center, Jerry Lucas. Budweiser loved the documentary and in NBA cities it played at least three times in prime time.

Jack Fierben was back in town in a local hospital fighting for his life against cancer. I visited him and he looked pretty bad. I notified his so-called best friend who never visited Jack but used Jack's illness to his advantage. The press was notified our director (how could that be when he had been fired) and dear friend was fighting for his life. I was ordered to have a big screen color TV put in his room. A gift from his employer. Jack wasn't watching television, he was trying to breathe.

Christmas was coming and I was to create a one hour special starring Pat Fontaine who was now acting as crazy as the prima dona by calling in once or twice a week saying she was committing suicide. After a couple of mad rushes to Pat's condo to find scratches on her wrists, I let that part of insanity out of my life. The infamous glass eye spun on the table wanting Christmas Eve with Pat Fontaine to be a really big show. Ray Carlson came aboard as co-writer and I produced. Film cameras covered the area like a blanket. Great footage of Christmas decorations in and out of stores, shoppers, Santa, the Budweiser famous Clydesdale horses all dressed in holiday gear was taken. The whole Christmas scene was filmed. Fred Rice sent fabulous Capitol Records soundtracks including Nat Cole's "The Little Boy That Santa Claus Forgot" that I built into a scene that pulled a great deal of favorable fan mail. I selected Lee Christian a young staff director to call the shots and he did an excellent job.

Final rehearsal went well but forty-five minutes before we hit the air Pat Fontaine was found in the ladies rest room drunk with her head in the toilet throwing up. The ladies at the station felt there was no way she could do the show, no matter how much coffee we gave her. Then I remembered a mature young lady I had wanted to add to the staff to do interviews but the glass eye said we had Pat Fontaine. The lady's name was Jane Flornoy and she would be perfect. On short notice, Jane came in and without rehearsal did a show including reading the many cue cards without a bobble. The audience was told Pat Fontaine "was ill."

I drove to Columbus to visit my mother. I could have slept forever in my old room being lulled to sleep by the sound of the Super Chief heading west. Eating in the kitchen with mom and visiting our old Thurman Avenue home where we lived until I was in 9th grade was about dead from the passage of time and decay. Barret Junior High was where I discovered basketball and Virginia Boyer. I sat in the Amp theater where I graduated from University High and remember many things. Memories that can never be erased of home, school and friends. What had happened to the dreams I had then? With regret I returned to work.

Dixie and the kids came in the week before Christmas and almost left at once when there was no bonus check. Kim, who was ten came to the station and was fascinated by my office. I had told the kids about my problem and Kim wanted to see the prima dona's show. I got him a ticket and he was standing in the line waiting to get into the studio when the prima dona swept in wearing her furs. I didn't see what happened but the staff filled me in.

When she reached Kim she put her hand on his head and asked, "Whose little boy are you?"

He looked her straight in the eye and said, "I'm the barracuda's son."

She jerked her hand away and demanded to know who let the little monster in. The staff roared with laughter as she swept into her dressing room. I loved it. Score one for us. Dixie refused to meet the realtors who were standing by to show homes. She wanted a divorce and I told her to see my attorney, Roger Garity, the former Prosecuting Attorney of Marin County. While I was at work the following day she and the kids flew home. Merry Christmas.

The NBA All-Star game was scheduled January 16, 1965, in St. Louis. Budweiser needed a documentary. I put together *The NBA – Road To Glory*. The guests were Bill Russell, Jerry West, Bob Pettit, Wilt Chamberlin, Red Aurback, Elgin Baylor and the Hawk's owner, Ben Kerner. Ed McCauley would host and I would write and direct.

CHAPTER FIFTY-FOUR

During January 1965 I must have set a record for round trip flights to San Francisco. A divorce hearing would be set. I arrived and it was cancelled. Dixie was "ill." Flying cost money and it left me little time for work. *NBA, The Road to Glory* was a winner and I started writing the story of boxing great, Willy Pep, as a documentary. I met with a depressed Bob Woods to see what could help. Although there were never any signs of alcohol abuse Bob had started drinking heavy when we were at NBC. Each morning he would drink an entire bottle of vodka before he came to work. Then have three Rob Roy's for lunch, a couple before dinner and two more after dinner. He was going to a rehab in California. The glass eye told me I needed to spend more time in my office and less in San Francisco and he was right. I knew Dixie would get big alimony and child support. I needed the job.

I heard Dixie was ordered to have a psychiatric exam after she tried to run my attorney down in the parking lot. He saved himself from injury and possible death by diving onto the hood of a parked car. He reported the incident and the judge said, "This case has to close before someone gets killed." That afternoon I was having a sandwich in Mill Valley, prior to my return flight that evening, at the only place I knew that had Scopatone, a wonderful device that showed artists looking alive as they sang their hits. Two lovely German girls and a song by Tony Bennett were my favorites.

A young guy I had never seen and would never see again set down at my table. "You're having trouble with your wife," he said.

"Yea, I'm going through a rough divorce," I replied.

"For $5,000 I can make it all go away."

"How could you do that?" I asked.

"Very simple. I'll waylay her car going up Rose Avenue and beat her to death with a ball bat. You will be back east and you'll be free."

"I can't do that. She's the mother of my children."

He stood and said, "You'll be sorry." Who was this guy? An undercover cop testing the water? Someone sent by her attorney or just a punk looking for some quick money? I will never know.

A week later my attorney had Dixie's psychiatric report. It had been found that she had three personalities. One was her own, the second was the one that hated the world and authority, and the last being she was Scarlett O'Hara who had been raped by a Yankee, and the Yankee was me. Now the case would move forward. I told Roger to hold off the next hearing until February as I needed to log some hours at work. It all went to hell the morning of February 8th. Roger called to tell me Dixie had beat my oldest son, Kim, with an iron poker. He had awakened during the night and heard his mother making sounds as if she was being hurt. He rushed up the stairs to help her and saw she was on the floor in front of the fireplace with a naked man on top of her. He beat the man with his little fists and the man rolled off his mother who was also naked.

She arose, grabbed the poker and beat him, saying he was destroying her life. I told Roger I wanted custody of my son and that I would be on the next flight west. I told the station manager my problem, and wise man that he was said I had to choose between that kid and my job. I resigned immediately.

The only flight west would be that evening and a heavy snow was falling. I was in the airport hours early and watched flights being cancelled praying my flight would not be one of them. The weather got worse but we were going, two thirds of the ticketed passengers refused to go. I made my way through the blinding snow to the plane and asked God to let me get to my little boy. The wings were icing up and there was a truck by each wing that sped down the runway at takeoff spraying the wings. Until we crossed the Rockies, the pilots kept spotlights on the wings, then at last I saw the lights of San Francisco.

The court battle was fierce but I won custody of Kim and Sunday visitation with Sharon and Sean. If and when the Mill Valley property was sold, the profit was to be equally divided between the three children. That never happened. When, in time, Dixie sold the home she pocketed all the money. The kids never got a dime. Dixie had asked the priest at Church of Our Savior in Mill Valley where Kim and Sean were choir boys and Sharon was involved in youth activities to testify and lie that I had abused her. He refused. In a fury she took the kids out of the

Church and enrolled them in private school at Marin Catholic.

There was no way I would be welcome in affiliated television and I didn't have money to return to Hollywood to follow my dream. I had big alimony, child support and private school plus Kim and I had to live. Roger pointed out to the judge that my income was greatly reduced. The senile judge said, "He made it once he can make it again." Who said justice isn't blind? No need to cry and whimper but turn to the one thing that had never let me down. Music!

I had to exercise my fingers and voice and learn some new hits like "King of the Road," "Downtown" and "It was a Very Good Year" as well as brushing up on the standards. I landed an eight week booking at the fabulous Fairmont Hotel that stands atop San Francisco's Nob Hill across the street from the Mark Hopkins. It was at the Fairmont that Tony Bennett first sang "I Left My Heart in San Francisco." I worked the Cirque Lounge with its murals of wild animals and the famous wrap lounge with its wild animal murals and wrap-around bar. It was the greatest room ever for solo piano and vocals. The piano was a Steinway and there was no microphone in sight. The sound system for voice and piano was built into the piano. You just sang. Piano and vocal blended and you sounded so good you never wanted to leave. The room changed talent every eight weeks and although I was offered a return date I had to decline. I needed a steady gig.

Imagine my happiness when I was offered three months at the Casa Blanca Hotel-Motel on the Miracle Mile in Redding, California. The site of grass lake fishing that was the best in the west. I was asked to bring a trio and I did, called the Skyliners. The group included my friend and bassist Lou Manning, sexy blond Marilyn Brown "The Talk of the Town" on drums and vocals and I had piano and male vocals covered. It proved to be fun and relaxing after St. Louis. Those days I loved to fish and each day would limit out on Rainbow Trout which Chef Ano prepared. The hotel featured top of the line Italian food plus prime ribs and steaks. I loved wading in the grass lakes to fish but the hotel, in addition to room and board, provided a speed boat for days I just wanted to kick back.

When I worked the Fairmont I went every Sunday to have Sharon and Sean as the court had ordered and Dixie refused to let them go. Imagine my surprise when I asked to take them to Redding and she said okay. It turned out to be a summer to remember. Fishing, boating and just having fun was the order of each day. My group, "The Skyliners," clicked with the clients. As always, we had our moments with the audience. A few days after opening Lou Manning with his "dog house" big string bass played a sensational solo on Duke Ellington's theme "Take the A Train" to a standing ovation. We then stayed up tempo with "Lullaby of the Leaves" that featured piano. A woman by the bandstand said she loved the bassist and wanted his name. Five times I told her "Lou Manning" but she never got it. When she asked the sixth time I said his name was Sam.

"Sam what," she asked.

I replied, "Sam Goatsmilk."

"Goatsmilk," she uttered.

"That's right" I said. Later she had Lou sign a menu and he signed, "Sam Goatsmilk." The rest of the engagement Lou was introduced as Sam Goatsmilk.

We lost Marilyn Brown the final three weeks as she had to return to LA to honor her contract with Capitol Records. Patti, a redhead from the bay area was the replacement. I had to keep working and I signed with Hal Morris a San Francisco agent who was singer/actor Tony Martin's brother. Hal liked to show everyone the engraved cigarette case Tony gave him. Believe me, Tony had the looks and the smarts in that family. Hal wore spats and was proud he had turned down a pianist/singer who wanted him to manage him. Hal said the man sang flat and he turned him down. The man in question was Nat 'King" Cole. We should all be so lucky to sing like Nat.

I wanted to go somewhere in the area with a trio. He said the only jobs open were for pianist/singers. So I started an open end run at The Chicken Shack in Concord, California in the east bay. The Shack was owned by Richard Bessemer who also owned a big club called "Richards" in the heart of Concord by the BART station where the commuters caught the train that would go under the ocean and deliver them for work and play to San Francisco. I wanted to move up to Richards. Hal said it couldn't be done. Mr. Bessemer never came to the Chicken Shack at night so I went to see him and presto, I was working at Richards. Hal was amazed and I paid him the commission.

It turned out to be the luckiest thing I ever did. I was happy being free and knew I never wanted to get married again. Kim and I were doing fine and women were poison. It was a Saturday night. Richards was packed. I looked to my right and the world stopped.

The most beautiful girl I ever saw had come through the door wearing a dark coat with a fur collar. I stopped playing and singing and stood up. The heavenly choir was singing "Where Love Has Gone." and my world stopped. In that instant, I knew this was the girl destiny meant me to be with, the person I would marry and share my life with. I didn't know how or why but I knew it would be forever. I wish I could tell you she felt the same vibes but she and her lady friend just wanted to be seated which they were, in the back of the room. I, at last remembered I was being paid to perform, so went back to work. The lady, this beauty, was with had been in several times before and was interested but the interest was one sided.

As I later learned she asked the beauty what she thought about my work and beauty said, "My mother would like him." Her mother was a classical trained pianist. As the evening progressed, the ladies moved up by the piano. I was so taken by this lovely creature, I was having trouble breathing. I didn't want them to leave so I asked them to join me for breakfast in the coffee shop. The friend with the beauty talked constantly until the restroom called.

Alone at last, I wanted to say, "Don't go home, let's get married," just like George Montgomery did in the movie *Orchestra Wives* where the actress accepted his offer. Not going completely overboard I asked, "Would you like to go to the beach sometime?"

She looked at me wondering why I would ask someone wearing a cocktail dress to the beach.

She said, "Possibly."

I lived at Richardson Bay at the time and maybe that's why I said beach. Her lady friend came back.

They left and I didn't have beauty's name. But come hell or high water I was going to have her.

The staff at both Richards and the Chicken Shack had never seen her before. Although the lady she had been with they knew lived in Concord. I presumed the girl of my dreams must also live here. I spent days going through stores and into places of business but no luck. A week later, the lady she had been with came in and during intermission I asked about her friend. She claimed she didn't know her last name although her first name was "Rena." Had no idea where Rena lived or worked. She was trying to start a relationship with me.

At least I had a first name. A week later I asked a client at Richards. He told me a girl answering her description with the name of Rena had been in real estate sales but didn't remember the company she worked for. From that time on, whenever I heard a person was in real estate I bent their ear. At last I hit pay dirt with an elderly husband and wife who were both in the real estate game. The woman said, "I bet you're talking about Rena Fletcher, a truly beautiful girl. She is not selling real estate anymore but works for a title company.

The man added that Rena was divorced and had a small daughter and owned a duplex but they didn't know where. They did give me the name of the title company. The next day found me at the Title Insurance and Trust Company on Concord Boulevard and there was my angel, more beautiful than ever, filling out papers for a client behind a desk sign that identified her as Rena Fletcher, Escrow Officer. I reminded her of our meeting and asked to take her to dinner Sunday, my day off but she wasn't interested. I knew her number was in the phone book and I knew how to use the phone.

When I first came to the east bay I told my agent I wanted to work for Sam and Syl Enea at the upscale Concord Inn, the classy "joint" hotel in that fast-growing community. I met Rena in March. Come April, I opened at the Concord Inn Sunday through Thursday with Babe Palette's Orchestra taking over Friday and Saturday. My calls to Rena for dinner were turned down so for a while I worked Fridays and Saturdays at Danny's Hideaway in exclusive Layette, California.

Living at the motel Alto in Mill Valley made it a long drive to and from work but I was so happy working for the Enea's plus I was a local call away from Rena. The middle of May I ended my work at Danny's. I had Friday and Saturday off. I called Rena for a dinner date and she could pick the day. Her answer was, "I don't think you realize, I'm not interested in a gin mill piano player." When I hung up I was crushed. I was desperately in love with her but what could I do? I waited a few weeks then called again and found the reason behind our not dating.

Her first marriage had ended due to her husband's abuse of alcohol which led to her mental and physical abuse and she thought that someone who worked around liquor, which I did, was a pretty good drinker and she was through with drunks in her life. At most I was a one cocktail drinker. When clients bought me drinks the waitress would bring a 7-Up disguised as gin and tonic. She took a chance, and we went to San Francisco and saw the movie *High Wind in Jamaica* with Anthony Quinn. For dinner she was expecting The Mark or The Fairmont. I had found out that her father had been a AAU Heavyweight Champion boxer in 1930 so I thought I'd surprise her by going to Lefty O'Doul's famous sports bar and restaurant in San Francisco. It was not a good selection. She had been there many times with her dad whose photo was prominent on the wall.

We talked about her hopes for the rest of her life. She talked for twenty minutes but my name was not included. She was so beautiful and I wanted her future and mine to be one. Things got better in June when we took her little daughter, Dana Lee for a picnic at Stinson Beach. A wonderful day as Dana Lee played in the ocean and sand. All three of us enjoyed our picnic lunch and spending time with my dream girl made it perfect. Rena and I had a wonderful courtship. She got to know Kim, Sharon and Sean and they got to know Dana Lee when they came to the Concord Inn where we swam, played a lot of miniature golf and had fun.

Rena and I visited her mother and dad. They made me feel like family the moment we met. For holidays we mingled with the entire San Francisco family. Uncle Jack and Aunt Iva, Aunt Lee, Rena's mother's sister and her husband Tony, Franco and wife Louise, Frank, Rena's dad and her mother Julie. What fun and what wonderful food. Sometimes Frank's father Tucker would join in.

My mother and I were always close and I wrote her about the beautiful lady that I was in love with. She may have been puzzled when I wrote regarding a super dinner Rena made for us when she invited me to her duplex. There was candlelight, wine, soft music playing, a tasty salad and dwarf chickens. I'm sure Mom didn't grasp "dwarf" chickens. What Rena served was stuffed cornish game hens. We had never had cornish game hens. When we had chicken we had big chickens. Mom would get the "dwarf" chicken story when she came to the Concord Inn to welcome in 1966 and spend a few days.

She flew in New Year's Eve morning and got situated in her room at the Inn. I had to work both cocktail hour and evening and I asked Rena if she would take my mother to dinner at the Concord Inn. There was a problem. She had accepted an invitation to a New Year's Eve party and had purchased a cocktail dress for the occasion. I didn't want to spoil her plans. She would take mom to an early dinner, then go to her party.

There was no time to go home and change clothes between dinner and the party so she wore her new dress which was low cut, worrying what my mother would think. They met and went off to dinner and I went to work. A couple of gentlemen in the dining room sent drinks to their table and dinner went fine. As they waited for dessert, mom asked Rena if she wasn't chilly and Rena knew she disapproved of her dress. After dinner, Rena brought mom into the lounge where I was working. They had a Cream Sherry and Rena went to her party and mom to her room. New Year's Eve ran until 2 AM and when I got to my room I was dead tired.

My phone jangled at 7 AM. It was mom. She had ordered room service breakfast for two and she wanted me to come now. I beat Room Service to her room where she was seated in an arm chair. I was still closing the door when she said, "If that girl will have you, you better get her. It's the best thing that will ever happen to you." I wasn't sure if my mother had lost it or if my hearing was out of order. Then she repeated the same lines again and added, "She is not only a beautiful person she has a beautiful soul. You can see it in her eyes." Room Service arrived and as we ate she went on about the beauty of the dress Rena had worn. She said, "If I were twenty years younger I would have one just like it." Rena had worried so much about wearing it. When Mom had asked Rena at dinner if she was chilly, it had nothing to do with her dress. Mom was sitting where an air vent blew on her and she was chilly. Rena would find my mother loved high fashions and the two of them loved to shop. I told mom we had visited her family in San Francisco and planned to take her to their home while she was visiting. We did and a delightful time was had by all. Rena introduced mom to miniature golf and she wanted to play four or five games every day. Her trip was all too short but she would be coming back in August for Kim and Sean's birthdays which were both in August.

CHAPTER FIFTY-FIVE

In January I wanted to buy Rena an engagement ring. The problem was alimony, child support, private school and just living. I was putting away tips and a few dollars a week toward a diamond wedding ring. Then I remembered a Greenbrier graduate can purchase one and only one miniature ring that is a duplicate of his class ring. I had her ring size and I ordered it. Although it arrived in three weeks, it seemed like it took forever. When it came I couldn't wait. I rushed to the Title Company. Somehow we wound up behind the office building and I told her what it was. She didn't want to accept it. But in time, it was on her fourth finger, left hand and we were engaged.

I felt I should ask her father for her hand in marriage. Rena said there was no need. She had been married and had a daughter. It was something I had to do, so I called Frank at his car dealership and made an appointment for lunch at the Jack Tar Hotel close to his office. We were seated. Frank ordered a Scotch and water and I had a real gin and tonic. We ordered lunch and while waiting for service he asked what he could do for me. I'm certain he thought I was going to ask about buying a new car. Imagine his shock when I said, "I'm in love with your daughter and would like your permission to marry her and make her my wife."

Frank looked up at our waiter saying, "Another Scotch please." There never was a better father-in-law than Frank Tucker. He was just a wonderful man in every way.

It was February 11th when Lee Giroux called that our friend Buster Keaton had died of lung cancer at his home in Woodland Hills. I will always remember this pleasant, humble man who had a world renown talent. On the last day as a guest on our show, he presented me with a copy of his book, *My Wonderful World of Slapstick*. Here was one of the greatest film stars of all time giving me his book in his warm friendly manner. He had told me he wanted to live to be one hundred. I wish he could have made it. He was thirty years short of his goal. Buster was seventy when he made the transition.

Rena and I selected St. Patrick's Day 1966 as our wedding day. We would not move into her duplex but rent an apartment at the Lani Kai complex that had a lake for the kids to play on. A couple of days before the wedding, we moved her furniture and my spinet piano into our second-floor unit. It was work but the real test came when the two of us took the piano up a flight of stairs to the second floor. We were almost at the top when it started to slip. With sweat pouring off, we got it under control, and at last it was in our living room. Kim and I would move our possessions in after the wedding. Dana Lee and Rena moved into our apartment, two days before the wedding, Rena stocked the kitchen with food for when we returned from our three-day honeymoon. I had Friday, Saturday and Sunday off but had to be at the keyboard Monday night. Rena was taking off Friday and Monday. Our dear friend, druggist John Radovitch, would have Kim and Dana as his guests while we were gone.

St. Patrick's Day dawned bright and sunny. Rena got Dana ready for John to pick up and she started to put on her makeup. Thank God she had bought some candles because the electricity was out in the entire unit and had been most of the night. Not a good omen when you're the bride and you're getting dressed for your wedding. The manager told her it would not be on until late afternoon. So she gave John everything out of the fridge because it would spoil before our return. Lights or no lights Rena was dressed and packed when I arrived.

Our plan was to get to San Francisco early, get married by a Justice of the Peace. We had both had big weddings before and this time it would just be us. After we were married, we would have our first lunch together as Mr. and Mrs. at the Top of The Mark Hopkins Hotel. Nothing is easy.

We were driving to Los Angeles in Rena's almost brand new Bonneville convertible. With our bags in the trunk, we left Concord with Rena driving. A few miles out of town the fan belt broke. Into a service station for a new belt. How could this happen to a new car? Before we reached the Bay Bridge the fuel pump went out. Another visit to a service station. A long wait for the part. More money down the drain but at long last we reached the Court House in San Francisco. The justices were at lunch and they would not be back. Hey, Bunkie, it's St. Paddy's Day and the whole world is Irish. I'm sure Rena wondered why, because I'm Irish I had picked this day, although she didn't mention it. Where was the fabled luck of the Irish? From no lights, to car problems, to no judges.

The kind lady gave us a small card for a Reverend Estreem at The Little Chapel of the Flowers on Valencia Street in San Francisco saying he would marry us. Back in the Bonneville we searched for The Little Chapel of the Flowers but the address on the card was an apartment building. After driving by three times, we stopped and went in. Sure enough, on a mailbox it said, Reverend Estreem, The Little Chapel of the Flowers. I thought it was very romantic. Rena thought I had gone off the deep end.

I knocked on the door and an elderly man dressed as a minister welcomed us to the Little Chapel of the Flowers. The only flowers were in the faded wallpaper and there was a tiny neon cross on the mantle. For the first time, Rena whispered, "This isn't legal." The minister identified himself as Reverend Estreem and asked if we had a witness. Since we had none he said it was not a problem. Going to the wall of the next apartment, he called out "Come over, Mabel, we have a wedding."

"This isn't legal," Rena whispered in my ear. The door opened and Mabel, an elderly woman with her hair in curlers wearing a bandana, entered. The ceremony went smoothly. I put the diamond and gold wedding ring on Rena's finger, kissed the bride, paid the Reverend, thanked Mabel, and I floated down the stairs as Rena said, "It wasn't legal. You noticed he asked you what ship you were on. He thinks you're a drunk sailor getting married before you ship out."

Here I am in the biggest romantic glow of my life. Legal or not, we went to the Top of the Mark for a late lunch and I called Rena's mother, Julie, to tell her she hadn't lost a daughter, she had gained a son. Julie cried. Our legal certificate of marriage came in next month's mail.

Our honeymoon destination was The Sportsmen's Lodge Hotel in North Hollywood, California. The hotel where the guests for the *Johnny Carson Show* stayed. A five story hideaway with beautiful gardens, swans, a waterfall, huge swimming pool, formal dining room Sportsmen's bar and stylist suites. It's a long drive down the coast highway we went a few miles inland for our first dinner as husband and wife at Pea Soup Anderson's restaurant in Buellton. Back to 101 by the pacific ocean to The Trade Winds at the Wagon Wheel Junction Restaurant row in Oxnard for Mai Tais then off to Suite 35 at The Sportsmen's Lodge.

On Saturday I kept a lunch meeting with an agent. The evening saw us at The Captain's Table for dinner with Cousin Ken Agee and his wife. The Matt Dennis trio entertained while we enjoyed the fabulous dinner which included hearts of palm salad which we had never tasted.

Sunday morning we had a silver fizz, bacon and eggs and coffee with my old bassist and friend Lou Manning and his wife Francis at the Colonial House in Oxnard. Bert Barer, my college professor, friend and announcer on Frankie Carle's radio and TV series, came by with wife Shelia and brought us a bottle of champagne for our first wedding present. Bert also took some great photos for our wedding book. The evening was hosted by my former student Conrad Holzgang now the Executive in Charge of Production for David Wolver whose credits include *Willy Wonka and The Chocolate Factory* and *Roots* and his career had just started. He was with his wife Joy and we all enjoyed the fabled Playboy Club on the Sunset strip.

I had to be at the keyboard come 9 PM so we left early Monday. We were anxious to see Kim and Dana Lee, get into our new digs and get family life started. The kids had a blast staying with John, and Kim gave us a wedding present of an oil painting of a lovely autumn nature scene. Rena and I love the autumn best of all the seasons and the painting hangs in my office.

As always, I was thinking of advancing my career and increasing my income. I felt I had to take things in steps. First I had to form a trio. Then expand larger into a major show group but never have more than seven members in the group. A couple of road blocks had to be conquered. First a club owner who would pay top money for a musical group. Second, a manager capable of getting solid bookings in major clubs and hotels across the United States. This meant travel. Most top groups only have one week a year at their home and I had just got married. There would be challenges ahead.

CHAPTER FIFTY-SIX

Shaboom...life was a beautiful dream. The only cloud being the weekends when we would drive to Marin to pick up Sharon and Sean for visitation as ordered by the Court but their mother would not release them. Then in early June, she had something personal planned for her weekends. They joined us for fun filled days in the Concord Inn swimming pool, Sean and Kim on the raft at Lani Kai, movies, pizza and night games at Candlestick watching Willie Mays and the San Francisco Giants. One memorable night after feeding our faces with hot dogs and popcorn at the ballgame, we crossed the Bay Bridge and found a pizza parlor that played silent films. I thought everyone was stuffed but the cry for pizza rang loud and clear so we piled out of the car, ordered pizza and on the screen was the movie I had made in 1928, *The Pie Eating Champeen*. The kids hollered and laughed and kept asking, "You call that acting?" Rena had never seen the film and we set through three showings and would have seen a fourth but it was getting close to midnight. I asked if the parlor owner was around so I could get the address of the firm which had sold him the film as I wanted to buy a copy. The owner was off that night and the girl had no idea how to contact him. I should have returned the next day but it was spring before I returned to find a diner where the pizza place had been and the former owner had died. I didn't worry. I would find the film with a distribution company in Los Angeles. I'm still looking.

I knew that I had to build a trio and later a show group to advance my career and bring in more money. I also knew that in time that would mean traveling and I wasn't about to leave my beautiful wife at home and I wasn't going to ask her to spend a great part of her life in lonely hotel rooms, in towns where she had no friends, while I worked. Any of the above would end a marriage that was the number one thing in my life. I had an idea. I had a meeting with Syl Enea and pointed out that I was doing top business in the lounge and people wanted to dance. Instead of having Babe Pallotta and his band Friday and Saturday for dancing why not The Bob Cawley Trio Monday through Saturday? Syl agreed and he set Friday, September 2, 1966, for our opening. This would be in two weeks.

On Sunday morning I told my bride that she would be opening with my trio in two weeks and she would be playing drums. We had to get over to San Francisco and buy her a full set of Slingerland drums. She was almost speechless. She had studied piano which she didn't like, tap dancing lessons which didn't take and although she loved to sing she had never appeared as a vocalist. But she had been a model working big shows with major names like Bud Abbott and Lou Costello. At the music store we bought a sparkling set of red Slingerland drums,

Zilgen cymbals, maracas the works and arranged a drum teacher for lessons seven days a week. He assured us he could develop top drum skills until he learned he had two weeks to teach her all the standard rhythms including the Latin beats. She would take lessons at night when I was at work. We took her drum set home and set it up by our piano. The next day I hired bassist, singer and former drummer, Lalo Reyes, who had been featured with Joe Loco, the Benny Velarde Orchestra in Las Vegas to give Rena seven days a week lessons. Rena had worked on getting the feel of her drums and on Sunday Lalo arrived for lesson number one. He asked if he could hear Rena play and I suggested a chorus of Rose Room.

When we finished there was dead silence then Lalo spoke. "Senor, could I have a drink?" Rena worked at the drums during the day and at her nightly session in San Francisco. She played to records, to my piano and listened to recordings of Dave Tough, Krupa, Rich and Ray McKinley. Like all young drummers when she first started, she had the tendency to turn the beat around. This was not a problem for music vets like Lalo and myself who just turned the beat with her. This only happened for the first couple of weeks then the beat was perfect. To hold down the pressure we limited her vocals and I did more group vocals. She and I did duets.

During this time, we had to get publicity pictures taken and started looking for gowns for Rena. For opening night she had a sensational gold lame sequined dress from Neiman Marcus that hugged every lush curve like her skin and she glittered and glowed under the spotlight. Lalo and I had our After-Six tuxes plus blue and red band jackets as alternates with our tux pants. When we came in to set-up for the opening, Sly had a big surprise for me. He had purchased a concert size Steinway that was perfectly tuned to 440 pitch. Wow! The portable Baldwin organ keyboard was atop the piano and within easy reach was a Celeste, an electronic piano, which gave the group a wide variety of sounds. Opening night went very well. Rena's parents were in the audience plus many friends including Jay Sebring trained hair stylists, Jess and Frank Hernandez. The dance floor was packed. Sam and Syl Enea were happy and so were we. Later when I went back stage I found my wife crying. "What's the matter sweetheart?" I asked. "A man who said he was a professional drummer told me I was the worst drummer he ever heard." "Honey, don't be upset. If this guy is such a hot shot why wasn't he working? Every good drummer in the area is working on weekends. Just remember he paid to listen to you while you were getting paid." A smile broke through and we headed home off on a new career together.

Sam and Syl were delighted with the group and four months later threw a Champagne and Cake party for us and celebrated with a long-term contract.

The trio had a brand new sound as Joe Taylor had replaced Lalo Reys with his stand-up electric bass and pretty trombone passages. Joe, from San Francisco had been featured with the Murray Arnold Trio and The Artists and Models in Las Vegas. We recorded our performance each evening which proved to be an invaluable tool in constantly improving our work. We added group vocals, lush trombone solos, and Rena and I did very well with duets and Rena's versions of

"So I Said Yes," "I'm A Big Girl Now," and "One More Ride on the Merry-Go-Round" were hits.

We generated large crowds and at certain moments people get out of control when alcohol takes over. The Steinway grand I played sat on the dance floor and Rena and Joe were on the stage above me. One evening a good-looking young lady wearing a full-length mink coat leaned over while I was singing and made a request. During the moment I took a breath I told her "next number." She said "now." I kept singing. Out of the side of my eye I saw a bright flash as the spotlight hit something metal. I ducked just as the blade of her straight razor missed my neck. A client at a ringside table saw the action and tried to stop her. She hacked his face into a bloody mess before security could disarm her and subdue her. The cut man was given first aid until the ambulance arrived to take him to the hospital. The woman was taken to Syl's office where she grabbed a steel mini file and attacked the security men before the police arrived and took her away. As soon as the blood was cleaned up, the trio played on. The woman, who was drunk, was the wife of one of San Francisco's most famous plastic surgeons. So it never made the papers. The woman's husband made the injured client's face almost as good as new. A huge cash settlement enabled him to buy his own nightclub.

Women are extremely dangerous in nightclubs. They will come upon the stage after you. A few weeks later a woman came on the stage while Rena was singing and tried to unfasten the front of her gown and reveal her breasts. Joe made the mistake of going into the audience playing a trombone solo. A woman grabbed his crotch and almost made him a soprano. It happens in Five Star Hotels and Supper Clubs as well as lesser locations.

Men will invite you for a drink or ask the girl in the group for a later date but women don't wait. One night the dance floor was packed when a young blond pushed her dance partner away then pulled up her sweater to reveal she was braless, pointed at Rena screaming, "I've got as much as she's got," before security ended her evening.

The New York Yankees' Joe DiMaggio was a regular visitor to the Concord Inn during his off season as he and Syl Enea were golfing buddies. One night we saw Joe, Syl, and a sidekick of Joe's, sitting at the back of the room. At intermission the sidekick approached Rena saying, "Joe DiMaggio finds you very attractive and would like to take you out for a late dinner." To which Rena replied, "If Mr. DiMaggio wants to take me out tell him to ask me himself." Later I mentioned the incident to Syl. Who told me Joe never asked a woman for a date. That way, he was never refused. A lot of guys like a "go between." I never understood it. Hasn't everyone heard the word No?

CHAPTER FIFTY-SEVEN

I came up with an idea for a stage upon the stage. Made of wood with hinges so it could fold and be carried. The top was plexi-glass and under the glass was a series of lights I could control from the piano that would enhance custom-made costumes Rena would wear while dancing to production numbers we would sing the lyrics in harmony while she danced. This would be a feature no other group would have. The songs she danced to told a complete story while the lyrics and the lighting from her stage would be the only lights in the room for a very dramatic and exotic effect. Audiences loved these numbers. Getting started, we selected the songs. "Johannesburg" (Blue veils), "Tangerine" (orange & silver sequins), "Swamp Girl" (green and black), and "The Legend of Tiabi" (red, silver and white with a full American Indian war bonnet). All costumes were brief and beautiful in design. Rena flew to Reno to engage Cleo of Reno, a top costume designer, to create her costumes plus gowns she would wear doing the regular portions of our performance. Cleo made a mannequin form so that later when we traveled and needed new gowns or costumes

Rena could call and order and a few days later they were delivered.

One evening our friend John Radovitch, who had looked after Kim and Dana Lee when Rena and I honeymooned, told us he had sold his drug store and was moving to Hawaii. He had never been there but movies and books had convinced him this was paradise. We hated to see him go but it turned out to be a major turning point in his life. He landed a great job, met and married a lovely lady, bought a beautiful home on the windward side of Oahu with a private beach. We would later enjoy a reunion in the islands. The group went into 1967 at full steam. We knew the music and lyrics to 3,500 songs including a tune called "Tiny Bubbles." Rena's cousin who lived in Hawaii sent us a lead sheet of this song which was rocking fans in the island and would soon be a hit around the world. We may have been the first group in California to play this song and it was every third request by our clients. We played and sang it so often several entertainment writers referred to us as the "Tiny Bubbles Band." The clients wanted it and we did it. Keep 'em happy.

During New Year's Eve the dance floor was packed when everyone stopped dancing and stood staring out the windows at the wing of the hotel across a strip of lawn. A just married couple had checked in, discarded their wedding garb and were consummating their marriage before a very large audience. The front desk called to tell them to shut their window blinds but they were not going to answer the phone at this point. An employee rapped on their door and called through that the entire hotel was watching them. All of a sudden the naked groom was off the bed, the bride was trying to cover herself as the window blinds closed to thunderous applause by the dancers. Happy New Year!

I wanted to start building us as a show group. All the pieces in the group were starting to fit when our bassist/trombonist, Joe Taylor required surgery. We had to find a replacement fast. There was no one available in the San Francisco Musicians Union so we called Local #47 in Los Angeles. All of the union offices have lists of musicians available. They put me in touch with Art West. He assured me he had played with big bands and trios on both bass and electric guitar plus could sing harmony. Rena is tall and I asked his height as they would be working side by side. He said he was six feet tall and was clean cut and single. He said he would like to find a studio apartment, and I said we would have several lined up for him to look at. He was booked and could arrive in Concord a week from Sunday. That would work because we had a bassist with the San Francisco Symphony available for the upcoming week.

My mother had come to live with us and be with Dana Lee and Kim while we worked. I stewed all week over West's arrival. I never liked hiring musicians I had never heard play. If I didn't like their work the union said I had to pay them a full two weeks salary plus travel but come hell or high water I had to have a replacement come Monday.

Art called Sunday just before the family sat down to breakfast. Said he was at a gas station on the edge of town and he had not had breakfast. I told him Kim and I would be right down. He followed us home to have breakfast with our family. His station wagon had his stand-up bass/guitar case and amplifier in the rear and a hard-looking woman smoking a cigar in the passenger's seat. Kim remarked that he sure had an old-looking wife. I reminded Kim that Art told me he was single. I got out of my car and shook hands and realized that at five-nine-and-half inches tall, I had two inches on him. So much for being perfect to stand beside Rena. I said I thought he was single and he informed me that he was and that the cigar-smoking phantom was his mother. Mom West shook my hand like the handle of the town pump and blowing a cloud of smoke in my eyes announced that I would love the way Artie sang "Rambling Rose" the Nat Cole hit.

They followed my car and when we arrived at our apartment, Lani Kai Apartments, Kim sprinted up the steps to tell Rena we had two guests to feed. Seated around the kitchen table after breakfast Mom West lit up another cigar and told us what a great vocalist we had hired. When at last she stopped giving us Artie's hype Rena told her she was sorry we had only set up studio apartments for Art to look at as we had thought he was single.

"Studio is just fine" was Mom's answer. "Artie and I always sleep together." My mother dropped her spoon, and time stood still. Kim's mouth was open. Dana Lee's eyes were bugging out and I thought my mother might pass out. Rena broke the spell by suggesting we go look at apartments. They took the second place they looked at and we left after telling Art we would rehearse at the hotel 8:30 AM the next day.

Thus started six weeks of hell. Art played bass like a kid would in a mad high school orchestra. His guitar work was slightly better but left a great deal to be desired. He had trouble with the lyrics of the production numbers so I told him to forget them, I would sing them.

Mom West and her cigar attended every rehearsal. She constantly yelled for Art to sing "Rambling Rose." One morning I told him to sing it. He did. I needed a drink. Mom blew clouds of smoke and made wild applause. We got Art outfitted in a tux and the show went on. Every night mom was at ringside smoking, drinking and calling out for Art to sing "Rambling Rose." I would like to tell you he got better with practice but this was not the case.

Rena and Art were up on the stage and behind them were mirrored walls. I was on the dance floor in front of the stage with my mic and various keyboards. I talked to Joe who was home from surgery and was still weak but thought maybe he could return in two weeks. I could not give Art notice until I was certain Joe was ready. As it turned out, Art made the decision for all of us.

At the end of six weeks, Saturday night, the room was packed with dancers and listeners.

All evening he had told Rena to tell me to introduce him singing "Rambling Rose." We were into the final set of the evening and I had just told Rena to tell him he would not be singing. We went into the first bars of a Latin number when I heard a huge crash, saw splinters of glass flying through the air, then Rena was flying through the air and crashed into the upraised lid of the grand piano and her bare back was bloody. Art had thrown his stand-up bass against the mirrored wall, shattering the glass, then it hit Rena so hard she went over her drums and off the stage onto the piano. Security had Art, his screaming mother, and his instruments out the front door in record time but restrained me from going after him. Rena's back was treated, the lid of the piano was raised and we continued as a duo.

Sunday Joe called to let us know he could come back if we needed him. Talk about a message from heaven, this was it. However, the mom and Artie show was not over. Only next time Joe would be involved.

Syl decided to bring in Louis Armstrong and his All Stars featuring jazz pianist Marty Napoleon and Hall of Fame clarinetist, Barney Bigard, who was co-writer with Duke Ellington of the beautiful "Mood Indigo" to alternate with our group for a one-night special event. There would be standing room only. We were thrilled to be working with Louis Armstrong the trumpet player who, as a young man, had come up from New Orleans to Chicago on a riverboat and brought jazz music to the entire world.

He was the first and became a legend. Although a good trumpet player, I felt he never came close to Harry James, Roy Elridge, Bunny Berrigan, Charlie Shavers or Chico Alverez for brilliance of trumpet performance. However, Louis was a great entertainer. His mannerism, comedy, and husky-voiced vocals on such hits as "Hello, Dolly" and "It's a Wonderful World" were terrific. We found Louis fun to work with. The All-Stars were as advertised with Barney Bigard playing solos to standing ovations. Marty Napoleon didn't play the piano, he beat it to death. In two sets he broke the pedals and four strings on the brand new Steinway, his keyboard work did not come close to his brother, Teddy who was pianist for the Gene Kruppa Orchestra. Teddy was featured on Gene's historic recording by his trio playing "Dark

Eyes" with Gene on drums, Charlie Ventura on sax and Teddy on piano.

One night early in the year, I saw Syl sitting at the back of the room with a very handsome man that I was sure I had seen before but couldn't remember where or when. During the first set, I remembered. When I did my disc jockey show on KPHO-TV, I played many Snader Teletranscriptions and one of the most requested films was of this man singing his theme song "Vienni Su," in Italian and English. This was the one and only Carl Ravazza. Carl who was featured violinist and vocalist with the Tom Coakley Orchestra in the mid-thirties took over the band when Coakley gave up music to practice law. Carl and the band played "Music to Hold Hands By" and recorded for Decca and Bluebird. After a record breaking engagement at San Francisco's Sir Francis Drake Hotel, he took the band on the road. They played top hotels with radio wires and had national exposure. Dates included The Adolphus in Dallas; Peabody in Memphis; Muehlback in Kansas City; The Nicolette in Minneapolis and the Lexington in New York. Engagements in San Francisco, his home town, were long runs at the St. Francis Hotel. When the big band era faded Carl became a headline single playing major night clubs from coast to coast for several years plus many TV guest appearances. Carl and his wife, Marcie purchased a ranch near Reno and put together Nevada Entertainment a very successful talent agency.

Carl was the most "alive" man I ever knew. He was always upbeat. Full of energy with sparkling blue eyes, a million dollar smile and a mellow speaking voice. He was very smart, great in business with creative ideas that got done and was straight arrow with the talent he managed. Carl was an old friend of the Eneas. He told Syl he had heard great reports about our group and wanted to sign a management contract with us and put us on the road as we had great potential. Syl asked him to wait until the following day to make his pitch, and after work, that night we talked things over in his office. He told me what Carl had said then offered me a "lifetime" contract for the group with pay increases each year. If they ever sold the hotel (which they did many years later), we would have a large cash settlement.

It was tough. Never was I offered a lifetime contract by anyone. I loved working for the Eneas, our kids were in school, we had a normal home life and we really liked Concord and our job, the money and the workplace. But I was still the kid who laid in his bedroom and went to sleep with the whistle of the westward bound Super Chief in my ears,...a rolling stone. When Carl made his pitch the next day, I signed on the dotted line.

Carl saw us for the next couple of years never expanding over four members. We were unique. A small group with a variety of sounds for dancing plus a show that featured each member as a solo act. He would keep close watch on our work and give us suggestions to make the package better. He also saw a future that included television and long run engagements in Las Vegas and Reno/Tahoe. We gave four weeks' notice at the Concord Inn, then hit the road to the Tyee Motor Inn in Olympia, Washington for six weeks. Followed by six days as headliners at the Ferris Hotel in Winnemucca, Nevada during rodeo week with supporting acts. Bob Mackey's Star

Broiler across the street from the Ferris would give first class competition as their headliners were Phil Spector's Group, "Ronnie and the Ronettes." Then off to four weeks at the Stockman's Hotel and Casino in Elko, Nevada which would be a major event for our group.

CHAPTER FIFTY-EIGHT

The first stop on what was to be a long journey on the road was the Tyee Motor Inn in Olympia, Washington.

We had purchased a new Chevy van to transport our sound system and amps. A rack running the van's length held Rena's costumes as well as changes of jackets and tuxes for the guys. Rena's stage and complete drum set, back-up lighting, instruments, that included a spinet piano that had been raised so I could play standing up. If a pianist in a show group sits down the audience thinks he is dead. Add my Baldwin compact organ and speaker, all the cords and plugs needed, and with makeup cases the van was packed. We were on the great adventure.

I drove the van with Kim aboard while Rena drove our Cadillac with mother, Dana Lee and our personal luggage while Joe drove his car. The Tyee was a beautiful Motor Hotel just an hour south of Seattle. This well appointed hotel had a beautiful showroom and an appreciative audience plus wonderful employees.

This was our home for the next six weeks. After

you spend years on the road most of the venues seem the same but a few have memories that remain forever. It was here Rena first felt real confidence as a performer. One evening during our show Joe Taylor, a superb musician, played a sensational trombone solo of the classic "Danny Boy" that would have made Tommy Dorsey green with envy. Joe got a big applause. Rena followed with a solo number and got a standing ovation. Joe turned to me saying, "I've been in music all my life and I get a little applause. She's been in the biz a year and she gets a standing ovation."

I laughed and said, "Joe, if you haven't noticed, there's a difference." When a beautiful girl in a glittering costume is in the spotlight she has the audience at her command.

We will always remember Tyee breakfasts fabulous fresh blackberry sundaes. Mounds of ice cream covered with fresh blackberries and blackberry juice and fresh baked cinnamon rolls. We never gained an ounce. The owner of the Inn took us out several times in his power boat for delightful hours. Near the end of our stay, Joe was not feeling well and would return to his home in San Francisco. We had three days before we opened in Winnemucca and since we would go through Reno we knew we could pick up a replacement bassist/guitarist from the Union to play this engagement.

In Reno I called the Union and was put in contact with bassist/guitarist/singer Frankie Carr who gave me an address where to pick him up the following morning. With Rena, Mother and Dana in the Cadillac and Kim and I in the van we took off at 7 AM to pick up our replacement. I parked in front and with Kim went to the screen door of the two-story house. I had no idea it was a bordello until a naked woman opened the screen inviting me in. Sending Kim back to the van I asked if Frankie Carr was there. The naked lady said he was upstairs and she would get him. I had a feeling this was not going to go well. Dressed in sports clothes Frankie wandered down the steps with his stand-up bass case and his guitar. Giving the naked lady a hug and kiss, he stepped out into the sunlight and I saw his face and hands were covered with running sores. I got his stuff in the van but he was not interested in riding in the van with me but took a seat by Rena in the Caddy as she drove to Winnemucca and the Ferris Hotel with mother and Dana in the rear. We arrived and got our equipment set up. As always, we provided a tux for the sideman and told him he could keep it. He never took it off during the six days that followed. Although rooms at the hotel were part of the package and Frankie checked in, Rena, Mother, the kids and I moved into a nice motel on the west side of town.

At the Ferris they were removing all the mirrors, paintings and anything hanging from the walls. The manager told us things got very rough when the cowboys and Indians came in after a year on the range. They also advised Rena not dance on her stage, as the year before the female vocalist had been attacked. Also Rena was not to wear costumes but street clothes as she played drums and sang from the rear of the stage. The two groups we alternated with, The Red Nix Combo and the Leland Pierce Band, did not have a female, so although we were the headliners, we played two shows back to back and the other groups alternated into the wee hours of the morning. While setting up, Rena went to the bar to get a Coke. She gave her order to the bartender who picked up a glass a cowboy had just finished and without washing it poured Rena's Coke into the same glass. Trust me, it was one of the longest weeks of my life. We wished we could have traded venues with Ronnie & The Ronettes across the street at Joe Mackey's Star Broiler. We met Mr. Mackey during the week and he expressed interest in booking us into the Broiler at a future date. That never happened as Joe Mackey and his entire family were killed in the crash of his private plane soon after our paths had crossed. Frankie Carr was a less than journeyman player on both bass and guitar. The fact that he sang falsetto failed to thrill the macho Indians and cowboys.

I spent every hour wondering who I could get as the third person in our group to open The Stockmen's. As it turned out, son Kim solved our problem. He was allowed to go out on the main street at night until 9 PM at which time he returned to Grandma and Dana at our motel. He was too young to enter the Star Broiler, Ferris or the Red Lion where there was entertainment, but he could stand outside and listen. After our second night in town, he told us that the greatest guitarist he had ever heard was playing as part of a duo at the Red Lion. Normally when a kid is high on a musician it's not someone you would want but Kim played and studied guitar and had listened to recordings of great guitarists at home. So on the third night Rena and I went to the Red Lion.

I had worked with Elmer Warner, a member of the Jazz Hall of Fame. I had played with Mundel Lowe on *The Kate Smith Hour* when Mundel was number one in the Downbeat pole and had worked with Lloyd Ellis, "The fastest guitar alive" considered one of the greatest guitarists ever, on my TV show with the "Four Deals" but I never heard anyone who could play like Phil Rivera. A Mexican-America from Tucson, Arizona who could play the most complicated piece of classical music ever written then dazzle on pop tunes, Rock and Roll and light a fire on jazz numbers. In addition to his work on his Super 400 guitar and his Fender electric bass, he was a first-class drummer who sang harmony. He had been a great infielder at the University of Arizona and had been drafted by the Cleveland Indians. He loved baseball but thank goodness music won out. Phil was leaving the duo at the end of the week and agreed to open with us at The Stockmen's. Phil became family as we would spend happy years together.

At the end of the week, I paid Frankie his salary plus a Greyhound ticket to Reno and left him at the bus station wearing his tux.

We drove to Elko where we saw our names on the marquee of the Stockmen's on the bill with the show group "Evalanie and the South Sea Island Review," the " Rod Fisher Duo" and the "Willy K Trio." We were booked for four weeks. On this day no one guessed that the big show groups would come and go but our show plus dance music would be held over for fifty-two all time record breaking weeks and we would be offered an additional six months if we would stay. The major show groups of that era played the Stockmen's. The "Bobby Rogers Show" featuring the Taylor Maids: "The Jade's & Jade Adorables;" the "Joe Maze-Marty O'Conlan Show;" "Paul Littlechief Show" with Baby Rae; "The Action Faction;" "Stevee

Vee" and "The Plush Sounds;" the "Frankie Fanelli Show" and others.

Our manager had told us to stay at Jay's Motel where the majority of show people stayed. We got mom and the kids settled then went down to the Stockmen's to meet the Entertainment Director, Dick Toothman, a pleasant man who was a joy to work with.

The hotel was owned by the Bilbaos, a Basque family from Spain, who were great to work for. The father was slowly turning the daily operations over to son, Danny, who was dynamic. A top business man and avid golfer. Danny started his annual golf tournament while we were there. The employees felt like family and it was a happy experience. Carl Ravazza sent us a telegram opening night with good wishes and two weeks later, he caught our last show as we had a late dinner in the coffee shop. When you're on stage you can rarely see beyond the second or third row due to the lights so we didn't see him mid-room. He had talked to Dick Toothman who extended our contract to "open end" with no termination date and increased our money to include a drummer. We would then be billed as the Bob Cawley Trio featuring Rena Winters. Playing rock and roll would break the veins in Rena's legs and she could still play a single drum or Fender bass (she had added this to her bag of tricks) solo but her priority was being out front as MC, singing playing Latin rhythms and dancing her production numbers.

Carl gave us a list of things to delete and things to add plus playing the current hits like "Born Free" "Ballad of the Green Berets" and "Strangers in the Night." Our drummer was Jimmy Lynch from New

York who could read any music put in front of him. He had played in the orchestras working the pits for Broadway shows when he was just sixteen. Jimmy who didn't smoke or drink, reminded folks of a young Burt Lancaster and could he play. Wow! I wouldn't trade him for Gene Krupa or Buddy Rich. His solo's got standing ovations and his tasty, overall work added so much to our total sound.

We kept in competition with the big show groups and enjoyed alternating with them. The Joe Maze-Marty O'Conlon Show was a blockbuster. Joe was one of the best comics ever and pianist O'Connor had been a key figure in the success of Vickie Carr while a line singer at the Stockmen's. Marty wrote a beautiful song titled "Lake Tahoe on a Winter Night." The talented Joe Maze went blind and ended his career and the show a few months after he worked the Redwood Room of the Stockmen's with us. Bobbie Gentry had also been a singer and line dancer.

We always enjoyed the Paul Littlechief Watusi Warriors Show that featured his wife, dancer, Baby Rae, who was a miniature Marilyn Monroe. They were a great couple. Paul, a handsome full-blooded Kiowa Indian was a top-flight frontman, singing, dancing and doing comedy routines with Baby Rae. He also featured Ronnie Redman on tenor sax, drummer/comic Jerry Rainey and Dick Bouchet a brilliant trumpet player from Las Vegas. Paul, who everyone would have liked as a neighbor or a friend, worked the Stockmen's twice with us and both times had a major crisis. No matter how high the rating of a hotel or casino, you can't control the public and their consuming of alcohol. Paul was doing a comedy routine when a young lady walked on the stage and hit him in the head with a full bottle of beer saying, "I hate Indians." Security got her out of the casino. Paul had a bandage put on his head and finished the show. This happened in the winter.

In the summer, the same woman came up on the stage and hit him again with a full bottle of beer this time landing in jail. Paul, Baby Rae and his show played across the country and he had a bright future in TV. Two years later, his son who had become a drug addict, would use a shotgun to kill Paul as he ate lunch in his home. His talented wife, Rae, gave up show businessman and became a horse trainer. Paul wasn't the only entertainer to encounter drunk clients.

Young Stevie Vee heading his Rock & Roll Plush Sounds Show was singing and came off the stage onto the dance floor where a drunk woman hit his hand holding the mic with a beer bottle driving the mic into his mouth, breaking his front teeth. You still want to be in show biz?

US Route 80 from Reno to Salt Lake City is a very busy highway and cuts through the city of Elko, a progressive and modern town famous for proximity to Bing Crosby's large ranch. The railroad tracks ran through the center of town and the Stockmen's Hotel and Casino was on the Southside of the tracks while the Commercial Hotel with the giant Polar Bear in a glass case was on the Northside. The Commercial had once presented the great Ted Lewis and Eddy Howard and his orchestra as featured attractions but now were heavy with Country-Western, Rock & Roll, strippers and novelty acts.

Down the street, the Red Lion had entertainment on a smaller scale. (Like most Nevada towns, with the exception of Las Vegas where prostitution is not legal although half of the yellow pages in the phone book lists "escorts," both male and female, you can call them to your hotel room or visit "fancy girls" working the famous strip.) Elko had two "joy houses," Betty's D & D, and Suzie's. Many travelers going both east and west stop in Elko and on the weekend we had huge numbers from Salt Lake.

Dana and Kim enrolled in school. My mother was with the kids while we worked and life was pretty normal.

CHAPTER FIFTY-NINE

We visited the famous Carlin Gold Mine near Elko and were amazed how heavy those solid gold bars were. We made many trips to Reno on our day off to visit with Carl to discuss the future and catch some of the acts playing the Reno–Tahoe area. At times we drove and other times we made the round trip on United Air Lines infamous "Vomit Comet." The flight went through the mountains not over them and it was like riding a roller coaster thanks to the turbulence. The passengers who had drank a lot the night before provided the flight with its nickname. In Reno, Rena visited Cleo for new gowns and costumes, and we danced at the Ponderosa to "Music by George," George Liberace and his orchestra.

Every fourth Monday, our friend and hair stylist Jess Hernandez would fly from Concord to Reno to keep Phil and I looking trim and neat. During one visit Jess slipped off the shoe shine stand at Harrah's Hotel breaking his ankle. In the future, he sent his younger brother Frank, also a Jay Sebring alumni, to take care of our needs. Frank, an accomplished make-up artist would be a key factor in our future.

Bob Dunn, a Green Beret, who had three tours of duty behind enemy lines in Vietnam, became a close friend as did Father Dave who would later be assigned to the Wind River Indian Reservation in Wyoming.

Rena was the subject of an interview for a newspaper feature. The young female reporter, anxious to write about Rena's glamorous life in entertainment, was shocked when she arrived to find her baking cookies for Dana Lee's class at school after working until 2 AM.

Appearing at the Commercial Hotel, Georgette Dante, an exotic dancer who worked with a large boa constrictor, lived next door. The maids would not clean her quarters while the big snake was loose, so Georgette would sit by the pool with the snake wrapped around her.

On Sunday night Georgette asked us to have dinner with her after our last show. We were two-thirds through the show when the audience started leaving. We didn't know what had happened until we saw the boa slithering across the dance floor. She had let the snake loose so we could close the show early. Needless to say, she and her co-performer were banned from the Stockmen's. She completed her engagement at the Commercial with a show to remember. During the close of her act, she set her body on fire with the stuff stunt people use in the movies. Herbie Day, a fine guitarist from Tupelo, Mississippi, played solid rock as she danced. Herbie, laying down hot licks moved off the stage to the dance floor. Georgette with her body on fire, her silver g-string flashing in the spotlight whirled and picked Herbie up, overhead. She was 5'11' and strong. Herbie was about

5'8". His guitar cord pulled loose and the cuffs of his pants caught fire as he yelled for help. Someone with a small fire extinguisher put the fire out on Herbie's pants as the whole thing brought a huge ovation and Georgette, her fire and boa left town for other engagements.

The Commercial's big entertainment room was 350 degrees from the Stockmen's. They catered to a different clientele. However, they had some top acts in their lounge and the very best was a young guitarist "song teller" Garn Littledyke. Garn should have been as big a star in the country field as Marty Robbins. He wrote and performed really great songs and had a unique singing style. The killer was the lack of good management. This truly great talent never got the personal appearances or recording exposure he deserved.

The Commercial came up with a couple of "name" acts for their showroom. First was Yale Basketball All-American and two-year NBA player with the Boston Celtics and the New York Nicks, Tony Lavelle. An excellent accordionist he had studied at Julliard and had appeared as an accordion soloist for the New Haven Symphony and appeared on several network TV shows as a guest. Nightclub goers in the East are more tolerant and his agent should have been shot for booking him into a showroom catering to men who considered themselves utterly macho. During his sports career 6'3" Tony with the super hook shot deserved the miles of print on sports pages from coast to coast. He had won the Helms Foundation Player of the Year Award as well as the NCAA Player of the Year Award in 1949 but now he was a nightclub entertainer in a hostile venue he should have never been booked into. We saw his opening which was also his closing the same night. The orchestra played, Tony came on stage dribbling a basketball singing the hit song, "Mame." It was obvious Tony was gay. There was a growing murmur through the crowd that was growing louder by the minute. Tony ended "Mame" and picked up his accordion and went into a rousing version of "Granada" as someone in the macho crowd yelled, "Let's hang the fruit." Chairs were pushed back and the crowd moved toward the stage. Lucky for everyone the hotel's muscular bouncers surrounded Tony and took him off stage and the showroom closed.

It was common on Sunday mornings to see new glass doors being installed at the Commercial. The bouncers, who enjoyed their work, threw troublemakers through the doors head first. Soon after the Lavelle debacle, the hotel booked Yvonne Zhivago, "The Passionate Pole," a stripper, as the new headliner. Things went well until Yvonne broke the number one rule to avoid trouble. Never come off the stage. She did and all hell broke loose. Wiggling her curvy body between tables she stopped in front of a table of applauding and cheering cowboys. She hooked her thumbs in her g-string and pulled it down. "You like?" she asked.

"You're damn right we like" was the reply as she was picked up, laid on the table and her g-string was being removed. Enter the bouncers and a full-blown fight was in progress. Miss Zhivago was removed to her dressing room before she could be violated, but the destruction of tables, glassware, chairs and other items was large and many clients flew through the glass doors including the cowboy who had her g-string. The management spoke to Miss Zhivago who promised to remain on stage. Of course, she didn't mean it. The following week she did the same thing, triggering another brawl with more destruction, and her engagement was terminated.

One snowy afternoon Rena was cooking and my mother was in the kitchen. Rena's concentration was on the stove and oven when she realized mother was not responding to conversation. When she looked around, Mother was gone and so was her overcoat. That started a frantic search. We piled the kids in the Cadillac and started driving the streets as the snow continued to fall. Elko has high curbs and we were afraid mother would slip and break an ankle or leg.

After an hour of driving, we returned home to call the police when a patrol car drove up with mother in the rear. The officer helped her out of the back and as she passed me going into the house she told me, "Give that man a big tip. He's a wonderful driver." The officer had seen this old lady trudging through the snow and fearing she would have an accident offered her a ride home. She gave him her address as 514 North Hague which was our address in Columbus. Realizing she had a memory problem, he drove her up and down every street in town trying to find her home. At last he gave up and was driving her to the police station where she would be warm until someone came to claim her. As they drove by the Stockman's, she told him that was her son's name blazing on the marquee. The puzzle was solved. He knew where the entertainers stayed and brought Mama home.

In snow country, we had fun. Sharon and Sean came up for the holidays and we snowmobiled in the nearby Ruby Mountains.

Rena's folks came up for a long enjoyable weekend.

Young men like the ladies and ladies like young men in the musical spotlight. Phil Rivera took this to heart and chalked up a score that many a so-called Romeo would have liked to have had. During the fifty-three weeks at the Stockmen's, he scored every show. Rena, Jimmy and I could not believe his success with the worst pickup line ever uttered. He would leave the stage when he was featured on the classical "Malaguena," "Quiemn Sera" or "Currito De La Cruz" while playing he would stop by a lady's table and say, "How would you like to have a groovy happening?" and presto, our dressing room was off limits. Fifty percent of his "scores" were married women whose husbands were gambling. A few minutes prior to show time, we could hit our dressing room long enough for Rena to put on a new gown while Jimmy, Phil and I changed jackets and ties. After the group on stage in front of us finished their act and the curtain closed, they had to remove their equipment while we brought on our equipment. Five minutes later the curtain would open automatically and we would be singing and swinging with "I Love Being Here With You" or "ETO Curtain Call" with Rena introducing the group. Phil Rivera from Tucson, Arizona, Jimmy Lynch, from New York, Bob Cawley from Columbus, Ohio, and herself from San Francisco, California. When introduced, we each took an eight-bar solo and Rena sang the closing eight bars. Without pause we went into an up-tempo medley of current hit Broadway show tunes and we were off and running for the next hour.

So many times, as the curtain opened and our

show started, a couple would be standing near the stage with the man berating a woman wondering where she had been the past hour. While she made excuses, our guitar wizard was just smiling as he played.

During the winter, I had my first formal dance with Sharon and Dana Lee while a band played. It's a very emotional moment when a father dances with a daughter and realizes they will soon be young ladies. Once in a while my mom and the kids would come to an early show.

One day we were closing the show and Rena was thanking the audience for coming when she felt something pulling at her skirt. She looked down to see little Dana Lee with tears streaming down her cheeks saying, "You didn't do my favorite song." Rena told the audience we had a request for one more song and we went into Dana's favorite, "Born Free."

Like most towns in Nevada, Elko had two bordellos. Betty's D & D and Suzie's. On Saturday morning the madam of Betty's would bring her girls into town to shop. Her place was a couple of blocks from the Stockmen's and was an easy walk. Just before Christmas Rena was coming out of a jewelry store as the madam and her girls were going in. The madam stopped Rena to invite our group down to Betty's for Christmas dinner and told her to bring a publicity picture so it could hang with others in their collection. The picture of *The Bob Cawley Show* with Rena Winters does not hang in Betty's Hall of Fame but Phil's solo picture does and he was very proud that his picture was on the mirror behind the bar across from a photo of Bing Crosby. Phil went down to Betty's on Christmas. He took his guitar and played carols so the girls and guests could sing before dinner was served. He was on our stage for our 9 PM show a happy camper.

Starting in early 1967, we spent time looking for a home in Lake Tahoe. Carl was working on a five year plan for 32 weeks a year in Las Vegas, 18 weeks in Lake Tahoe, Reno and Carson City giving us a two week vacation. At that time, they were constructing lovely condos right on the water at the North Shore of the Lake and Carl bought a couple as investments. We really wanted a house and over time we found a perfect three-bedroom home on a half acre just one block from the Lake with a view and big shade trees.

Our search had taken us until late July. We were ready to make the down payment on July 30th. We would fly with Carl to Las Vegas on Monday, July 29th to sign the contract with Major Riddle for 32 weeks a year, for five years, at the Top of the Dunes Hotel & Casino on the famous Las Vegas strip.

The 19th of July Carl was bothered by a small hernia and the doctor said it should be removed. Carl wanted to wait until August but the doctor insisted he have the operation sooner. Carl went into St. Mary's Hospital in Reno. We flew down and visited him a couple of days after the surgery and he looked in perfect health. Those blue eyes were sparkling and he was full of plans for the future. He had our flight to Las Vegas booked to leave Reno before noon on the 30th and to return to Reno that evening. We flew down on Saturday the 28th from Elko and saw him in the hospital. He would be going home that evening. Carl loved to read bio's and we took him a brand new book about the life of producer Billy Rose. We told him we would be coming on the early flight from Elko

Monday, come to his office, and we would all fly to Las Vegas.

Needless to say we were on a high. It all came down Sunday night when we were coming off stage after our midnight show. We were passing the group coming on when one of their musicians said, "I'm sorry to hear about your manager."

"What are you talking about?" I asked.

"I heard the news on the radio. He died at the hospital this evening."

There went the future, the life we had planned, the home at Tahoe. I didn't believe it until I saw the headlines in the Sunday paper. "Carl Ravazza dies in Reno." Carl was just fifty-eight. An autopsy proved he had bled to death internally. His surgeon had cut a main artery while removing the hernia. This surgeon had killed a patient just two years before by cutting an artery while removing a hernia. Killing Carl cost the surgeon a million dollars paid to Carl's widow, Marcie. It didn't bring Carl back and it didn't bring back our future plans; however, the surgeon kept on operating.

Carl was barely cold when agents came around wanting to manager us. The first was Bobby Morris, an arrogant former drummer for Louis Prima now an agent. Bobby liked to say he invented the "shuffle rhythm" but I remember hearing black drummers play it years before. Bobby showed up unannounced at a rehearsal, said he would manage us and teach Jimmy Lynch how to play drums. Remember, Bobby had never heard us. He only knew Carl was very high on our group and had big plans for us. He asked us to play something and I selected "Sing, Sing, Sing" which had a 32-bar drum solo. We went into the song at break-neck speed and when Jimmy was turned loose on the solo he showed Bobby Morris he knew more about playing drums than Bobby would ever know. Bobby walked out during the last of the solo never to be heard from again.

Agents came and made their pitch, but none of them were like Carl. Summer rolled into fall and we still hadn't signed with an agent. During the fall Rena and I decided to try gambling on a very limited cash basis. I think we were the only group to play Elko that didn't gamble. In those days in Nevada if you were booked into a casino for six or eight weeks, the casino paid you for the entire length of your contract the first day you worked. Of course, they hoped you would leave the bulk of your money on the crap and poker tables or in the slot machines. That's why Eddie Fisher and others played such long engagements. They gambled all their money then borrowed more and couldn't pay it back. The casino would provide room and board and pay the band backing them and they repaid the borrowed money by playing additional weeks without pay.

One group that came into the Stockmen's gambled away their entire six-week salary before they opened. Their guitar player put his guitar, amplifier and shoes in a pawn shop raising money to gamble which he lost. He begged Phil to let him use his Super 400 guitar and amp. Phil also gave him a pair of shoes. The leader of the group had cash wired from home to pay their hotel bill and provide food for their Nevada stay.

Rena and I knew they didn't build those casinos and hotels by paying out big winnings. One morning as we were leaving work, I put a nickel into a slot machine and hit for forty dollars and a ticket for a Friday drawing. The next Friday we were having coffee and pie in the restaurant when I heard the number of my ticket being called in the casino. To my surprise I had won a $3,500 fishing trailer It was really nice with a kitchen, shower, sleeping areas for two and all the bells and whistles. The following day, I sold the trailer to the casino for $2,500 and that ended my gambling and the casino passed a rule that no employee could ever win a drawing. Rena hit for $2,000 plus on Bingo and bought me a beautiful Longine wristwatch in hammered gold with diamonds at 12-3-6-9 on the face, My all-time favorite watch. Dick Toothman offered us an additional six-month run in Elko and it was very tempting.

It was time to move on and we excepted an "open end" contract from the Crystal Bay Club at North Shore Lake Tahoe. We closed the Stockmen's on December 22nd. Rena', Phil and Jimmy had the flu and someway amid snow and a lot of ice Sharon and I loaded the van, including the piano, for the move. We traveled icy roads to the lake and rented an apartment at Incline Village that was on the second floor that could only be reached by ice covered iron steps. We opened at Crystal Bay during a blizzard on December 26th. The road to California was closed due to heavy snow but we had loads of tourists that were trapped by the blizzard and the music and gambling were up and running. We had to buy a shovel as our Cadillac was buried in snow each night while we worked. We had to shovel the snow off at 2 AM then slowly follow the snow plow along the edge of the lake (there were no guard rails) to Incline Village then slowly climb the ice covered stairs to our apartment.

One night we shoveled snow like crazy only to uncover the wrong Cadillac. We then had to uncover our car and wait an hour for the next snow plow.

Bad weather or not, there was plenty of talent in the area. Jackie Gayle at Harold's; Glen Campbell at Harrah's, Reno; Ed Ames and Jerry Van Dyke at Harrahs, Frank Goshen at Harveys Tahoe. There was Jack Jones and Rich Little at the Sahara Tahoe. We headlined the Crystal Bay Club.

Down the road, the celebrated vocal group "The Vagabonds" were working. Some nights we would stop by and catch their act. It was here we first heard the song "Yesterday I Heard the Rain." May found us splitting the bill with the Joe Rossi Trio at the Holiday Inn in Reno which also welcomed Buck Owens and his Buckaroos. The Holiday Inn was by the Truckee River where divorced women threw their wedding rings when their quickie divorces were final. The engagement there went very well until one evening an electrical storm knocked out our amps. Joe Rossi who was unhappy because our group with Rena's dancing was outdrawing his act, refused to let us use his amps for the remainder of our show. Ours were repaired by show time the following day and we buried his group for the remainder of our run.

Competition was keen at Reno and the Lake Tahoe with Juliet Prowse, Jimmie Rogers, Rusty Draper, Roger Williams, Jimmy Dean, Phyllis Diller, Fats Domino, the June Taylor Dancers, Page Cavanaugh Trio, The Modernaires, Jades & J'Adorables, April Stevens, Evalani and the South Sea Island Review, plus one of the greatest pianists I ever heard, Rene Paulo. We spent time seeing Rene and a country duo with short hair and lots of talent working in a tiny club down Virginia Street. Their names – Willie Nelson and Wayland Jennings. We tried a variety of agents in the months ahead as we did a lot of traveling with my mother, Dana Lee and our tiny Chihuahua "Trinket" who could fit in my overcoat pocket, plus the guys.

CHAPTER SIXTY

In Alaska, we visited the Ice Flow in Captain Cook's inlet, Portage Glacier and Mount Alyeska, while Trinket would scamper over Earthquake Park. After Easter, We returned to the lower forty-eight, played Lewiston, Idaho where we found a bakery that produced the world's best lemon pie.

Phil was ill and was replaced by a local bass player, Don Bennet, an expert musician. While playing on stage, the area where Don was playing his doghouse bass, gave way and all we could see was his hand still playing at the top of the instrument. He never missed a beat. We helped him back on the stage and the show went on.

A couple of nights in Lewiston we shared the bill with trombonist Sy Zenter and his orchestra. They were riding the crest of the music world with their hit single of "Up The Lazy River."

With Phil in good health again, we played Waterloo, Iowa which was buried in snow. Opening night we drove back to our motel where the drive was hidden by snow drifts. Aiming for the motel housing, we drove until we hit two sharp bumps. Dead tired at

3 AM we fought our way through snow drifts to our room. Before 7 AM the manager was knocking on the door to tell us we had driven into the shallow end of the drained swimming pool, which was now covered totally by snow.

Next came a tour of Oregon which included Meford, Salem and Portland.

We opened the New Year at Milwaukee, a venue that made Alaska seem like Palm Springs. From my point of view there is no place in the world as cold as Milwaukee in January.

Cold? You better believe it. We stayed at a first class motel but you could write your name in the frost on the inside of the storm door. We did love the venue, Frenchy's, rated as a top ten American restaurant with a worldwide reputation.

Hot buttered rums awaited each arrival and it was a happy place to perform before major clients that included immortal football coach Vince Lombardi, his wife, Marie and record producer, Mitch Miller.

What an "on order" menu they had. Tonight at dinner you could enjoy Norwegian Reindeer Steak served sautéed with Hunter's sauce and wild rice at $7.95 or maybe you're in the mood for Wild African delights – Rib and Chops of Lion, only $11.50. Or maybe have African Lion Ragout at $7.75 or Chopped Sirloin of Lion or Savory Lion Steak, or perhaps your choice is Kangaroo Tail. All available on order along with fresh peaches, strawberries and corn-on-the-cob in mid January.

Art Torgolson, Frenchy's manager, gave Phil and I a surprise birthday dinner that was fit for royalty. We never forgot Frenchy's.

We had no idea of the turbulence 1970 would

SILENTS TO DIGITALS

bring. Nixon widened the war to Cambodia and Americans spit on our returning troops. At Kent State University, four students were killed and eleven wounded by National Guard; the trial of the Chicago seven; Charlie Manson and his "family." Black Panthers, Bobby Seale and Huey Newton, Janis Joplin and Jimi Hendrix were only twenty-seven when they died of drug overdoses as the drug culture moved into mainstream with young America. Indians took over Alcatraz. A crippled Apollo 13 made its way back from space and on Earth Day millions protested pollution of their own space ship.

On the flip side, the song machine kept playing. "A Boy Named Sue," "Hair," and "Aquarius" would be the big hits.

We were headed to Sioux City where we would have another kind of night to remember.

Phil had been on the road for years and had an offer of a top position with the University of Hawaii in the music department and would leave after we played Sioux City.

Jimmy Lynch had a wife and two children in Las Vegas and one required very expensive surgery to correct a hearing problem. Although very well paid, he needed more money. I knew that Ray Anthony was getting ready to hit the road with his new "Book End" show that included girl vocalists Anita Reyes and Kitty Oliver; pianist Arnold Ross, brother Leroy Anthony on tenor sax and comedian, vocalist and super bassist, Dave Leonard. The show would be fabulous if he could get a sensational drummer. I called Ray and told him about Jimmy, sent photos and an audio tape. Jimmy was to report to Ray as soon as we finished our closed engagement of four weeks. Phil and Jimmy had become more than musical associates, they were family and we hated to see them go but in life you have to do what it takes to make your life complete.

While Phil and Jimmy went on new paths Rena and I would return to San Francisco to hire new musicians and build four new shows in the three weeks before returning to the road.

In the meantime, Sioux City had its problems. A big club built up three tiers with tables around the dance floor but the stage was quite small. So small that Rena's portable stage had to be set on the dance floor in front of the permanent stage.

You knew there would be trouble and it came on the final show of our stay. A lot of mother's don't teach young men to respect women and "busy" fathers fail to slap them in the head enough to get the message across. In entertainment you get a lot of mouth from both male and female customers and it rolls off your back but when they touch you or come on the stage, all bets are off. I remember the night at the Turf Club in Yakama when two would be tough guys came in with two floozies. They took a ringside table and started ethnic insults directed at Latino Phil Rivera. It got worse. We were in the third show when one of the clowns stepped on the table, then on to the stage to, "Change that Mexican's face." Phil was playing the solid Fender bass. Flipped the bass in the air then made a swing his old baseball manager would have loved connected with the guys head knocking him beyond his table onto the dance floor. Phil flipped his bass back, kept playing as they carried Mister Tough Guy away.

Sioux City was different. These four young jerks were after a girl and this girl was my wife. They had gotten drunk through three shows and by the fourth show the remarks were gutter dirty. Rena was dancing and we were singing "Tangerine" as she whirled in her silver and orange costume. She had maracas in both hands as she twirled. When her back was turned, one guy reached out and pulled on her bikini panties. She felt it, the audience saw it. She kept smiling, and dancing but switched the maracas to her left hand. When she faced the pants puller she smashed his glasses and broke his nose with a Marciano-type right cross. He went flat on the floor with blood running everywhere as Rena received a standing ovation as she went to her dressing room leaving Phil, Jimmy and I to close.

We thought the excitement was over but we were wrong. Into our last super fast closer, I looked up to the third row to see a woman in her early forties throw off her mink coat and start walking down to the stage, throwing off her clothes with a middle aged man begging her to stop. Before stepping on Rena's stage she removed her silk panties and naked, except for high heel slippers, went into wild gyrations while her escort cried, begging her to stop. We could play longer than she could dance and in time she collapsed. Her man gathered her up and their friends gathered up her clothes and the story was over. Well, not quite over. A reporter and photographer for the newspaper had been in the audience and the story and photos were front page. It turned out her husband was a big time politician in their state. I wonder where his career went following his wife's performance?

Home in San Francisco, we got busy. A couple of people suggested I quit the road, buy a house and work piano bars. In my young years I had tried this route and found out fast why piano bar players are drunks. What is it that possesses people who work at regular jobs makes them think anyone wants to hear them sing? If they want to sing, buy a piano, learn to play and sing at home. Sing to records, sing in the shower but don't sing in public. This feature affects amateurs who should know better. Danny Thomas, a great talent and nice guy used to come to dinner at Jimmy's in Century City with his wife Rose Marie, a lovely lady, who liked to sing. Sing she did but not like Julie London, Peggy Lee or June Christy, but in her style which was no style at all.

Manufactures made fools of America's young with the making of endless guitars so they could hang the instrument around their necks and wiggle and twist like their favorite rock stars or even smash the guitars like the rockers who thought this was the ultimate in show biz. Millions never learned to play three basic chords, but many of their heroes didn't play either. The guitar solos were played by the studio musicians with years of study and practice.

The other great sin was when they made amps and mic's available to the general public. Brain surgeon's tried to be recording stars. Everyone forgot that only a lucky few have real talent.

No time to cloud our minds, we needed to get to work. Our new show group would be with a youth accent and a new agent.

We never found an agent manager like the late Carl Ravazza although we tried. We had major agents including Abe Meyers, MCA, The Belmont Agency and Dick Shelton from McConkey but with the exception of Abe Meyers, never met them, or their reps face to face. I did know agent Jack Kurtz and would have liked working with him but things never worked out. We signed with Max Bordy in Chicago. I never met Max although he handled us to the end. He made two promises that he kept one hundred percent. One, we would never miss a day of work and second, at every engagement our income would increase. We believed and he delivered.

Five things killed the music business.

1. Woodstock which opened concerts for the young.
2. San Francisco's "Summer of Love" gave us hippies, free love and a monster supply of drugs.
3. "The Beatles." The British invasion was England's revenge for throwing them out during the revolution.
4. Television. During World War II Adolph Hitler predicted that television would be the opiate that would help certain factions to control their countries. If it's on television it's true? Wrong. We have managed news and programs so bad they would have been laughed out of the studios during the Golden Age of television. Maybe men rebelled at dressing up to see a live performance or women, who rarely cooked but shoved everything into the microwave while they got fat and lazy, just wanted to slump in front of the television, slurp beer and watch. Something killed the music business.

5. Greed closed the ballrooms and the theaters and in Nevada closed the lounges where shows by Louis Prima, Bobby Sherwood, Mary Kay and others had thrilled thousands for free and this same audience spent money in their casinos. In Nevada there is never enough. Close the lounges put in more slot machines. It was happening but Max knew where there were still top paying venues. The jumps were farther apart and the chances of death or destruction on the highway rose but the band played on.

The only restriction we put on Max was no more double billing. Working with the Louis Armstrong show had caused major problems thanks to Marty Napoleon and the time with Frank Fontaine who had played a character named "Crazy Guggenheim" on the *Jackie Gleason Show*. Jack, like a master of his art, dumped Fontanne but we had him and an ego larger than Madison Square Garden. Rehearsals were disaster, then when on stage he would sing songs that we had never rehearsed and always overstayed his stage time.

Sy Zenter and his orchestra were okay. The band did what they did and we did our show.

By far and away the best "guest" act was the guy who was the greatest Light Heavyweight Champion of them all who could have been the Heavyweight Champion of the World had he just boxed and not tried to knock out the Champ, Joe Louis. Billy Conn was handsome. The "Sweet Science" had left no marks on his perfect features. His movements were graceful and audiences loved him plus, Billy could sing. We would have liked to work with Billy forever but show biz was not his interest. His heart was with his wife and children back in Pittsburgh. Billy did work as a greeter at the Stardust Hotel and Casino in Las Vegas where one night a high roller gave him $9,500 just to stand beside him for a half hour. No matter how you slice it, that's easy money.

CHAPTER SIXTY-ONE

We selected two young musicians from Elko. Roland Davis and Bobby Chan, real name Chan Stenovitch who's father headed Nevada's Highway Patrol. At that time in America, women of all ages were gaga over the live performances, TV appearances and records of a British entertainer named Tom Jones. Although still young and the fact that his sexy movements and tight pants excited the ladies, his face was turning old from the life style he lived. In Roland, we had a fresh young man, six foot tall with a mass of blond curls and a fabulous personality who not only was an outstanding bassist but was a singer who could out Tom, Tom Jones and he wore tighter pants. In addition to Tom Jones songs, he also had his own unique vocal style. Women of all ages invited him into their bedrooms but Roland wasn't interested. He was in the first blush of young love and was engaged to a girl back home. Bobby Chan, whom we liked to introduce as the illegitimate son of oriental detective, Charlie Chan, was a smiling, good looking young man the kind of guy when he turns fifty will appear to be thirty. Bobby was a very good drummer who could come down front and do a good vocal with tons of boyish charm. While women wanted to drag Roland into the nearest cave, they wanted to baby Bobby.

Three intense weeks of rehearsal and we opened at the Holiday Inn in Springfield, Illinois. The show was a smash hit. Manager Lacy Brooks loved it as it packed his room, that is he loved it until his wife caught a show the second week. I was called in and told that Mrs. Books thought that between Rena and Roland the show was too sexy and to tone it down. I told him I would, but of course we didn't change a thing. On our final night we played to standing room only like we had from the start.

At Mankato, Minnesota we went down to the college to see a pre-season workout of the NFL Minnesota Vikings, then known as "The Purple People Eaters" under Coach Bud Grant. We took Trinket, our tiny Chihuahua and set her down by our feet. Suddenly Grant was in a personal red alert screaming into his bullhorn "get that dog off the field." Without fear Trinket stood on the fifty yard line wagging her tail. I wish I would have had a video camera as for the next five minutes these monster players dove through the air trying to catch her to no avail. They were sitting panting and coach's face had turned purple when Trinket swished her tail and strolled to the sidelines. What I had seen of the Vikings attempted tackles, it figures it would be a long season.

The fall saw us back in Sioux City at a different club than the one where the naked lady had danced. We were held over then hit Chicago's Conrad Hilton while Rod McKuen was knocking them dead at Mr. Kelly's on Rush Street. We caught Rod's show and got to reminisce about our TV show from *Hungry I*.

RENA WINTERS

Next came Cheboygan then a hop to beautiful and historic Mackinac Island where Rena and I rode a tandem bike everywhere with the scent of lilacs filling the air. It was very romantic.

This was the summer we returned to Columbus to play the Olentangy Inn a truly beautiful resort hotel adjacent to Ohio State University. It was the first time our show worked outdoors and it was great out on the big patio. We pulled the same crowd as we had during our stay at the Neil House and was able to spend lots of time with Cousin's Ken Agee, Bob Shumaker, Bobby Chandler and their wives as well as old school friends. Dana Lee was on summer vacation and we had many good times. A tour of Minnesota followed and we did Minneapolis, Rochester, Sault St. Marie, and Duluth.

CHAPTER SIXTY-TWO

We did the state of Washington from Spokane to Kennewick. The happiness boys from Elko took turns driving the van while Rena and I alternated in the Caddy. At last we were back in Georgia with four weeks in Miami to follow. It was our closing night when I got the call. We had a standard rule in our group, since we would be traveling all night to the next job, everyone rested and never drank on the last night. At this time, we had planned to drive to Miami in the daytime so no one rested and everyone had a drink.

The call couldn't have come at a worse time. Roland, the young entertainer who had all the tools to be a major star or at the very, very least a contender, as Marlon Brando had uttered in the movie *On The Waterfront* had his brains turned to mush and he was going home to marry his first girl friend, to have the cottage with babies on the floor and work in a drug store. These young guys never learn that there's more ahead than they left behind and the window to the job opportunity would never open again. I never advise people regarding their love lives. They have to live with their decisions. Bobby Chan was suddenly homesick, so we lost half our show. They were replaced by non singing drummer Dieter Mantel and a good guitarist performer, Ted Allen, who had a drinking problem and a lousy attitude.

Max was on the phone and when he called me "Bobby sweetheart" I knew we were in real trouble. During the years, several ladies have called me sweetheart but no one, including my family ever called me Bobby. Max told me there had been a slight change in plans and we were getting more money. I reminded Max we were leaving in the morning when he dropped the bombshell. No Miami and we were leaving tonight driving from deep in Georgia to Aberdeen, South Dakota where we would do our first show at 7 PM Dakota time for the American Legion Convention. "Don't worry, baby, you can do it. They're goanna love you," was Max's closing as he hung up. Don't you adore show biz?

A dead tired group cleaned the stage and dressing rooms, packed the van. Rena was driving the Cadillac with Dieter and Ted asleep and me driving the van half asleep and we headed north to the "Pheasant Hunting Capitol if the World."

We ate meals served at Mcdonald's' and once when we stopped to gas up, Rena fell asleep in the car with her head against the ring horn. Consuming gallons of coffee, we arrived in Aberdeen around 6 PM. Found the hall and set up. Still time for a hot dinner. Wrong. Every restaurant in town was closed and dinner at the convention was over and their kitchen was closed. We had last had a Big Mac and a shake about 1 PM but we could not eat until breakfast the following day. At that moment everyone in the group hated each other, our agent and Aberdeen. At 7 PM we came on swinging. When I introduced Ted who had been sipping from his flask, he stepped to the mike telling the Legionnaires he could whip any guy in the room. I managed to defuse that with a joke and the show rolled out smooth. Sometime during our week's stay Max called to say that Miami was out and we would hit the Ramada Inn in Fort Dodge, Iowa.

Ted Allen had to go and once again I turned to a local chapter of the AFM for help. From the St. Louis chapter, I got Billy Clark who according to our phone conversation had worked with big bands, shows and was tops as a guitarist, bassist and vocalist. The last thing I told him was that it was a clean-cut group, no long hair or hippie attire.

The trip from Aberdeen provided the near miss that could have been fatal. Rena and Dieter in the Caddy were ahead of me as we drove on the freeway around Chicago in late afternoon traffic. In an explosion, both rear tires on the van blew out and the van went into a spin. The other drivers managed to miss me as I spun down an off-ramp deep into Chicago's South side. Coming to rest at the ramps end, I saw a garage. The workers managed to get the overloaded van to the garage where cash and a paid up credit card got two new tires and I was back in business. I got to Fort Dodge in time for dinner.

After my hectic day, I was in the shower when a knock on our door brought Rena face-to-face with Billy Clark, our new musician. She told him I was showering but would be right out. She gave me the news that my new player had arrived then threw herself on the bed rolling gales of laughter. I knew why when I opened the door to see a gaunt apparition with hair down to his shoulders. "I told you to get a haircut," I said. "I did" he replied. This was the start of the Billy Clark saga.

Billy drove an old station wagon with several old worn-out tires tied on top that looked as worn as he did. I never rehearsed on the road unless there was a hot Top 40 tune we wanted to add but I rehearsed Billy seven days a week from 10:30 AM to 1:30 PM, the time was wasted. He played badly, he was lost on group vocals and his solos were sick comedy. One night, a woman who I thought wanted to make a request, pulled his hair trying to prove to her girlfriend he was really a girl.

Billy, Dieter and I were rehearsing, Rena was sitting at the bar when heavenly deliverance arrived. A young clean-cut man with a guitar case and a suitcase set down, orderd a Coke and started listening. Rena moved down and engaged him in conversation. He was Chuck Hurt from Missoula, Montana. He had just worked with a group playing Fort Dodge that had broken up and he was headed home since no job was available. Rena asked him what kind of a guitar he played and he said a Gibson Super 400. She knew this cat could play. She asked him to wait a minute as she left the bar for the showroom. Calling me aside, she told me my worries were over. My new player had just arrived and he played a Super 400. In a heartbeat, I was paying Billy his salary and transportation costs and let Dieter know the rehearsal was over. Without a note being played, Chuck opened that night. He played, he solo sang what would be my favorite version of the hit "Cabaret." When he put his guitar in play with his classic interpretation of

"Moonlight In Vermont" you could have heard a pin drop. Great on group vocals, he was the perfect guy and believe me this cat could play.

Doing shows now was a delight. Chuck's private life soared also. He met a lovely girl, in Fort Dodge and they were married. In their future, there would be a beautiful little girl they would name Carla. That would be later. In the meantime, we enjoyed each other's company off the bandstand.

An then came a phone call I never thought I would get. Jimmy Lynch was leaving the *Ray Anthony Book End Show* and wanted to come back. That was the ultimate. With Jimmy driving the beat, we could compete with any show group in the land.

I want it known that I have always liked Ray as a person, a co-worker and a musician. The job he did hosting the *Stars of Sound* TV special on NBC was top quality and he was fun to work with. Although I told my co-producer, Fred Rice I thought Ray might be tough to work for because he demanded perfection. Rena and I saw it one night when we were at the famous Bimbo's in San Francisco where Ray and his Orchestra were playing. Something went wrong. Ray stopped the music and fired his pianist and sent him off the stage.

Earlier, in Las Vegas I saw Benny Goodman fire Wardel Grey, one of the all-time tenor sax greats when he played a wrong note. Benny chased him off stage and we never heard or saw Wardel again. A week or so later, he was murdered in a Las Vegas alley just a stone's throw from the famed Las Vegas strip. There were no second chances when you worked for "The King of Swing."

Although a little shocked by both firings in public,

later I would fire Sean, my youngest son, off the stage when for the fourth straight night he played the intro to "The Shadow Of Your Smile" incorrectly. This happened on a busy Saturday night. He was welcomed back on Monday and he never played the intro wrong again.

I knew how much the extra money meant to Jimmy and asked when he was leaving Ray. He told me everything was fine until they played the Fontenbleu Hotel in Miami, As he had done before, Ray introduced Jimmy as his great young drummer from New York featured on the great drum classic, "Sing, Sing, Sing." Jimmy's solo turned on the room and he received a seven minutes yelling, applauding, standing ovation. When the ovation had stopped Ray took the mic to announce to the packed house. "He's not that good."

For all purposes Jimmy's life in the show was over. He never played a solo again, just kept the rhythm. You don't get more applause than the boss.

I never understood this mind set. I wanted all my players and singers to get applause, it showed what a smart guy I was to hire them and it made me work harder on the keyboard and vocals.

The big thing was that Jimmy was going to join us when we opened the Torch Club in South Bend just a couple of blocks removed from Notre Dame University.

We were in for four weeks and would be followed by the fabulous Ink Spots and their backup band.

During set-up, the manager told me he wanted the show to play loud and never have silence between numbers but play a musical riff with a solid drum beat. This was a most unusual request until I got in tune with what was going on. This was a mob-owned club and they had business to conduct in the alley right behind the stage where a three-sided concrete waste area stood. The family used this area to discipline the women who worked in their bordello's and their screams would vanish in the loud sounds we made on the other side of the wall. It was very hard on Jimmy who set with his back to that wall. He wanted to go out and engage the punks doing the beatings but wiser heads prevailed. We played to full houses and many evenings the then Chief of Police of this historic town sat front and center in the audience.

We visited the Notre Dame campus, the Golden Dome, Touchdown Jesus and the mystic of Notre Dame football with Knut Rockne, George Gipp and their long list of All Americans.

In Cherokee, Iowa, we played at one of the most beautiful clubs ever built and it was located in the center of a cornfield. It was huge and the Harry James Orchestra had just left and we would be followed by Buddy Rich and his band. They alternated big bands and show groups. I told the manager I didn't think we could fill this room. He said he didn't care if anyone came just play your shows. The mob owned this beauty spot and maybe they laundered money but whatever they did was their business. Speaking of business, I was wrong. I don't know where the audiences came from but they came and not in overall's but dressed to the nines like Las Vegas crowds used to do.

Life was quiet in Cherokee until the morning the police called saying they had arrested a man who claimed to be part of our show and would we come down to headquarters. On arrival, we found Jimmy

Lynch shivering in his grey jogging suit. Jimmy, a real health nut who didn't smoke or drink and worked out every day had been running when the police picked him up. What Jimmy didn't know was that he was jogging outside the state insane asylum and the inmates wore grey jogging suits just like his. Instead of checking if any inmate had escaped they called Jimmy over to their car and when he told them he was drummer, they took him down. One cop told me that lot's of inmates say they are drummers. We got Jimmy out of there and to a warm breakfast. Among Jimmy's great solo's was the eighteen bars he did on the old Charlie Barnet hit, "Cherokee." I always announced it with a wink and smile for Jimmy.

We were playing Bemidji, Minnesota, when the call came that my mother had died in Mill Valley, California.

Rena had known hours before the call but didn't wake me. In the wee hours, Mama had awakened her saying she was going to be with my father, that our marriage was solid and we didn't need her.

We made arrangements for cremation and Mother was laid to rest between my father and beloved Uncle Howard in the family plot in West Jefferson, Ohio, close to where she had been born. Later, there would be a beautiful Memorial service where she had prayed and watched her son grow up as a choir member and altar boy.

The Canyon Lakes Club in Rapid City, South Dakota, was next. This was a very special spot that would later be destroyed by a flood.

At the foot of the majestic Grand Teton Mountains we played the famed Rancher Lounge in Jackson Hole, Wyoming, one of the greatest vacation spots in our western states. Jackson offered the biggest ski mountains in America and a wide variety of accommodations and restaurants.

Max alerted us that we would return to Nevada for a Christmas opening at The Theater Lounge at the Carson Nugget. Dana Lee would fly home from the Samuel Ready School in Baltimore where she had excellent grades and was a member of the Field Hockey Team and Rena's parents would visit... maybe. There was 132 inches of snow on Donner Pass with more snow due Christmas Eve. Getting to Nevada would be dicey. They made it a day later.

I think we knew in our hearts this would be our last go around in Nevada. The American Federation of Musicians was crumbling and all because of Nevada greed. Frank Sinatra played Las Vegas with a twenty-three piece orchestra but brought thirteen of the group from California. His studio musicians were guys who could cut his complicated arrangements. No problem, the casino paid their traveling scale. This did not set well with the local musicians union. They demanded that the casino's hire additional local musicians who would sit in the basement, drink and play cards while the shows played. They were being paid the local rate as if they were working. The casino's said no. At once, all the large orchestras that had backed the big production shows were gone. When a production show had been cast and ready, musicians in either New York or Hollywood cut the tracks and the stars sang to them. Audiences thought there were large orchestras playing behind the scrim. It's only a tape recording. "Yes, but what happens when the cast changes and singers do the numbers in different keys" That's no problem. Modern technology enables us to transpose the tape to any key we desire.

At first very slowly, then with speed, non-union groups sprang up in the small venues. Then Las Vegas found out what Los Angeles was doing with the young, upcoming Rock groups. All along the fancy Sunset Strip the club owners charged the groups for the opportunity to play their venues. The kids paid for the long shot of a possible shot at a recording contract and stardom. When my oldest son Kim told me he had paid Garraras, one of the top clubs on the Sunset Strip for a one week engagement I was dumbfounded. When club owners don't pay me, I don't play.

We grabbed the big black headlines of the Reno Orbit newspaper in Reno. We were headlined over the Carpenters, Bobby Darin, Gaylord & Holiday, Phyllis Diller, Woody Allen, Joey Heatherton, Della Reese and that duo playing down the street, Willie Nelson and Wayland Jennings. Both Rena and I had large photos on the page and Chuck and Jimmy had first class reviews. The area was overpowered with great acts, Liza Minnelli, Burt Bacharach, Louis Jordan and the Tympani 5, O.C. Smith, Count Basie Orchestra, Jay P. Morgan, Jackie De Shannon, Rich Little, Doc Severson and Bill Cosby.

When we opened on December 23, 1971 we were at the peak. Everything we did worked in spades. I only wish it would have been filmed.

Our stay at Carson pleased the owners who planned to have us return the following year. When we closed, Phil Harris and his show moved in and we went across the United States to the VIP Club in Greenville, South Carolina.

We arrived to find Rena's photo dominated the Piedmont Times plus lots of good press about out show. We noticed there were a lot of Confederate flags in town but failed to get the meaning. We would. The VIP Club was a bottle club which meant you had to buy a bottle of booze and order set ups. When you left your remaining booze it would be numbered and placed in a locker to be kept for your return. I never saw a bottle go into a locker, the clients drank every drop then hit the highway.

Our opening show started with the ETL Curtain Call, where everyone in the group is introduced. When Rena introduced the group vocally she noticed not a single Southerner was included. We went into a medley of show tunes from current Broadway hits. The final show we saluted was The Great George M" and the song was "Yankee Doodle Dandy." The sound generated by the redneck audience was the sound of a lynch mob. Without a breath we did a medley of Creedance Clearwater hits to calm things down. The Civil War is still on in Greenville.

Rena's dressing room was behind the kitchen which was behind the stage at the VIP club. She had three minutes to change which she did twice each show. As she raced back and forth the black chefs and kitchen staff would waive their knives and spoons and cheer her with "Yayaya" and "Go Girl Go."

Sunday's we were off and would go down to The Fireside Inn for dinner and listen to Charlie Spivak who played "the sweetest trumpet in the world" and his small group that featured his wife, one of the truly great girl singers of the big band era, Irene Day. Charlie remembered he and I worked the "Hijinx Show." The Spivak group was the resident band at the Fireside and I wondered if Charlie thought about those fabulous nights when his band broadcast from New York, Chicago, Los Angeles and he worked in major movies.

We left Greenville alive which I had doubted we would opening night, to play seven weeks in the Chaparral Room of the Golden Rooster Club atop the beautiful Inn of the Golden West in Odessa, Texas. "The Jack Rabbit Capitol of the World."

They had life-sized cutouts of Rena dancing in her blue veils on every floor by the elevators inviting patrons to meet her at the Golden Rooster.

In Odessa, the area was agog with cases of young women who had been abducted from oil company offices leaving their shoes under their desks. Their murdered bodies would be found later at various sites where oil was being drilled. I was as fascinated by the case and it was the major topic of conversation. One night talking to a customer at the bar, I said I would bet every one of the women had been murdered when the moon was full. I didn't realize the man I was talking to was a detective. I found out at 7 AM the following morning when four detectives knocked on my motel room door. They had checked their files, and sure enough all the women had been murdered during a full moon, and was I ready to confess? When the murders started, I was a couple of thousand miles away and at that point didn't know Odessa or where it was located. During the time we were in their fair city, every hour was accounted for. The cops were disappointed. They thought they had a quick solution. The story got newspaper headlines and brought clients to the showroom to meet the group leader who had thrown out the clue about the "Full Moon Murders." In the meantime, Rena had many invitations from Texas oilmen to fly with them in their private planes to see their oil drilling operations. All requests were turned down with a smile. The killer of the women taken from their offices was solved with his arrest a month after our engagement.

In Wichita, Kansas, we played both the Candle Club and the Twin Lakes Club. We played the Plantation House in Alexandria, Louisiana whose walls were decorated with large paintings of exotic art (nudes). Texas and the Wichita Falls Country Club where tornado warnings sounded each day and we could see tornadoes swirling in the distance but they never came close.

Then back again in Texas at the deluxe Midland Texas Country Club, the club of future United States President George Bush. SR and his family welcomed us.

First night we left the club the greens were being sprayed as we walked to our car. Rena wondered why fire hoses were stretched over the cement walks when the sprinklers covered everything. On closer examination, we found these were not fire hoses but fat, seven foot rattle snakes enjoying the warmth of the concrete walks. We stepped very gingerly after our first encounter.

Max was setting up a new tour when Rena suggested we leave the music business.

Dana Lee was ending her year at boarding school and she could come home and we could live like a normal family. Just as important was where our future was going. When Carl Ravazza died so did our opportunity for a major recording contract and TV guest shots. Producer Howard Koch had Rena come to Hollywood with the idea of a studio contract. When he saw how tall she was that went out the window. With the exception of Rory Calhoun, Burt Lancaster, and a few others all leading men were small and you couldn't have woman tower over them.

I talked to Max. He said we had three years left where he could get us big money. We really had two options. First was to run our group into a country western act which we could have done but would have to play a lot of low end clubs while building a reputation in that area and of course no production numbers, just picking and singing. He really wanted us to move the group to Europe where he had many contacts, and we could extend our musical careers for at least ten years. The folks in Europe were very loyal to groups even when they had passed their prime. If asked Dieter, would go, he had no ties. I never asked Chuck and Debbie. With a baby on the way I never thought Europe would seem like a good idea. Music has always been my life and I wanted to go forward. As it turned out, destiny stepped in and made the decision.

On the Monday we started our final two weeks in Midland, Rena received a call from an executive from the Red Carpet Realtors of America offering her a one-year television contract for a daily thirty-minute show. She would be the hostess and do something very novel. Using her background as a real estate agent and title officer she would sell homes on television. Just not any television but on KPHO-TV in Phoenix where twice before I had been number one.

She accepted and told me if I desired, I could replace her and go on with the show. Our marriage came before any show. I could find solo piano jobs in the Valley of the Sun or maybe form a trio.

We all said tearful goodbyes when we closed. Dana Lee flew in and we packed the costumes, organ, piano, portable stage and sound equipment and headed down the desert for a new life.

CHAPTER SIXTY-THREE

Dana Lee was home for keeps. We found a nice apartment and settled in and also started looking for a location to build a family home in Scottsdale.

The station was anxious for Rena to start working on her show when suddenly everything stopped when the doorbell rang the night of July 24, 1971, and we opened it to find a collection of reporters and photojournalists from the *Arizona Republic* newspaper. We let them in and they were shaking our hands and offering congratulations. They hit us with a bolt of lightning. We had been selected by a national screening committee headed by Doctor Lynn Bartlett, Professor of Family Living at the University of Miami, as Arizona's 1971 All-American Family. Our family would represent Arizona and compete in the Grand Finals of the National Family Search which would be carried on national television in August.

Prior to leaving, the *Republic* ran full pages of colored photos, interviews and stories about our family and the phone rang and letters followed from Phoenix Mayor Jack Williams and United States Senators Barry Goldwater and Paul Fanning.

Having always been a big fan of Phoenix, I was thinking of calling Jack McElroy to see if he would like for me to come into Durant's with a trio. I never made the call. We were too busy.

We flew to Florida with other families from the west to be greeted by popping flashbulbs and endless interviews at Lehigh Acres Vacation Villa in Florida which is north of Tampa on the Gulf Coast.

I had no idea how our names turned up in Florida and I still don't but they had. We had been selected to the All-American Family team, so don't look a gift horse in the mouth. Start acting All-American.

The families from all fifty states and the District of Columbia would be quartered while being judged for nine days on an almost twenty-four-hour basis eating, playing, handling themselves in a variety of forums, cooking ability and talent. In addition, we were involved with the United States Saving Bonds program who would present us with Award Plaques, a $300 Vacation Villa at Lehigh Acres, a 1972 Dodge. U.S. Saving Bonds and Grolier Library personnel would make the awards to the family who won the competition on the television special to be co-hosted by 'Miss Florida Orange Juice," recording star Anita Bryant and "Hollywood Squares" domo, Peter Marshall. Entertainment would be "The Cowsills" a popular group of that era.

We had no allusions regarding the top prize. The average family had four children and we had one. Had Kim, Sharon and Sean, who were in private school in California, been with us it might have been a different story but we still did our State proud. We did some re-writing of the lyrics to "I Love Being Here With You." We all sang, I played, Rena and

Dana Lee danced and we won the entertainment award hands down. Then there was the day when the All-American mothers went into the huge hall where each had a new Tappan Range waiting to be used to create a family meal. Rena took second place with her Ranch Chicken, still the best meal I have ever enjoyed.

You put all those families together and you get a real mix. Not with the kids. They all played together and the accent is on having fun. The adults are a different story. We had two black families in the contest. One family, black power advocates, gave a university professor and his family constant insults calling them "Uncle Toms" and worse.

One night at dinner, a young boy did something to displease his father who jerked him out of his chair and proclaimed that all-American or not he was taking him outside to get his attitude adjusted.

Lehigh Acres was new and processing shakedowns to be sure everything was in perfect order. We had a very comfortable room with a double bed and a single for Dana Lee. We had gone to bed the second evening in Florida when Rena went to the bathroom. I was almost asleep when I heard her make the loudest and most piercing screams I have ever heard. Rena had never screamed before and she hasn't screamed since, but this night she awoke the All-Anericans that stayed on the hotel's first floor. Turning on the light, I saw the problem. Every square inch of the floor was covered with big black Palmetto bugs crawling. We were moved to a higher floor. We were told Palmetto bugs don't like heights. I packed Dana Lee, who could sleep if cannons went off by her head, to our new digs. Next morning the bug people were spraying everything in sight.

Although Lehigh Acres had lovely swimming pools what could be more exciting to the kids than an old-fashioned swimming hole beneath big shade trees complete with rope swings? They loved it until the day a big alligator came out of its depth. All the kids got out safe and Animal Control took the reptile to Gator Alley. The old swimming hole was never used again.

The nine days were hectic but fun. The hour-long television show was a success and although we met Anita Bryant and Peter Marshall we had no idea they would play a big role in our futures.

Tired but happy we flew home.

Rena was one busy lady as the KPHO staff worked to get her show ready for air. During each week with her trusty Nikon camera in hand, she would visit and film Red Carpet's most desirable real estate.

They selected a sports announcer as her side kick but the combination didn't click. Their biggest problem was the show. Red Carpet wanted the slides presented to look like film rolling through and the station didn't have a director or technical director including program director, Fred Huff, who could handle it. Panic was at the boiling point with everyone wringing their hands. They didn't want to lose this valuable account. Who can direct this show they all asked? Rena smiled, "My husband can." So for the third time, I became a part of the KPHO team. Not as a performing artist, but head of the new Documentary Department with a smiling, talented sandy aired cameraman, Neil Bobrick, who would later be a key element of ABC-TV's vampire series *Dark Shadows*. Neil and I were a team from the second we met. Our first job was to get a sidekick for Rena. Enter my ex-co-worker and soon-to-be best friend, Bob Corrigan, whom I had worked with on the series "Danger, Wild Cargo." If Neil and I made a potent team behind the camera Bob and Rena were a super team up front.

I had the problem that the station just didn't have fast enough equipment or skilled enough personnel to do the show. Told about an excellent technical director at a Tucson station, we hired him and the station facilities to package a halfhour show to be aired on KPHO during the following week. Every Saturday morning, we traveled to Tucson and by lunch everything was in the can.

The show and the selling of real estate prospered.

CHAPTER SIXTY-FOUR

The Red Carpet Realtor, five days a week shows, proved to be the beginning of the phenomenal years to follow. While in Arizona I directed *Celebrity Series* and wrote and directed a documentary called *Spaghetti Joe – In Search of Yesterday* about Joe Spanola's career.

Forming my own production company, many shows followed. Many through my association with Tino Barzie such as two Frank Sinatra, Jr shows, one in Las Vegas and one in Burmuda.

During this time, I also directed for 20th Century Fox *The Juliet Prowse Spectacular*, in Las Vegas, which turned out to be the last television appearance for Juliet, she died not too long after.

After four years of Red Carpet shows, we moved back to Los Angeles. I continued producing/directing and writing various television series, such as *Stars of Sound, Fit for Life, Peter Marshall – One More Time*, and the series *Jerry Vale's World* all followed.

During ensuing years there were the following shows: *The Tamara Rand Show, Myth or Reality* starring Rena, *Hawaiian Honeymoon Secret, A World*

Full of Music, My Little Corner of the World, which won the Freedom's Foundation and American Family Heritage Awards, *Sound Factor, The American Rifleman, The American Hunter, Shoot For the Gold, The American Rifleman II, Alive* – winner of the Bronze Halo Award, *The 8th Erotic Film Awards, The King is Coming, Pia Zadora in London, Musical Reunion, It's Not Easy Being a Bartender* – starring son Kim, *Rock Star, Aids, The Global Explosion* – nominated for an Emmy, *The Law and the Lady*, and *Happy Birthday American Federation of Nations*. The above shows produced twenty-seven Emmys which I am very proud of.

There were also many commercials, too numerous to mention or remember.

After the Northridge earthquake, our children had grown up and moved from the Los Angeles area, Rena and I moved to Las Vegas where I intended to semi-retire and write. I wrote three books, *In Search of La Dura, Components of Murder*, and *Target Tayopa*.

I raised money to do a movie entitled *Treasure of Tayopa* which starred Rena and did very well in distribution worldwide, playing in theatres and on compact disc.

During this time I also wrote a song entitled "Puerto Vallata" on a trip to Mexico with Rena who wrote the words, which was included on an audio cassette disc entitled *America* by Hilltop Records. We envisioned it as a hit for a Latin artist; however, when recorded by Hilltop it was performed more as a modern rock and roll song.

I wrote a script entitled *Black Star* with Brendan Walsh of Canada, about America's first black marshall, which was produced in Canada.

After moving to Las Vegas, I was approached by the College of Southern Nevada to teach writing courses. Novels, Short Stories, Creative Writing, Screenplays and production and music courses. I only agreed to teach for a brief period of time, perhaps six months; however, this continued for the next twenty years of my life until my death at ninety-two.

ABOUT THE AUTHOR

Multi-talented Rena Winters has enjoyed an outstanding career in the entertainment industry as a writer, talent, producer, production executive and as a major TV and Motion Picture executive.

At the College of Southern Nevada, Rena is an adjunct instructor teaching Creative Writing courses. She makes her home in Las Vegas, Nevada and works in her spare time as an editor and ghostwriter.

To learn more about Rena Winters and discover more Next Chapter authors, visit our website at www.nextchapter.pub.

Silents To Digitals
ISBN: 978-4-82416-619-7
Mass Market

Published by
Next Chapter
2-5-6 SANNO
SANNO BRIDGE
143-0023 Ota-Ku, Tokyo
+818035793528

17th January 2023

Printed in the USA
CPSIA information can be obtained
at www.ICGtesting.com
LVHW031040191123
764349LV00021B/1450